2019

THE PUBLICATIONS OF THE BEDFORDSHIRE
HISTORICAL RECORD SOCIETY
VOLUME 95

WILLINGTON AND THE MOWBRAYS

After the Peasants' Revolt

Dorothy Jamieson

THE BEDFORDSHIRE HISTORICAL RECORD SOCIETY

THE BOYDELL PRESS

First published 2019

A publication of
Bedfordshire Historical Record Society
published by The Boydell Press
an imprint of Boydell & Brewer Ltd
Bridge Farm Business Park, Top Street, Martlesham, IP12 4RB
and of Boydell & Brewer Inc.
668 Mt Hope Avenue, Rochester, NY 14620–2371, USA
website: www.boydellandbrewer.com

ISBN 978–0–85155–082–4

ISSN 0067–4826

The Society is most grateful for financial support from the
Simon Whitbread Charitable Trust and other donors who have
helped make the publication of this volume possible

Details of previous volumes are available from
Boydell and Brewer Ltd

A CIP catalogue record for this book is available
from the British Library

The publisher has no responsibility for the continued existence or accuracy of
URLs for external or third-party internet websites referred to in this book,
and does not guarantee that any content on such websites is,
or will remain, accurate or appropriate

This publication is printed on acid-free paper

Printed and bound in Great Britain by
TJ International Ltd, Padstow, Cornwall

Contents

Preface

One Monday evening, in late 1997, Chris Pickford, then Bedfordshire County Archivist, invited a group of members of Bedford National Trust Association to visit Bedfordshire and Luton Archives and Record Service to look at two sixteenth-century documents relating to Willington which, with the help of Samuel Whitbread, had been purchased for the collections. Chris opened a cardboard box, and I saw that it was full of rolls of parchment and wondered about the lives of the men who had written them some 600 years ago. So began a long programme of research which has led to the production of this volume for the Bedfordshire Historical Records Society.

Transcribing and translating manor court rolls is an absorbing task; the handwriting, some of it very beautiful, but much of it almost illegible, is often cramped and sometimes faded and dirty. Then there is the language; Latin, of course, but with its use of Medieval abbreviations, words and phrases. Inevitably many records have been damaged and destroyed over the centuries. They may be crumpled, torn, or just not there at all, and the collections of documents which remain may give a limited historical picture. But whatever the problems, when there are eureka moments and when a difficult puzzle has been solved there is cause for celebration. There is considerable satisfaction in deciphering documents written by people with very different lives to ours but with similar human feelings.

No accounts or manor court rolls exist for Willington before 1382. Although we have no evidence to indicate why manorial records before this date have not survived, many manorial records elsewhere were destroyed during the rioting in 1381 known as the Peasants' Revolt. This account ends, not in 1540, when important changes of land-holding and estate management occurred as a consequence of the dissolution of the monasteries but in 1522, because significant changes took place in Willington soon after this date, and the years that follow are part of a different story.

The writing of this volume would not have been possible without the preservation of documents by the Duke of Norfolk and the Duke of Bedford. His Grace the Duke of Norfolk gave his kind permission for me to visit the Archives at Arundel Castle to study original texts, for which he holds the copyright. Bedfordshire Archives hold the Russell Collection of documents from the Bedford Settled Estates of the Dukes of Bedford at Woburn Abbey on long-term loan.

The Willington court rolls have been translated from the Medieval Latin over a period of several years, with much assistance. It would not have been possible to complete the translations without the help and encouragement of Kevin Ward, James Collett-White, Dr Bridget Jones, Stephen Gibbs and other fellow local historians and students. I am most grateful for their help; without them the task would never have been finished.

The preparation of this volume would not have been possible without the work done in the second half of the twentieth century by John Stevenson Thompson. Mr

Thompson was by profession an aeronautical engineer, working in research at Farnborough and Thurleigh. After he retired he regularly spent two mornings a week, in the then Bedfordshire County Record Office, translating medieval documents from Latin into English, so making them accessible to later researchers such as myself. His work has enabled me to access information from the Willington bailiffs' accounts, the Blunham manor court rolls and the Eggington court rolls. I am proud to have been able to put into print some of the results of his work.

Sincere thanks are due all the staff of Bedfordshire Archives for their consistent patience and expert assistance; to Stuart Antrobus and Sylvia Woods, who gave considerable assistance by proof-reading the text during the later stages of its preparation; and to Frank Fattori, chairman of Willington Local History Group, for digitising the sketch map of Willington.

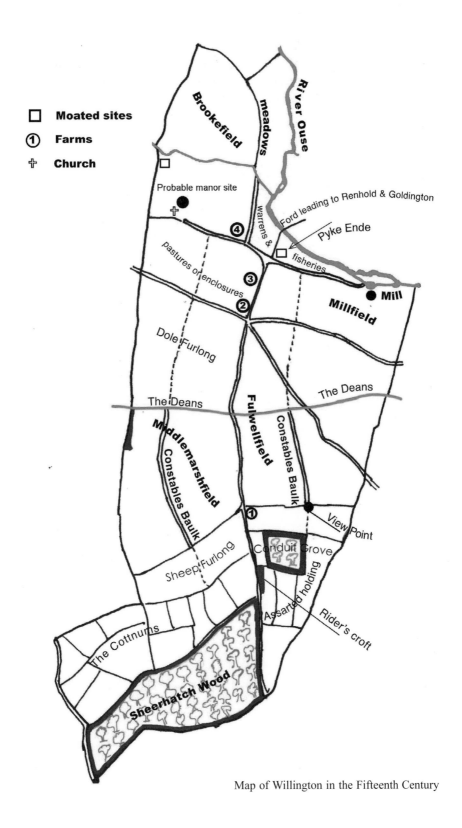

- ☐ Moated sites
- ① Farms
- ✝ Church

Brookefield

meadows

River Ouse

Probable manor site

Ford leading to Renhold & Goldington

Pyke Ende

④

warrens &

fisheries

pastures or enclosures

③

②

Millfield

Mill

Dole Furlong

The Deans

The Deans

Fulwellfield

Constables Baulk

Middlemarshfield

Constables Baulk

①

View Point

Sheep Furlong

Conduit Grove

Assarted holding

Rider's croft

The Cottnums

Sheerhatch Wood

Map of Willington in the Fifteenth Century

Chapter One

The Evidence

This book is primarily concerned with the documentary evidence for the history of Willington from 1382, the year after the Peasants' Revolt, to 1522, which was the date of the last surviving manor court roll before the manor was bought by John and Joan Gostwyk in 1529. Numerous documents relating to Willington manor are extant for the period.

The central theme of the volume is the story of the co-operation of the bailiff, manor elite and the other tenants to regulate and control their own affairs within the context of the management of the Mowbray lords' and ladies' councils and their officials. The prestigious and powerful Mowbray family was at its most influential at the end of the fourteenth century and in the early fifteenth century when they became Dukes of Norfolk and Earls Marshall of England, but they had financial problems before the male line died out in 1476. Willington was part of the dower of Katherine Neville, widow of the second Duke of Norfolk, from 1432, and the extant records document consistent management by her, her third and fourth husbands, their stewards and their councils October 1448-May 1482. The Mowbrays enjoyed close, but often dangerous, relationships with the English kings and their courts. Their properties and lands included Willington, Bedford Castle, Bromham, Cardington, Cople, Haynes and Stotfold in Bedfordshire and part of Wing in Buckinghamshire.

The text draws on the information contained in primary sources from several collections. Because the sources are incomplete, analysis of the information is problematic, but it is clear that serfdom lingered on throughout the 140 years covered by this volume, that tenants worked together under the leadership of local bailiffs, and that by the end of the fifteenth century villein tenure was almost as secure as free tenure.

Then, as now, the inhabitants were dependent on the landscape in which they lived. The geology, topography and archaeology of the landscape help to put information from the early documents and other records into context.

In his introduction to *The Making of the English Landscape*, W. G. Hoskins says that, 'everything is older than we think', and this is very true of Willington.[1] The landscape of Willington manor and parish can be described as a palimpsest: something which has been rewritten or redrawn at least once. The landscape, in which the settlement was – and is – placed, contains evidence of an earlier, hidden history, predating the parish boundaries. Human beings lived in Willington from prehistoric times, and invasions by the Romans, the Danes and the Normans left their mark.

---

[1] W. G. Hoskins, *The Making of the English Landscape* (London, 1995), p. 10.

Geological evidence

Willington's complex geology has influenced the choice of sites for settlements over the centuries. Beds of clay cover the greensand ridge in the south and lie below gravel terraces further north. Evidence of prehistoric habitation has been found during recent investigations by archaeologists prior to the extraction of gravel in the north-west of the modern parish; evidence of late Iron Age and Roman settlement has been found where the clay beds and the gravel terraces meet.

In the medieval period, the huge banks of gravel and sand along the southern bank of the river Great Ouse led to the development of rabbit warrens, which were sources of food and income for the lords of the manor, and moated sites were developed on the outcrops of clay at the east and west of this river bank, near the Blunham and Cople boundaries respectively.

Heavy clay soils are ideal for the building of moats, and Bedfordshire is believed to be the county with the densest concentration of medieval moats in the country. [2] Although they are often associated with extensive wood clearances, in Willington they were not associated with clearances on the greensand ridge, but are found where the clay soils and sub-soils extend to the river bank to the east and west where there may have been drainage problems, and where they may have been boundary markers intended to mark changes of land-ownership to traffic passing by on the river.

A moated site, known today as the Danish Camp, lies to the east; [3] a moated site, known as the Pond Garden in the eighteenth and nineteenth centuries, lay to the west, until being filled in during the twentieth century. There was a third moated site in medieval times, but although a description of the manor site in 1376 survives, no trace of it, or its moat and drawbridge, has so far been confirmed.[4] The logical position would have been between the church and Brook Field (formerly Brookefield, Brookefeild), near where the Tudor dovecote and stables stand today. A sketch map based on a drawing from an eighteenth-century map shows the Tudor farm buildings adjacent to the church but also shows three nearby ponds which may have been the remnants of the moat of the earlier manor house. [5]

The heaviest clay soils are to be found on the crest of the greensand ridge, which is covered with boulder clay. The land gradually slopes down to the north over an area of Oxford clay and then across gravel terraces to areas of alluvium along the river banks.[6] Beds of Oxford clay lie beneath the gravel terraces where, in some places, the gravel is less than half a metre deep. The most fertile soil seems to have been in Brook Field, north of Willington church, which before 1382 formed part of the demesne lands, the home farm of Willington manor. In 1507, this field was described as being divided into strips, but these strips may have existed much earlier.[7]

---

[2]   S. R. Coleman, 'Monuments Protection Programme', *South Midlands Archaeology*, vol. 20 (1990), pp. 3–5.

[3]   G. Edmondson and A. Mudd, 'Medieval Occupation at 'Danish Camp', Willington', *Bedfordshire Archaeology*, vol. 25 (2004), p. 220.

[4]   M. Bailey, *The English Manor, c1200 – c1500* (Manchester, 2002), p. 59.

[5]   Alan Cirket, *Sketch Map based on Gostelow Map 1779*, Bedfordshire Archives and Records Service (BARS), R1/75.

[6]   R. White, *Willington Parish Essay* (unpublished, 1978), BARS, PL/AC2/57.

[7]   D. Jamieson, *The Terrier of the Prior and Convent of Newnham of its Land and Tenements in Willington 1507*, unpublished transcription and translation, BARS, AD 325.

The medieval open fields were laid out over clay soils north of Sheerhatch Wood on the northern slopes of the greensand ridge. These extended to the waterway known as The Deans, which ran east to west in the central part of the manor, and almost to the river in the north-east corner of the manor near where the mill, mentioned in the Domesday Book, was situated on the river bank.

In medieval times the different soil types were farmed in the most efficient way: open fields on clay lands for arable; gravel terraces and grass verges of paths and lanes for grazing; sandy banks for rabbit warrens; and the most fertile fields enriched with river alluvium for the lord's demesne.

Topographical evidence

When the parish boundaries were first drawn, Willington was part of the Wixamtree Hundred, which may have been a Saxon estate with its centre at Old Warden. The hundred comprised the manors of Blunham, Moggerhanger, Willington, Cople, Cardington and Eastcotts at the northern edge, and the modern parishes of Old Warden, Northill and Southill to the south. Willington and Cople were much smaller than the other manors in the Wixamtree Hundred and may have originally been one unit. The greensand ridge and Sheerhatch Wood, at the southern boundary of Willington, formed the spine of this estate and the shape of the parish boundaries and pattern of connecting lanes, either side of the ridge, suggest that the wood may have been shared by more than one parish for the keeping of pigs, or for the collection of fallen branches and surplus trees for buildings or for fuel in the medieval period. [8]

There is evidence to show that the boundaries of Sheerhatch Wood changed at different points in the manor's history. Field boundaries and field names on the earliest detailed map of Willington (the Gostelow map of 1779) indicate that Sheerhatch Wood once extended further north and that there had been extensive clearances, or assarts.[9] Several enclosures, named Cottnums, between the northern edge of the wood and the southern edge of the fields, were cleared, although it is not possible to date these assarts with certainty. They may have been cleared by the Beauchamps in the two centuries after the Norman Conquest, or by the Mowbrays, to provide more land in response to rising population in the decades before the Black Death in the fourteenth century: 'but it is more likely that peasants cleared lands for themselves, perhaps with the lords' encouragement or permission.'[10] The enclosures were named Barnyard Cotnum, Barn Cotnum and Stockings Cotnum; three enclosures were called Hill Cotnum, and there were various other versions of the name. A document related to Cranfield, dated about 1140, describes the service of a man who held a cotland there: 'He works 2 days a week and does carrying service on foot', but there is no similar evidence of dues performed by holders of

[8]   Sheerhatch is the modern spelling of the name of the wood; earlier records use slightly different spellings such as Sherehatch, Shirehatch or Shirehatche.
[9]   Thomas Gostelow, *A Plan of the Estate of Her Grace the Duchess of Bedford and Robert Palmer Esquire, lately purchased of His Grace the Duke of Marlborough, in the Parish of Willington in the County of Bedford 1779,* and the map book, BARS, R1/75. The map was drawn five years after Willington and other Bedfordshire properties were bought by Gertrude, Dowager Duchess of Bedford, with her agent Robert Palmer, during the minority of Francis, Duke of Bedford.
[10]   Christopher Dyer, personal communication, 17 September 2016.

cotland in Willington.[11] The assarts named Sheep Leys and Sheep Furlong in 1779 suggest that the clearances may have been made at a time when it became more profitable to keep sheep than grow crops. An area of replanted ridge and furrow, found within the wood at the end of the twentieth century, suggests that at one time the area of cultivation extended further than today.[12] Angela Simco described the remains of a wood bank and external ditch round the east part of the woodland, and also identified a raised platform with the remains of a hollow way running from it in a north-north-westerly direction, which may be all that remains of a keeper's house and the access to it.[13] A deep rectangular hollow a few metres inside the eastern edge of the wood may be the remains of a sawpit.

The manor's open arable fields were recorded in 1507 as Millfield, Fulwell-feld, Midlemarshfeild [sic] and Brookefeild [sic], but in the eighteenth century the Gostclow map shows them as Conduit Field, Michaelmas Field, Mill Field and Brook Field.[14] They were laid out over a landscape divided into strips running north from the woodland on the crest of the greensand ridge towards to the river. The ditches and tracks which divide the landscape into strips may have been a way of draining the heavy land, or of providing access from the river to the woodland on the ridge, though it is possible that they were the remains of a designed landscape: perhaps a Saxon field system.

Five roads meet at the Willington crossroads, Wood Lane, Bedford Road, Station Road, Barford Road and Sandy Road. Five-way junctions are unusual and may mark former medieval meeting places or entries into land-holdings. There may have been another five-way junction at the south-west of Willington parish, at the western end of Sheerhatch Wood, where the greensand ridge crosses the Willington/Cople parish border. Tradition has it that this was the meeting place for Wixamtree Hundred, and was where Deadman's Oak once stood.[15]

It has been suggested that Wood Lane was formerly a green lane running past the medieval Goggs Hall (near where Hill Farm stands today) and the east end of Sheerhatch Wood to the ancient common of Beeston Leys.[16] The road, to which this green lane from Willington was connected, also gave Blunham, Chalton and Moggerhanger, in the north-east of the hundred, access to Beeston Leys, Sheerhatch Wood and Deadman's Oak. Running north from the village crossroads, this track

[11] Joyce Godber, *History of Bedfordshire, 1066–1888* (Bedford, 1969), pp. 34–5.

[12] Three National Trust volunteers and the late Angela Simco were granted permission by the Shuttleworth Estate to undertake an informal archaeological exploration in 2000. They found wood banks, tracks, a possible house platform and an area of ridge and furrow, Simco, *Unpublished Letter and Report to the Author, 6 February 2003*.

[13] Angela Simco concludes that: 'The limited results of the field visit indicate that Sheerhatch Wood merits a complete archaeological survey. It clearly has a complex history, with part at least having been cleared for agriculture in the middle ages. The internal banks suggest that the northern part of the wood may have survived clearance and was separated from the ridge and furrow area by an east-west track. Further work should clarify the extent and layout of the internal boundaries and ridge and furrow, and investigate the nature of the possible keeper's house.' Angela Simco, personal communication, 6 February 2003.

[14] D. Jamieson, *The Terrier of the Prior and Convent of Newnham of its Land and Tenements in Willington 1507*, BARS, AD 325.

[15] F. W. Marsom, 'The Meeting Place of Wixamtree Hundred', *The Publications of Bedfordshire Historical Record Society*, vol. 25 (Streatley, 1947), pp. 1–3.

[16] *Ibid*, p. 1.

continued along today's Station Road, across the site of the original village green, on which the Methodist church now stands, and straight on along the track towards the river, across today's cycle track and to the site of a ford across a tributary of the river Great Ouse. This track was still in use in 1900 and was shown on Jefferys' map of 1765.[17] The wide grass verges on Station Road suggest that flocks of sheep, other animals and pedestrians passed along this way in earlier times on their way to the ford, and on to Castle Mills and Bedford. From before the Domesday Book the ford, near the downstream, eastern boundary of early estates belonging to Aschill of Ware and later the Beauchamps, connected Willington to Goldington and to their other lands which were situated on both sides of the Great Ouse.[18]

There is no clear documentary evidence of the use of a ford in medieval times, or of the use of the river for transport. This is not surprising as: 'travel was such a routine matter; the vast majority of journeys, whether of people or goods, were simply not recorded.'[19] Navigation up the Great Ouse is recorded as far inland as Lavenham, but: 'the upper reaches were impeded to a marked degree by fords, shallows and mill dams.'[20] The Domesday Book records that in 1086 the stretch of river either side of Willington contained four mills; two in Great Barford, one at Willington and another in Goldington.[21] A submerged stone barrage across the Great Ouse near the site of the former Bedford castle was constructed to direct water to flow through the King's Ditch built in the tenth century, but was also probably part of the town defences by blocking the river approaches to the town.[22]

Although the documentary sources for Willington manor do not contain any direct references to the use of the river for transport, there is an intriguing hint in the bailiff's account 1388–89:

> And to the same Receiver General with 33s. 4d. for the price of 20 quarters of oats delivered to the lord's avener at Hynton, near Cambridge;[23] 6d. for the cost of the men bringing the said oats; 12d. for the cost of one man taking 24 partridges for the use of the lord's household; 12d. for the cost of various men taking 32 rabbits and carrying them with the partridges to Hynton aforesaid.[24]

The transport of goods by water was far cheaper than by road, by a factor of up to six.[25] The above passage suggests that partridges and rabbits were carried by

---

17   Thomas Jefferys, *The County of Bedford* (London, 1765). No trace of the ford remains today, but the map shows a ford which was described in the *Bedfordshire Times and Independent*, 'Round the County', 4 August 1899, p. 3, cols. 1 and 2. The author of the article, 'A.R.', describes the ford as being just west of the moated site known today as the Danish Camp and says that: 'This ford is still useable, and the road to it, now covered by grass, is traceable across the meadows towards Renhold.'

18   Aschill of Ware was the Saxon thegn who held Willington before the Norman Conquest.

19   James F. Edwards and Brian Paul Hinde, 'The Transportation System of Medieval England and Wales', *Journal of Historical Geography*, vol. 17, no. 2 (April 1991), p. 124.

20   Dorothy Summers, *The Great Ouse – The History of a River Navigation* (Newton Abbot, 1973), pp. 22–3.

21   John, Morris, ed., Veronica Sankaran and David Sherlock, *Domesday Book 20: Bedfordshire* (Chichester, 1977), section 23, nos. 7, 11, 36, 39.

22   Matt Edgeworth, *Fluid Pasts: Archaeology of Flow* (London, 2011), p. 92.

23   An official responsible for the horse's food.

24   *Willington Bailiffs' Accounts*, BARS, R8/62/2/6, or J. S. Thompson, ed., *Bailiffs' Accounts for Willington and Certain Other Manors, 1382 to 1397*, BARS, CRT 130 Willington 11, p. 22.

25   Edwards and Hinde, 'The Transportation System of Medieval England and Wales', p.129.

horse or horse and cart, while oats, which were much less perishable, travelled the cheapest way possible, that is, by boat.

East of Wood Lane and Station Road there is evidence of a north/south boundary, which was already beginning to disappear in 1779. Immediately north of the road to Sandy the hedge line had been lost by 1779, but it could still be seen crossing Mill Piece, almost to the river. South of the road to Sandy part of the boundary between that road and the greensand ridge was described as Constables' Baulk. Until recently the position of this boundary was partially marked by hedges and continued across the waterway known as The Deans, passing the site of a Tudor conduit house, marked on Jefferys' map of Bedfordshire, and on later maps.[26] Further south, the boundary continued to a feature marked by Gostelow as Cuckoo Pen, a lozenge-shaped enclosure situated at the northern edge of the medieval extent of the wood and still marked today by hedges. From Cuckoo Pen views over the vale of Bedford, to the north-east and north-west, open out.

To the west of Wood Lane/Station Road another boundary, also named Constables' Baulk, can be seen. There may have been a similar lozenge-shaped enclosure at the southern end of this western Constables' Baulk, but twentieth century drainage works have obliterated any evidence. Today the baulk exists as a broad track, standing higher than the fields either side, with a ditch to east and west, and runs from the northern edge of Sheerhatch Wood towards the river. Today's Balls Lane is not exactly aligned with this track, but follows its approximate line towards the main village street, Church Road. The parish boundary between Willington and Cople also marks one of these early boundaries.

Archaeological evidence

Archaeological investigations and aerial photographs show that this medieval landscape was laid out over an earlier prehistoric and Romano-British one.

Archaeological investigations on the gravel terraces along the riverbank on the boundary with Cople, during the twentieth century, have revealed evidence of human habitation during the Neolithic and Bronze Ages. These investigations, with the use of aerial photography and other surveys, suggest an early ritual landscape with ring-ditches, linear enclosures, pit alignments, isolated burials, barrows and mortuary enclosures.[27]

A probable Iron Age triple boundary, to the east of Station Road and leading almost to the river, has been identified from aerial photographs, and similar ditches have been found elsewhere in the Ouse valley. Aerial photography has also revealed traces of part of a Roman road, between a settlement near today's town of Sandy and the ford over the Great Ouse at Bedford, passing across the southern part of Willington parish, entering what became the open fields, in the east, just north of Sheerhatch Wood. It led through the manor to what has been described as the most complex crop mark in the county.[28] More than a hundred

[26]   Jefferys, *The County of Bedford*, 1765.
[27]   Albion Archaeology, *Archaeological Desk-based Assessment, Bedford River Valley Park Bedfordshire* (unpublished, 2007), p.13. Produced for Bedfordshire County Council on behalf of the Marston Vale Trust.
[28]   S. R. Coleman, Historic Environment Information Officer, Central Bedfordshire Council, personal communication, 2012.

Roman coins from the second to the fourth centuries AD have been found at two find-spots near this crop-mark.[29]

Field walking has shown that there was a substantial wood bank at the western side of the southern end of Wood Lane and that Sheerhatch Wood is still surrounded by a ditch. East of the substantial wood bank was a small three-field estate, with its own piece of woodland, The Grove, which in medieval times may have been the site of Coppyd Hall, occasionally referred to in the fifteenth century court rolls and held by the Maryon (or Maryan, Marion) family.

Other archaeological investigations have called into question the theory that the moated site, traditionally known as the Danish Camp, at the north-east of the manor had Danish origins.[30] Bedford, with its crossing of the Great Ouse, was a Scandinavian stronghold taken by King Edward the Elder in 914, but evidence of a Danish settlement in Willington has not been found. There is evidence of a later high-status building on the bank above the river east of the ford, and pottery finds indicated that: 'occupation was quite tightly defined between the early twelfth and mid-thirteenth century.'[31] This building, on a bank above the flood level of the river, would have been a natural look-out giving views to east and west, and northwards across the flood plain and up the slope towards Renhold. Occupation may have ended in 1265, on the death of the last Baron of Bedford, when Willington and other parts of the estates of the barony passed to the Mowbrays by marriage. They may have built themselves another medieval manor house further to the west, near the church, but so far no trace has been found.[32]

Documentary evidence from the eleventh century to 1382
The Domesday Book for Bedfordshire makes it clear that Willington existed before the Norman Conquest of 1066, and was one of Aschill of Ware's many land-holdings in the county. It was situated in an important strategic position; being almost the first point at which visitors, welcome or unwelcome, travelling upstream by boat, entered his lands.

Bedfordshire was one of the two English counties where land values reduced dramatically at the time of the Norman Conquest; the other one was Yorkshire.[33] Most Bedfordshire manors which were in the army's path suffered losses of between 20% and 40% of the value of their lands, and many suffered losses of 50% or more.[34]

[29]   Bedford Borough Council, Historic Monument Record, Willington Finds List.
[30]   Jane Hassall, 'Excavations at Willington, 1973', *Bedfordshire Archaeological Journal*, vol. 10 (1975), pp. 23–40 and Edmondson and Mudd, 'Medieval Occupation at 'Danish Camp', Willington', pp. 208–21.
[31]   *Ibid*, p. 208.
[32]   There is an account of the Mowbrays tenure of Willington, with detailed references in William Page, ed., *Victoria County History of Bedfordshire* (VCH), vol. 3 (London, 1912), pp. 262–3.
[33]   Robin Fleming, *Lords and Kings in Conquest England* (Cambridge, 1991), p.124n. Bedfordshire is not mentioned by R. Welldon-Finn in *Domesday Book, a Guide* (London, 1973), p.83, where, when describing the decline in land values, he says that they cannot be all attributed to the Norman armies, but that: 'bad weather, poor harvests, disease and the flight overseas of many native land-owners would also be factors.'
[34]   G. Herbert Fowler, *Bedfordshire 1086: An Analysis and Synthesis of Domesday Book*, Bedfordshire Historical Record Society (BHRS) Quarto Memoirs, vol. 1 (Aspley Guise, 1922), p. 31. Fowler notes the loss of seed-corn and plough oxen at the time of the invasion; bad harvests and taxation retarded the return of prosperity. Failures in harvests resulting in famine are chronicled for the years 1071 and 1082. It is not known why Willington did not suffer as so many other manors did.

Willington was not the worst affected but was reduced to one third of its former value. In 1068, the Domesday Book recorded that the value of Willington had risen above its pre-1066 value by 1086: 'Total Value £7; when acquired 40s; before 1066 £6.'[35] It had become one of almost sixty holdings held by Hugh de Beauchamp.[36] The data about loss of values, contained in the Domesday Book text, was used by Herbert Fowler to plot the route of the Norman troops when they travelled north-wards from London to subdue the English counties.[37] He calculated that the Norman armies travelled west to east along the Great Ouse taking provisions and devastating communities as they went.

In 1086 Willington supported thirteen villeins and eight serfs, there were two mills (under one roof) worth 12s., significantly less than other mills on some nearby manors, and one hundred eels worth 7s. Willington consisted of ten hides and was a double five-hide unit, with land sufficient for nine ploughs, though there were only eight. One five-hide unit formed the demesne, with three ploughs. The other five-hide unit was held by thirteen villeins with five ploughs. By 1086 it had become the only vill in the Wixamtree Hundred to be valued at more than it had been before the time of King Edward.

The number of pigs recorded (forty) was low when compared with the hundred pigs in the neighbouring manor of Cople. The pigs in Willington may have been grazed in the common woodland either side of the waterway known as The Deans, which runs east to west across the landscape, at the foot of the northern slope of the greensand ridge. The much larger area of common pasture in Sheerhatch Wood may have been shared with the manors of Cardington, Cople and Northill, and was perhaps excluded from the survey.[38]

The Beauchamps became barons of Bedford, and Willington continued to be part of their estates until 1265, when the last baron died childless. His estates were divided between his four sisters. Willington was part of the inheritance of his sister Maud and became part of the huge honour of the Mowbrays, the property of her husband Roger de Mowbray, and part of her dower after his death in 1266. After her death, Willington, and some of her other lands in Bedfordshire were held by her second husband, Roger le Straunge, until his death in the early fourteenth century. He was named as the lord of Willington in the Hundred Rolls for Bedfordshire 1275–76 in the section on Wixamtree (Wyxconestre): 'Roger le Straunge held the regality in Wyburn [Willington] but it is not known by what warrant.'[39] During the years between the death of Maud de Beauchamp in 1273 and the Peasants' Revolt in 1381, members of the Mowbray family only held Willington directly for twenty-seven years, for most of the time it was handed over to in-laws, or the Crown or its nominees.

---

[35] Morris, *Domesday Book 20: Bedfordshire*, section 23, no. 11.

[36] *Ibid.* He held lands in Stoddon Hundred, Bucklow Half-Hundred, Wixamtree, Clifton, Flitt, Barford, Manshead, and Willey Hundreds, some of which were sub-let.

[37] Fowler, *Bedfordshire 1086: An Analysis and Synthesis of Domesday Book*, p. 79.

[38] Morris, *Domesday Book 20: Bedfordshire,* section 23, nos.10, 49–55, 56.

[39] J. S. Thompson, ed., 'The Hundred Rolls of 1274 and 1279', in John Thompson, ed., *Hundreds, Manors, Parishes and the Church: A Selection of Early Documents for Bedfordshire*, BHRS, vol. 69 (Bedford, 1990), p.10.

Lay subsidy records for Bedfordshire in 1309 and 1332 survive.[40] Willington's tax assessment in 1309 was lower than those of neighbouring manors, and the manor had the dubious distinction of being the only one in Bedfordshire to be re-assessed; an increment was taken and the taxes increased.[41] The tax was assessed by the village community, organised by them and paid by them, and was not directed by the lords of the manor. The differences between the two assessments that year suggest some tax-evasion. The table below shows that the *incremento* raised more tax; prosperous tax-payers were required to pay more (with the exception of the lord of the manor) and fewer poorer people were charged. The taxes raised on the manor in 1332 were higher, and no *incremento* was deemed necessary.

Summary of lay subsidy data for fourteenth century Willington.

Tax paid by villagers or inhabitants	1309	1309 incremento	1332
The lord of the manor	16s. 8d.	14s. 3¼d.	13s. 2¼d.
Paying 2s. and above	2	4	8
Paying 20d. and under 2s.	0	3	7
Paying 16d. – 19d.	0	2	6
Paying 13d. – 15 ¾ d.	0	1	2
Paying 10d. – 12 ½ d.	12	6	4
Paying 6d. – 9 ½ d.	24	8	1
Paying under 6d.	0	2	0
Total number taxed	39	27	29
Average payments	9½d.	1s. 7d.	1s. 8¾d.
Total tax paid	46s. 8½d.	55s. 5¼d.	61s. 7¼d.
Total assessed value of the manor	£58 7s. 8½d.	£69 5s. 11¼d.	£46 4s. 0¾d.

Although a detailed examination of these taxes is outside the scope of this book, the lay subsidy records for Willington show fluctuating fortunes for some families, evidence of movement of families in and out of the manor and changes in the distribution of wealth. The lord's taxes were reduced and the number of people paying higher taxes grew. In 1309 twenty-four men paid smaller sums, less than 9d. The number of poorer people paying tax was reduced to ten in the increment and to one in the 1332 assessment.

In 1309, in addition to the lord of the manor, the two men paying more than 2s. were Roger Gostwyk, paying 2s.¾d., and Walter Pecke, paying 2s.¼d. When

[40]   S. H. A. Hervey, ed., *Two Bedfordshire Subsidy Lists 1309 and 1332*, Suffolk Green Books 18 (Bury St Edmunds, 1925). Carolyn Fenwick's book, *The Poll Taxes of 1377, 1379, and 1381. Part 1 Bedfordshire-Lincolnshire*, also includes Bedfordshire figures but several parishes, including Willington, are missing. The tax payable in 1309 and the increment of 1309 was one twenty-fifth, giving valuations of the manor of £58 7s. 8½d. and £69 5s. 11d. respectively. In 1332, the tax was one fifteenth from country manors and one tenth from the town; the valuation of Willington manor that year was £58 7s. 8½d.
[41]   Hervey, *Two Bedfordshire Subsidy Lists 1309 and 1332*, pp. 47–8, p. 133. *Incremento* is either the dative or ablative form of the Latin for 'increase'.

the increment was made later that year, Gostwyk's payment increased more than three-fold to 6s. 10d, and Walter Pecke was not taxed. A new man, Walter James, possibly a new bailiff, paid 7s. 2½d., and the total number of men paying more than 2s. rose to four. Geoffrey Rider, who had paid 6¼d. in the first assessment, was taxed at 18¼d. in the increment and two members of the same family paid 15¾ d. and 18 ¾d. respectively. No members of this family were taxed in 1332, although they became a force to be reckoned with later in the century, disappearing from the records in the early fifteenth century. The Gostwyks continued to flourish. Although the tax they paid reduced by more than half in 1332 the family was to have a major influence on life on the manor for the next four hundred years.

In 1332, of the eight people who paid more than 2s., five paid double the amount they paid in 1309. There were three new names, of which one may have been a member of a gentry family; the other two were a reeve and a shepherd.

The reduction in the value of the manor shown in the table suggests an apparent decline in prosperity, and it has been suggested that bad harvests from about 1316 may have led to financial difficulties for the poor and contributed to the fall in the total value of the taxes collected in 1332 throughout the county.[42]

Some wood clearances on the manor took place later in the century. In 1366 the third John Mowbray accused his stepmother, Elizabeth de Vere, his father's second wife and widow, of laying waste the manor. She was fined an estimated £938 18s. for destroying hundreds of trees and allowing buildings to fall into decay.[43] An inquisition on her estates in Bedfordshire was held in 1376.[44]

The information in contemporary official documents from the fourteenth century, when the demesne of the manor was still managed directly by the extended Mowbray family, shows that there was a pattern of mixed farming, with cereals and other crops being grown in the arable fields and horses, oxen, cows, sheep and pigs being reared.[45] After the demesne lands were leased out the court rolls show that the pattern of mixed farming continued.[46]

The effects of the Black Death of c.1348 and the disputes between the different lords of the manor and the tenant farmers in Willington are unclear, but something was sufficient to drive the Mowbray lords to lease out their demesne lands before 1382, after which time more details are available about the management of the manor and the lives of the people who lived there.

Documentary evidence 1382–1522

Manor court rolls for Willington survive 1394–1674, but are most numerous for the period 1382–1482. The 101 rolls on which this volume is based date 1394–1522. Fifty-three of the rolls are for courts held in the autumn, usually called views of frankpledge with court, or occasionally views with court. The remaining forty-eight rolls are for courts held in the spring, and usually called halmoots, or, in later years,

42   Godber, *History of Bedfordshire,* p. 97.
43   VCH, vol. 3, p. 263. There is a reference to Elizabeth de Mowbray rebutting a charge from her stepson in 1366 of pulling down cottages in the village. She claimed that the tenants had died of the plague, however this evidence is unreliable.
44   *Ibid.*
45   *Ibid.*
46   *Willington Manor Court Rolls, 1394–1674*, BARS, Box R212, Roll 1, April 1394.

courts baron. At the views of frankpledge, payments of fines for brewing ale and baking bread were paid, and manorial officials were usually appointed. Land transfers, the management of fields, fines for petty crime and the imposition of by-laws took place in both the autumn and spring courts.

Most of the Willington manor court rolls are kept by Bedfordshire Archives and Records Service as part of their Bedford Settled Estates (Russell Collection) Archives.[47] Eight rolls, dated 1463–72, are kept in the British Library.[48] These rolls were purchased by the British Museum in 1881 from the widow of A. J. Horwood, a barrister. Transcriptions of the rolls held by the British Library are kept by Bedfordshire Archives and Records Service.[49] Translations of all the Willington manor court rolls can be found on the Bedfordshire Archives and Records Service website.[50]

There are forty-two rolls April 1394–1426, of which sixteen form a complete series of two rolls a year for the eight years October 1413–April 1421, by which time the manor was held by John Mowbray. There is a single roll dated 1440, with lists of costs for new buildings, after Katherine Neville had been widowed.

There are fifty-one rolls 1448–83, of which eighteen form a complete series of two rolls a year for the nine years October 1450–June 1459 when Katherine Neville was married to her third husband, John Beaumont, first Viscount Beaumont. There is a complete set of sixteen rolls for the eight years October 1462–May 1470, during the time when Thomas Rokes was steward, which includes the eight rolls held in the British Library. Three of this series of rolls have the name of Katherine Neville's fourth and final husband, Sir John Woodville, who took precedence over her, in the heading. There is a further short complete series of six rolls for the three years October 1473–April or May 1476 when Katherine Neville is named alone.

Rolls from the time of the Howards, Dukes of Norfolk, are dated September 1515, March 1520 and March and December 1522. There are four rolls from the time of John Gostwyk and his wife Joan, dated 1537–40 inclusive, and then no further rolls until October 1556.

The series of eleven Willington bailiffs' accounts 1382–97 is not complete; it also includes nine accounts for Haynes, and individual accounts for Wing, Linslade and Sheerhatch Wood.[51] Accounts for four years are missing (1383–84, 1391–92, 1393–94 and 1395–96) and the evidence in the remaining accounts suggests that in these missing years changes took place because of disputes about rents and holdings. The collection of bailiffs' accounts are the only surviving accounts of the Mowbrays prior to the first Duke of Norfolk's exile in 1398, and overlap the first five Willington manor court rolls. All these accounts are held by Bedfordshire Archives and Records Service.

The British Library holds a bailiff's account of Willington manor 1457–58, with the accounts of Bedford Castle, Bromham and Ickwell and references to Cardington

---

47 *Willington Manor Court Rolls, 1394–1674*, BARS, Box R212.
48 *Willington Manor Court Rolls, 1463–72*, British Library, Add Ch. 26813/1-8.
49 *Willington Manor Court Rolls, 1463–72*, transcription by Joyce Godber, BARS, CRT 130 Willington 4.
50 *Willington Manor Court Rolls, 1394–1674*, translation by Dorothy Jamieson, BARS, http://bedsarchives.bedford.gov.uk/CommunityArchives/Willington/WillingtonManorCourtRolls/WillingtonManor CourtRollsIntroduction.aspx. There is a general introduction to the rolls and each roll is summarised.
51 BARS, R8/62/2/1-11, and Thompson, *Bailiffs' Accounts for Willington*, BARS, CRT 130 Willington 11.

and Southill.[52] Arundel Castle Archive holds another account for 1480–81; *Wyllyngton Account of William Paryssh, Bailiff and Reeve there at the time within.* [53]

Arundel Castle Archive also holds the receiver's accounts for Willington for 1421–22 with details for Bedford Castle, Newnham, Bromham, Linslade, Wing and Seagrave. [54] Ministers' accounts for Framlingham, Willington and other manors are kept by the Suffolk Records Office, 1486–87, 1502–3, 1503–4 and 1508–9. [55]

Other evidence still extant for the years 1382–1522 includes a terrier of Newnham Priory listing its lands in the manor in 1507. [56] The terrier includes the names of major tenants and land-holders. The Jefferys' map of 1765 and the Gostelow map and map book of 1779, both held by Bedfordshire Archives and Record Service, provide evidence of the layout of the manor in the eighteenth century. [57] The village layout may have been similar four hundred years earlier.

No surveys, rentals or extents for Willington survive, but the records described above show how the absentee lords of the manor of Willington managed their resources there. Their administrators safeguarded their lord's interests and preserved the value of their assets after the demesne lands had been leased out. The information found in the records, showing how they responded to growing confidence among the tenants and changing social conditions on the manor during the period 1382–1522, will be delineated in the following pages. The purchase of the manor by John and Joan Gostwyk in 1529 meant that the story of medieval Willington came to an end. Management of the manor by absentee landlords ceased for the next two hundred years.

[52]   *Willington Bailiff's Account, 1457–58*, British Library, Add Ch. 657.

[53]   Arundel Castle Archives, A1328.

[54]   *Willington Receiver's Accounts 1421–22*, Arundel Castle Archives, A1642.

[55]   *Compoti of all the Ministers of Thomas, Earl of Surrey, for Manors of Framlingham at the Castle, Kettleburgh, Hacheston, Peasenhall, Kelsale, and Willington (Bd.)*, Suffolk Record Office, HD 1538/225/6.

[56]   D. Jamieson, *The Terrier of the Prior and Convent of Newnham of its Land and Tenements in Willington 1507*, BARS, AD 325. Newnham Priory terriers, or land books, also exist for Bedford, Biddenham, Southill and Toddington. See Appendix 1.

[57]   Jefferys, *The County of Bedford*, 1765 and Gostelow, *A Plan of the Estate of her Grace the Duchess of Bedford and Robert Palmer Esquire ... 1779.*

Chapter Two

The Decline of Serfdom and the Peasants' Revolt

Some historians divided the past into periods or eras, and some identified major historical turning points. In contrast to these artificial attempts to divide history into units, researchers now examine continuity and change; features which were formerly used to identify periods, eras or turning points are recognised as the results of earlier developments and are seen to contribute to later ones.[1] The Peasants' Revolt of 1381 has often been identified as an historical turning point leading to the end of serfdom. But, while significant, it should also be seen as part of a longer transitional process.

The decline of serfdom after 1348
Social conditions, which were at least partly the results of the Black Death of about 1348, and further outbreaks of the plague later in the fourteenth century, brought about changes in the relationships between landlords and tenants and led to conflicts between them, not only in England, but also on the continent of Europe.

As a result of the depopulation caused by the plague landlords found it difficult to keep tenants under the old terms. Gradually conditions of tenure changed, and serfdom began to disappear even before the Peasants' Revolt of 1381, which started in the towns of Essex in response to the government's imposition of a national poll tax.[2] While it is possible that the Peasants' Revolt had some influence on life in Willington, Joyce Godber wrote:

> The Bedfordshire villages were surprisingly quiet, as were those in Buckinghamshire… Perhaps it was the lord, rather than the customary tenant, who was getting the worst of things on the small Bedfordshire manors, and the poll-tax alone was not sufficient to incite the freemen to rise.[3]

Even though the disturbances in Bedfordshire seem to have been few, at Willington the Mowbray family seemed to accept that change was inevitable. Their power base was too far away, at Epworth on the Isle of Axholme, to effectively control difficult villein tenants, so by 1382 the holdings had been rearranged, a new extent agreed or imposed and a new way of life begun. In the years to come change in Willington as elsewhere: 'was mostly brought about, not by organised

---

[1]   These ideas are discussed at length in John L. Watts, ed., *The End of the Middle Ages: England in the Fifteenth and Sixteenth Centuries* (Sutton, 1998).
[2]   Richard Britnell, 'Land and Lordship, Common Themes and Regional Variations', in Ben Dodds and Richard Britnell, eds, *Agriculture and Rural Society after the Black Death: Common Themes and Regional Variations* (Hatfield, 2008), pp.163–4.
[3]   Godber, *History of Bedfordshire*, p. 102.

violence, but through a long-drawn out accumulation of petty acts of obstruction and insubordination by the peasantry.'[4]

Although the evidence from the bailiffs' accounts and the manor court rolls is incomplete, they suggest that the people of Willington were given greater control of their own affairs after the Peasants' Revolt. The bailiff at the time of the revolt, Robert Gostwyk, a free man of the village, continued in post for over ten years, and was succeeded by another man of similar status for about a year (William Pecke), but from 1394 the bailiff was named as William Ridere, a villein tenant. From 1404 he oversaw a second jury sworn in at every view of frankpledge to verify that: 'the tithing men, constable and tasters of ale spoke well and faithfully and concealed nothing', ensuring that at least twenty-four heads of household from the manor participated in the legal process.[5]

Rising labour costs and stable grain prices also contributed to change, and most lay and church landlords had let parts of their lands by about 1400, or abandoned the system of direct farming completely. The farming of manors directly to provide for the market or the landlord's table gave way to a policy of leasing the demesnes and living off the rents. On some manors demesnes were let out to manorial tenants piecemeal, a few acres at a time for terms of a year or two, on others they were leased whole over the longer term to one individual. The manor of Willington was farmed directly by the lords of the manor until an unknown date some time before the date of the first surviving bailiff's account 1382–83.

Customary tenants had been expected to perform boonworks as part of their rents, but in 1382–83 the demesne lands were let to: 'various bondsmen tenants and certain tenants at will of Willyngton.'[6] As a result, boonworks for the lord became unnecessary.

The lord of the manor found the manor less profitable from about 1400 and throughout the fifteenth century. The Mowbrays attempted to protect their property and their income, but the bailiff and tenants acted together to negotiate better terms, as shown by the bailiffs' accounts and the manor court rolls, which provide evidence of negotiations over entry fines, heriots, rents and services. During these processes the disappearance of servile status was gradual but inexorable.

Changing relationships between lords and tenants after 1382

It is possible that Willington suffered badly from the plague and that this may have led, in part, to a rearrangement of the holdings, the preparation of a new extent and free tenure.[7] A copy of the new extent which described this rearrangement of lands has not survived but the new arrangements reduced the customary burdens on the tenants while protecting the financial interests of the Mowbrays.

---

[4]   E. B. Fryde and N. Fryde, 'Peasant Rebellion and Peasant Discontents', in E. Miller, ed., *The Agrarian History of England and Wales*, vol. 3, 1348–1500 (Cambridge, 1991), p. 750.

[5]   BARS, Box R212, Roll 7, October 1404.

[6]   The passage at the end of this account describes them as, 'four acremen formerly bondsmen tenants', *Willington Bailiffs' Accounts,* BARS, R8/62/2/1, and Thompson, *Bailiffs' Accounts for Willington*, BARS, CRT 130 Willington 11, p. 1.

[7]   Godber, *History of Bedfordshire,* pp.101–2. In this context 'free' must be taken to mean that there were reduced boonworks and manorial services. Tenants still had to obey the custom of the manor, which included obligations to attend the manor court and pay rents.

The lands were not free, in the modern sense of the word, for any of the tenants on the manor. The language used in the accounts before 1400 reminds the customary tenants that many of them used to hold their lands in bondage, as molemen, acremen or cottars. Free tenants whose lands could be inherited and who held their lands by charters, which provided evidence of ownership, were also required to attend the manor court and observe the custom of the manor. They paid small rents which today might be considered to be ground rents. Customary tenants, no longer in bondage and now usually described as villeins, paid much larger rents than the freemen for standard sizes of holdings, a messuage and half a virgate (about ten acres on this manor) or a messuage and eight acres. Their tenancies were much less secure at that time, being held at the lord's will or for one life. Five tenants, presumably on small-holdings, paid their rents in kind by a pound of pepper or a chicken or two 1382–97.[8]

The inequality of the payments between villeins and free men continued throughout the fifteenth century. The rents paid by the free tenants increased slightly during the period 1382–1482, from a total of 6s. ½d. in 1382–83 to 6s. 10½d. by 1481; but they were very small amounts when compared with 13s. 4d. paid throughout the period by each villein tenant for a messuage and standard holding.

The Mowbrays' decision to let out the demesne lands, instead of farming them directly, led to life changes for most of their tenants. The customary tenants were no longer required to provide the unspecified boonworks. The tenants who rented parts of the demesne lands were able to cultivate fields on the most fertile soil of the manor, but they found, however, that the new extent arranged by the lord's council or his steward imposed extra charges of 32s. for lands that had previously been included in their rents. They protested, and the bailiff, Robert Gostwyk, supported them and discussed the problem with the lord's council. The final paragraph of the first surviving bailiff's account 1382–83 was added in a different hand and records:

> Out of which [is] requited to the accountant [that is, the local bailiff, Robert Gostwyk] 32s. above owed for rents of four acremen formerly bondsmen tenants, because the above said total had been allowed to farmers[9] of meadow land and demesne pasture without payment except £25 6s. 8d. above, owed both for the aforesaid rents and for the aforesaid meadow lands and pasture this year, as the accountant swears on his oath over the present account, since when he has spoken with the council of the lord, and from that he will be able to enquire into the truth of the matter and to certify etc.[10]

It appears that Robert Gostwyk allowed arrears of 32s. a year to accumulate until 20 August 1393, by which date they had reached £18 3s. 3½d.[11] He retired or died in that year and the arrears were written off, but the rents were raised. Robert Gostwyk had enabled the men who held the demesne lands to obstruct and defy the lord's attempts to raise the rents for more than ten years.

8   BARS R8/62/2/1-11, and Thompson, *Bailiffs' Accounts for Willington*, BARS, CRT 130 Willington 11, pp. 1, 3, 7, 11, 15, 20, 24, 28, 32–3, 38, 42.
9   'farmer' in this context refers to the verb 'to farm', meaning to pay rent.
10   BARS R8/62/2/1, and Thompson, *Bailiffs' Accounts for Willington*, BARS, CRT 130 Willington 11, p. 3.
11   BARS R8/62/2/1-9, and Thompson, *Bailiffs' Accounts for Willington*, BARS, CRT 130 Willington 11, pp. 3, 6, 9, 13, 17, 22, 26, 31, 35.

The rents of the former demesne land continued to have a far from straightfor-ward history, overcharging continued to be resisted and over the years the tenants negotiated for the rents to be reduced. They continued to feel that they were being ill-used, and by April 1421 two parts of the demesne lands of the manor were without tenants and a special meeting was held outside the court: 'to agree with the lord's tenants the rents of the demesne land there.'[12] More than thirty years later the tenants of all the demesne lands refused to cultivate them: 'On this day came the tenants who held the demesne lands with meadowland, and they surrendered them into the hand of the lord before the feast of the Annunciation of the Blessed Virgin Mary next in the future etc.'[13] The rents for the demesne lands had been reduced to £18 by 1481 from £25 6s. 8d. in 1382–83. The lord's income from the standard holdings also reduced.[14]

Economic and social status of tenants after 1382

On some manors the marks of villeinage lingered on into the sixteenth century, but at Willington the letting out of the manorial demesne by the lord of the manor at the end of the fourteenth century began the process which eventually led to greater freedom and equality for the former bondsmen and their families. Most labour services, and some dues, were replaced by money payments by the middle of the fifteenth century. In addition, tenure by several lives and the development of copy-hold began to offer more security to villein tenants whose tenancies became more like those of free tenants.[15] However, payments in kind, usually a pound of pepper or two or three capons, are recorded in the Willington bailiffs' accounts 1382–97, and some payments in kind lingered on, being recorded in the court rolls until the death of Katherine Neville in 1482, although by this date tenants may have paid a cash equivalent.

While some of the burdens of serfdom and customary tenure disappeared as early as the end of the fourteenth century, most tenants continued to be unfree at least until the middle of the fifteenth century and were described as villeins. The lord still considered the villein tenants to be his property and those who tried to abscond from the manor were ordered to return, though there is no evidence that they did so.

The custom of the manor, and the granting of messuages and other land-hold-ings, established in 1382, continued while the Mowbrays adjusted their manage-ment strategies in response to changing economic conditions and the demands of their tenants. Following the period for which all the court rolls except one are missing, 1427–47, significant changes had taken place; the payment of heriots after a death or the surrender of a holding had almost completely died out and tenancies were increasingly granted for three lives or for periods of years.

There were significant differences between the prosperity of the individual tenants on the manor, but these differences seem not to have been related to the

---

12   BARS, Box R212, Roll 30, April 1421.
13   BARS, Box R212, Roll 42b, May 1454.
14   *Willington Receiver's Accounts 1421–22*, Arundel Castle Archives, A1642.
15   A. C. Jones, *The Customary Land Market in Fifteenth Century Bedfordshire* (unpublished PhD thesis, 1975), University of Southampton, p. 9. BARS, 163, book no. 5229.

free or villein status of the individuals. Both free and unfree tenants were elected or appointed to manorial offices, taking up the posts of bailiff, constable, ale-taster, and assessor of fines. Most men aged over twelve, whether free, of villein status, or servants were enrolled into tithings under the leadership of a tithing man, and each man was expected to guarantee the good behaviour of the others.

Although customary tenants are named in all the court rolls, free tenants on the manor were seldom named until the second half of the fifteenth century. Their land holdings were outside the customary business of the court. The early bailiffs' accounts 1382–97 simply say that they, as a group, paid 6s. ½d. for their rents;[16] but in the later accounts of 1457–58 and 1481–82, freemen are named as John Norman, John Abel, Robert Partriche, Robert Miton, Robert Warner, John Cawde, John Miton, Thomas Stoughton, John Gostewik the elder and the prior of Newn-ham.[17] The spellings may be different in the two accounts, but they are clearly the same men, or their sons. After 1482 the Abel, Cawde, Norman, Partrych (or Partriche, Partryche) and Stoughton families are no longer mentioned in the rolls, but the Gostwyk (or Gorstwyk, Gostewik, Gostwick, Gostwyke), Miton (or Myton) and Warner families continued to live on the manor. At the end of the sixteenth century the Gostwicks were still playing a major part in the manor's history.

In 1382 the fisheries were leased to the vicar, John Dowe, for ten years; he was presumably of higher social status than most other tenants.[18] The mill, dovecote and warren were also rented out; the miller is named as John Phille 1386–87.[19] In the account of 1389–90, Richard Pullet of Wilstead is named as leasing the dovecote.[20] These three tenants came from outside the manor and are assumed to have been relatively prosperous individuals of free status.

As discussed above, most of the men named in the accounts and court rolls would have been villeins or unfree tenants, but all tenants who were granted lands through the manor courts promised fealty, that is loyalty, to the lord and were expected to attend the courts twice a year at Easter and Michaelmas time. There is one notable exception in 1474:

> Also they said that John Myton, who held certain lands from the lady closed the days of his existence after the day of the last Court on the Sunday next before the Feast of the Purification of the blessed Virgin Mary [2 February] in the xiij° year of Edward iiij° [30 January 1474] whose heir is John Myton, the chaplain, and so he came to Court and said that he owed no other services to the Lady except suit of Court at the feast of Saint Michael the Archangel [Michaelmas, 29 September]. Therefore a day was given for enquiry by the tenants until the next Court.[21]

---

16   BARS R8/62/2/1-11, and Thompson, *Bailiffs' Accounts for Willington*, BARS, CRT 130 Willington 11, pp. 1, 3, 7, 11, 15, 19, 24, 28, 32, 38, 42.
17   British Library, Add Ch. 657; Arundel Castle Archives, A1328.
18   BARS, R8/62/2/1, and Thompson, *Bailiffs' Accounts for Willington*, BARS, CRT 130 Willington 11, p. 2, under rents (*firmae*).
19   BARS, R8/62/2/4, and Thompson, *Bailiffs' Accounts for Willington*, BARS, CRT 130 Willington 11, p. 11.
20   BARS, R8/62/2/7, and Thompson, *Bailiffs' Accounts for Willington*, BARS, CRT 130 Willington 11, p. 25.
21   BARS, Box R212, Roll 56, April 1474.

As so often happens, the records of the next two courts are missing, so there is no evidence of the court's decision, and this John Myton's name does not reappear in the court rolls. The Miton family was free and appeared in the rolls 1394–1559; they regularly contributed to the community by holding the post of assessor of fines and on this occasion, at least, as chaplain.

None of the charters, or legal documents, by which some privileged tenants of the manor held their lands have survived, but they were referred to at intervals during disputes over ownership, often after a death. The tenant holding the land may have been free, or the lands held may have been free, or both. One such holding was that of the Maryon family, who appear in the court rolls 1395–1475, and held Coppyd Hall, which may have been the small estate with its own little three-field system at the southern end of Wood Lane shown on the 1779 Gostelow map. Members of the Maryon family stood as surety or made pledges for other tenants 1395–1412. John Marion's right to have a dovecote was challenged in 1425, when he admitted that: '[he] made his Dovecot about the fourth year of the reign of the late King Henry IV [30 September 1402–29 September 1403].'[22] The result of this challenge is not known. Lady Elizabeth Maryon was regularly excused from attending court 1458–69. Some of her lands were taken over by other tenants in 1465, and the court ordered that they should be returned to her. This holding and this family must have been free. Other similar families and holdings have not been found. The Gostwyk, Miton and Partrych families were all influential with extensive holdings, but most of their lands seem to have been spread out among the open fields, meadows and pastures of the manor.

Despite close examination of the sources, no evidence of systematic exploitation of the tenants by the Mowbray lords has been found in the second half of the fifteenth century; as far as can be ascertained the Mowbrays used progressive and humane management techniques.

Changes in estate management 1382–1461
In theory, all land was held from the king in the medieval period, but several levels of tenure might intervene between the Crown and the local manorial lord. The word 'manor' had two meanings after the Norman Conquest; at first it meant a residence or a unit of estate administration, but by the fifteenth century it had also come to mean a piece of landed property with tenants over whom the lord held a court: 'If there was no Court, there was no manor.'[23] A manor was said to require at least two free tenants otherwise it ceased to exist and became a 'reputed manor'.[24] However, there was great diversity of local custom and local language.

No evidence of a written custom of the manor of Willington has survived, though it formed the basis of life on the manor. Customs can be inferred from the by-laws and other business of the manor courts, and a list of rules, from 1599, survives.[25] The custom may have been generally ignored by the end of the sixteenth century, causing the Gostwicks' then steward, William Butler, to write a list of rules and

---

[22]   BARS, Box R212, Roll 35, October 1425.
[23]   P. D. A. Harvey, *Manorial Records*, Archives and the User, no. 5 (London, 1999), p. 2.
[24]   Kevin Ward, *Society of Archivists Diploma Training Manual, Module G 'Estate Archives' Units 2–9* (unpublished, 1995), pp. G.2.1-G.9.14.
[25]   See Appendix 2 and Appendix 3 respectively.

penalties in the manor court roll. William Butler was very diligent, and the roll lists the common fines and the rents paid; most interesting perhaps are the fines for not having bows and arrows.[26]

Evidence for estate management in the later fourteenth and the early fifteenth centuries includes the bailiffs' accounts for Willington and Haynes 1382–96, prepared under the lordship of John Mowbray's younger brother, Thomas (John died in 1383); seven surviving court rolls from the period when the manor was held by Sir Thomas de Rempston, 1399–1406; and ten rolls from the period when the manor was held by Queen Joan, second wife of Henry IV, 1406–12/13 during the minority of John Mowbray.

The records indicate that the lords of the manor rarely visited, but that their steward visited twice a year for the manor courts, accompanied by other members of the council and surveyors or clerks. Although these other visitors are not named, it has been possible to identify most of the stewards.

William Rees is first identified as head steward 1392–93, a position he held for at least eighteen years. He seems to have continued in post during the years when the lord of the manor was Thomas Mowbray, throughout the period when the Crown granted Willington to Sir Thomas de Rempston, and during the early years of Queen Joan's administration. No steward's expenses were recorded in the time of Thomas Mowbray, but during the time of Thomas de Rempston the expenses claimed varied between 23d. and 3s. for each court. At this early date, the expenses for the two different types of courts, the view of frankpledge with court in the autumn and the customary court in the spring, were similar. In the later 1400s the view of frank-pledge became more lucrative than the spring court as more business began to be transacted in the autumn.

John Boteler became steward for Queen Joan in 1410 and last appears in the rolls in June 1423.[27] During this period the expenses increased slightly but remained below 4s. until Willington, and other Mowbray manors, were returned to John Mowbray (the fifth) in 1413.[28] John Mowbray set about establishing control of his inheritance, and in October 1413 and April 1414 Boteler's expenses increased significantly. John Mowbray continued to send stewards to visit Willington manor twice a year from 1414, and there is evidence that the steward, surveyors and other council members visited at other times, especially when it was necessary to negotiate lower rents with the tenants of the demesne land.[29] They occasionally referred difficult decisions to the lord's council.[30]

[26]   BARS, Box R212, Roll 74, October 1599.
[27]   He was not named as steward May 1412–October 1415, but it may be reasonable to assume he was steward during those years. He was named as under steward in 1418.
[28]   BARS, Box R212, Roll 15, October 1413, in which John Mowbray is first mentioned in the heading of the manor court rolls. An account of his early life can be found in Marilyn Roberts, *The Mowbray Legacy: The Story of one of England's Great Medieval Families; with Genealogical Tables of Famous Descendants including Anne Boleyn, Elizabeth I, Sir Winston Churchill, Diana, Princess of Wales, Audrey Hepburn, George Washington, Thomas Jefferson and George W. Bush* (Scunthorpe, 2004), pp.97 – 99, and Lucy B. Moye, *The Estates and Finances of the Mowbray Family, Earls Marshall and Dukes of Norfolk, 1401 to 1476* (unpublished PhD thesis), Duke University, USA, pp. 7–8.
[29]   BARS, Box R212, Roll 30, June 1421.
[30]   BARS, Box R212, Roll 9, October 1407; Roll 15, October 1413; Roll 23, October 1417; Roll 35, October 1425.

The manor court rolls show that under the stewardship of John Boteler buildings were allowed to fall into disrepair while a villein family, the Ryderes, dominated the courts.[31] A William Rydere may have been succeeded by his son on the jury as a William Rydere the younger is mentioned from 1417. There were also two men named John Ridere (or Rydere).[32] John the elder was a juror 1394–1417 and John the younger until about 1423.[33] They were both involved in fights; John the elder in 1395 and John the younger in 1418. A Thomas Ridere (or Rydere) was also a juror 1394–1417 and assessor of fines for many years.[34]

In May 1417 Thomas Bekyngham was appointed head steward, a post he held until 1423/4. Initially Bekyngham's expenses were slightly higher than Boteler's, and the lord's income from the view of frankpledge with court in the autumn began to exceed the income from courts in the spring. In five consecutive years, beginning in May 1416, Thomas Bekyngham brought other officials with him that resulted in the increased costs.[35] The retirement of William Ridere after 1418 from the position of bailiff, the appointment of Robert de Wyllyton (Welyngton, Wilton) as warrener in January 1419,[36] two visits by the steward in spring 1421,[37] and the conviction of the woodward, John Kempston, for dishonesty and concealment in April 1421[38] suggest a determination by the lord and his steward to establish greater control over the manor.

Under the stewardship of Thomas Bekyngham, the number of holdings without tenants became unacceptable; two cottages and a holding that had belonged to Felicia Prentys were difficult to let, and part of the demesne lands were farmed by the bailiff on behalf of the lord for about two years.[39] Two main problems were identified, the most pressing of which was the state of the buildings. In addition, it was also said that in the time of the former steward, John Preston, one tenant had demolished an insethouse, which may have been a substantial farm building with accommodation for people and perhaps animals.[40] Although demolishing buildings was unusual, many tenants tried to avoid repairing them.

The manor court rolls show that John Mowbray maintained his building stock by threatening his tenants with penalties when they did not repair their buildings. In the eight years after his lands were returned to him, that is October 1413-October 1420, thirty-eight tenants were listed as having buildings which needed repair. Most of these tenants were villeins; although some free men were included the most prestigious free families, such as the Gostwyks and the Maryons, were not. Four women, twenty men who served on the jury of the manor court and the miller were

---

31   Before 1400 this family name was often spelt as Rider, but Ridere was also used. Ryder, Rydere were common alternate spellings, and in 1417 a double name, Ryder Tayllour appears.
32   BARS, Box R212, Roll 23, October 1417.
33   BARS, Box R212, Roll 2, October 1394; Roll 22, May 1417; Roll 33, October 1423.
34   BARS, Box R212, Roll 2, October 1394; Roll 22, May 1417.
35   Prior to his appointment to head steward.
36   Arundel Castle Archives, A1642.
37   BARS, Box R212, Roll 30, April 1421.
38   Ibid.
39   BARS, Box R212, Roll 21, October 1416; Roll 22, May 1417.
40   BARS, Box R212, Roll 23, October 1417. John Preston was mentioned only once, in Roll 23, 6 October 1417: 'And that in the time of the steward, John Preston, John Gaubryel took from the lord one Messuage and 10 acres of land for the term of his life, on which messuage the same John destroyed one Insethouse with a solar that is still not put right.' No other information is known regarding his stewardship.

all threatened with penalties of various sizes (from 6s. 8d. to 40s.) if repairs were not made promptly.

In October 1413 seven tenants had ten buildings needing repair between them which varied in size between a pig sty and a grange.[41] The court roll reports that five buildings were immediately repaired but penalties of 10s. were threatened for each of the others. In addition five further tenants were given timber to repair unspecified buildings and were threatened with penalties of 20s.

Thomas Tele, who was a juror, was threatened with a penalty of 20s. in April 1415 because his insethouse needed repair;[42] in October 1418 he had a ruined grange, for which he would have to pay 6s. 8d. if it was not repaired;[43] and in October 1419 he and eleven other tenants had, 'divers ruined and defective buildings' and were all expected to pay a penalty of 40s. if they did not repair them.[44] By May 1420 the buildings had been repaired, with the exception of those belonging to Thomas Tele: 'Thomas Tele, the lord's villein, who held two messuages with two half-virgates of land from the lord, according to the custom of the manor by rendering service to the lord and 26s. 8d. a year has left the lord's demesne of his birth and removed all his goods and chattels and but where he [is] not known.'[45]

At the end of the period 1413–20, five tenants had still not repaired their buildings and were each threatened with huge penalties of 40s. but were given still more time: 'because the said tenants are paupers and the greatest penury of money exists between them.'[46]

The steward, Thomas Bekyngham, had become aware of another problem. There is evidence that members of the village elite sought to conceal the thefts of John Abel:

> They present that by night, in the Autumn in the eighth year of the reign of Henry Vth, John [12d.] Abel caused damage[47] and took and carried away sheaves of corn and property valued at 2s. from the goods and chattells of John Gaubryel, against the peace of the lord king. Therefore he is amerced. And that the same John [4d.] Abell [sic] illegally took goods from John Kempston by the lord's bailiff. Therefore he is amerced. And the tithing men [12d.] have concealed and are amerced. [48]

The men of the main jury, who had concealed these offences, were fined 12d. Concealment by the jury was almost unprecedented in Willington, and the reason for the concealment in unknown. The steward's expenses for this court are high, 7s. 3d., providing some indication of his concern.[49]

The receiver's accounts 1421–22, suggest that this was a difficult period in the history of the manor. William Ridere was in arrears, and two former warreners owed money, although earlier bailiffs' accounts 1382–97 indicate that this was not unparal-

41   BARS, Box R212, Roll 15, October 1413.
42   BARS, Box R212, Roll 18a, April 1415.
43   BARS, Box R212, Roll 25, October 1418.
44   BARS, Box R212, Roll 27, October 1419.
45   BARS, Box R212, Roll 28, May 1420.
46   BARS, Box R212, Roll 29, October 1420.
47   *Noctans*, no exact translation for this word has been found. *Noct* has been used elsewhere to refer to illegal night-time activities, and the noun *nocumentum* refers to harm, damage, nuisance, harmful thing.
48   BARS, Box R212, Roll 29, October 1420.
49   BARS, Box R212, Roll 29, October 1420.

leled. In 1423, John Kempston, the woodward, became keeper of Sheerhatch.[50] His appointment was not without its problems, and in 1426 he was threatened with a fine of 100s. and was later heavily fined for not repairing the fences round the wood.[51]

Throughout this period the Mowbrays made changes to their management structure and arranged that at least two of their officials were local men. They appointed Robert de Wyllyton to live on the manor as warrener from 1419, and Roger Hunte, from nearby Roxton, was first named as steward in October 1425. [52]

The appointment of Robert de Wyllyton, described as surgeon and as warrener for life by John Mowbray in letters patent at Rouen in January 1419, is recorded in the receiver's accounts 1421–22. His wages were 2d. a day, the same as the bailiff, and were paid to his wife in two instalments while he was away:

> And £8 2s. 8d., should be answerable as paid in money to Robert Wyllyton, surgeon and warrener of Willington, as put below in title of fees, which the lord earl put in his letters patent at Rothomagn [53] on the 24th day of January in the 6th year of Henry 5th [1419] granted 2d. a day for keeping the Warren of Willington and of the wood of Shirehatche for the term of his life from the issues and profits of the manor there, just as William Walter,[54] formerly warrener there formerly had from a grant from the lord, as long as the said Robert manages his office well at the usual terms, that is to say in full payment of the aforesaid wages from the 24th January in the said 6th year until Michaelmas in the 9th year [1421] of the same king, for 2 full years and half a year and 66 days, taking for a day as above, therefore the total due is £8 2s. 8d. [364 days a year paid for] by two discharges for the said Robert, into the hand of Margaret his wife at Willington from the first date, at Willington on Wednesday next after the Feast of Pentecost in the eighth year of the same king [29 May 1420] containing £7 16s. 8d. and the other on 15th December in the 9th year [1421] of the said king, containing 6s., in full payment of the said wages up until the Michaelmas in the 9th year of the said king [29 September 1421] notwithstanding the date of the last discharge.[55]

Robert de Wyllyton's family name is not known, but he was almost certainly a free man, and Robert was a name used by three free families on the manor; the Gostwyks, the Mitons and the Partryches. Lands and sinecures were given by the Mowbrays as rewards for good service; Robert de Wyllyton was paid a fee of 60s. 8d. a year from 1419 to after 1432 and seems to have been appointed in response to the concerns about arrears and missed payments.[56]

Two quarter shares of the demesne land were still without tenants in April 1421 and buildings continued to need repair:

---

[50]   BARS, Box R212, Roll 32, June 1423. In this roll John Kempston is at first referred to 'the wode-ward' when he surrendered his holding, but at the end of the roll he is referred to as the 'keeper of Shirewood'. This may have been a sinecure.

[51]   BARS, Box R212, Roll 36a, April 1426; Roll 36, September 1426.

[52]   BARS, Box R212, Roll 35, October 1425. He was also steward for Fen Stanton in Huntingdonshire and became speaker of the House of Commons and the second baron of the exchequer.

[53]   Most likely Rouen, the Latin word for which is *Rotomagense* or *Rothomagensis*.

[54]   This may be a scribal error as Walter is not used as a family name in earlier rolls. It may have been Waryn or Warner, although the only mention of a William Waryn seems to have been in 1409, BARS, Box 212, Roll 11, April 1409. Waryn may have been an occupational alias for the man who was the warrener. Members of the Waryn (or Waren, Wareyn, Waryner) family appear in the rolls 1394–1481 or later.

[55]   Arundel Castle Archives, A1642.

[56]   Moye, *The Estates and Finances of the Mowbray Family,* p. 425.

THE DECLINE OF SERFDOM AND THE PEASANTS' REVOLT 23

So, in the expenses of the steward and other surveyors the same day 3s. 3d. And in the expenses of Thomas Bekyngham and others being there for one day and one night, that is to say on 17th day of June to agree with the lord's tenants the rents of the demesne land there, for everything which is paid in cash 4s. 1d. [57]

The results of this meeting are not known. The list of other holdings without a tenant continued to increase so that by 1426 the steward, Roger Hunte, was letting out holdings rent-free to men that he hoped would repair the buildings. One of these men was William Launcelyn, who assumed more importance in the manor later in the century.[58]

In 1426, Roger Hunte claimed expenses for two courts. In April he claimed 4s.1d. for himself and other surveyors.[59] This provided a generous meal, parchment for the rolls and ink for writing. In September expenses of 6s. 4d. were claimed providing a meal of bread, beer and a wide variety of protein foods for him, 'and many other visitors' with two bushels of oats, presumably for the horses.[60] Some tenants may have thought that the new steward would be lenient as there had been two thefts of animals, one housebreaking and one assault drawing blood. Nor did the constables and ale-tasters perform their offices properly.[61] These offences were all punished by the manor court under Roger Hunte's stewardship.

Evidence of relationships between the lord and his tenants during the years 1427–47 is largely missing. There are no extant rolls for the period with the exception of the surviving court roll of 1440.[62] After the death of John Mowbray in 1432, Willington became part of the dower of his widow Katherine Neville so depriving her son, and later her grandson, of the income from these lands.[63] Evidence of the management of the manor during the lifetime of Katherine Neville's second husband, Sir Thomas Strangeways, has been lost, but the later surviving rolls show that she and her last two husbands administered the manors which formed her dower in a consistently stable way so that they escaped most of the problems experienced by the rest of the Mowbray estates from the mid-1440s.[64]

The Mowbrays usually insisted that tenants repaired the buildings on their holdings, but the court roll of 1440 shows that Katherine Neville was prepared to invest in the manor by building a large barn for a new tenant. The roll is short, about 380 words. Attached to it are two small pieces of paper or parchment, one of which contains the cost of a new barn for Thomas Wyltshyre.[65]

When the series of court rolls begins again in 1448, Katherine Neville had married her third husband, John Beaumont. They, and their steward, began to elect new constables approximately every two years 1450–71, so sharing the role and

57   BARS, Box R212, Roll 30, April 1421.
58   BARS, Box R212, Roll 36a, April 1426; Roll 36, September 1426.
59   BARS, Box R212, Roll 36a, April 1426.
60   BARS, Box R212, Roll 36, September 1426.
61   BARS, Box R212, Roll 35, October 1425.
62   BARS, Box R212, Roll 37, April 1440, and additions.
63   Dower was a widow's right to hold a proportion (normally one third) of her deceased husband's land for the rest of her life, Bailey, *The English Manor*, p. 242. Willington manor court rolls show that each time that Katherine Neville remarried her new husband took precedence over her in the heading of the courts, despite being of lower social status.
64   Moye, *The Estates and Finances of the Mowbray Family*, pp. 67–8
65   BARS, Box R212, Roll 37, April 1440. See Appendix 4.

involving more of the tenants in the control of the community. This programme continued under a new steward, Thomas Rokes, who held the post from 1457 until at least 1474, continuing after the death of John Beaumont and through the years of Katherine Neville's fourth marriage to John Woodville, 1465–69.

The contents of the roll of October 1448 contain little evidence to indicate that the court business was in any way unusual, apart from one section which contained information about Thomas Wyltshyre and William Launcelyn:

> And that Thomas Wyltshyre has not repaired the holding called Trykats. And on this the aforesaid Thomas Wyltshyre came and granted it to William Launcelyn for a certain sum of money for repairing it because he made his withdrawal, and that the aforesaid William would be answerable for the aforesaid repairs. Therefore the aforesaid William Launcelyn was charged with the aforesaid repairs. And therefore the aforesaid William Launcelyn was ordered to make the repairs of the aforesaid tenement, lately held by the aforesaid Thomas Wylt-shyre before the next, and if not the aforesaid tenement will remain in the hand of the lord because of no repairs and no tenants.[66]

Thomas Wyltshyre, for whom the barn was built in 1440, had not apparently made a success of farming, and the arrangement with William Launcelyn was that the latter would repair the former's buildings. This was the beginning of a series of speculative ventures by William Launcelyn in which he obtained holdings free of charge because he agreed to the cost of repairs; he was also paid to repair buildings for other tenants. Unfortunately, he was very slow to keep his part of these bargains.

In May 1452 the rolls record that the steward and his visitors stayed with the Launcelyn household, though it is not known where that household was.[67] This is the only occasion where the name of a host is recorded, and the reason for this is unclear. The main branch of the Launcelyn family held the nearby Mowbray manor in Cople, and William Launcelyn had previously rented much of the medieval manor site in Willington. The expenses recorded at the end of the roll were not unduly expensive; it is not evident whether the steward and his visitors stayed overnight.

> In expenses of the steward and visitors with the Launcelyn household 5s. 6d.
> In expenses for parchment and paper for the roll and the survey 4d.
> Sum total of the last 2 Courts 13s. 10d., also for certificate 7s. 4d. [68]
> Therefrom in expenses of the steward at the aforesaid Courts 10s. 2d.[69]

William Launcelyn was linked to the repairs of several buildings at this time and the court roll is dominated by lists of buildings needing repairs and holdings needing tenants.

John Beaumont and Katherine Neville tackled the problem of letting the demesne lands when their steward and surveyors, who visited Willington in May 1449,

66   BARS, Box R212, Roll 38a, October 1448.
67   It is not known whether they stayed in the manor house at Willington or at the Launcelyn manor in nearby Cople. BARS, Box R212, Roll 40b, May 1452.
68   BARS, Box R212, Roll 40a, October 1451; Roll 40b, May 1452. The totals for these two courts are correct. The profit to the lord from these two courts was 3s. 8d. No details of this certificate have been found.
69   BARS, Box R212, Roll 40b, May 1452.

divided them into twelve lots. And in 1449 thirteen tenants agreed to take them at reduced rents, which amounted to £18 a year, for three years on certain conditions:

> John Rodland one lot and a half
> John Myton one lot and a half
> John Yarwey the elder one lot and a half
> John Palmer and John Flaunders [torn edge] two lots
> John Bawde the elder one lot
> Randolph Bawdewyn one lot and one quarter
> William [torn edge] of Couphyll [Cople] one quarter [70]
> John Goode half a lot
> Robert Warner half a lot
> William Starlyng and John his son one lot
> William Launcelyn holds the hall yard, le Orcharde and half of Thalde Well
> [The Old Well, field name].[71]

The sizes of the redistributed lands varied.[72] It was agreed that the lord would pay the tenants 8s. each year for the three years to compensate for losing the right to ploughbote, which was the right to take wood from the commons.[73] They would also be allowed to, 'enter upon the Fallow pasture and meadow land' at Lady Day in the third year, as well as other benefits.[74] Although the tenants gave notice in the court roll of May 1454 that they intended to surrender the demesne lands in the following year no further redistribution of the lands is recorded.[75] The rents for the demesne lands were still £18 a year in 1480–81,[76] but they had returned to the rent charged in 1384–85, £27 6s. 8d., by 1487.[77] There continued to be difficulties in finding tenants for all the customary lands and in persuading the tenants to repair their buildings.

In October 1454 there were new concerns.[78] The common way was obstructed by branches in two places and tenants were ordered to clear them; William Launcelyn had not repaired a malt kiln; the goods and chattels of an important tenant, Robert Partrych, had to be taken to repair his holding; and there had been a 'violent wind' the previous winter.[79] The steward and extra officials came to inspect the damage and the repairs; their expenses were 7s. 8d.

In April and October 1457 and July 1458, in the first three courts immediately after he was appointed steward, Thomas Rokes established a pattern of control which was consistent with the control that John Beaumont and Katherine Neville had used in the previous nine or ten years.[80] In April 1457, when he stayed overnight in Shefford, and when the court at Willington was dominated by the need to

---

[70]   It is very probable that the lost surname was Launcelyn as that family held a manor in Cople until at least the sixteenth century.
[71]   BARS, Box R212, Roll 38b, May 1449. Lack of punctuation in the original document means that it is not clear whether William Launcelyn held the hall and the yard, or the hall-yard.
[72]   The assarted lands north of Sheerhatch may have been part of the former demesne. They are shown divided into twelve on the Gostelow map.
[73]   Ploughbote is not mentioned elsewhere in the documents.
[74]   BARS, Box R212, Roll 38b, May 1449. That is, 25 March.
[75]   BARS, Box R212, Roll 42b, May 1454.
[76]   Arundel Castle Archives, A1328.
[77]   Suffolk Record Office, HD1538/225/6.
[78]   BARS, Box R212, Roll 43a, October 1454.
[79]   BARS, Box R212, Roll 42b, May 1454.
[80]   BARS, Box R212, Roll 45b, April 1457; Roll 46a, October 1457; Roll 46b, July 1458.

repair buildings, he immediately agreed that an old timber from one tenancy could be reused on other holdings and arranged for timber from the lord's woods to be given for repairs.[81]

Villein tenants or labourers resident in Willington at that time must have been looking outside the village for employment, for Thomas Rokes ordered that:

> The labourers by the day who are resident and belong to the Lete are not to accept labouring outside the vill. They are able to have sufficient services and payment within. Under a penalty of 40d. payable to the lord and the Church in equal portions, as and when they are found guilty to the contrary.[82]

This is a unique entry in the rolls and suggests that although some of the villein tenants wanted to work outside the manor, the steward asserted the lord's right to compel them to only work there. There is no clear evidence that the tenants obeyed, just as there is no evidence that the men who had earlier in the fifteenth century left the manor to live elsewhere ever returned when ordered to do so. The sharing of a fine between the lord and the church suggests that the steward knew that imposing a penalty of this size for working outside the village would be unpopular.

In July 1458 the court was again dominated by the need to repair buildings, and two tenants surrendered their holdings.[83] New tenants were found. Three years later, in October 1461, Thomas Rokes dealt with infringements against the lord's property and the custom of the manor; a butcher sold meat without heads, and the miller, Simon Usshere: 'took excessive toll at the bin and not on the lady's land for two years against the statute concerning which is proclaimed, causing nuisance to all the villagers.'[84] He was fined and ordered: 'not to take toll from now on, after the date of this view with Court, at the bin.'[85] And there were other problems on that day: 'John Fitz Geffrey esquire of Thirlye [Thurleigh] in the county of Bedford, [had] this day at Court, for fishing within the head of water of the lady in the Wall of the church's byn on the land of the mill and from there he took 2 small pikes without permission.'[86]

The stewards' expenses recorded in the rolls from 1448, and during the 1450s, were generally high, suggesting that more officials attended the court than usual; most Willington rolls give some details to justify the costs. In October 1448, the expenses of the steward and other surveyors of 8s. 1d. included the expenses at Bedford.[87] The expenses for May 1449 included 4d. for parchment for the roll and the ink and paper for Willington and Cardington. In October 1450 the steward claimed 4s. 4d., which included payment for fuel.[88] From this year onwards expenses for the courts held in the autumn and the spring in Willington

81   BARS, Box R212, Roll 45b, April 1457.
82   BARS, Box R212, Roll 46a, October 1457.
83   BARS, Box R212, Roll 46b, July 1458.
84   The palaeography here is difficult, 'b' and 'v' being very similar, but seems to be *byn*. There was no evidence of a vineyard in Willington, so this is probably is what it says, a bin for storage (for grain). It seems that the tolls charged on milling the tenants' grain should have been charged in public, outside the miller's enclosure.
85   BARS, Box R212, Roll 49a, October 1461.
86   BARS, Box R212, Roll 46b, July 1458.
87   BARS, Box R212, Roll 38a, October 1448.
88   BARS, Box R212, Roll 39a, October 1450.

were claimed together, and claims for expenses appear to have been settled annually.

Large expenses were recorded for four courts after the appointment of Thomas Rokes; in April 1457, 7s. 6d.;[89] in October 1457, 6s. 9d.;[90] in July 1458, 6s. 8d.;[91] and in October 1461, 7s. 8d.[92] John Beaumont is not mentioned again in the rolls after that date, after which the steward's expenses reduced and were usually between 3s. and 5s. for the next twenty years.[93]

Expenses were consistently high during times of management change as with the appointment of Thomas Rokes 1457–58; after the death of John Beaumont 1460; and in 1481 when Katherine Neville was very old, and presumably her heirs were preparing to assume management of the manor (6s. 8d.). After this date the expenses ceased to be recorded.

Management of Willington manor had became more business-like under the control of John Beaumont and Katherine Neville, and the costs of holding the courts reduced after 1461 under the steward they appointed in 1457, Thomas Rokes.[94] The manor of Willington was on the edge of Katherine Neville's dower, managed separately from the parts of the estates under the control of her son and later her grandson. The pattern of co-operation between trusted local manorial officials and regular twice-yearly visits from the steward continued until Katherine Neville's death, when Willington became part of a large group of properties that included Framlingham Castle.

Management of land transfers, heriots and copyhold
When land became available, the lord's steward, assisted by the bailiff, preferred to grant a vacant holding to another tenant immediately, but this was not always possible, either because the buildings were ruined and needed repairs, or because no new tenant could be found. From just after the Peasants' Revolt until the early sixteenth century it was usual for all Willington tenants to hold their messuages, tenements and land on the understanding that they would repair and maintain their buildings, fences and fields at their own expense. It was only on rare occasions that the lord paid for major repairs or for new buildings, although they often provided some of the materials to enable them.

This was because the woodlands of the manor were a regular, though fluctuating, source of income for the lord. Underwood from Sheerhatch Wood was cropped in rotation and sold from different parts of the wood.[95] It generated 6s. 8d. an acre until

[89]   BARS, Box R212, Roll 45b, July 1458.
[90]   BARS, Box R212, Roll 46a, October 1457.
[91]   BARS, Box R212, Roll 46b, July 1458.
[92]   BARS, Box R212, Roll 47, October 1458.
[93]   '...by 1461 the Mowbrays were heavily in debt. The fourth duke (1461 to 76) and his council attempted to stave off bankruptcy by consolidating the inheritance, and their efforts were assisted by a partial recovery of estate revenues. These financial problems may not have affected Katherine Neville and her dower but the clear reduction in steward's expenses after 1461 suggests that attempts were being made to curb expenditure.' Moye, *The Estates and Finances of the Mowbray Family,* abstract.
[94]   Thomas Rokes was first mentioned in April 1457 (Roll 45b) and last mentioned in April 1474 (Roll 56).
[95]   Underwood was small bushes and shrubs growing beneath the trees. It could include trimmings from oak and alder coppice stools, but this is not mentioned in the documents.

1396–97, when the price increased to 7s.[96] Acres of more valuable wood and under-wood were sold 1389–90 and 1390–91 at 40s. an acre. In 1421–22 the receiver's account includes a figure of £17 4s. 3d. for the sale of wood and the profits of the dovecote, but the individual amounts are not given.[97] The price for an acre of under-wood had increased to 8s. by the time of the next surviving account, 1457–58, when the lord's income for eight acres and twenty-six perches was 65s. 8d.[98]

The first references to trees being supplied for repairs begin soon after the manor was granted to Queen Joan.[99] In April 1407 William Webbe was expected to pay for the wood that he was given: 'William [2d.] Webbe agrees that certain wood was delivered to him to repair his house and he owes 4d. to the lady which should be raised. And the said William is at mercy for the aforesaid amount.'[100] In April 1409 he had not used the five trees with which he had been supplied, and he was threatened with a penalty of 2s. if he did not do so, even though the Queen had already begun to supply some timber for repairs without payment. In the same roll, another tenant, Nicholas Shaxton, was threatened with a penalty, this time of 40d., for not using eight trees.[101] At the same time the court recorded that each new tenant agreed to: 'maintain, sustain, repair and put right the said tenement at his own expense except for large timber from the lady' and fourteen men were given a total of more than one hundred and fifty trees for repairs.[102] They were each threatened with a penalty of 40d. if they did not use them for repairs before Michaelmas, that is, within five months.

After October 1452 it was sometimes agreed with the lord's steward that timber laths and withies would be supplied for repairs. The court record of that year states: 'the aforesaid John Yarwey will well and competently maintain and sustain all the buildings being in the said messuage in thatch, carts and enclosures. And the lord will provide timber, laths, withies and the carpentry-work as is necessary during the aforesaid term.'[103] In May 1454, when John Norman and his wife were granted two holdings, the record includes details of the conditions under which most holdings were granted at that time.[104] They agreed that they would:

> submit to and will carry out a check midway and will put right and repair the buildings of the tenement. And at the end of his aforesaid term he will suffi-ciently repair and [illegible] when he demises and surrenders his premises. The lord will provide timber, laths and withies for him to make repairs as and when required during the aforesaid terms.[105] And he made fealty to the lord and no heriot after his death or withdrawal. And he gave one capon as entry fine to the lord.'

96   BARS, R8/62/2/11, and Thompson, *Bailiffs' Accounts for Willington*, BARS, CRT 130 Willington 11, pp. 47.
97   Arundel Castle Archives, A1642.
98   British Library, Add Ch. 657.
99   The first court roll which names her as lady of the manor is Roll 8, October 1406.
100 BARS, Box R212, Roll 8b, April 1407.
101 BARS, Box R212, Roll 11, April 1409.
102 Ibid.
103 BARS, Box R212, Roll 41a, October 1452.
104 BARS, Box R212, Roll 42b, May 1454
105 Timber, withies and laths were also supplied for some holdings granted in the following rolls: BARS, Box R212, Roll 46a, October 1457; Roll 51a, October 1464; Roll 52a, October 1465; Roll 53a, April 1467.

Other tenants were required to agree to the condition of their buildings being examined during their tenancy,[106] and on another occasion it was said that buildings had been previously repaired by the lord.[107]

After the appointment of Thomas Rokes in 1457 the emphasis on tenants to keep their buildings in good repair increased. The court roll for that date includes lists of buildings needing repair and the timber allowed for the repairs.[108] Additional costs of 40s. 7¼d. were incurred to pay workmen and buy materials and equipment for the manor, and underwood was sold for a total of £4 14s. 7d., which more than paid for the repairs.

Timber and underwood continued to be important into the sixteenth century; for in his advice to his son, written about 1540, John Gostwyk wrote: 'I charge you never to lett your fermor your woodes, nor underwoodes, but to have certen loodes of woodes assigned [to] him, by you, or your deputy for his fewell. But lett him never have ploughbote or cartebote, for then you will distroye your timber.'[109]

Holdings usually became vacant on the death of a tenant, or when a tenant was no longer able or willing to look after the holding, but on four occasions holdings of a messuage and ten acres or half a virgate of land were surrendered for the use of another person. No financial arrangements are mentioned, but they may have been made as a way of helping elderly tenants retire.[110] In 1409 John Lygtfot agreed to pay Christina Verne a tenth of his estate in money and grain.[111] On very rare occasions a tenant was deprived of his or her holding because it was not being looked after properly. Once granted a holding, the head of the household, almost always a man, but occasionally a widow or a free woman, was required to swear loyalty to the lord and promise to attend the manor court twice a year.

Over a period of thirty-two years, 1394–1426, twenty-two deaths of tenants were recorded in Willington, nineteen of which were men. All except one of the vacant holdings formerly held by men required payment of a heriot. The other three tenants who died were widows, and no heriots were due according to the custom of the manor.

Customs varied in detail from manor to manor, but at the next court after a death, the death would be reported and the heir, if there was one, would come forward to be admitted to the holding and would agree to pay the heriot.[112] On some manors this would relieve him from paying an entry fine but at Willington, at the end of the fourteenth and start of the fifteenth centuries, both were payable. From 1394–1426 it was quite usual for a widow to take over her late husband's holdings.[113] Sometimes the phrase 'on her own' is used in the rolls which may imply

[106] BARS, Box R212, Roll 44b, April 1456.
[107] BARS, Box R212, Roll 43b, May 1455.
[108] BARS, Box R212, Roll 47a, July 1459.
[109] A. G. Dickens, 'Estate and Household Management in Bedfordshire, c. 1540', in BHRS, vol. 36, *The Gostwicks of Willington and Other Studies* (Streatley, 1956), p. 44.
[110] BARS, Box R212. Roll 11, April 1409; Roll 42a, October 1453; Roll 55a, March 1474; Roll 60b, May 1482.
[111] BARS, Box R212, Roll 11, April 1409.
[112] Ward, *Society of Archivists Diploma Training Manual*.
[113] BARS, Box R212, Roll 1, April 1394; Roll 9b, April 1408; Roll 10, October 1408; Roll 12, October 1410; Roll 13, April 1411; Roll 14, October 1411; Roll 17, October 1414; Roll 23, October 1417; Roll 25, October 1418; Roll 36a, April 1426.

that a widow would lose her holding if she remarried.[114] After 1448 it become usual for men and their wives, or men, wives and their sons, to be granted holdings jointly so that it became unnecessary for a widow or the sons to go to court to claim the family holding.

In the earliest surviving court roll of 1394 there were five land transfers: three messuages, two with ten acres and one with eight; one toft with five acres; and a 'certain parcel' of demesne land.[115] Two of the messuages were transferred on the death of the former tenant. One of the messuages with ten acres of land, and the toft with five acres, were granted through the court roll and 'at the will of the lord', meaning that the lord could evict the tenant for not taking good care of his holding.[116] The messuage and eight acres, which had previously been held in bondage, was again granted in bondage through the court roll. The widow of a deceased tenant was granted her late husband's messuage and ten acres for her life according to the custom of the manor, and the parcel of demesne land was granted to two men to hold for their lives at the will of the lord. In later court rolls, when a holding is granted to more than one person for their lives, the text makes it clear that it can be held by the surviving partner until his or her death.

In 1394, heriots of different sizes were paid on the surrender of the three messuages and the toft. They were respectively one bull calf, valued at 40d.; one ewe with one suckling lamb, valued at 18d.; a platter valued at 12d.; and a new heriot of 6d. Usually the animals were sold and the lord's income from the sale appeared in the accounts under 'perquisites of court'. Each new tenant, except the widow, also paid an entry fine or premium. Thomas Starlyng, who was granted the largest holding, paid the largest heriot and promised to make: 'annually the same rent and services just as his father John customarily rendered and made.'[117] He provided the names of three men as pledges to guarantee the payment of the entry fine or premium and another new tenant provided the names of two different men as pledges for a smaller holding.

The bailiffs' accounts and court rolls for Willington include more detail about how heriots were administered 1394–1426. They were paid on a large number of customary, standard-sized holdings which had formerly belonged to serfs. The holdings were described as having been formerly held in bondage, or formerly held in bondage by acremen, or formerly held in bondage by molemen.[118] There were twenty-eight messuages and thirty-four half-virgates, or ten acres, which were: 'formerly held in bondage now handed over to various tenants of the lord to hold freely'.[119] There were also four holdings of a messuage and eight acres each: 'formerly held in

[114] BARS, Box R212, Roll 9b, May 1408; Roll 14, October 1411; Roll 17, October 1414; Roll 21, October 1416; Roll 23, October 1417.
[115] BARS, Box R212, Roll 1, April 1394.
[116] The meaning of this term 'through the court roll' is unclear.
[117] BARS, Box R212, Roll 1, April 1394 (first entry on Roll).
[118] BARS R8/62/2/1-11, and Thompson, *Bailiffs' Accounts for Willington*, BARS, CRT 130 Willington 11.
[119] The size of a virgate varied, but was often about thirty acres. The size of virgates in Willington is unclear; the standard holdings may have varied in size and fertility. In Thompson's unpublished transcripts of the original Willington bailiffs' accounts he says that the standard sized holdings were 'now leased.' However the use of 'lease' is misleading as it implies a formal document and a fixed term of years. In this context the words 'were granted' or 'were handed over' are more correct. Thompson, *Bailiffs' Accounts for Willington*, BARS, CRT 130 Willington 11.

bondage by acremen, now handed over to four tenants of the lord to hold freely'.[120] Heriots were paid for most of the above messuages and half virgates or eight acres throughout this early period and were also charged on smaller land-holdings and individual cottages, suggesting that the payment of heriots indicated a low-status tenant who had been granted a customary holding.

The payment of a heriot appears to have become much less usual during the period 1427–47, although the court rolls which would have contained the details have been lost. Before 1427 payments of heriots were commonplace, but by 1447 they had virtually ceased although there is reference to a 'new' heriot of a horse being paid in October 1451,[121] and of a heriot of a capon being paid in October 1453 when a holding was surrendered.[122] The tenant to whom this holding was granted then paid 12d. as an entry fine and heriot. Subsequent court rolls begin to state that no heriot is due, and in 1475 the roll says, 'no heriot because none is customary' implying that the older form of customary tenure had been supplanted by a copyhold tenure with fewer liabilities.[123] There was, however, a rare mention of services still due as part of the rent in 1461, when:

> John Fraunceys and Agnes his wife and John their son took one messuage with a garden and a nearby croft and ten acres of land and meadow with appurtenances, lately in the holding of John Palmere, from the lady, to have and to hold it for the terms of their lives and whichever of them lives longest, at the will of the lady, according to the custom of the manor by services, rendering therefrom 10s. a year to the lady at the usual terms there and suit of the common court and all the customary services due therefrom.[124]

John Fraunceys, Agnes his wife and John their son paid an entry fine of just two capons, worth 8d., and it was agreed that they should not pay a heriot at the end of their tenancy.

After 1447, the numbers of land-transfers reduced dramatically. During the period 1448–82 it was much more common for lands to be granted for terms of two or three lives to a man and wife, a mother and son, or a man, his wife and sons or assigns; or leased for periods of up to twenty years, and on one occasion, sixty years.[125] On several occasions a tenant was granted two or three holdings. The first recorded incidents of this significant change in the pattern of land transfers were in the court roll of October 1452.[126] A dwelling and ten acres was granted for three lives and a messuage and eight acres was granted for twenty years. The new tenants of these holdings each paid entry fines of one capon worth 3d. In October 1466, Thomas Baylemont and his assigns leased a holding for twenty years.'[127]

---

[120] BARS, R8/62/2/1-11. Very similar wording continues to be used in the accounts held by the Duke of Norfolk, A1642 (1421–22) and the account held by the British Library, Add Ch. 657 (1457–58).
[121] BARS, Box R212, Roll 40a, October 1451.
[122] BARS, Box R212, Roll 42a, October 1453.
[123] BARS, Box R212, Roll 55b, March 1475.
[124] BARS, Box R212, Roll 49a, October 1461.
[125] BARS, Box R212, Roll 41a, October 1452; Roll 41b, May 1453; Roll 42b, May 1454; Roll 43b,May 1455; Roll 44a, October 1455; Roll 44b, April 1456; Roll 46a, October 1457; Roll 52a, October 1465; Roll 53a, April 1467; Roll 53b, October 1466.
[126] BARS, Box R212, Roll 41a, October 1452.
[127] BARS, Box R212, Roll 53b, October 1466.

Thomas Baylemont's name appears in the records until 1474, but his family name may have been misspelt by later scribes, because a Thomas Baylmond is still serving as a juror in 1481.[128] In April 1467, Richard Floure (or Flowre) and his assigns leased a toft and ten acres for twenty years, but his name only appears in the records until 1478.[129]

Deaths of free tenants and the inheritance of their free lands were not part of the business of the manor courts, and because of the changes in tenancy agreements for customary tenants only six deaths of customary tenants were recorded in the thirty-five year period 1448–82, but they resulted in a variety of outcomes. In October 1453 John Palmer's widow and his sons took his holding, 'for the term of her life and of whichever of them lives longest' and 'were admitted as tenants by a copy.'[130] In October 1458, John Clerke died holding two messuages and twenty acres owing money to the lord. The bailiff was ordered to take all his goods and chattels.[131] When Geoffrey Palmer died in October 1464 his widow was admitted to her husband's holding but was asked to produce evidence of her title at the next court.[132] He had held his fields by a charter, or perhaps by copyhold, and Margerie was able to provide the required proof. At the same court William, the heir of John Passewater, was said to have paid a relief for his father's lands, which were held by knight's service, but the amount he paid is not recorded. The deaths of John Myton and John Coke were both recorded in April 1474, but neither inheritance was straightforward. John Myton's son, the chaplain, also called John, claimed that he: 'owed no other services to the Lady except suit of court at the feast of saint Michael the Archangel' and the tenants were unsure what lands John Coke had held; so enquiries were held in both cases.[133] The records of the following two courts have not survived, but John Myton does not appear in the later rolls and John Coke disappears from the records after 1478.

No records survive to show whether the experiments with granting holdings for numbers of years were repeated, and holdings continued to be granted for between one and three lives, according to the custom of the manor. Only once is it recorded that a new tenant challenged the custom; after the death of John Myton in 1474 when his heir, John Myton the chaplain: 'came to court and said that he owed no other services to the Lady.'[134]

The later court rolls show a surprising return to some earlier terms of tenancy. In November 1478 two tenancies were held jointly with another person, in one case the man's wife, and in the other 'one following', and were described as being held 'at will of the lady', who was the elderly Katherine Neville.[135] Capons were paid as entry fines for these and another holding. In October 1481 the term 'at the will of the lady' was again used, after a gap of many years, and in the rolls for that court, and the court of May 1482, the conditions of tenure of holdings specified for the

128   BARS, Box R212, Roll 60a, October 1481.
129   BARS, Box R212, Roll 53a, October 1467; Roll 59a, November 1478.
130   BARS, Box R212, Roll 42a, October 1453.
131   BARS, Box R212, Roll 47, October 1458.
132   BARS, Box R212, Roll 51a, October 1464.
133   BARS, Box R212, Roll 56, April 1474.
134   BARS, Box R212, Roll 56, April 1474.
135   BARS, Box R212, Roll 59a, November 1478.

first time that tenants must not sub-let their holdings without permission. As before, they were required to maintain their buildings, except that: 'as and when it becomes necessary for repairs, he will take from the lady, through her assigns, timber, withies and laths.'[136]

No details of the granting of customary holdings are contained in the rolls which date from just after Katherine Neville's death, but the return to earlier terms of tenure suggests that just before the end of her life the management of the manor was already in the hands of her heirs.

The incidence of exacting a heriot does not seem to have been related to the relative wealth or status of individual tenants. In the early rolls, for example, heriots are paid by tenants described as being in bondage, or being a serf. When, in 1408, Matilda Tele paid a new heriot of a cow (5s.) on the death of her husband she was described as 'being free', as was Emilia Fesound, who paid a heriot of a heifer (40d.) after the death of her husband.[137] No heriot was payable by the heirs after the death of a widow.

The size of the heriot may have had some relationship with the tenant's ability to pay, or to the value of the holding. It could vary between a money payment of 6d. and a horse worth 13s. 4d. In many cases it seems to be equivalent to about a half-year's rent, but the court rolls do not make it clear how the sum was calculated, or by whom, nor do they explain why the heriot is sometimes described as 'new' as in 1418, when two 'new' heriots were paid by John Gaubryel's heirs:

> Heriot of one bullock valued at 10s. fealty

> John Gaubryel who held one Messuage and 8 acres of land from the lord by service [and] 8s. a year, and with other services according to the custom of the manor, closed his existence after the day of the last Court, after whose death a new heriot of one bullock valued at 10s. falls due to the lord.

> Heriot of one cow valued at 5s. fealty

> The same John held one cottage from the lord ... [and] ... after his death a new heriot of one cow valued at 5s. falls due to the lord.[138]

His widow, Matilda, claimed the holding, but in May of the next year, 1419, she surrendered the cottage which was then granted to John Budenho, for his life, but no heriot was to be charged after his death or withdrawal.[139] The roll does not explain why a heriot was charged on John Gaubryel when he held the cottage but not on John Budenho. The difference, on this occasion, may have been related to status as John Gaubryel was a customary tenant and John Budenho may have been a member of a minor gentry family, which held land on the southern slopes of the greensand ridge.

Tenants who held land 'by copy' were given a copy of the entry in the manor court roll, which recorded the granting to them of their holding or holdings, and proved their entitlement to the land and buildings and the conditions under which

[136] BARS, Box R212, Roll 60a, October 1481; Roll 60b, May 1482.
[137] BARS, Box R212, Roll 9b, April 1408.
[138] BARS, Box R212, Roll 25, October 1418.
[139] BARS, Box R212, Roll 26, May 1419.

they were held. Explicit evidence of copyhold tenure at Willington is not found until the second half of the fifteenth century. In October 1450 the court roll states: 'that John Clerk has a ruined tenement from the lord and it should be repaired as appears above in the copy of the day of the last View.'[140] The record of the previous view of frankpledge has been lost, but in May 1452 the position is made quite clear: 'the holding that John Clerk the younger held is ruined and totally broken down. The lord made repairs once in his main term. And afterwards the aforesaid John maintained [them] as appeared in his Court copy and he asks for a plea with the lord.'[141]

There is no mention of copyhold in the next court roll, dated 4 October 1452, but copyhold admissions to three holdings were made in October 1453. The conditions under which one of them was to be held were clearly stated:

> To this View came William Legge and surrendered one Messuage and 10 acres of land lately held by John Palmere, into the hand of the lord for the use of Richard Wyneld. For which he was accustomed to render 10s. a year, and nothing fell due to the lord as heriot, except a capon. And following this the aforesaid Richard Wynyld came and took the aforesaid Messuage and land from the lord, to be held by himself and Agnes his wife for the terms of their lives and whichever of them lives longest, rendering therefrom 10s. a year. And the aforesaid Richard will well and competently repair and sustain all the buildings being in the said Messuage and at the end of his term will sufficiently repair the aforesaid to hand over and demise [them]. And each of them is answerable for an examination of the said Messuage and land at the middle of the term and it will be entered and will be divided, for which the lord will provide timber for the same Richard [and] necessary laths and withies for making repairs as often as were needed during the aforesaid term. And he gave 12d. to the lord as entry fine and heriot, and made fealty to the lord. And he was admitted as tenant, by a copy and no heriot after his death or withdrawal. And he owed suit twice a year etc.[142]

This passage demonstrates the practice of surrendering a holding for the admission of another tenant. Although this may have involved some sort of payment between the two parties, this is never mentioned in the court records. The payment of a heriot of one capon suggests that by this date payment of a fine on death or withdrawal was a symbolic token payment rather than a significant contribution to the lord's income. The record of the second copyhold admission is briefer:

> To this Court came Matilda Palmer and took one Messuage and 10 acres of land with its appurtenences, lately held by John Palmer her late husband, from the lord, to be held by her and her sons for the term of her life and of whichever of them lives longest, rendering therefrom 13s. 4d. a year to the lord, paid at the usual terms there. And the aforesaid Matilda and her sons will well and competently repair and sustain all the buildings being on the tenement at their own expense. And they were admitted as tenants by a copy and made fealty and owed suit twice a year.[143]

---

[140] BARS, Box R212, Roll 39a, October 1450.
[141] BARS, Box R212, Roll 40b, May 1452.
[142] BARS, Box R212, Roll 42a, October 1453.
[143] *Ibid.*

Another copyhold admission to a messuage and ten acres of land and a meadow for a man and his wife is recorded in May 1454.[144] In October the same year a messuage and ten acres was surrendered, and when no tenant was found it was taken by the bailiff without a copy; presumably the lord hoped to arrange a copyhold tenancy at a later date.[145] Although elsewhere copyhold tenancy eventually became almost as secure as freehold tenancy, at Willington it continued to be held for only two or three lives, under more and different conditions.

After these few recorded admissions, in the early 1450s, there is no further mention of copyhold in the Willington court rolls until March 1520. This roll is damaged, so the text is incomplete, but the lord of the manor asks that each tenant: 'shows at the next court what acres of land and meadowland he holds from the lord, both by copy and at the lord's will, and how much of the demesne land, under a penalty for each offence of 6s. 8d.'[146] Copyhold must have been important at that date, but some holdings were still held 'at will' or under special terms because they were parts of the demesne land.

All but five of the forty-one court rolls for the years 1394–1426 contain records of land transfers, of the forty-six rolls 1448–82 more than half contain none. The reduced number of land transfers recorded in the court rolls from the middle of the fifteenth century suggests that copyhold tenure was established and in regular use in Willington from that date. Manorial incidents associated with land transfers lessened, entry fines and heriots fell out of use; and the former customary tenure became more secure, so fewer land transfers were recorded.

On some manors changes in the value of lands and property were reflected in the entry fines, for example in nearby Blunham where they were sometimes at least ten times the annual rent.[147] This was not the case in Willington where rents were comparatively high and entry fines were comparatively low before the mid-fifteenth century, after which they disappeared or were reduced to one or two capons or chickens.[148]

The land-market in Willington has been described as 'demonstrably low' with little traffic in small parcels of land, and the Mowbrays seem to have discouraged fragmentation of holdings into smaller units, but details of the market in free lands are not available.[149] Tenants were certainly forbidden to let or sublet all or part of their holdings without permission in the years 1415–23, but then no reference is made to permission being necessary until much later in the century. In October 1481 and May 1482, in the last two rolls before Katherine Neville died, there was a change in language suggesting that her heirs were already taking over adminis-

---

[144] BARS, Box R212, Roll 42b, May 1454.
[145] BARS, Box R212, Roll 43a, October 1454.
[146] BARS, Box R212, Roll 62, March 1520.
[147] *Blunham Manor Court Rolls*, BARS, L26/51. An entry fine of 20s. was paid for a messuage and eight acres for which the annual rent was 2s. In 1417, 32s. 6d. was paid for a messuage and a quarter of virgate of land (about eight acres) for which the annual rent was 2s. In 1430, an entry fine of 3s. 4d. (40d.) was paid for a cottage and curtilage (messuage) for which the rent was 8d. a year. In July that year an entry fine of 2s. 6d. was paid for two messuages and two quarter virgates of land for which the annual rent was 26s. 8d.
[148] In the years 1452, 1454, 1455, 1461, 1478, 1481 and 1482.
[149] P. D. A. Harvey, 'Tenant Farming and Tenant Farmers - The Home Counties' in E. Miller, ed., *The Agrarian History of England and Wales*, vol. 3, 1348–1500 (Cambridge, 1991), p. 674.

tration of the manor. In these two court rolls the phrase: 'And there is no permission for the said … to rent out the said Messuage with any of its appurtenances without the lady's permission' is used as part of the records of the transfer of lands to John Pecke, John Yarewey, William Yarewey, John Waren, William Jerman and William Flawnders.[150]

The mill, the fisheries and the warrens were sometimes leased to prosperous tenants, usually from outside the vill. Securing a tenant for the rabbit warrens required flexibility on the part of the Mowbrays, who encouraged tenants to keep them by offering inducements. When William Launcelyn took the warren in 1465, for his life, the court roll reads:

> And in the future the lord will provide brambles, for the said William, for putting above the holes for the said rabbits in the aforesaid Warren. And if it comes to pass that anyone hunting or fishing or taking geese contained within the aforesaid fisheries or warren, the lord should prosecute in his own name by a brief against the hunters, fishers or takers of geese so taken from the keeping of the said William Launcelyn. The aforesaid William should take each and every revenue recovered against them by legal means and all amercements made against them in whatever court of the lord's tenants being held there for his total aforesaid term to his own proper use, without any contradiction.[151]

No offer of help with legal fees was made in 1475 when the warren was granted to Willington tenant Thomas Passewater on a forty-year lease, but he was offered dead trees and prunings from trees to cover the rabbit holes.[152] After only seven years the warren was granted to Richard Godfrey Esquire and William Fitzhave Gentleman.[153] It seems that members of the gentry had greater negotiating skills because the court roll reads:

> And furthermore the lady will provide brambles for the said Richard and William to put over the holes of the said Rabbits within the aforesaid warren. And if it should come to pass that anyone takes the fish or takes geese from the fisheries or the warren then the lady will bring a brief in her own name against the hunters or fishers taking from the said Richard and William, at her own expense.

Disputes over important issues relating to holdings of lands or buildings were occasionally referred to the lord's council. In October 1425 the steward referred the question of three men in the village holding dovecotes to the council, claiming that: 'they do not have sufficient free land to occupy and keep the said Dovecotes.'[154] As so often happens, the records of the following one or two courts are missing, so that it is not possible to discover what action the lord's council took. In May 1455 the tenants all supported John Stones who said that he needed a barn on his holding. They protested to the lord's council that: 'no-one should put a tenant into a tenement

[150] BARS, Box R212, Roll 60a, October 1481; Roll 60, May 1482.
[151] BARS, Box R212, Roll 53a, October 1465.
[152] BARS, Box R212, Roll 55b, March 1475.
[153] BARS, Box R212, Roll 60b, May 1482.
[154] BARS, Box R212, Roll 35, October 1425.

for holding and servicing himself, without having a barn there.'[155] In April 1457: 'the lord obliged the tenants to build the barn for John Stones'.[156]

Temporary reductions in rents are described in the court rolls and accounts as 'allowances' and may have been given when especially bad weather and poor harvests caused great hardship. Holdings which had ruined buildings, and so were unattractive to new tenants, were sometimes offered completely rent-free on condition that the new tenants made the necessary repairs. Powerful tenants like William Launcelyn did not always keep their side of the bargain without determined action by the manor court.

The Mowbrays adjusted to changes in economic and social life during most of the fifteenth century, but under their stewardship the leaders of the village negotiated good terms for themselves and their neighbours. The differences between free and villein status for tenants became less important and their joint action forced reductions in rents. There was increasing security of tenure as holdings were granted for three lives or were held on leasehold or copyhold tenancies.

After the death of Katherine Neville control of Willington by the Mowbrays came to an end, as all her direct descendants had predeceased her. The last two Willington court rolls of the fifteenth century, dated October 1481 and May 1482, contain few details about the tenants and concentrate on land transfers, perhaps reflecting the interests of the Howards, Dukes of Norfolk, based in Arundel, who inherited the manor. The Duke of Norfolk became one of the great survivors of Henry VIII's court, but the sparse evidence in the few Willington manor court rolls of the early sixteenth century makes it difficult to draw firm conclusions about life in Willington as Henry VIII came to throne.

---

[155] BARS, Box R212, Roll 43b, May 1455.
[156] BARS, Box R212, Roll 45b, April 1457.

Chapter Three
Willington, Blunham Greys and Eggington

This chapter examines Willington and its records within the context of two other rural Bedfordshire manors, Blunham Greys (also called Blunham with Girtford) and Eggington. There are translated records, concurrent with Willington, for both these manors.

It is possible to examine Willington in some detail because of the large collection of manorial documents which survive from the late fourteenth to the early sixteenth centuries. Characteristics specific to the manor are the limited influence of religious institutions on its history and the fact that it was held by landlords who did not live there, so being managed by a network of friends and relatives who formed the lord's council, or by their officials and employees. The tenants had opportunities to work together, to organise themselves and negotiate lower rents under the leadership of the bailiff who was almost always a local man, 1382–1483.

Manors were territorial units under the administration of a lord and often part of a larger estate. The three manors of Willington, Blunham Greys and Eggington were all lay manors, although the lord of the manor of Willington, Lord Mowbray, was patron of Newnham Priory. Willington was part of the extensive Mowbray estates, and its bailiff held some responsibility for the collection of rents from other smaller properties.[1] Blunham Greys was adjacent to, and downstream of, Willington on the south bank of the river Great Ouse and was also in the Wixamtree Hundred. It had links with nearby lands in Girtford. Ownership of this manor passed to the de Grey family, of Wrest Park, in 1389, and it was part of their wider estates.[2] The court of the small manor of Eggington, situated in the south-west of Bedfordshire, is presumed to have been part of a larger holding centred on Leighton Buzzard and was held by members of the Chyld (or Child) family until 1433, after which it passed to the Man family.[3]

Willington was a quiet rural settlement of between 1,600–1,700 acres on the south bank of the Great Ouse, east of Bedford. The boundaries of the manor were coterminous with the boundaries of the parish.[4] The court rolls show that

---

[1]   VCH, vol. 3, p. 262. Mowbray lands in Bedfordshire included Bedford Castle, Willington and manors and/or other Bedfordshire properties in Bromham, Cardington, Cople, Haynes, Stotfold and elsewhere, and part of Wing in Buckinghamshire. While substantial numbers of rolls survive for Willington, there are only a handful of rolls from the other manors, although the bailiffs' accounts for Haynes provide interesting information about the management of the park there.

[2]   The de Greys became Earls of Kent in 1465. They held the manor until the death of Henry de Grey, Lord Chamberlain, Lord Steward and Lord Privy Seal, who became Duke of Kent in 1710.

[3]   J. S. Thompson and K. T. Ward, 'Eggington Court Rolls (1297–1572)', in John Thompson, ed., *Hundreds, Manors, Parishes and the Church: a Selection of Early Documents for Bedfordshire*, BHRS, vol. 69 (Bedford, 1990), p.185.

[4]   Although not particularly rare, single-manor parishes have been estimated to constitute 10% of the manors created in England.

the lord's woodlands, which comprised Sheerhatch Wood on the greensand ridge in the south and The Grove on the north slopes of the ridge in the south-east, were important assets, and that their use by tenants was carefully controlled by the keeper of Sheerhatch or the woodward.[5] There is no evidence that tenants had common rights in the woodlands in the fourteenth and fifteenth centuries. The lord's officials and the jurors of the court together regulated the use of the common fields and the maintenance of paths, tracks and boundaries within the manor. From 1404 there were two juries at the courts, each comprising twelve tenants, so that at least twenty-four tenants were involved in some way in the court process during the fifteenth century.[6] The bailiffs' accounts 1382–97 describe the income from the manor and the landholdings including the demesne lands, which were recorded as 590 acres of arable land, twenty-one acres of meadow, and forty-nine acres one rood of pasture; a total of 660 acres and one rood. But the medieval scribe had apparently made a mistake; from 1388–89 onwards the demesne arable lands were recorded as 190 acres, making a revised total of 260 acres one rood. It is difficult to estimate the sizes of the half-virgates and other customary land holdings; the extent of the free holdings is unknown as are the extents of the woodland, the warren and the fisheries.

A market and a fair had been granted to Blunham in 1314, and Blunham Greys was one of three manors in the vill.[7] There is no mention of either the market or the fair in the manor court rolls for Blunham Greys, but the variety of business recorded, including the number of pleas of debt, suggests commercial activity of some sort. The manor had good communication links with local and national networks because of its position adjacent to the Great North Road and to the river Ivel, a tributary of the Great Ouse. There was a bridge over the Ivel from 1270 or before, and there was a ford at Girtford, providing easy access to the market at Potton.[8] It is difficult to estimate the size of the manor accurately. In 1086 the land which later became the manor of Blunham Greys was described as four hides one virgate held by the abbot of St Edmunds, and half-a hide held by Countess Judith; a total of less than five hides. Willington (at about 1,660 acres) was a ten-hide holding in 1086, so Blunham Greys manor may have been approximately half the size of Willington manor, perhaps 800 acres.[9]

Eggington manor was situated in one of the several hamlets in Leighton Buzzard parish, where the soil was loamy and much of the land was laid to grass and used as pasture. The size of the manor is unclear, but in 1589 it was said to have comprised 160 acres of land held by under-tenants paying quit rents and eighty acres of demesne.[10]

---

[5]   VCH, vol. 3, p. 262, states that there were 183 acres of woods and plantations in Willington parish in 1905, approximately 12% of the lands there, but there is no similar data about the area of the woodlands in the late fourteenth and the fifteenth centuries.
[6]   BARS, Box R212, Roll 7, October 1404.
[7]   Godber, *History of Bedfordshire*, pp. 50–1.
[8]   Godber, *History of Bedfordshire*, p. 71.
[9]   VCH, vol. 3, p. 228 gives the size of Blunham parish, which included Moggerhanger and Chalton, as slightly over 3,020 acres, but this includes the two townships. There were also five manors recorded over time in Blunham and no data in the extant records enables their relative areas to be calculated.
[10]   VCH, vol. 3, p. 299.

The limitations of the evidence in the bailiffs' accounts, the manor court rolls and other manorial documents make estimates of the populations of the three manors unreliable. It is possible to count personal names in court rolls and use a multiplier of 4.5 to reach an estimate, but suitably detailed court rolls for all three manors are only available in 1413.[11] In that year the names from a detailed roll for Willington number forty-one,[12] from Blunham Greys sixty[13] and from Eggington thirty-two,[14] suggesting tentative estimated populations of 180, 270 and 136 respectively. In 1471 the estimated population for Willington was 153.[15] The only extant comparable document of this date is for Blunham Greys when the Blunham Charter was signed by thirty-six tenants. This suggests that Blunham Greys' population was in the region of 164.

There are no court rolls extant for the period 1435–1500 for Eggington, but it is possible to estimate population for all three manors in the later part of the fifteenth century and early part of the sixteenth century. At Willington in September 1515 a court roll contained thirty-two names suggesting a population of 144.[16] A rental for Blunham Greys dated 1457 contained seventy-two names, an estimated population of 324,[17] and a survey in 1498 contained sixty names, giving an estimated population of 270.[18] At Eggington, the long and detailed court roll of November 1506 contains twenty-five names suggesting a population of 112. By June 1529 the number of names in the Eggington court roll had dropped to twelve, an estimated population of fifty-four, and the size of the jury had reduced from eight to five.[19] These population figures can only be estimates, based on incomplete evidence. The low figures for both Willington and Eggington in the early 1500s may have been due to a reduction in administrative diligence in Willington by the Howard family, based in Arundel, and the death of William Man of Eggington some time between 1514 and 1529.[20]

Although Willington and Blunham Greys were neighbouring manors, both on the south bank of the Great Ouse, there are few interrelated references in the documents. The Willington rolls record five instances relating to Blunham Greys: in 1417 William Flandyle of Blunham falsely accused John Abel of Willington and was fined 2d;[21] in 1420 Richard Hende, son of John Hende of Southmylne (South Mill), and William Denyas of Blunham, son of John Denyas, the butcher of Blunham, hunted in Willington Warren and took rabbits without permission, and faced prosecution;[22] in 1423 William Starlyng of Willington brought a case against John Rydere in the court of the Lord de Grey at Blunham, when he should have taken it to the

---

11 A multiplier of 4.5 assumes that an average of a man, his wife, one or two children and a servant or labourer is represented by each name that appears on the court rolls.
12 BARS, Box R212, Roll 15, October 1413.
13 *Blunham Manor Court Rolls*, BARS, L26/51, m 1, October 1413.
14 Thompson and Ward, 'Eggington Court Rolls', pp. 207–10.
15 BARS, Box R212, Roll 54a, October 1471.
16 BARS, Box R212, Roll 61, September 1515.
17 *Blunham Rental 1457*, BARS, L26/154.
18 *Blunham Survey 1498*, BARS, L26/212,
19 Thompson and Ward, 'Eggington Court Rolls', pp. 221–3.
20 Thompson and Ward, 'Eggington Court Rolls', p. 221.
21 BARS, Box R212, Roll 23, October 1417.
22 BARS, Box R212, Roll 29, October 1420.

Willington court, and was fined 12d;[23] in 1440 Thomas Wryght of Blunham was paid 3s. 4d. for the carriage of twenty-eight spars for repairs to a building;[24] and in 1450 two men from Blunham broke into Willington Grove and stole four oaks, and a third man stole three oaks from Sheerhatch, they were each fined 40d.[25]

The court records

Detailed comparison of the three manors is difficult due to the limitations of the evidence. Even the court rolls extant for Willington, although numerous, are incomplete; many of them may have been lost, damaged or destroyed, or the courts may not have been held. The court records for Blunham Greys, although very numerous, are condensed into a short period of time, 1415–57. The nine court records included for Eggington are part of a much larger collection dating from 1297–1572, which, given the nature and operation of that particular manor at that period, are largely concerned with land transfers. The only years when there are rolls extant from all three manors are 1413–26, and these do not form a complete series.

Court records were important to the lord, not only because the income derived from the business of the manor court contributed significantly to his income but also as legal documents. They were preserved to provide proof of titles to land and other property within the manor, evidence of customary by-laws and agreements which benefited the lord and the community of tenants, and to record licences to brew or sell ale and bake bread on the manor. Some informal business arrangements made between tenants outside the courts may not have been documented, and there are occasional examples of tenants sub-letting all or part of their holdings.

Written records of manorial courts, which every manorial lord had the right to hold, began to appear in the mid-thirteenth century when some extant records suggest that courts were held every three weeks. Generally it is thought that a powerful lord with many unfree tenants was able to impose more onerous regimes on the manors under his control.[26] But the records for Blunham Greys, for instance, show a more stringent regime than that at Willington, despite the Mowbrays, who held the latter manor, being significantly more powerful than the de Greys. The records for Blunham Greys include long lists of fines or amercements and occasional distraints and attachments, especially between October 1447 and November 1448 when assaults and pleas of debt were particularly frequent.[27] In the roll dated 5 October 1447 there were ten assaults and fines of 4d. each were paid.[28] Seven debts are recorded in the Girtford section of the roll. In the roll dated 8 October 1448 there were twenty-seven assaults for which fines of 12d. each were paid and a further assault, 'against the watchman of the lord King against the peace' for which the fine was 3s. 4d.[29] There were eight pleas of debt in the Girtford part of the roll.

23   BARS, Box R212, Roll 32, June 1423.
24   BARS, Box R 212, Roll 37, April 1440.
25   BARS, Box R212, Roll 39a, October 1450.
26   Bailey, *The English Manor*, pp. 7–8.
27   BARS, L26/54, Court 13, m 6, October 1447; Court 14, m 6 dorse, November 1447; Court 15, m 5, March 1448; Court 16, m 5 dorse, May 1448; Court 17, m 9, October 1448; Court 18, m 7, November 1448.
28   BARS, L26/54, Court 13, m 6, October 1447.
29   BARS, L26/54, Court 17, m 9, October 1448.

At Willington the manor courts seem to have been run more co-operatively. Fines were paid for breaches of the custom of the manor, there was no physical punishment and it was rare for a tenant to be deprived of his or her holding; disputes with the tenants were solved by negotiation where possible. The manorial court rolls for Eggington contain very few details of life on the manor. This small private seigniorial court was almost entirely concerned with the transfer of land, and only one statement of manorial custom is recorded, in 1298.[30]

Manor courts can be divided into two groups; the views of frankpledge, sometimes called views with court or leet courts, which gave the lord of the manor the power to administer rights of jurisdiction which had been granted or franchised by the Crown; and the customary courts, also called courts, little courts or halmoots, which later became known as courts baron. The distinctions between the essentially franchised and locally determined customary jurisdictions are often blurred and cannot be presumed by the title of a court at a given date.

At Willington a view of frankpledge with court, sometimes called view with court or leet court, was held in the autumn. A customary court, or halmoot, was held after the view in the autumn and then without a view in the spring. One hundred and one rolls are still extant 1394–1522 and have been transcribed and translated by the author, with the assistance of other specialists in medieval Latin and palaeography.[31]

About 130 court records for Blunham Greys and Girtford survive for the years 1413–57 (an average of almost three a year) translated by J. S. Thompson. The pattern of survival is very uneven and is completely different from either Willington or Eggington because in some years the records of several intermediate courts, referred to as little courts (*curie parve*), are still extant, although many of them are very short. The year for which there is the most complete record is 1432 from which ten rolls are still extant, but all the rolls for 1452–54 inclusive are missing. The pieces of parchment are all approximately ten inches wide and eighteen or twenty inches long. They are sewn together at the upper edges into four rolls of varying sizes by one stitch on the upper edges of the parchment. The details of a court in Girtford, a hamlet between Blunham and Sandy, which was first mentioned in the thirteenth century, are recorded within the court rolls for Blunham Greys at the end of the views of frankpledge; seventy-one records of these courts survive.

A unique feature of the Eggington manor court rolls, of which thirty-two survive, is the variation in the sizes of the pieces of parchment on which they are written.[32] The courts at Eggington were described as 'court' until 1500, when the term court baron began to be used. It is likely that these courts did not meet more frequently

---

30   Thompson and Ward, 'Eggington Court Rolls', p. 188 and pp. 193–226.
31   The majority of the rolls, which are of varying sizes, are to found in the Russell Collection held by Bedfordshire Archives and Records Service and deposited on long-term loan by the Dukes of Bedford. For the most part they are in reasonable condition. A further eight rolls are held by the British Library. Some of the latter are very difficult to read but were transcribed with a short commentary by Miss Joyce Godber in the twentieth century. BARS, CRT 130 Willington 4.
32   'Medieval manorial rolls in fact varied a good deal in size and shape; to take two extreme examples, both from Bedfordshire, nearly all the courts for the Loring family's manor of Chalgrave 1278–1313 are entered on a single roll 20 feet long, new membranes being added as court followed court, while another early fourteenth century roll, from Eggington, measures less than 5 inches square.' Harvey, *Manorial Records*, p. 42.

than twice a year although the tenants promised to attend court every three weeks when entering into tenancies.[33]

Despite the varying survival and condition of the manor court rolls there are similarities in layout and content which can be attributed to written guides and sets of instructions dating from the late thirteenth century for the use of clerks.[34] There is no evidence in the rolls about the practical production of the documents, though occasionally they seem to have been written out in advance with details added and alterations made later. Details of the names and lifestyles of the clerks who wrote them are not given, and although the similarities of format, headings and language suggest some sort of instruction there is no evidence of where or how the clerks were trained, or whether they lived on the manor they recorded or were visiting as part of the lord's household. Men with the family name Clerk (or Clerke) lived in Willington 1397–1483, but it is not clear if members of this family had been educated at, or had other links with, nearby Newnham Priory and so become clerks.

The Willington court rolls show that a few pence were sometimes paid for purchases of parchment and ink, probably from Bedford,[35] but the variety of different sizes of parchment used at Eggington suggests a more unreliable, and perhaps cheaper, local source. The Willington documents also provide a hint of how the rolls were stored; following details of John Usshere's nine-year lease of the watermill in the October 1413, the roll says: 'which certain deed remains in the bag of rolls of Bedford.'[36]

The rolls were legal documents and were written in Latin, but there were occasional hints of the French language in the Willington rolls; names of some landscape features or buildings begin with the definite article *le*. The use of vernacular English in some practical contexts is found in descriptions of repairs to Willington mill, *goyngere* referred to the mill machinery and *hengys et hoks* (hinges and hooks) were bought in 1440.[37] The production of the Blunham Charter in English in 1471 suggests that at least some of the tenants of that manor were literate.

Administration of the manors

At Willington, the lord of the manor was usually mentioned in the heading of the court roll, although the steward held the court. Reginald, Lord de Grey, is only mentioned once in the Blunham Greys headings, in 1418. At Eggington, the lord was usually named and may have presided over the court.[38] At first, the lords of Eggington were members of the Chyld family, but in the roll of 1433 the heading states that the lady of the manor was, 'Christiana formerly wife of John Man' who may have been a daughter of William Child (who was named as lord of the manor in 1425). A William Man succeeded her in 1500. The courts of all three manors used regnal years and saints' days to indicate the dates on which they were held.

33   Thompson and Ward, 'Eggington Court Rolls,' p. 187.
34   Harvey, *Manorial Records*, p. 43.
35   12d. was paid: 'In the expense of parchment and paper for the Courts and rolls, and ink for Bedford, Wylyngton, Cardington and Bromham.' BARS, Box R212, Roll 45b, April 1457.
36   BARS, Box R212, Roll 15, October 1413.
37   BARS, Box R212, Roll 37, with additions, April 1440.
38   Thompson and Ward, 'Eggington Court Rolls', p. 188.

An owner of an estate who found that he was unable to manage it himself might employ someone as a bailiff to run the property on his behalf or lease out the manor for a number of years, or a term of lives, and collect a pre-determined rent.[39] In the late fourteenth century the Mowbrays did both in Bedfordshire. They leased out Haynes Park as one unit at the same time as they employed a bailiff at Willington. The bailiff was sometimes referred to in the Willington bailiffs' accounts as the accountant and also served as rent collector to other local manors. In addition, the Mowbrays employed members of the gentry to act as stewards, to hold the manor courts and take on the role of receiver for payments from Bedfordshire and receiver general for all their estate accounts. The de Greys of Wrest Park ran their manor in Blunham Greys with the assistance of a bailiff.[40] Although no bailiff is named in the headings of the rolls one was elected from a shortlist prepared by the tenants. Other manorial officials were also elected, but further details of how the de Greys ran their estates are sparse. At Eggington manor, the Chyld and Man families seem to have run the courts largely by themselves; a steward was mentioned only once, in 1413.

Essoins recording tenants' excuses for absences from court nearly always appear after the heading of the court roll. All male tenants, whether free or unfree, were expected to attend the manor court and were fined for non-attendance. Women were not expected to attend the court unless they held lands in their own right, either as a free woman who had inherited lands from her father or as a widow who continued to hold her husband's lands after his death. At Willington there were usually one or two essoins at each court, but in October 1422 there were six, and sometimes, in the 1460s, four or six tenants were excused. Essoins at Blunham Greys reached their highest number of eleven in October 1433. At Eggington there were no references to essoins in 1413 or 1425. Some of the later courts included the heading 'Essoins' and then noted that there were none.

The jury at Blunham Greys, like that of Willington, usually consisted of twelve men, and throughout 1413–37 it was regularly led by a John Lety, senior or junior. As at Willington, the men were referred to as tithing men or jurors. Twelve jurors are named for Blunham Greys and eleven for Girtford in October 1455, although Girtford's jury was usually smaller; juries of three, four, five or six men were not unknown. The jury at Eggington was described as the homage in 1428, but the number of jurors was not given.[41] From 1500 the size of the jury of this manor court varied between five and eight, and the jurors are named.

At Willington, a second jury is first recorded at the end of the view of frank-pledge in October 1404. Its purpose was to verify: 'that the tithing men, Constable and Tasters of Ale spoke well and faithfully and concealed nothing.'[42] The importance of the second jury to the Mowbrays is made clear by the number of times the jurors are named and the variety and status of the participants. The sworn men in

---

[39]   Harvey, *Manorial Records,* p. 4.
[40]   Elections of bailiffs are recorded in BARS, L26/51, m 10, October 1417, and L26/51, m 12, September 1418. Elections of a reeve, the ale-tasters and the hayward took place in October 1429; two constables were elected in April 1430, BARS, L26/53, m 9 (ii), April 1430.
[41]   Homage has at least three meanings depending on the context. It may mean the act by which a villein tenant accepts the superiority of his lord; the group of men forming the jury at the manor court, usually twelve; or the 'whole homage' may mean everyone who is expected to attend the manor court.
[42]   BARS, Box R212, Roll 7, October 1404.

the second jury were first named in October 1416, very soon after Thomas Bekyn-gham was appointed steward. John Gostwyck and John Maryon, two important free tenants, led the lists of jurors on the second jury four times before 1426. The names of those on the second juries 1448–81 included a mix of established and new tenants. There was no second jury after 1481. In Blunham, there are hints of a second jury for the views with court and the views of frankpledge. In October 1416, tenants John Simmond, Robert Kempe and their associates state that: 'the aforesaid jury have presented all things well and have concealed nothing, on their oath.'[43] Similar phrases were used in 1455, 1456 and 1457. There was no second jury in Eggington.

At both Willington and Blunham Greys the bailiff was appointed by the lord, as were other paid officials, but the manorial officers, that is the constable, the ale-tasters, the assessors of fines and the hayward, were usually elected at the views or leet courts.[44] Unfortunately, the rolls do not explain in detail how elections took place or who was entitled to vote. It is known, however, that in 1417 the tithing men of Blunham Greys produced shortlists from which the steward selected the bailiff and the hayward.[45]

Two ale-tasters and two constables were usually elected at Willington, but after October 1461 the roles were often combined.[46] Being a constable in Willington did not protect a man from being accused of minor crimes.[47] There were also two assessors of fines at each court, who were often members of the Miton family.[48] There would also have been a clerk to the court, but it is not clear whether he was a Willington tenant or whether he travelled with the steward.

At Blunham Greys there were two assessors of fines; two ale-tasters, who some-times did not do their jobs properly; two constables; a hayward; and a clerk. At Eggington, because of the infrequency of the surviving documents, the pattern of assessors of fines is more complex. None were mentioned 1413–33; two are mentioned in the court of July 1435; two are named in the courts of October 1500 and July 1501; none are mentioned in November 1506; the whole homage were listed as assessors in June 1514; no assessors were recorded in June 1529; and in August 1531 the roll once again says, 'Affeered by the whole homage.'[49] There would have been a clerk.

The prior of Newnham Priory was the most frequent absentee from the court at Willington and usually paid fines for default. In the 1390s there were three occa-sions when six or seven people defaulted, and eight absentees were recorded in 1410 when there was a new steward. After that date the numbers were usually much lower, although six absentees were recorded in March 1522. Defaulters in Blunham Greys were recorded at most courts, reaching a maximum of seventeen in

43   BARS, L26/51, m 7 and m 7 dorse, April 1416; m 8, October 1416.
44   Although the records may indicate that these officials were elected, the performance of a manorial office may have been a condition of some tenancies.
45   BARS, L26/51, m 10, October 1417.
46   BARS, Box R212, Roll 49a October 1461; Roll 50c, October 1462; Roll 52a, October 1465; Roll 60, October 1481.
47   BARS, Box R212, Roll 2, October 1394; Roll 5, October 1397; Roll 7, October 1404; Roll 10, October 1408. In these years the constable was fined 2d. on several occasions.
48   Referred to as 'affeerors'.
49   Thompson and Ward, 'Eggington Court Rolls,' pp. 207–23.

September 1435. At Blunham Greys the abbot of Warden avoided coming to court, much like the prior of Newnham at Willington. At Eggington most tenants who did not come to court were fined 2d., but in 1500 and 1501 two persistent offenders were each fined 4d.

The Willington views of frankpledge generated more income than the other courts, with the highest incomes in 1383, 1385 and 1395. In the fifteenth century the incomes gradually reduced, and sometimes the courts in the spring operated at a loss. The Blunham Greys views of frankpledge generated more income than the manor's intermediate courts and the largest sum, of £4 3s. 5d. was recorded in May 1457. Other relatively large sums were recorded in April 1444 and October 1447. At Eggington, in June 1425, the total income from rents and labour service (that is, working days) was recorded as: 'total of rents overleaf, 16s. 8d.: and working days overleaf, 7½ days.'[50] In 1433 and 1435 the total of the court was nil and no mention of a total appears in the other rolls.

Stewards' expenses for Willington were always mentioned and occasionally the steward is said to have stayed overnight. In April and September 1426 the rolls describe in detail the costs of generous meals after the courts, which were 4s. 1½d. and 6s. 4d. respectively. These costs included oats for the horses and parchment for the rolls.[51] At Blunham, stewards' expenses were not mentioned until April 1456. In December 1456, they were considerable, amounting to 8s. 4d., and in May 1457 they were 8s. 6d. plus 18d. for shoeing the horses. Expenses for intervening courts were lower.[52] No stewards' expenses were recorded for Eggington.

Transfer of land and buildings
Transfers of land, the passing of by-laws to regulate the lives of the local community, the use of open fields, pasture and common land, and orders to repair buildings and local infrastructure were recorded at the views of frankpledge and other courts. The lord was most interested in surrenders of holdings, admissions to properties and other transactions which generated income, but where a roll states that a property was transferred for the use of another named person, it is generally assumed that the former owner reached some sort of business arrangement with the new tenant which did not generate any income for the lord.

At Willington an average of three land transfers were recorded in each roll before and including 1426, with an average of one heriot paid in each roll. Women sometimes took over the lands of their late husbands; some held them for several years, others soon surrendered them. Manorial estate assets such as the warren, the fisheries and the dovecote were leased for periods of years, and some holdings were leased out after 1448, when the numbers of land transfers on the manor reduced, perhaps due to the evolution and development of copyhold.

Detailed records of land transfers were kept at Blunham Greys, but there is evidence that some transfers of land took place without the knowledge of the bailiff

---

50   Thompson and Ward, 'Eggington Court Rolls', p. 212. Kevin Ward notes that the scribe had made a mistake, and the total of rents should have been 17s.
51   BARS, Box R212, Roll 36, September 1426; Roll 36a, April 1426.
52   BARS, L26/54, Court 39, m 18, December 1456; Court 43, m 17, May 1457; Court 38, m 16 dorse, June 1456; Court 40, m 18 dorse, December 1456; Court 41, m 18 dorse, January 1457; Court 42, m 18 dorse, April 1457; Court 44, m 17 dorse, May 1457.

or the steward 1415–55. Most orthodox entries recording transfers of land begin with a phrase similar to that used in 1425: 'At that court, Thomas Wrygth [*sic*] came and took from the lord …'[53] However, it is clear that some transfers had taken place before the court convened as one new tenant later: 'came and acknowledged that he held from the lord a messuage with appurtenances' and he made fealty.[54] Matters were not always quite so simple, in April 1443 the court record states: 'William Botiller [was] tenant of certain land, late William More's, also a river meadow and 2 acres 3 roods of land lately Bustryches, in what way it is not known.' The bailiff was: 'ordered to seize the land and meadow … and take the proceeds of it.'[55] Five years later two other men, also with the family name Botiller, neglected to pay annual rent for land that they had taken over from Emma Chapman and Alice Bandewyn, who were presumably widows, and in October 1448 the bailiff was ordered to: 'take these lands into the lord's hands and receive the proceeds.'[56]

Widows paid heriots in Blunham Greys to take over their late husbands' holdings, and in 1418 a widow was granted his messuage and land on condition that she stayed single and paid an entry fine of 15d.[57] In 1443: 'to that view came Alice Berkewell, and gives to the lord as fine (15d.), according to the custom of the manor, for the lands and tenement which Henry Bekewell [*sic*], late husband of Alice herself, held of the lord.'[58]

In the Willington bailiffs' accounts 1382–97 the free tenants of Willington, Cople and Cardington paid rents of 6s. ½d., 7s. ¾d. and 5s. 1½d.; a total of 18s. 2¾d. Thirty-six messuages with thirty-four half-virgates and sixty-four acres of land and a croft were said to be held freely. Although it is not entirely clear what this meant, it is assumed to indicate that the lands were free of labour services on the demesne, which had been granted to bondsman tenants and certain tenants at will at Willington before Michaelmas 1382. By 1457, the rents from the free tenants had increased to 6s. 10 ½d. and they were still at this level 1480–81. Most lands at the end of the fourteenth and the beginning of the fifteenth centuries were granted, 'at the will of the lord' or for one life, but by the second half of the fifteenth century lands were more often let for two or three lives. On rare occasions they were leased for a number of years, and some tenants held more than one holding. At Blunham Greys, the granting of messuages or cottages for three lives (a man, his wife and their heirs or assigns, usually their son) begins much earlier than in Willington and is first recorded – twice – in October 1414 with entry fines of 20s. for both.[59] In 1413, the roll contains a reference to a messuage and half virgate of land said to be, 'as appears in the extract of the court roll', that is, by copyhold. It was granted to a bondsman who also paid an entry fine of 20s.[60] Copyhold tenancies appear much later in the Willington rolls.

With one exception, the land transfers at Eggington by conveyance or inheritance took place before a court was held; the details were later recorded, and in effect

---

53   BARS, L26/53, m 1 dorse, October 1423.
54   *Ibid.*
55   BARS, L26/54, Court 1, m 1, April 1443.
56   BARS, L26/54, Court 17, m 9, October 1448.
57   BARS, L26/51, m 10 dorse, May 1418.
58   BARS, L26/54, Court 1, m 1, April 1443.
59   BARS, L26/51, m 1, October 1414.
60   BARS, L26/51, m 2, October 1413.

registered, at the court. In the fourteenth century many holdings were said to be held 'by service', and occasional details of the boonworks or labour services required from tenants were also kept. By the fifteenth century this phrase was no longer used. Some lands could be inherited and tenants paid heriots for certain holdings on the death of a tenant.[61] Selected single acres of land should have been let 'at will' or for one life but in practice were sold or transferred without the lord's permission. From 1433 lands are described as being 'held freely', at least fifty years later than when the phrase was first used at Willington. In 1500, the Eggington roll records that questions were being raised about the tenants' rights to their holdings:

> Also they present that various tenants hold certain lands for which they have not paid rent or other payment, but they do not hold because they owe rent as appears in a court roll of 12th Henry VI; and similarly that some entered into the fee of the lord as appears there; therefore it is ordered to distrain them against the next court to show how and by what service they hold.[62]

At Willington the size of holdings varied, but many were of standard size.[63] Rents for the former demesne lands were reduced over time following negotiations between the tenants, the lords' steward and other officials. Rents for the mill, the fisheries and the dovecote also reduced. In Blunham Greys parcels of land recorded in the rolls were smaller than in Willington and rents appear to have been lower, although the much larger entry fines levied there brought in more income from the Blunham Greys courts for the de Grey family than the Mowbrays received from Willington.[64] As P. D. A Harvey notes:

> The once-for-all payment on entry may often have affected the level of rent; this appears clearly in early fifteenth century Bedfordshire, where at Blunham the annual rent for a half-virgate might be no more than 2s., with an entry-fine of 20s., while at Willington, a couple of miles away, the half-virgater paid 13s. 4d. a year in rent but an entry-fine usually of only 8d., or 1s.[65]

Other patterns can be seen elsewhere and it has been suggested by Harvey that rents may have been fixed by bargaining with the individual tenant.

> At Eggington the holdings varied in size, and there was a wide variation in rents perhaps due to the productivity of the land and other factors such as the extent of the services which were due from the tenants. In 1413, the rents were between 9d. for half a messuage without any land being mentioned, and 5s. 6d. for a messuage with appurtenances, further details of which were not given.

At Willington messuages were granted with half a virgate of land, which is assumed to be about eight acres, for 13s. 4d. in 1382–83.[66] They were still being rented out for the same sum in 1480–81.[67]

---

[61]   Thompson and Ward, 'Eggington Court Rolls', p. 191.
[62]   Thompson and Ward, 'Eggington Court Rolls', p. 217.
[63]   BARS, R8/62/1/1-11, and Thompson, *Bailiffs' Accounts for Willington*, BARS, CRT 130 Willington 11, pp. 1–45.
[64]   Harvey, 'Tenant Farming and Tenant Farmers - The Home Counties', p. 669.
[65]   *Ibid.*
[66]   BARS, R8/62/1/1, and Thompson, *Bailiffs' Accounts for Willington*, BARS, CRT 130 Willington 11, p. 1.
[67]   Arundel Castle Archives, A1328.

The pattern of holdings established in Willington in 1382 was maintained throughout the fifteenth century, and there is no clear evidence of land being divided into smaller units. In Blunham Greys, information in the rental of 1457 shows very clearly that land had been divided into many small units.[68] There were forty-two free holdings and a further forty-five small holdings described as being held by 'tenants at will' or by copyhold. The Blunham Charter was negotiated in 1471 between Edmund, Earl of Kent, and thirty-six tenants and allowed for portions of land to be sold under certain conditions to people already living on the manor, although heavy dues were payable to the lord when these sales took place.

> Firste we will and grant yf yt shall be lawfull for every tenante of our Sayde Lordship to bye & sell theyre Messuage, Cotage, lande tenemente and all other tenures of theres theare, to enie other tenante of ours there in manner and forme as ensueth, reserving to us such Fyne, gersume and dutie as shall growe to us by righte and custom of the Sayde fermre.[69]

The 1498 Blunham survey records that there were about a hundred holdings held by copy or 'at will' with rents varying between 1d. and 14s. 2d. a year.[70] The trend was towards many smaller units in Blunham Greys and larger land-holdings in Willington, where some families held more than one unit.

In earlier centuries tenants-in-chief, such as the Beauchamps of Bedford and the Mowbrays, were required to provide a horseman to fight for the king; this later changed to a money payment for knight's service, or scutage. This was not an annual land tax but was levied by the king when extra income was required - such as to fight wars or pay for family weddings. At Willington it was passed on from the landowner to his free tenants and was mentioned twice, in 1410 and 1464.[71] It was mentioned at the end of the thirteenth century in Eggington and once in the Blunham Greys rolls, in 1447.[72] The records do not indicate what proportion of knight's service was paid in relation to a particular unit or parcel of land or the amount of tax levied.

Rental payments in kind, involving capons or chickens or an occasional pound of pepper, were recorded in the Willington bailiffs' accounts at the end of the four-teenth century, and such payments continued to be accepted until 1509,[73] although by 1457–58 rents in kind at Willington had largely been replaced by a money payment.[74]

> And for 15d,, being the value of two capons as rent from the tenants there this year as in the preceding account, and for the value of one pound of pepper from Robert Warner this year nothing, because this is the annual payment to the lord, delivered to the Auditor, for their fees by ancient custom sum total 15d.[75]

68   BARS, L26/154.
69   *The Trewe copye of Blunham Charter, made unto them by Edmonde, Late Earle of Kent*, BARS, L26/229, CRT 130 Blunham 7.
70   BARS, L26/212.
71   BARS, Box R212, Roll 12, October 1410; Roll 51a, October 1464. In both cases knight's service was paid by free men, but the size of the tax is not given.
72   Thompson and Ward, 'Eggington Court Rolls', p.190 and 193; BARS, L26/54, Court 12, m 4, April 1447.
73   The last reference to payments of capons or chickens are found in BARS, Box R212, Roll 60a, October 1481; and in Suffolk Record Office, HD1538/225/2-6, 1487, 1503, 1504, 1509.
74   British Library, Add Ch. 657.
75   *Ibid.*

At Blunham Greys capons were paid as part of the rents of holdings, as entry fines, or for permission to hand over holdings to another tenant, at least fourteen times 1419–57. On one occasion the court entry read: 'A cottage was taken by a man for his life, for 5s. a year and 2 capons at Christmas.'[76] This condition is not mentioned elsewhere in the Blunham Greys records. At Eggington no payments in kind for rents are mentioned 1382–1522, and although heriots are often recorded there is only one occasion when details are given; a horse worth 6s. 8d. in 1413. Although the payment of heriots at Eggington continued to be expected for messuages and tenements into the sixteenth century, long after they had been expected for holdings in Willington,[77] the court roll of 1529 records that three heirs, Thomas Doget, William Gurney and Edmund Wadlowe had avoided paying them.[78]

All Willington, tenants were required to swear fealty to the lord when taking over a holding although demands on villein tenants to work in the lord's fields and help to bring in his harvest had disappeared when the demesne lands were let 1382–83. At Blunham Greys all tenants were also required to swear fealty when taking a holding. But there, the requirement to perform labour services, usually at harvest time, was often ignored, and it became normal for money fines to be paid instead. The same requirement to swear fealty was also imposed at Eggington, but by November 1506 all was not well. Tenants were avoiding paying heriots or rents and also avoiding swearing fealty to the lord.

Tenants in Willington were forbidden to sublet, although there are occasional references which suggest that some tenants had labourers or other people living in cottages on their holdings, as witnessed by a court entry of 1478:

> To this [court] came Thomas Huett and took from the Lady one Cottage next to the Cottage in the holding of William on one side and the Cottage in the holding of John Bardolph on the other side. To have and to hold by himself and one following at the will of the lady, according to the custom of the manor.[79] Rendering therefrom to the Lady 12d. a year and suit of Court and for [entry] fine 1 capon. And he made fealty etc.[80]

A greater emphasis on this rule can be seen in 1481 and 1482 when six holdings were granted on condition that the new tenants agreed not: 'to let any of the said messuage with its appurtenances without the lady's permission.'[81] At Blunham Greys, although the charter of 1471 makes it clear under what conditions lands could be sold, there is no mention of lands being sublet, but some details in the Eggington rolls suggest that it occasionally took place there.[82]

The evidence in the court records for Willington, Blunham Greys and Eggington suggests that the emergence and development of copyhold tenancies took place at

---

76   BARS, L26/54, Court 4, m 2, October 1443.
77   The last charge of a heriot in Willington was of a horse worth 8s. in October 1451, BARS, Box R212, Roll 40a. After that date the rolls note, 'no heriot after withdrawal' for several years and then cease to mention the charge at all.
78   Thompson and Ward, 'Eggington Court Rolls', p. 222.
79   The 'one following' may have been a relative, or someone else to whom Thomas Huett sought to pass the cottage after his death.
80   BARS, Box R212, Roll 59a, November 1478.
81   BARS, Box R212, Roll 60a, October 1481; Roll 60b, May 1482.
82   Thompson and Ward, 'Eggington Court Rolls,' p. 190.

different dates. Early Willington court rolls, 1394–1411, refer to land being held 'by or with' the court roll, but there were no explicit references to copyhold on the manor until 1450, and even then the references are few.[83] After five references during the next few years there were no more until March 1520. Copyhold is mentioned only four times in the 130 Blunham Greys rolls 1413–57. In Eggington, mention is made of a, 'copy in the court of John Child, son of John Child' at the end of a roll in 1413, but the meaning of this is unclear. Copyhold was first mentioned explicitly there in 1572.

Details of holdings by freemen in Willington were not usually recorded in the court rolls, and few details of tenants' status were given in the important re-negotiations of rents for the demesne lands held in 1421, 1449 and 1454.[84] At Blunham, the status of freemen is also unclear although the rolls include the names Butler and Pecke, the names of families known to be recorded as free tenants in the Willington records.

At Eggington, as previously noted, most land transfers took place outside the court but were later recorded and registered there. No mention of the status of tenants is included in the documents although it is thought that: 'despite the variation of technology, it is most likely that the rolls are at all times concerned with free socage tenants.'[85] However, the requirement for many tenants to work in the lord's fields as part of their rent and the continued payment of heriots suggests that medieval custom persisted and that at least some tenants were unfree.

The courts at Willington attempted to protect the lord's woods, warrens and fisheries, and the common fields and meadows from trespass and theft by the tenants and by men from outside the manor. A new lessee of the warrens must have been especially concerned in 1482, for in that year the lady of the manor, Katherine Neville, agreed to prosecute on his behalf anyone found stealing any of his game or water birds.[86] There are no details of comparable arrangements on Blunham Greys or Eggington manors.

In both Willington and Blunham Greys manors the tenants became more demanding as the fifteenth century progressed. At Willington, the lord's officials and members of his council were involved in negotiating changes with them. At Blunham, the charter of 1471 between the lord and his tenants witnesses their joint agreement to the conditions under which lands and buildings might be sold. There is no evidence to show how the Man family at Eggington dealt with any similar changes, but it is recorded that the tenants were resisting the payment of rents and heriots by the end of the century.

Income from the courts
The business of the courts enabled the lord of the manor to raise income in various ways including the payment of fines for non-attendance, unless excused as essoins. Payments for default of attendance at the views of frankpledge or views with court were more complex in Blunham Greys than at Willington, and separate lists were

---

[83] BARS, Box R212, Roll 39a, October 1450.
[84] BARS, Box R212, Roll 30, April 1421; Roll 38b, May 1449; Roll 42b, May 1454.
[85] Thompson and Ward, 'Eggington Court Rolls', p. 190.
[86] BARS, Box R212, Roll 60b, May 1482.

made of tenants in both Blunham Greys and Girtford throughout the period October 1413–May 1457. Tenants were fined for non-attendance by varying amounts: 1d., 2d., 3d., or multiples of these. The procedure for calculating the fines is unclear, but it appears that the status of the tenant influenced the fee. Bondsmen paid 1d. and members of the gentry paid 4d., but occasionally both a tenant and his servant each paid the same fee of 2d. Some fees of 12d. or 18d. may have been a single payment for a series of defaults. Elizabeth Waryn of Girtford paid 18d. on 12 October 1415, nothing on 22 April 1416, and then 18d. on 15 October 1416, which the roll says was, 'remission of suit of court up to the feast of St Michael.'[87] A year later, she again paid 18d.: 'as a fine for remission of suit of court up to the feast of St Michael next to come, and a boonwork.'[88] The next mention of her is found in October 1420, when she paid 4d.[89] No essoins were recorded at Eggington, but fines were collected from tenants who defaulted.

Common fines were a regular form of income for the lord. Originally a payment to the county sheriff for ensuring the proper administration of the view of frankpledge, this fee was later paid to the lord as part of his income. At Willington, common fines are described as such in the court rolls 1394–1522 except in October 1425 and 1458 when there are entries describing them as a 'fixed fine'. No details of how these fines were calculated are given in the views, but in the Willington bailiffs' accounts 1382–97 under 'perquisites of court' there are entries, '12s. for a common fine of bondsmen tenants of Willington.'[90] This amount continued to be paid each year at the view of frankpledge or the view with court in the autumn until October 1425. Records of the views of frankpledge and other courts for the next twenty-three years have been lost.

The court rolls after 1448 show that the fixed amount of 12s. for common fines had been abandoned and the fines reduced. Amounts of about 7s. were usually paid. On 26 October 1457 the view of frankpledge records that: 'Charged and sworn by various articles concerning the Court, they [the jurors] present that they gave 7s. 9d. as common fine on this day',[91] but the bailiff's account for 1457–58 shows the common fines were being described as rents of assize and that instead of being paid by former bondsmen were now being paid by freemen:

> … and for 6s.10½d. for the rents of free tenants of the aforesaid lord this year paid at the terms of Easter and at Saint Michael the Archangel, that is to say from John Norman, John Abel, Robert Partriche, Robert Miton, Robert Warner, John C[B]awde, John Miton, Thomas Stoughton, the prior of Newnham, John Gostewik the elder.92

The accounts were kept, 'in the bag of rolls of the Court of the aforesaid Lord.' A similar passage in the Willington account of William Paryssh, bailiff and reeve,

87   BARS, L26/51, m 8, October 1416; m 7, April 1416; m 7 dorse, April 1416.
88   BARS, L26/51, m 10, October 1417.
89   BARS, L26/52, m 4, October 1420.
90   BARS, R8/62/2/1-11, and Thompson, *Bailiffs' Accounts for Willington*, BARS, CRT 130 Willington 11, pp. 2, 5, 8, 12, 16, 21, 25, 29, 34, 39, 43.
91   BARS, Box R212, Roll 46a, October 1457.
92   British Library, Add Ch. 657.

1480–81, suggests stability.[93] The same free men paid the same rents, and after twenty years the accounts were being kept in the same place.

Court rolls from the time of John Gostwyk, in the late 1530s, describe the fixed fines differently, as head silver and land silver: '5s. 6d. They say on their oath that they gave land silver to the lord on this day with two pence remaining in the lord's hands for the lands in the lord's hands … And they give two shillings to the lord on this day for head silver.'[94] In 1540, 5s. 8d. was given to the lord for land silver and 16d. for head silver, 'apart from the people residing in the fine house or lord's mansion.'[95] By the end of the sixteenth century many more tenants paid head silver and land silver, and the rolls finally give more details of how the amounts were calculated.[96]

Although the term land silver does not appear in the court records for Blunham Greys, the term head silver was sometimes used 1413–57, many years before it was used at Willington. At Blunham Greys common fines of 10s. were paid in the autumn, and 6s. 8d. in the spring.[97] They were paid less frequently at Girtford where fines of 12d. were paid in the autumn. Although the common fines were usually described as such it appears that the de Greys employed different clerks who sometimes described these common fines in different ways, the expression 'common fines for head silver' appears 1432–51 in views of frankpledge in the autumn and spring.

The views of frankpledge or the views with court show that men aged over twelve were expected to enrol into tithings. At Willington, fees of 2d. were paid by fathers or employers to enrol their sons or employees. Men were admitted to tithings at intervals until 1522[98] although no fees for admittance were paid after 1422.[99] Even before that date fees for admittance were not paid for some men.[100] It seems that young men from established Willington families were admitted free of charge.[101]

Tenants of Blunham Greys and Girtford were enrolled into tithings on several occasions 1414–55, and no fees were charged. In October 1443 the roll records that: 'Thomas Wryghte (2d.), John Broun (2d.) and Thomas, servant of John Breton remain outside a tithing and refuse to come, therefore they are amerced.'[102] Other men refused to join in October 1433, April and September 1435, and October 1448. They were fined 2d. each.[103] There are no records of refusals to join a tithing at any

93 Arundel Castle Archives, A1328.
94 BARS, Box R212, Roll 65, October 1537.
95 BARS, Box R212, Roll 68, November 1540.
96 BARS, Box R212, Roll 73, April 1594; Roll 74, October 1599.
97 BARS, L26/51-54.
98 BARS, Box R212, Roll 64, December 1522.
99 The last court in which fees for entering tithings were paid was BARS, Box R212, Roll 31, October 1422.
100 Men entering tithings are mentioned in the following rolls: BARS, Box R212, Roll 3, October 1395; Roll 6, October 1403; Roll 12, October 1410; Roll 14, October 1411; Roll 15, October 1413; Roll 17, October 1414; Roll 21, October 1416; Roll 25, October 1418; Roll 27,October 1419; Roll 29, October 1420.
101 BARS, Box R212, Roll 6, October 1403; Roll 14, October 1411; Roll 17, October 1414; Roll 27, October 1419; Roll 29, October 1420.
102 BARS, L26/54, Court 4, m 2, October 1443.
103 BARS, L26/53, m 14 dorse, October 1433; L26/53, m 16 (iii), April 1435; L26/53, m 17, September 1435; L26/54, Court 17, m 9, October 1448.

time in Willington, suggesting a more co-operative attitude among the tenants there. There is no mention of tithings, or tithing men, in the Eggington rolls as this was beyond the court's jurisdiction.

Standard fines, usually amercements of 2d., were charged in both Willington and Blunham Greys for a variety of offences.[104] A 2d. fine was often levied in Willington for an unauthorised brewing, a minor breach of public order, or for buildings needing repair and ditches needing scouring. At the end of the fourteenth century fines of 6d. were charged for breaking the peace, and thefts of a sickle and hares from the warren. Tenants were warned of larger penalties for more serious offences; in 1395 William Tele was threatened with a penalty of half a mark (6s. 8d.) to make sure that he repaired the highway to the mill, which he had ploughed up.[105] In Blunham Greys bakers, brewers, butchers, fishmongers and chandlers were fined 2d. or more for offences related to the sale of goods, which may in practice have been a tax on sales. Leaving a dung heap, or a pile of timber, on the king's highway also attracted a standard fine there. In October 1415, six women and a man who washed linen in the lord's close were amerced 1d. each.[106]

The courts at Willington and Blunham Greys recorded the rights and obligations which generated income for the lord; the activities of the tradesmen and women on the manors, brewers, bakers, millers and butchers, all feature in the records. Brewers and bakers were monitored by the courts to ensure that they paid the assize of bread and ale, which was essentially a form of licensing. In Willington, twenty-three brewers paid fines for their brewings in 1394, but the number of brewers gradually reduced until there were only two of them in the early sixteenth century and only one brewer by the time John Gostwyk bought the manor in 1529. No baker was mentioned in the Willington court rolls until the early sixteenth century and then only occasionally.

At Blunham Greys the number of brewers varied and was sometimes as low as six, but every few years the numbers peaked at nineteen or twenty. The numbers of individual brewers and brewings recorded each half year varied significantly. In May 1436 there were twenty-four brewers and seventy-nine brewings; in September that year there were fifteen brewers and fifty-eight brewings. In April 1441 there were twenty-four brewers and ninety-three brewings; in October that year there were twelve brewers and seventy-three brewings. There was more mention of sales of ale than at Willington and of petty crime connected with it. The word 'ganoker' for ale-seller is sometimes used.

Bakers in Blunham Greys are mentioned in almost all views of frankpledge. Although in 1413 the only baker was Matilda Finch, who paid no fine for baking bread, there were usually two bakers each paying 2d. or 3d. twice a year. In the years 1422–24 and 1427 much higher fines were paid, but the reasons for this are not given. For two years at the end of the Blunham Greys series of manor court rolls, October 1455-May 1457 there were three bakers, Thomas Taylor, who had

---

[104] To be amerced is to be 'at mercy' or obliged to the lord. The rolls indicate that a payment to the lord was paid, though occasionally no fee is charged for the first offence, or for an offence which is considered of minor importance, or for which there were extenuating circumstances.

[105] BARS, Box R212, Roll 3, October 1395.

[106] BARS, L26/51, m 6, October 1415; m 6 dorse, October 1415.

first baked in April 1441, John Verne who had baked from October 1443 and Walter Boteler, who was new.

The millers of Willington and Blunham Greys were regularly fined for taking too much toll. The millers in Willington were accused of charging unjust toll, or using a measure without a seal, fifteen times 1394–1455 and paid various fines for this of 2d., 3d. or 4d. In October 1458 the court noted: 'that Simon [12d] Usshere took excessive toll against the terms of the statute, that he took toll twice, where he should only have taken it once. Therefore he is amerced.'[107] And he was ordered to stop doing it, under a penalty of 6d. 8d. This did not seem to discourage him as he was amerced yet again in 1461.[108] The pattern of evidence of increased fines suggests that while the miller's misdeeds had been tolerated by the Willington stewards during the earlier part of the fifteenth century, as they provided a small annual income for the lord, in the middle of the century the taking of too much toll became less acceptable. Simon Ussher was fined 12d. on two occasions for collecting too much toll in 1458,[109] and on one occasion in 1461.[110] When John Wodehyll was miller, he was fined 4d. in May 1472, the only recorded occasion when this fine was paid in the spring. [111] A fine of 2d. appears for a final time in December 1522, in the last roll surviving before the manor was bought by John and Joan Gostwick in 1529.

At Blunham Greys the miller was fined regularly for overcharging or taking too much toll 1415–51 and, as at Willington, fines of 2d., 3d. or 4d. were paid. There was also a mill at Girtford, although the courts seldom record the fines paid there. A mill-way was referred to three times in the Eggington court rolls, being referred to as 'le Mullewey' in June 1377, 'Westmylleweye' in December 1428 and 'Millwaie' (written as 'le Mylwaye' in a draft document) in April 1572, but there is no reference to the mill itself, nor of any petty crime associated with it.[112]

Butchers also feature in the rolls of Willington and Blunham Greys, although the Willington references are relatively scarce. In 1410 John Prentys was involved in a dispute;[113] in 1426 William Starlyng of Welyngton, described as a butcher of Bedford, stole malt worth 18d. from the watermill, 'of the lord next to Willington' and was fined;[114] and in 1461 Henry Maye was fined 2d. for selling meat without heads.[115] In contrast, the references to butchers in Blunham Greys are numerous; the first mention of a butcher being in 1417 when John Bocher of Blunham was recorded selling rotten fish.[116] In 1420 he was accused of selling rotten meat.[117] The next year John and Walter Bocher feature in the court roll for selling, 'stinking and alluring meat'.[118] The records show that butchers in Blunham Greys continued to

[107] BARS, Box R212, Roll 47, October 1458.
[108] BARS, Box R212, Roll 49a, October 1461.
[109] BARS, Box R212, Roll 47, October 1458.
[110] BARS, Box R212, Roll 49a, October 1461.
[111] BARS, Box R212, Roll 54b, May 1472.
[112] *Eggington Court Rolls*, BARS, X301/1/6 recto, 10 recto, 16 recto; and Thompson and Ward, 'Eggington Court Roll', p. 212 and p. 225 respectively.
[113] BARS, Box R212, Roll. 12, October 1410.
[114] BARS, Box R212, Roll 36, September 1426.
[115] BARS, Box R212, Roll 49a, October 1461.
[116] BARS, L26/51, m 8 dorse, May 1417.
[117] BARS, L26/52, m 4, October 1420.
[118] BARS, L26/52, m 5, October 1421.

sell rotten meat or to overcharge their customers and were fined about thirty-five times, until May 1457.[119] It was usual for two or three butchers to be named in each view of frankpledge and occasionally for one of them to be from outside the manor.[120] They were fined 2d. each, except in September 1435 when the three butchers were each fined 3d.

At the end of the fourteenth century the customary holdings on Willington manor were let on the understanding that the tenants would keep them in good repair. The first surviving roll records that: 'Thomas Taillour, Edward Tailour [*sic*], John Berde and John Wattes hold from the lord in bondage and have ruined and defective houses. They are given days until the next [court] to repair and mend these under penalty of forfeiture.'[121] Penalties paid by the customary tenants in Willington when they did not keep their buildings in good repair were a regular source of income for the lord 1394–1522, but free tenants of free holdings were not liable. In April 1409 the entry recording a transfer of land on the manor reads:

> And to this Court came Cristiana Verne and surrendered one Messuage and half a virgate of land into the hands of the lady for the use of John Lygtfot. To be held by the same John by Court roll according to the custom of the Manor for the term of his life, rendering therefrom to the lady 13s. 4d. a year, and all the customs and services owed therefrom. And the aforesaid John will well and sufficiently provide the said Cristiana with mixed grain and money in proportion to a tenth of his estate during all her life.[122] And the said John ~~maintains~~ will maintain the said holding at his own expense except for large timber, through the pledges of Robert Myton and Thomas Heryng. And he gave 12d. as premium and made fealty.[123]

Not only is this entry a rare example of a new tenant providing a pension for someone, but it records that he is not required to provide 'large timber' for his building repairs. In Blunham Greys tenants were ordered to repair ruined tenements and buildings promptly or pay a penalty of 10s. or 100s.[124] There are no such details in the Eggington rolls.

Lords of the manor expected the natural assets within their manors to provide revenue. The Mowbray lords of Willington, for example, were determined to protect the value of their trees and the proceeds from their woodlands. Sales of timber to men from outside the manor were an important source of income for them, and after the middle of the fifteenth century the rolls record an increase in these sales. It was usual, at least in Bedfordshire, for the lord of the manor to provide timber for repairs and for the tenants to provide the labour.[125] The distribution of free timber to the tenants for repairs was carefully controlled and the lord and his officials dealt

[119] BARS, L26/54, Court 43, m 17, May 1457.
[120] *Ibid.*
[121] BARS, Box R212, Roll 1, April 1394.
[122] Her surrender of her holding to his use, and his agreement to pay her a pension, suggests that she may have been his mother-in-law, or his mother who had remarried and been widowed a second time.
[123] BARS, Box R212, Roll 11, April 1409.
[124] BARS, L26/53, m 4 dorse, October 1426, penalties of 6s. 8d. were threatened; L26/54, Court 13, m 6, October 1447, penalties of 20s. were threatened; L26/54, Court 15, m 5, March 1448, penalties of 20s. were threatened.
[125] Godber, *History of Bedfordshire,* p. 123.

with requests for building materials on an individual basis. No records of free timber being distributed to tenants are found in the Willington court rolls which survive after May 1482. The Blunham Greys and Eggington documents show even stricter control; there are no records that timber was distributed for repairs to buildings although tenants were ordered to repair them or build new houses.

The playing of illegal games attracted regular fines. In Willington it was ordered in 1397 that: 'no-one shall play the game called Quoyte in the future under a penalty of 12d.'[126] And in October 1467 it was ordered that:

> Henceforth none shall play at tennis at anytime of the year if they are 12 years of age or more and not as such unless at the feast of the nativity of the lord[127] and not for money within the vill, unless they have sufficient, under a penalty for each of 40d. and a punishment of imprisonment for one day and a night.[128]

Six years later, in 1473, the order was being disobeyed and the: 'tithing men and Constables presented well and faithfully and furthermore they said that Robert [4d] Wareyn, Thomas [4d] Mores, servants of Nicholas [4d] Cruce played tennis against the statute. Therefore they are amerced.'[129]

In Blunham Greys playing tennis was forbidden in entries 1431–36. In October 1431, not only were nine tenants fined for playing tennis, but another two were fined for playing dice.[130] A further six were fined for playing tennis in October 1433,[131] and five were fined in May 1434 for playing tennis and, 'other unlawful games'.[132] Five more were fined for tennis in September 1435:

> Amercements 10s., penalties ordered. And that Robert Bocher (3s. 4d.) John de Ware (20d.) Thomas Swetyng (20d.) Henry Baker (20d.) Thomas Taylour (20d.) are common players at tennis, to the annoyance of the whole community and contrary to the statute and therefore they are amerced. And it is ordered that they give it up, under penalty of 3s. 4d.[133]

The last mention of tenants playing tennis was in September 1436, when six people paid fines, but the playing of dice and other unlawful games continued.[134] In April 1451 Nicholas Tayllour and John Wodec assaulted each other and were said to be: 'common players of dice and chequers and other unlawful games.'[135] In October 1455 three others were fined for being: 'unlawful players of dice and chequers and other unlawful games.'[136]

At Willington several pleas of debt were dealt with in 1396, 1408 and 1410; but in other years there were very few or no pleas. Occasional cases were settled out of court or referred to the court at Bedford. The last mention of debt recorded was in 1463

---

[126] BARS, Box R212, Roll 5, October 1397.
[127] 'xij' is written superscript in the document which may indicate that 'the feast of Christmas' includes the twelve days following.
[128] British Library, Add Ch.26813/3, October 1467 and BARS, CRT 130 Willington 4, p. 6.
[129] BARS, Box R212, Roll 54c, October 1473.
[130] BARS, L26/53, m 11, October 1431.
[131] BARS, L26/53, m 14 dorse, October 1433.
[132] BARS, L26/53, m 15, May 1434.
[133] BARS, L26/53, m 17, September 1435,
[134] BARS, L26/53, m 17 dorse, September 1436.
[135] BARS, L26/54, Court 32, m 12, April 1451.
[136] BARS, L26/54, Court 35, m 15, October 1455.

when: 'It was ordained in Court, by the agreement of all the tenants, that no tenant henceforth shall prosecute another tenant, outside the demesne for debts, nor for trespass, unless they should exceed 40s., under penalty of 20s. forfeited to the lady.'[137]

Pleas of debt were very common in the courts of Blunham Greys and Girtford. It was usual for there to be several each year, but in some years the numbers were much higher.[138] In 1449 the records from seven courts survive and reveal that there were 130 pleas of debt that year. The reasons for the debt culture at Blunham Greys and Girtford are unclear, but it is in contrast to the situation at Willington and Eggington.

When fines were not paid, distraints or attachments could be employed. These involved the temporary seizure of land, property or goods and chattels, and were used to force a tenant to pay a fine or a penalty. They were rarely used in Willington but were much more common in Blunham Greys where distraints were taken for not doing customary labour services or boonworks, for staying on a holding when it should have been passed on to someone else, or as a surety for a debt or for building repairs. Attachments, often horses or carts, were taken for larger value items. At Eggington distraints were used regularly as the lord or his officials did their best to collect debts which arose because of illegal land transfers by the tenants or from heriots due following their deaths. There were six distraints for not paying fealty to the lord in February 1433 and seven distraints in July 1435 for the same reason. In 1500 the roll states that various tenants were distrained for non-payment of rents but neither the numbers nor the names are given; a further ten tenants were distrained in November 1506.[139] Fewer appear in later rolls and no debts for any other reason appear in the Eggington rolls 1413–1514.[140]

By-laws and life on the manor
No written record of the customs of the manor of Willington exists, but some of the orders agreed in the courts appear to act as a means of recording and reinforcing manorial custom. The Blunham Greys rolls contain some evidence of customs on the manor including the keeping of dogs. No details of manorial custom were found in the Eggington rolls.

By-laws controlling the use of land in Willington were made on ten occasions 1411–70, but the greatest number were made in September 1415 in relation to making drains in the fields, keeping sheep and calves in enclosures, payments for keeping pigs on the manor and specifying in which fields bullocks should be tied up.[141] Tenants who had encroached on other neighbours' lands were fined and ordered to return them. By-laws were agreed at regular intervals in the court records but became more frequent in the 1460s while Thomas Rokes was steward.

At Blunham Greys orders were agreed about the management of the pasturing of animals and geese and the use of the sown fields after the harvest, but there were

137 British Library, Add Ch.26813/1, and BARS, CRT 130 Willington 4, p. 2. This was intended to ensure that pleas for petty crime and small debts went through this court, and that the lady got the income from them.
138 In 1416 (38); in 1432 (70); in 1448 (59).
139 Thompson and Ward, 'Eggington Court Rolls', pp. 213–220.
140 BARS, X301/1/8-14a and Thompson and Ward, 'Eggington Court Roll', pp. 207–21.
141 BARS, Box R212, Roll 18a, Michaelmas 1415.

continual infringements relating to the land. In July 1414 the account of the hayward revealed that seventeen men and one woman were fined for trespassing in the lord's meadows and fields;[142] and in 1432 it was said that eleven people trespassed in the fields sown with corn, barley and peas.[143] Problems with the control of dogs were first reported in 1423 when: 'John Bocher (2d.) has a dog of red colour which has killed sheep, therefore he is amerced. And he is ordered to put the said dog outside the township, under a penalty of 6s. 8d.'[144] The same problems occurred again in 1455 when: 'John George and Robert Devyas have dogs unleashed, therefore they are ordered to tie them up or to take them out of the village before the feast of All Saints [1 November] under a penalty of 6s. 8d.'[145] In 1443 it was reported that twelve headlands were too large, a boundary marker had been ploughed up and an unlawful road had been made to the mill.[146]

The precise status of tenants in Willington in terms of villeinage and free tenancy is seldom mentioned, but differences in status are evident. At Blunham Greys bondsmen are occasionally mentioned throughout the rolls and a long list of tenants was made in 1498 in which free and villein tenants were listed separately.[147] No tenants are described as bondsmen in the Eggington rolls. Some villein tenants from Willington moved away from the manor or found work elsewhere even though this was forbidden; there is no evidence to suggest that these men returned. Similar restrictions were not apparent in Blunham Greys or Eggington.

There is some evidence for the occupations of the free tenants; there were brewers, bakers, butchers and millers at both Willington and Blunham Greys, and it can be assumed tenants worked as builders and carters. In Willington a tailor and a weaver are mentioned on rare occasions, and there is a suggestion of a basket weaver too. In Blunham Greys, between two and five fishmongers are listed as overcharging or selling rotten fish in thirty-four rolls 1417–57. Fish must have been an important part of the tenants' diets as on several occasions men were also fined for fishing in the waters controlled by the lord. Chandlers also appear in the Blunham Greys rolls: 'William Morris (2d,) and William Bedford (2d.) are chandlers and have sold candles for too much contrary to statute, therefore they are amerced.'[148]

Pledging took place when an established tenant guaranteed the behaviour of someone else or agreed to provide financial support, but the practice seems to have disappeared from most manor courts by the early fifteenth century.[149] The bailiff and other established men of Willington pledged regularly for the good behaviour of others until about 1460. The term was used again in 1470 and in 1522. In the Blunham Greys records, pledges were provided by the constable or other established tenants almost every year 1413–20, then less frequently; the last recorded occasion being in 1455. A major source of income for Joan Child of Eggington was the payment of a fine of 40s. paid in December 1413 by two tenants for wardship

---

142 BARS, L26/51, m 3, July 1414; m 3 dorse, July 1414.
143 BARS, L26/53, m 13, September 1432.
144 BARS, L26/54, Court 1, m 1, April 1443.
145 BARS, L26/54, Court 35, m 15, October 1455.
146 BARS, L26/54, Court 1, m 1, April 1443.
147 BARS, L26/212; L26/154.
148 BARS, L26/53, m 22 dorse, April 1441.
149 Harvey, *Manorial Records*, p. 49.

of a boy who was heir to a messuage and other property but was still a minor.[150] Two pledges were made in connection with this. No similar sources of income in connection with wardships have been found in the Willington or Blunham Greys court records.

The courts at Willington and Blunham Greys had the right to try minor breaches of the peace involving wounding, instances of anti-social behaviour and petty crime. The most violent incidents in Willington were recorded in the view of frank-pledge of October 1394, and later there were occasional reports of assaults using fists or sticks; in the second half of the fifteenth century metal objects were used. A greater variety of violent acts were recorded at Blunham Greys. There were disturbances 1416–19 said to cause 'great alarm' to the residents. Then, in 1444, there were problems with 'night-wanderers'. In 1448 there was an ambush and assault as well as twenty other assaults, followed by sixteen assaults in 1449. On 4 November 1449 Richard Bocher and William Naseby were ordered not to assault each other: 'Also it is ordered, by the whole court, between Richard Bocher and William Naseby, that if either of them offend against the other, either by assault or insult, he will lose 13s. 4d., one half of the money to the lord and the other half to the church of Blounham.'[151] William Naseby caused further problems in April 1450 when he was found guilty of assaulting Richard Bocher and his wife, being fined 4d. for each. [152] In May 1450 William was fined 2d. because he was in debt to the chaplain, and he paid 13s. 4d. to the court for breaking the above order not to assault Richard Bocher.[153]

In the 1460s some Willington tenants blocked tracks and attempted to enclose common tracks, roads leading to their properties and a common field to exclude others. In Blunham Greys people were excluded from parts of the manor by tenants frequently leaving piles of dung or timber on the 'Kings highway' or by building a wall across it.[154]

The operation of the manors

Despite the fragmentary nature of the records it can be seen that there were differences in the management and operation of the three manors. These differences almost certainly owed most to the different administrative and judicial systems of the times and the ways in which communal customary law developed, regulated and governed the lives of the tenants. Their lives may also have been influenced by the geography, topography and communication networks within which they were each situated. In Willington, in particular, different management styles of the lords of the manor, and the influence of certain stewards, bailiffs and groups of tenants, can be seen.

The management of Blunham Greys seems to have resulted in an onerous regime and problems of a commercial nature as evidenced by the large numbers of debts,

[150] Thompson and Ward, 'Eggington Court Rolls', p. 209.
[151] BARS, L26/54, Court 25, m 11 dorse, November 1449.
[152] BARS, L26/54, Court 27, m 10, April 1450.
[153] BARS, L26/54, Court 28, m 10, May 1450.
[154] BARS, L26/54, Court 43, m 17, May 1457.

distraints, attachments and violence. The lack of detail in the Eggington court rolls prevents any firm conclusions being reached about circumstances there.

The tenants in Willington probably benefited from the well-organised administration of the Mowbray estates. The regular involvement of many men in the manor court process seems to have resulted in an effective form of local and communal governance of life across a single-manor parish with complete and effective control of its own open fields. Furthermore, links with the outside world were the result of regular visits by the Mowbray's stewards and officials, and the bailiff travelled outside the manor to meet them and their receivers. The Mowbray accounts for Willington show reducing income to the lord from rents and the perquisites of court, with growing arrears for the Mowbray family, but the history of the Gostwicks of Willington shows that at least some yeoman farmers did rather well there in the fifteenth and early sixteenth centuries.[155]

---

[155] H. P. R Finberg, 'The Gostwicks of Willington', in BHRS, vol.36, *The Gostwicks of Willington and Other Studies* (Streatley, 1956), pp. 48–138.

Chapter Four

Life on the Manor

The bailiffs' accounts and manor court rolls for Willington, though not a complete record, provide information about the administration of this single manor parish by an important medieval family, the Mowbrays, and about aspects of the lives of those that lived there. It is possible to draw some inferences on topics such as population, mobility, co-operation, crime, work and standards of living. Many of the issues that arise through examination of these topics echo those of communities today including violence, anti-social behaviour, theft, fraud and debt.

Other areas are more difficult; while there were differences in the wealth and status of tenants on the manor, gradations in social status are harder to identify. Free men did not usually serve on the court juries or as tithing men, but both they and villein tenants were elected to manorial offices – as bailiff, constable, ale-taster and assessor of fines. The lives of women also present problems. The most powerful woman was Katherine Neville, but many other women will have participated actively in the life of the manor. However, in the manor court rolls, their names are exceeded by the names of men in the proportion of ten to one and there is little detail about their domestic existence. Evidence of their influence is largely represented by their calling the hue, their work as brewers and the management of their own holdings on widowhood.

After the death of Katherine Neville's fourth husband the rolls are less detailed than previously, although there are still records of land transfers, buildings needing repair, petty crime and disturbances of the peace. By the time of her death in 1482/83, the rolls contain very little information about the lives of the tenants.

Population and mobility
It is thought that up to one third of the population of England may have died of the Black Death, 1348–69, and this may also be true of Bedfordshire.[1] Another tangible effect of the plague was that land fell out of cultivation and buildings fell out of repair. Although difficult, it is possible to tentatively assess the impact of the plague on Willington. It is known that in 1366 there were complaints that the widow of the late Lord Mowbray had: 'committed waste by destroying the trees, digging up the land and allowing the buildings to fall into decay.' Part of her defence was that the tenants had died of the plague, although it is not possible to gauge whether there was an element of dissimulation in her reply.[2] In addition, there seem to have been a number of vacant holdings on the manor before the first court roll in 1394.

---

[1] Godber, *History of Bedfordshire*, p. 99.
[2] VCH, vol. 3, p. 263. A reference of De Banco, R., 425, m.144 is quoted.

The estimates of the population of Willington 1394–1522, which are summarised in the following table, are based on the numbers of names mentioned in a selection of manor court rolls, as far as possible at intervals of ten years, and increased by a multiplier of 4.5. This multiplier is based on the assumption that each name represents a household and that the average household consisted of two adults, one or two children and a servant.[3] Before 1394 the evidence for the population of Willington is fragmentary; there is no reliable evidence of the population between the Black Death in 1348 and the first surviving view of frankpledge in October 1394.

Much earlier, in 1302, lists of tenants were recorded in the lay subsidy data. In that year thirty-nine tenants are named in the original Willington tax list, but an increment was prepared which gives a different picture of the population and the tax liabilities of many tenants. The increment seems to contain an additional eight names, but this figure may be inaccurate because of irregular spellings.[4] Using the same multiplier of 4.5 and an estimated forty-seven names, the two lists suggest a population of just over 200.[5]

The view of frankpledge of October 1394 contains fifty-nine names, which includes eighteen men and women involved in calling the hue and twenty-three brewers, suggesting a population of 265 at that time.[6] The view of frankpledge of the following year, October 1395, is unusually long and detailed and contains seventy names. It contains details of three assaults; of seven young men joining tithings with the names of their fathers or employers; the names of twelve tenants involved in calling the hue by committing offences or giving evidence against others; and the names of five women.[7] This untypical court roll, which would provide a population estimate of 315, shows how difficult it is to calculate an accurate population count for the manor, especially as the roll of May 1396 only contains twenty-seven names.[8] Greater detail in the rolls, such as that of 1395, may be attributed to greater diligence by the steward or his clerk or following a change of bailiff.[9] Despite these uncertainties, it seems that the population of Willington in the late fourteenth century and throughout most of the fifteenth century varied between 160 and 230 persons. The evidence suggests that there was not the disastrous reduction in population in Willington which was experienced elsewhere due to the Black Death or that Willington's population recovered well afterwards.

---

3   This method was used by Professor Raftis and his students when working on the court records of Ramsey Abbey near Huntingdon. They indexed all court appearances of named individuals to reconstruct family relationships in L. R. Poos and R. M. Smith, 'Legal Windows into Historical Populations' in Z. Razi and R. Smith, eds. *Medieval Society and the Manor Court* (Oxford, 1996), p. 300.

4   Positions of names in the two lists suggest that Johanne Dauid was Johanne Dauy in the increment and that Wilmo le Carter and Rogero le Ryder may have been Willo Gotobedde and Roger Dauy.

5   In the increment seventeen tenants had their liability for tax removed. Eight men had their liability for tax more than doubled: Roger Gostwick, Roger Ryder, Geoffrey Ryder, Henry Ryder, Laurence the cleric, Roger David, David Avenant and Robert Bole; presumably they were the men who produced the original list.

6   BARS, Box R212, Roll 2, October 1394.

7   BARS, Box R212, Roll 3, October 1395.

8   BARS, Box R212, Roll 4, May 1396.

9   BARS, R8/62/2/9-10, and Thompson, *Bailiffs' Accounts for Willington*, BARS, CRT 130 Willington 11, p. 32, p. 38. William Pecke was bailiff at the end of the accounting period 1392–93, but accounts for the period 1393–94 are missing.

Most of the population estimates below have been calculated from the names occurring in the view of frankpledge with court records held in the autumn, as these are more detailed than the courts held in the spring.[10] The exception is the court record for 1440, which is the only record extant for the period 1426–48.[11]

Estimates of the population of Willington (at approximate intervals of ten years)

Year	Document	No. of names	Population estimate	Notes
1394	View of frankpledge with court, Roll 2, October 1394	59	265	This detailed roll contains a long list of tenants involved in calling the hue and cry, committing petty crime and anti-social behaviour, and brewing.
1404	View of frankpledge with court, Roll 7, October 1404	41	More than 185	More tenants attended this court than were named because it was the first court at which a second jury was called, but their names were not given.
1414	View of frankpledge with court, Roll 17, October 1414	27	122	This was the first roll in which the new lord of the manor, John Mowbray, was named in the title. The steward, John Boteler, had worked for the former lady of the manor, Queen Joan, second wife of Henry IV. The lack of detail may be due to lack of motivation on his part; he was later demoted to under-steward. Thomas Bekyngham replaced him in 1417 as head steward.
1425	View of frankpledge with court, Roll 35, October 1425	47	212	The new steward, Roger Hunte of Roxton, produced a very detailed court record which suggests a rise in population, but may be due to his careful record-keeping. Names of the second jury were still not given.
1440	Court, Roll 37 with additions, April 1440	35	158	There is less detail in this court record as it is not a view of frankpledge, but it is important because of the additions which follow it and because no other court records exist from this period. Although forty-two names are listed, seven of these were probably workers from outside the manor.
1450	View of frankpledge with court, Roll 39a, October 1450	45	202	Names of the second jury of the court are included in the record. Three men from Blunham are named and eight holdings are listed as being without tenants, so the estimate may give an inflated figure.

[10] For the years 1382–1426 and 1440–83; the rolls are too few in number after 1483 for the evidence to be considered reliable.
[11] BARS, Box R212, Roll 37, April 1440.

1461	View of frankpledge with court, Roll 49a, October 1461	43	194	John Beaumont, the lady of the manor's third husband, died, but a capable new steward, Thomas Rokes, who visited Willington in 1457, held the court. The second jury was named.
1471	View of frankpledge with court, Roll 54a, October 1471	34	153	This roll is short and only ten men are named in the main jury. The names of the second jury of the court were included in the record. The reasons for an apparent drop in population are not known, but ten of the following eleven court rolls are short or very short, suggesting that Willington was being neglected by the aging Katherine Neville and her officials.
1481	View of frankpledge with court, Roll 60a, October 1481	44	198	This roll is of moderate length. No steward is named, but it is possible that the Howard family was anticipating Katherine Neville's death and preparing to take over the manor. Names of the main jury and the second jury were included in the record.
1522	View of frankpledge with court, Roll 64, December 1522	29	130	Thomas, Duke of Norfolk held the manor at this time. The court roll is short; no second jury is mentioned or named.

In 1407, while the manor was held by Queen Joan, a tenant withdrew,[12] and in 1408 seven deaths were reported and eight holdings became vacant.[13] Two further deaths were reported in October 1410 and April 1411, and the population seems to have fallen to its lowest point in 1414 before gradually rising and levelling off in the sixteenth century.

It is possible that poor wheat and barley harvests, reported in 1400–1 and 1409–10, may have contributed to a reduction in the population of Willington in the early fifteenth century.[14] But it is also possible that the reduced number of names in 1414 was due to changes in record keeping by John Mowbray's steward and clerk. However, it has been considered that tell-tale signs of a low or falling population are vacant holdings, arable reverting to rough pasture, low or falling rents and entry fines, the accumulation of rent arrears and so on, and it is possible that these signs can be seen in Willington.[15] There had been vacant holdings on the manor before the first court roll in 1394 and eight holdings were surrendered in the next ten years.[16] Problems in finding tenants increased October 1407–April 1409 when

[12]   BARS, Box R212, Roll 9, October 1407.
[13]   BARS, Box R212, Roll 10, October 1408.
[14]   C. Dyer, *Standards of Living in the Later Middle Ages: Social Change in England c1200 – 1500* (Cambridge, 1989), pp.262–3.
[15]   John Hatcher, *Plague, Population and the English Economy 1348 – 1530*, Studies in Economic and Social History (London, 1977), p. 33.
[16]   BARS, Box R212, Roll 2, October 1394 – Roll 7, October 1404 inclusive.

Thomas Starlyng abandoned his two holdings. One or two other surrenders were listed at each court.[17]

The last roll to have survived from the period when Queen Joan held the manor suggests that in 1412 her steward was preparing to hand Willington back to the rightful heir, John Mowbray. John Carter, William Webbe, and perhaps William Herynge, were deprived of their holdings because they had not maintained them sufficiently well, and four other tenants surrendered theirs.[18] The roll does not explain why the four tenants surrendered their holdings, but two of them were increasing their lands. John Treket surrendered one messuage and half a virgate of land on which he paid 2s. a year rent and was granted a larger holding: 'one toft and 8 acres of land called Milond, and one Messuage with one headland of land, of half an acre of land' for which he agreed: 'to pay 10s. a year for the said Messuage and for the headland 2s.' John Rodland was granted John Treket's former holding and the holding surrendered by Agnes Shaxton, so that he had two holdings. Records of the following two courts, which would have been held in October 1412 and spring 1413, have not survived, but in the first surviving court roll after John Mowbray regained his inheritance only one tenant surrendered his holding.[19]

Vacant holdings, falling rents and entry fines continue to be evidenced in Willington, especially during the later fifteenth century; entry fines gradually disappeared and some tenants continued to hold more than one holding, but conversely a gradual increase in population apparently took place after 1414. A new steward, Thomas Bekyngham, was first mentioned in May 1416 and was named as head steward in May 1417. He continued in post until Autumn 1423/24 and, at first, tenants were soon found for vacant holdings, but from 1420 it became more difficult. In that year another tenant, Thomas Tele, who had held two messuages and two half virgates left the manor, adding to the number of vacant holdings.[20] Lists of holdings without tenants began to appear in the court rolls from April 1421, and a meeting took place in June that year: 'Thomas Bekingham [sic] and others being there for one day and one night, that is to say on 17th day of June, to agree with the lord's tenants the rents of the demesne land there.'[21]

Estimates then suggest a gradual increase of population in the second half of the fifteenth century, reaching 198 in 1481. The apparent reduction in population during the early sixteenth century may have been due to changes in management and record keeping. The surviving Willington manor court rolls of 1515, 1520 and 1522 continue to include many of the items found in the rolls of the late fourteenth century, especially in 1522, but in 1515 and 1520 the details are few.[22] However, it is also clear that enclosure, engrossment and depopulation of rural settlements at the end of the fifteenth and the beginning of the sixteenth centuries were concerns

17   BARS, Box R212, Roll 9, October 1407 – Roll 11, April 1409 inclusive.
18   BARS, Box R212, Roll 14b, May 1412.
19   BARS, Box R212, Roll 15, October 1413.
20   BARS, Box R212, Roll 28, May 1420.
21   BARS, Box R212, Roll 30, April 1421; Roll 32, June 1423; Roll 3, October 1423.
22   BARS, Box R212, Roll 61, September 1515; Roll 62, March 1520; Roll 63, March 1522; Roll 64, December 1522.

elsewhere. A statute of depopulation was declared in 1489 and a commission was set up by Cardinal Wolsey in 1517 to investigate the problems.[23]

A general depopulation of agricultural areas during the years 1495–1520 may have been due to an increase in enclosures and sheep farming for which fewer workers were required. It has been argued that: 'for many farmers, sheep were the one bright spot in an unpromising rural economy and that this induced many landlords to convert more land to pasture.'[24] In Bedfordshire, sheep farming was prominent in the south of the county in the late fifteenth and early sixteenth centuries, but the Willington rolls show that sheep had been part of a pattern of mixed farming since the late fourteenth century or earlier.[25] Sheep cotes, pens, shelters and folds appear occasionally on lists of buildings needing repair and in orders about the management of the commons and life on the manor. The values of individual animals are sometimes given. In 1395 a sheep was valued at 5s.;[26] in 1412 and 1415 sheep were required as heriots, and were each valued at 2s.;[27] in 1425 a sheep was stolen from a tenant but only valued at 10d.[28]

References to sheep in the court rolls do not increase in number as the fifteenth century progresses suggesting that there was no dramatic increase in the size of flocks held by tenants until the sixteenth century. In about 1540 John Gostwyk advised his son to keep: 'three or four hundred ewes in Willington fields' of which sixty were for the use of his household.[29]

Although several generations of some families lived on the manor for long periods the court rolls for Willington show regular evidence of short-term mobility. In 1394 and 1395 eight and nine men respectively made single appearances in the court rolls, far more than in any later years.[30] These two rolls are long and detailed and describe difficult years on the manor when some holdings were without a tenant. The appearance of the new names suggests that the bailiff may have obtained agricultural labourers from elsewhere to work for him and to care for vacant holdings.

About one hundred new names appear in the court rolls 1404–25. They include members of the local gentry, some paid employees of the lord or lady, workmen or tradesmen and some people who lived outside the manor. About eighty-five of these names are first found in the views of frankpledge, held in the autumn. The names include some of the lord's employees or members of his council and some people who went on to settle on the manor, but about forty people appear to have only stayed on the manor for one or two years. They included: John Clement, John Derby, Henry Maydewell and Thomas Naseby who joined tithings; men from Blunham who trespassed in Willington woods; and John Longhar and Thomas Pridde who were found guilty of theft. There was also a small group of unsuccessful entrepreneurs, Elene Aylebryht, a brewer; John Sangyle, a smith; Adam Spredelyngton, who rented the

---

23   Joan Thirsk, *Tudor Enclosure*, Historical Association 41 (London, 1958); Peter Gwynn, *The King's Cardinal: The Rise and Fall of Cardinal Wolsey* (London, 1990).
24   Christopher Dyer, *A Country Merchant 1495–1420* (Oxford, 2012), pp. 9–10; pp. 23–4.
25   Godber, *History of Bedfordshire*, p. 139.
26   BARS, Box R212, Roll 3, October 1395.
27   BARS, Box R212, Roll 14b, May 1412; Roll 19, October 1415.
28   BARS, Box R212, Roll 35, October 1425.
29   A. G. Dickens, 'Estate and Household Management in Bedfordshire, c. 1540', in BHRS, vol. 36, *The Gostwicks of Willington, and Other Studies* (Streatley, 1956), p. 42.
30   BARS, Box R212, Roll 2, October 1394; Roll 3, October 1395.

dovecote for a year; and at least one unsuccessful tenant, Roger Yotte (or Gotte), who was granted a messuage and ten acres in 1406 and surrendered it the next year. It is possible that some of the other new names were employed by the more prosperous tenants on their holdings for periods of a year, or perhaps two; but there is no indication of this in the documents. In May and October 1416 four new names are recorded, perhaps connected with the need to deal with dilapidations.[31] John Mowbray's bailiff had compiled a long list of buildings needing repair, including two insethouses and four granges. Repairs to the mill were also necessary as four trees were requested for cogs.

Incomers from the gentry included Richard Marable, about whom very little is known, in 1416. He is named as the lord's bailiff in the early part of the view of frankpledge, though William Ridere is named as bailiff near the end of the document.[32] Robert de Wyllyton, the warrener, appears 1419–26 and beyond. Roger Hunte of Roxton is mentioned in the roll of October 1425.[33] He was the lord's new steward, and the meals provided to the officials after the courts for which he was responsible were documented in detail.[34]

Four new names are recorded in October 1448 and again in July and October 1458. In 1458 they may have been linked to a new steward, Thomas Rokes, who is first mentioned in the rolls in 1457. Three new names were also mentioned in May 1470, soon after Katherine Neville took over sole lordship following the execution of her fourth husband, John Woodville, and when two tenants needed to repair both the halls and barns on their holdings.[35]

Forty-seven people are recorded as having lived on the manor for between one and three years 1448–83. A few may have been farm labourers who signed up to work for more prosperous tenants; some may have been craftsmen who stayed for a short while before moving on; two were Emma and John Skynner who only appear once in the records because Emma was accused of running a bawdy house and was escorted out of the manor by the bailiff.[36] At least two men were assaulted, William Pepyn with an open dagger and William Jarmeyn (or Jerman) with an iron fork. Both seem to have decided not to stay, but many of the new tenants seem to have wanted to settle in the village; they took over holdings or participated in the life of the manor in other ways.[37]

Control and co-operation

Before the end of the fourteenth century few country people were free, being tied to the lord of the manor and required to work on his demesne lands as part of the rent of their holdings. Villein tenants continued to be considered the property of the lord, and the lord's officials ordered the return of men who left the manor. When John Rydere Tayllour, son of Thomas Tayllour, left Willington to live in Renhold

---

31   BARS, Box R212, Roll 20, May 1416; Roll 21, October 1416.
32   BARS, Box R212, Roll 21, October 1416.
33   BARS, Box R212, Roll 35, October 1425.
34   BARS, Box R212, Roll 36, September 1426; Roll 36a, April 1426.
35   British Library, Add.Ch.26813/8, May 1470.
36   BARS, Box R212, Roll 40a, October 1451.
37   British Library, Add Ch. 26813/7, October 1469; BARS, Box R212, Roll 59a, November 1478.

in 1417, the court demanded that he should be seized and returned,[38] as it did in 1419 when John Rydere the younger also withdrew.[39] The latter's father may have sympathised with his son, for he agreed, 'to sustain and render service' for his son's holding for the next five months. When a third serf, Thomas Tele, left the manor in 1420 the tenants were ordered to enquire where he was; demands for the return of these three men do not seem to have produced any results as their names do not appear in any later court rolls.

Not only were the villeins the property of the lord but also their lands, buildings and some equipment. In 1395, a villein, Henry Plassher (or Plasshe), appeared before the court several times for a variety of reasons and was fined because: 'the aforesaid Henry sold one lead vessel, under bondage, without permission and the value of the said lead vessel is put at 40d. in respect of which the bailiff is responsible.'[40] This vessel was very valuable, perhaps a brewing vat or other large storage vessel.

Villeins were also liable to pay the lord for certain rights such as fines for a daughter's marriage or the education of a son. However, in Willington only one fine for merchet is recorded. John Rydere paid 2s. for the marriage of his daughter Agnes in 1414. The fine was to be: 'two shillings and no more … as he is exceedingly poor and in need.'[41] There must have been several other marriages between villein tenants but this single example suggests that the marriage of Agnes had special significance. She may have wished to marry someone from outside the manor, or who was a freeman; or perhaps the steward wished to emphasise her family's servile status for some reason.

Life on the manor appears to have been regulated in part by 'the statute', a legal framework referring to Acts of Parliament which survived from at least 1215. These are never quoted in detail in the manor court rolls, but knowledge of them must have resided with the steward who would have had some legal training. Legal handbooks were written from the thirteenth century, some very small, so that they could be carried in the pocket of a robe.[42] However, although legal concepts may sometimes have been quoted to justify decision-making, the law, as practiced in the manor court, was very flexible and varied according to local custom and precedent.[43] At Willington, the statute is mentioned eight times 1408–22.[44] In the latter year, the miller was noted as having taken, 'excessive toll against the statute.' The statute is quoted three further times 1458–73. In 1458 the miller featured once again;[45] he reappears in 1461 for a similar offence.[46] In the same roll the butcher is

38   The use of a double surname is very rare in the rolls, occurring on only one other occasion. BARS, Box R212, Roll 22, May 1417; Roll 26, May 1419; Roll 28, May 1420.
39   BARS, Box R212, Roll 26, May 1419.
40   BARS, Box R212, Roll 3, October 1395.
41   BARS, Box R212, Roll 16, April 1414.
42   M. T. Clanchy, *From Memory to Written Record: England 1066–1307*, 3rd ed. (Oxford, 2013), plate 16.
43   Anthony Musson, *Medieval Law in Context: the Growth of Legal Consciousness from Magna Carta to the Peasant's Revolt* (Manchester, 2001), p. 10.
44   BARS, Box R212, Roll 10, October 1408; Roll 12, October 1410; Roll 17, October 1414; Roll 19, October 1415; Roll 25, October 1418; Roll 27,October 1419; Roll 29, October 1420: Roll 31, October 1422.
45   The miller was Simon Usshere. BARS, Box R212, Roll 47, October 1458.
46   BARS, Box R212, Roll 49a, October 1461.

also amerced: 'Henry [2d.] Maye is a butcher and he sold meat without heads, in his workshop, for excessive gain against the statute.' And in 1473 the statute was quoted when it was written that the: 'Tithing men and Constables presented well and faithfully and furthermore they said that Robert [4d.] Wareyn, Thomas [4d.] Mores, servants of Nicholas [4d.] Cruce played tennis against the statute. Therefore they are amerced.'[47]

Responsibility for law and order was, in part, invested in the office of constable, which had duties that included arresting felons and dealing with local disorder. Constables were usually elected by the tenants of the manor from villein families, although no details of the electoral process used are given in the records. Members of the free Warner family served 1413–15, 1458–59 and 1465–68, other free families from whom constables were elected were the Partrych family in 1416, the Myton family in 1448 and the Gostwick family in 1538.

There appears to have been a single constable 1394–1412, but his name is not given before 1405, when Adam Warde was appointed and remained constable during the years when Queen Joan was lady of the manor. In 1413, after John Mowbray successfully claimed that his lands, including Willington, should be returned to him from the Crown, two constables were appointed, and the rolls indicate that it was usual for two constables to be appointed from that date. The first two constables, John Bande and John Warner, served together for about ten years, and sometimes also served on the main jury or as ale-tasters.[48] The pattern of appointments 1426–47 is unclear as all the rolls except for that dated April 1440 have been lost, but from 1448 it appears the Mowbray management team intended to change constables every two years, although there were problems finding suitable candidates 1455–58.

Some constables avoided the performance of their duties. In October 1394 there were fights and bloodshed and the constable was amerced 2d. on six occasions. The reason for these fines is not clear, the scribe has simply written: 'The constable [2d.] because he himself has not [pledged] therefore he is amerced.'[49] The constable continued to be amerced and fined 2d. on several more occasions 1397–1408.[50] The reason for the fines becomes apparent in 1404 - it seems that the constable had been expected to collect amercements, outside the court, as they occurred:

> John Cartere the elder justly [called] the hue on the said John [3d.] by the pledge of the Constable and the Constable [2d.] has not had his amercement so he is amerced. and that Agnes [6d.] Blodlatere unjustly called the hue by a certain examination pledged by the constable and the constable [2d.] has not had her amercement, therefore he is amerced.[51]

The constable paid similar fines in October 1413 and September 1423, but none were paid after that date.[52] In April 1467 the constable was fined 2d. for a malthouse which needed repair.[53]

[47]   BARS, Box R212, Roll 54c, October 1473.
[48]   BARS, Box R212, Roll 15, October 1413.
[49]   BARS, Box R212, Roll 2, October 1394. In the following passage two men, John Flaumyll, and Robert Bonde, each paid amercements of 4d., so must have been considered the ring-leaders.
[50]   BARS, Box R212, Roll 5, October 1397; Roll 7, October 1404; Roll 10, October 1408.
[51]   BARS, Box R212, Roll 7, October 1404.
[52]   BARS, Box R212, Roll 15, October 1413; Roll 34, September 1423.
[53]   BARS, Box R212, Roll 53a, April 1467.

Residents of the manor were also responsible for maintaining law and order through use of the hue and cry, by which they could accuse neighbours of anti-social behaviour or petty crimes in the manor court. In October 1394, eight hues were called by four men and three women:

> Also that Adam Abel justly [called] the hue on John [2d.] Warwyk who is amerced with the pledge of the constable.
>
> And that John Starlyng' justly [called] the hue over John [2d.] Warwyk who was amerced by the pledge of the constable. The constable [2d] because he himself has not [pledged] therefore he was amerced.
>
> And that Beatrix Starlyng justly [called] the hue on John [2d.] Abel etc, with the pledge of the constable Also and the constable [2d.] because he himself has not [pledged] therefore was amerced.
>
> Also that Margaret Tele justly [called] the hue over Richard [2d.] Cartere who was amerced, with the pledge of the constable.
>
> Also that John Starlyng justly [called] the hue over Robert [4d.] Bonde with the pledge of Richard Starlyng.
>
> Also that Alice [2d] Hoppere unjustly [called] the hue on John Miton, therefore etc with the pledge of the constable and the constable [2d.] because he himself has not [pledged] therefore was amerced.
>
> Also that John [2d.] Pelle drew blood from Alec Wayte with the pledge of the constable. Also the same Alec justly [called] the hue over the said John [2d.] with the pledge of the constable, and the constable has not asked and therefore is amerced.[54]
>
> And that John Wayte justly [called] the hue on over John Eames therefore etc with the pledge of the constable. The constable [2d.] has not [asked] and is amerced.[55]

Calling the hue occurred at the views of frankpledge held in the autumn, but after the appointment of Thomas Bekyngham as steward in 1416 the hue is seldom recorded; twice in 1417 and 1420, then once in 1423 or 1424, 1425, 1450 and 1457.[56]

Pledging

A system of personal pledging was probably in place in Willington before 1381, but the first surviving record appears in the court roll of April 1394 when Edith Starlyng asked to continue to hold her late husband's holding and was given time to find sufficient security. She was unable to find a member of the manorial elite to pledge for her, that is, to guarantee that she would be able to pay the rent and maintain the fields, hedges, watercourses and buildings in good repair, and so surrendered the holding at the next court.[57]

---

54 The amount of this amercement is not written in the document
55 BARS, Box R212, Roll 2, October 1394.
56 BARS, Box R212, Roll 23, October 1417; Roll 29, October 1420; Roll 34, September 1423; Roll 35, October 1423; Roll 39a, October 1450; Roll 46a, October 1457.
57 BARS, Box R212, Roll 1, April 1394; Roll 2, October 1394.

Men of some social standing on the manor, such as the bailiff, constable, or other member of the manorial elite, might on occasion agree to provide a pledge, which would be described today as a guarantee or surety. At the end of the fourteenth century pledgers at Willington seem to have been appointed by the bailiff or the steward and include some men whose names rarely appear in the rolls and who may have been free tenants. The constable pledged on nine occasions in the view of frankpledge of October 1394 and was fined 2d. each for five of them, 'because he himself has not [pledged]', which is presumed to mean that he had not made sure that the individuals for whom he pledged obeyed the orders of the court. None of the people who provided pledges for tenants were fined after 1408; from that date it became usual for the court to threaten tenants who had not completed their repairs, as ordered, with large penalties.[58] The penalty for a broken mill pond in May 1408 was 5s.;[59] in April 1411 it was 40s.[60] When Adam Warde did not repair his ruined buildings in October 1410 he and his pledgers were threatened with a penalty of 20s., which increased to 40s. at the next court.[61] The problem does not recur, so they must have repaired rather than pay the penalty.

Pledges might be used to verify an excuse for essoins or non-attendance at court, support the use of the hue and cry by another tenant, guarantee the truth of a plea to settle a debt, or guarantee that a would-be tenant had the necessary skill, workers or finances to work a holding successfully. Pledges might also guarantee the good behaviour of someone accused of a breach of the peace or other petty crimes. It was usual for new tenants to need two guarantors when they entered a holding; a new miller needed three or four guarantors until after 1476.[62]

Personal pledging appears to have died out in some places by the late fourteenth or early fifteenth centuries.[63] In Willington guarantees for rents and repairs largely disappeared by 1420 and guarantees for pleas of debt, hue and cry and petty offences became rare; the last one appears in 1450.[64] Pledges for essoins continued until 1522, but it became increasingly common for these to be given by the bailiff.[65] However, a new use of pledging appeared 1448–56 when William Launcelyn pledged to repair other tenants' buildings in return for money payments. He exploited this system for commercial gain and the repairs he promised were much delayed or not made.

When Queen Joan was lady of the manor, 1406–12/13, a total of twenty-four men and one woman provided pledges for other less fortunate tenants to be granted messuages, land, or cottages, or to repair buildings on their holdings.[66] Several of the tenants they helped seem to have been vulnerable members of the community. Although the details in the rolls are incomplete it appears that at least seven of the tenants surrendered their holdings almost immediately or died soon after. The constable provided ten pledges; the Rydere family pledged thirteen times; the Myton

58   BARS, Box R212, Roll 9b, May 1408.
59   *Ibid.*
60   BARS, Box R212, Roll 13, April 1411.
61   BARS, Box R212, Roll 12, October 1410; Roll 13, April 1411.
62   BARS, Box R212, Roll 57b, May 1476.
63   Bailey, *The English Manor*, pp.185–6.
64   BARS, Box R212, Roll 39a, October 1450.
65   BARS, Box R212, Roll 63, March 1522.
66   BARS, Box R212, Roll 8, October 1406; Roll 8b, April 1407; Roll 9a, October 1407; Roll 9b, May 1408; Roll 10, October 1408; Roll 12, October 1410; Roll 13, April 1411.

family pledged thirteen times; the Heryng, Gaubryel, Sherbourn and Gostwyk families each pledged four or five times. There may have been more because on two occasions the men who pledged for the mill were mentioned but not named. In this period some tenants wishing to be granted holdings found their own pledges as surety for rent and repairs. The phrase, 'he provided pledges' appears in eight rolls.[67]

The steward, Thomas Rokes, appears to have tried to revive the system of pledging on the manor but without success. He pledged for a new tenant of a cottage and eight acres of plough land in April 1474; two brewers in October 1474;[68] a new tenant of a messuage and ten acres of land in March 1475, and in that same year for Thomas Passewater who took the fisheries and the 'waters of the mill';[69] a tenant's repairs in October 1475;[70] and a new tenant in April 1476.[71] The only other man from the manor who pledged during the 1470s was the bailiff who pledged for three essoins in October 1475; no other tenants were prepared to provide surety for any of their neighbours.[72] The last recorded use of pledging of any sort in Willington was in 1522.[73]

Crime and disorder

The end of the fourteenth century was a disturbed period in the life of the tenants with relatively frequent assaults, debts, trespass and thefts. While there are no clear links between the number of brewers and the levels of anti-social behaviour, it is possible that alcohol may have had a role to play. It may be no coincidence that the lists of brewers in 1394 included twenty-three names and recorded forty-four brewings, and in 1395 included twenty-five brewers and fifty-five brewings; much greater than in later years.[74]

Problems with alcohol, the ale-tasters and the brewers may have been a factor in the arguments described between four families in 1420, but they may equally have been the result of changes brought about by the steward, Thomas Bekyngham, and by the appointment of a new manorial officer, Robert de Wyllyton, by Lord Mowbray while fighting in France:

> John Bande the elder and Robert Partrych the constables present that Emma (3d.) Fesound unlawfully called the hue on John Grace by the pledge of the constables. And that John (6d.) Abel assaulted Thomas Starlyng against the peace of the lord king. Therefore he is amerced. And that Hugh (2d.) Webbe assaulted Richard Bawdewene and Agnes his wife against the peace of the lord King by the pledge of Richard Parker. And that Agnes wife of Richard Baudewene rightly called the hue on the said Hugh (3d.) by the pledge of the aforesaid.[75]

[67]   BARS, Box R212, Roll 8, October 1406; Roll 8b, April 1407; Roll 9a, October 1407; Roll 13, April 1411; Roll 18a, Michaelmas 1415; Roll 19, October 1415; Roll 24, April 1418; Roll 26, May 1419.
[68]   BARS, Box R212, Roll 56, April 1474; Roll 55a, October 1474.
[69]   BARS, Box R212, Roll 57a, October 1475.
[70]   BARS, Box R212, Roll 57a, October 1475.
[71]   BARS, Box R212, Roll 59a, November 1476.
[72]   BARS, Box R212, Roll 57a, October 1475.
[73]   BARS, Box R212, Roll 63, March 1522.
[74]   BARS, Box R212, Roll 2, October 1394; Roll 3, October 1395.
[75]   BARS, Box R212, Roll 29, October 1420.

The frequency of pledges on the manor before 1482

Intervals of years	Pledges for essoins	Pledges for hue and cry and petty offences	Pledges for entry to holdings	Pledges for rent for holdings and building repairs	Pledges for pleas of debt
1394–97 Rolls1–5	2 pledgers named, 3 men essoined	21 pledges by 8 men (14 by constable)	8 pledges for 8 holdings	4 pledgers for rent and repairs of mill, 4 pledgers for other repairs	None
1403–9 Rolls 6–11	1 pledger named, 2 not named, 4 men essoined	8 pledges by 3 men (1 by the constable)	22 pledgers for 11 holdings	2 pledgers for 1repair	7 pledgers for 5 pleas of debt
1410–14 Rolls 12–17	4 pledgers named, 6 men essoined	8 pledges by the constable	20 pledgers for 10 holdings	2 pledgers for 1repair	6 pledgers for 3 pleas of debt. Other pleas entered without pledgers
1415–19 Rolls 18a–27	3 pledgers named, 15 men essoined	6 pledges by 3 men (5 by the constables)	25 pledgers for 13 holdings	2 pledgers for 1repair	2 pledgers for 1 plea of debt
1420–24 Rolls 28–34	4 pledgers named, 12 men essoined	4 pledges by 3 men (2 by the constable)	None	1 pledger for 1 repair	None
1425–26 Rolls 35–36a	1 pledger named (the beadle), 1 man essoined	None	None	None	None
1440 Roll 37	None	None	None	None	None
1448–54 Rolls 38a–43a	3 pledgers named (including the bailiff), 1 not named, 5 men essoined	None	None	3 pledgers for rent and repairs of the mill. Robert Rydere could not find a pledge for the repair of his malt-kiln in 1448[76]	1 pledger for one plea of debt (the bailiff). A further plea was resolved without a pledge
1455–59 Rolls 43b–47a	1 pledger named twice (the bailiff), 'the community' named twice, 1 not named, 13 men and 1 woman essoined	Hue and cry called but no pledge given	None	2 pledges for 2 repairs (by bailiff)	None

1461–64 Rolls 49a–51a[77]	5 pledgers named, 1 not named, 6 men and 1 woman essoined (latter 3 times)	None	None	None	None
1465–69 Rolls 51b–BL7	1 pledger named 3 times (the bailiff), 'the community' named once, 1 not named, 2 women essoined 3 times, 21 men essoined	None	None	None	None
1470–74[78] Rolls BL8–56[79]	1 pledger named (the bailiff), 5 men essoined	None	1 pledger for 3 holdings (the steward)	1 pledger for 1 repair (the vicar)	None
1475–79 Rolls 57b–59b	1 pledger named (the bailiff), 3 not named, no pledger given once, 5 men and 2 women essoined	None	1 pledger for the watermill (the steward)	1 pledger for 1 repair (the steward)	None
1480–82 Rolls 60a–60b	No pledgers named, 2 men essoined	None	None	None	None
1515–22 Rolls 61–64	1 pledger named, 1 not named, 5 men essoined	None	1 pledger for 1 holding	None	None

[76] Excludes Cardington. BARS, Box R212, Roll 38a, October 1448. This roll effectively marks the end of the system of tenants pledging for the repairs of their neighbours' buildings. William Launcelyn was either paid by the tenants to do the repairs or was ordered by the steward to carry them out; and he did his best to avoid doing these repairs.

[77] Ibid.

[78] Increase in activity perhaps caused by the new steward Thomas Rokes.

[79] The rolls at this point are out of sequence. Roll 56 is dated April 1474, but Roll 55b is dated March 1475.

The roll for October 1421 has not survived, but in 1419 there was a change in ale-tasters; William Ryder and John Myton were replaced by John Bande the younger and John Myton. By 1422 the number of brewers had reduced from thirteen in 1420 to seven, and the income for the lord from brewing fines had reduced from 32d. to 15d.

Although the level of recorded petty crime was much higher in 1394 than in later years, the period 1394–1426 seems to have been generally difficult for the tenants, with relatively high levels of disturbance. Changes of lord and bailiff during this period may have been contributory factors. The bailiff, Robert Gostwyk, retired or died in August 1393 after being in post for at least eleven years and was succeeded by William Pecke, a member of the local gentry who lived outside the manor. By the end of September 1394, during the year of the first surviving manor court roll for Willington, he had been replaced by William Ridere, from a Willington family of villein status, who continued as bailiff until at least 1418.[80] The relatively high levels of petty crime throughout the period may have been due to dissatisfaction among the tenants with William Pecke as bailiff and resistance to the diligence of William Ridere after he was appointed.

The period 1395–1415 was one of recession, felt by most agricultural communities.[81] Poor wheat and barley harvests, 1400–1 and 1409–10, may also have contributed to the increase in crime levels.[82] It may be surmised that poor harvests led to real difficulties for tenants and their families and resulted in thefts and short tempers. The rolls do not contain clear evidence of these causes, though two men from the same family, Adam and John Abel caused trouble at the end of the fourteenth century and early fifteenth century with a variety of offences, the most serious being in 1420 when John was fined for stealing sheaves of corn and his wife was found to be a disturber of the peace.[83] Hard times could also have led to housebreaking, cutting down hedges to use for fuel, stealing from neighbours' fields and poaching game in the lord's woods.[84] A later period of high recorded crime in Willington, 1450–54, seems not to have been caused by bad harvests but may have been due to the consistent and careful management of the manor by the officials of John Beaumont, leading to changes in the management of the court and to more careful record keeping. The Mowbrays' steward for the years 1448–56 inclusive is not named, but in these years William Launcelyn, a member of a nearby gentry family, held lands and buildings, perhaps even the manor house, in Willington and may have been a cause of conflict.

Launcelyn was an example of a member of the gentry who was determined to add to his holdings and to exploit his neighbours. He was accused of not paying his common fine in autumn 1452, and in the years 1448–57 he had the use of some holdings rent-free on the understanding that he would repair the buildings; he did

80   BARS, R8/62/2/10, and Thompson, *Bailiffs' Accounts for Willington*, BARS, CRT 130 Willington 11, p. 38.
81   R. Britnell, 'Markets and Incentives: Common Themes and Regional Variations', in B. Dodds and R. Britnell, eds, *Agriculture and Rural Society after the Black Death* (Hatfield, 2008), pp.13–14.
82   Dyer, *Standards of Living,* pp. 262–3.
83   BARS, Box R212, Roll 29, October 1420.
84   BARS, Box R212, Roll 23, October 1417.

not do so. He was also paid by some tenants to repair buildings for them, but again, he did not do so.[85] His active involvement in the life of the village ceases shortly after the appointment of a new steward, Thomas Rokes, in 1457.

Violence on the manor before the middle of the fifteenth century involved the use of fists, poles, sticks, batons and muck-forks, but later there was an increase in knife crime. Daggers were used in 1454, 1468 and 1469. This change in practice should perhaps not be interpreted as a symptom of greater dissatisfaction or violence because recorded levels of crime were still low. The influence of the Wars of the Roses may have been felt by country people, or some men may have had more disposable income with which to obtain knives because of greater levels of relative prosperity.

Incidence of petty crime and anti-social behaviour

Date	No. of rolls	Hue and cry	Assault	Antisocial acts	Theft	Neglect[86]	Debt
1394–97	5	15	6	5	10	17	1
1404–9	8	8	2	4	1	13	11
1410–14	7	7	2	3	11	8	7
1415–19	10	6	5	8	7	11	2
1420–24	8	3	3	8	12	11	0
1425–26	3	1	1	1	4	8	0
1440	1	0	0	0	0	0	4
1448–9	2	0	0	0	1	5	0
1450–54	9	1	8	4	6	17	2
1455–59	9	1	8	4	4	20	1
1460–64	6	0	1	7	5	9	0
1465–69	10	0	7	1	4	24	0
1470–74	6	0	7	6	1	14	0
1475–79	6	0	5	0	0	5	0
1480–82	2	0	3	0	1	6	0
1515–22	4	5	1	0	0	Implied	0
1537–40	4	2	0	0	0	Implied	0

While anti-social behaviour and violent crime was an issue so too were other more insidious crimes associated with land, agriculture and property, which took a variety of forms. Some tenants tried to enclose parts of their lands and discourage access to them by others. Members of an established family of freemen, the Partrychs, were confident enough to close the common way over their lands in

85 BARS, Box R212, Rolls 38a, October 1448; Roll 39a, October 1450; Roll 39b, May 1451; Roll 40a, October 1451; Roll 40b, May 1452; Roll 41a, October 1452; Roll 41b, May 1453; Roll 42a, October 1453; Roll 42b, May 1454; Roll 43a, October 1454; Roll 43b, May 1455; Roll 46a, October 1457.
86 This column includes trespass, watercourses needing cleaning, re-routing watercourses and failure to cultivate fields and trim hedges, also ploughing extra land, overstocking commons and blocking access to properties and fields by enclosures or other means.

1455 and 1456, but they encountered great opposition from the manor court.[87] They later seem to have fallen on hard times.[88]

Other members of the community tried to plough land without permission. In the west of the manor in Midlemarshfield, somewhere near the parish boundary with Cople, there seems to have been a feature named Willington Mere, or *Le Mare*. Although 'mere' may indicate a boundary, here its use is ambiguous. It was adjacent to the parish boundary, but evidence provided by the name of the open field, by entries in the court rolls, and by the low-lying nature of the area today, suggests that this was an area of land that was difficult to drain. John Fage ploughed illegally at Willington Mere in May 1464.[89] He was fined 2d. and:

> He was ordered to put it right by the next cultivation under a penalty of 6s. 8d. Also they say that John Fage made one drainage channel on the other side of the half an acre of land there. Therefore he is amerced. And he was ordered to put it right before 15 days under a penalty of 40d.

Later illegal ploughings by Fage and by Richard Hatley appear in the court roll for October 1468 when the feature was described as Willington Mare.[90] In October 1469, however, it seems to have been referred to as Willington Baulk.[91] Willington and Cople tenants were ordered to dig a drainage channel from the Mare in 1470.[92]

Failure to repair buildings or clear ditches was the most common cause of fines. Tenants were also found to have taken away hedges, sold trees from their holdings, failed to obey the rules of the common fields or the use of land belonging to others. There were thefts from more prosperous tenants and poaching by tenants and outsiders was often proved, though probably more often not detected. There were sporadic arguments and fights. Tenants attempted to encroach on the lands of others, enclose some parts of their lands and the common lands by planting hedges, or close common ways over their properties, especially in the years 1463 and 1467–70.[93]

Crime was not restricted to people of lower social status; men of high social status also transgressed and ignored the custom of the manor. In October 1425 three local men including the vicar were brought to court for having illegal dovecotes on their land. They may have used the rearing of pigeons to support an unusually luxurious lifestyle; the birds would have been an important source of extra income:

> Also they say that Robert Myton, John Marion and the reverend Robert, the vicar of the church there, have Dovecots within the lord's demesne and that they do not have sufficient free land to occupy and keep the said Dovecots therefore etc.[94] And that the said Robert Myton acknowledged he made his Dovecot in the first year of our said lord king [Henry VI, 1 September

87   BARS, Box R212, Roll 43a, October 1454; Roll 43b, May 1455; Roll 45a, October 1456.
88   BARS, Box R212, Roll 44a, October 1455; Roll 45a, October 1456.
89   British Library, Add.Ch 26813/2, May 1464.
90   British Library, Add.Ch 26813/5, August 1468.
91   British Library, Add.Ch 26813/7, October 1469.
92   British Library, Add.Ch 26813/8, May 1470.
93   British Library, Add.Ch.26813/1-8.
94   The vicar in 1421 was Robert Calyser, followed by a Robert Chapman, no dates given, Hugh Chapman was listed as incumbent in 1432. BARS, Fasti/1/Will and Gordon Vowles, *The Parish of St Lawrence, Willington, Its Church and its Vicars* (Willington, 2016).

1422–31 August 1423] and that the said John made his Dovecot about the fourth year of the reign of the late king Henry IV [30 September 1402–29 September 1403] and that the said reverend Robert, the vicar's, Dovecot was made by one of his predecessors within the 13th year of the reign of king Henry IV lately king of England [30 September 1411–29 September 1412] and the said Dovecots were placed in respite until Roger Hunte shall have spoken with the lord's council etc.[95]

Roger Hunte, the new steward, intended to take advice from the lord's council, but its advice is not recorded as the following roll has not survived.

Women too feature as perpetrators of crime and were linked to a variety of anti-social behaviours. In 1420 John Abel was accused of thefts and damage, and Agnes, his wife, was fined 12d. for being a: 'common chatterbox and disturber of the peace within the neighbourhood.'[96] This was a large fine, but the scribe may have omitted other alleged crimes as the entry appears to end in mid-sentence. Much later women were involved in assaults and thefts; in 1471 Elisabeth Redy and Elisabeth Langton were described as *ingulaciones* or *jugulaciones* and, 'disturbers of the lord King's peace.'[97] They were fined 4d. each.[98]

Detailed evidence of crime at this early date in Bedfordshire is sketchy. However, when compared with Blunham, where there was a vibrant mix of debt, petty crime and anti-social behaviour, Willington was a haven of peace and tranquility.

Entrepreneurial activity – work, wages and wealth
The prosperity of an agricultural community benefited from access to local fairs and markets, especially in a land-locked county like Bedfordshire, where water transport was unreliable due to the width of the river bed and the obstruction of deeper channels by mills and weirs. Water transport is not mentioned directly in the Willington court rolls, and Willington tenants may have transported much of their produce to market on foot, by cart or by pack-horse, or by walking their animals to sell to butchers on other manors or in the towns.

Bedford was in decline in the fourteenth and fifteenth centuries, and this decline must have limited the prosperity of the surrounding manors. Fortunately, Willington was situated within walking distance of other markets. Blunham market closed in the early fourteenth century, but Potton, Biggleswade, Shefford and St Neots markets were within reach.[99] Regional markets in Cambridge were accessible by road and river. Fairs, which drew people from further afield, lasted for three days and coincided with a church holiday were held in Bedford (four miles distant), in Elstow (five or six miles distant) and Biggleswade (seven or eight miles distant).[100]

Although a wide variety of meat, fish and fowl was produced on the manor, either for local consumption or for sale in nearby towns, the fisheries and the dovecote were held by members of the gentry from outside the manor, and the woodlands

---

[95]   BARS, Box R212, Roll 35, October 1425.
[96]   BARS, Box R212, Roll 29, October 1420.
[97]   R. E. Latham, *Revised Medieval Latin Word-list* (Oxford, 1965). These descriptions are clearly meant to be offensive but exact translations are not available.
[98]   BARS, Box R212, Roll 54a, October 1471.
[99]   Godber, *History of Bedfordshire,* pp.117–8, 155–6.
[100] Godber, *History of Bedfordshire,* pp. 50–1.

and the lord's right of free warren were kept under the lord's control, thus denying most tenants the opportunities for entrepreneurial activity that were available to the gentry. In 1474, when a tenant attempted to build a rabbit warren on his holding he was immediately dealt with: 'Thomas Cramfeld from now on should not have a rabbit warren on Willington Mere, under a penalty of 6s. 8d.'[101] Occasional references in the rolls suggest that some tenants supplemented the income from their holdings by part-time commercial activity or work as builders and craft workers. Felicia Prentys, who had surrendered her holding by May 1416, may then have made baskets as she bought five heads of willow in 1418 for 6d.[102]

Tenants were given timber to repair their houses and farm buildings suggesting that most of them had some building skills. In 1455, when John Stones complained that he did not have a barn on his holding the decision of the council was that: 'the lord obliged the tenants to make one building on the holding which John Stones held' so it is clear that they were expected to have the necessary aptitude.[103] Where building workers were employed in fifteenth century England, wage rates varied between town and country; rates for building workers were higher in large towns where there was considerable demand for craftsmen. Carpenters at Willington and Haynes were paid 3½d. or 4d. a day, much less than the wages paid in London (6d. a day), Oxford (6d. a day) or Stratford on Avon (5d. a day).[104]

There is evidence on the manor for a number of other trades. In 1415 the smith is named as Robert Tele,[105] followed by John Sangyle[106] and then John Smyth, who had a forge with defective thatch in 1425.[107] In 1451 members of the Fischere family were described as weavers.[108] Henry Maye the butcher was mentioned in 1461. He had a yard in the village from which he sold, 'meat without heads for excessive gain.'[109]

The court rolls contain details about bake-houses on the manor when they needed repair or replacement during the fifteenth century. They seem to have belonged to well-established Willington tenants and were timber-framed constructions separate from other buildings. John Salt was given recycled spars, studs and a horizontal timber for his bake-house in 1457, and in July 1458 John Morbo'rn (or Morbourne, Morboune, Morburn, Morborne) was given half a rood of underwood and posts and wall plates for his.[110] It seems that at least two bake-houses had tiled roofs.[111] There is one single mention of an oven in May 1472 but no further details, although in October 1465 not only was the bailiff, John Yarwey, allowed large timber and some withies but also: '8s. in money for making a new bake-house in his holding.'[112] The eight shillings may have paid for a new oven. The

---

101 BARS, Box R212, Roll 55a, March 1474.
102 BARS, Box R212, Roll 25, October 1418.
103 BARS, Box R212, Roll 45b, April 1457.
104 Dyer, *Standards of Living*, p. 220.
105 BARS, Box R212, Roll 15, October 1413: Roll 17, October 1414.
106 BARS, Box R212, Roll 27, October 1419.
107 BARS, Box R212, Roll 35, October 1425.
108 BARS, Box R212, Roll 39b, May 1451.
109 BARS, Box R212, Roll 49a, October 1461.
110 BARS, Box R212, Roll 46b, July 1458.
111 BARS, Box R212, Roll 54c, October 1473.
112 BARS, Box R212, Roll 52a, October 1465.

single payment of 2d. by William Lentewheat for baking bread in October 1461 eventually led to most bake-houses being unused and neglected in the sixteenth century.[113] Twelve were listed as needing repair in September 1515.

The miller was not usually a Willington man, but there is no evidence to indicate how he was recruited. In 1382–83 the rent of the mill was 106s. 6d., but the rent was increased to £6 (120s.) in 1384–85. No miller is named until John Phille (or Fille, Fylle)[114] who rented the watermill for a year at £6, 1386–87.[115] He renewed his lease for seven years in 1387–88 at a lower rent of 106s. 8d. and again in 1396–97 at the same rent for a further three years. There was another extension to the lease in October 1397. The bailiff's account 1396–97 state that this was for a further three years but the court roll states:

> Also John Fille came to this Court and took from the lord the mill of Wylton with the pond of the same mill, To have and to hold the aforesaid mill with the aforesaid pond and the branches of the trees growing around the aforesaid mill and with the herbage growing in pond of the aforesaid mill pond and with the fishery below the gates of the same mill. The aforesaid John Fille to hold the mill from last Michaelmas until the end of the five years next following, rendering to the lord 8 marks [£5 6s. 8d.].[116]

He continued as miller until about 1411.[117] There were complaints that the mill pond and mill dam needed repair from 1408.[118] The dam was still not repaired in April 1411 and: 'John Fylle the miller and his pledges were ordered to make the mill Dam good and sufficient before the next [court] under a penalty of 40s.'[119] The dam was not repaired, and when John Usshere took a nine-year lease on the mill from October 1413 he was given timber to carry out the repairs and paid a £20 deposit.[120] He was not asked to provide pledges or guarantors. The lord's officials agreed to provide:

> one limb for the same John to repair and put right the said Dam during the aforesaid term. And the said John and his assigns will hand over the said mill, the stones for milling and all the Machinery pertaining to the said mill and the mill Dams at the end of the term of the tenancy well and sufficiently repaired.[121]

John Ussher continued as miller until c.1425, but the mill was described as, 'ruined and defective, because of the lord's neglect' in June 1423.[122]

In May 1452, Thomas Myller took a six-year lease, with the support of three local men as pledgers, John Cook, John Myton and John Yarwey, suggesting that the steward was not convinced that he would be able to pay the rent or pay for the

113 BARS, Box R212, Roll 49a, October 1461; Roll 61, September 1515; Roll 62, March 1520; Roll 63, March 1522; Roll 64, December 1522.
114 BARS, Box R212, Roll 3, October 1395: Roll 14, October 1411.
115 BARS, R8/62/2/4, and Thompson, *Bailiffs' Accounts for Willington*, BARS, CRT 130 Willington 11, p. 11.
116 BARS, Box R212, Roll 5, October 1397.
117 BARS, R8/62/2/5, and Thompson, *Bailiffs' Accounts for Willington*, BARS, CRT 130 Willington 11, p. 16.
118 BARS, Box R212, Roll 9b, April 1408.
119 BARS, Box R212, Roll 13, April 1411.
120 BARS, Box R212, Roll 15, October 1413.
121 *Ibid.*
122 BARS, Box R212, Roll 32, June 1423.

repairs.[123] The mill was closed for nine weeks for, 'certain repairs and makings of the same' in 1455.[124] In 1459 further repairs were undertaken.

Simon Usshere is named as miller in 1458,[125] followed by Thomas Gybon (or Cebon) in 1462,[126] William Watt in 1469, [127] John Wodehyll in 1472, [128] and Thomas Passewater in 1475. These men seldom appear elsewhere in the documents, but in March 1475 Thomas Passewater was granted the mill, the mill waters, the fisheries and rabbit warren on forty-year leases. The Passewater family had lived on the manor since 1448 or earlier, but the forty-year lease proved to be too ambitious because in April 1476 he surrendered the mill.[129]

The fortunes of the mill and the miller fluctuated in the ninety years 1386–1476. John Phille had held the mill for twenty-six years 1386–1412, and John Ussher, who succeeded him, held it from 1412 to at least 1425, but in the second half of the fifteenth century the tenancies of the mill were shorter and substantial repairs were needed. The rents had reduced to 40s. a year by 1476 suggesting the mill must have become less profitable, possibly indicating a reduction in cereal production and an increase in the keeping of sheep.

Sheep farming was the business of two Willington tenants, Henry Yarwey and William Wryght, who together employed a shepherd in 1415.[130] Surplus wool produced by them, and others, may have been exported to the Continent when Bedfordshire wool merchants negotiated large contracts, at first with the king and later with The Staple (the centre of distribution) in Calais, but most owners of small numbers of sheep on Willington manor probably kept their flocks as part of a pattern of mixed farming, to feed their households and sell at market.[131]

Henry Yarwey's and William Wryght's shepherd is not named in the court rolls, but men with the occupational surname Shepherd are mentioned from 1410 and appear to have been unpopular and aggressive.[132] One of them joined a tithing, but the others only appeared in the rolls when they had been involved in fights or in the theft of animals. The Shepherd family history contributes to the impression that these men, who lived on the edge of the community and were not involved in the cultivation of the common fields, were more likely to be involved in assaults and petty crime than those who were subjected to the discipline and self-control imposed by co-operative farming practices.

Acts of theft and housebreaking against Robert Cooke, Robert Fesaunt, John Gostwyke, William Taylor and the Stoughton family suggest that these may have been relatively prosperous families and that others, such as the Shepherd family, found life much more difficult. While most tenants had to undertake the work on their holding themselves, these more prosperous families would have employed servants and temporary workers when they needed extra help.

---

[123]   BARS, Box R212, Roll 40b, May 1452.
[124]   BARS, Box R212, Roll 44a, October 1455.
[125]   BARS, Box R212, Roll 47, October 1458.
[126]   BARS, Box R212, Roll 50c, October 1462.
[127]   British Library, Add.Ch.26813/6, April 1469.
[128]   BARS, Box R212, Roll 54b, May 1472.
[129]   BARS, Box R212, Roll 57b, April/May 1476.
[130]   BARS, Box R212, Roll 19, October 1415.
[131]   Godber, *History of Bedfordshire,* p. 118.
[132]   BARS, Box R212, Roll 12, October 1410.

In the years 1395–1422 John Smyth, Thomas Rydere, John Bande and John Gost-wyke all employed servants who were entered into tithings.[133] They were probably all young men from outside the manor, who may have lived in the households of their masters and received some training, but their surnames are not given. On three occasions the masters of these servants paid fines of 2d. for them to be enrolled.[134] The rolls contain no further evidence of servants being entered into tithings until 1522, when: 'William Spenser servant of Thomas Myton, William Feyre servant John Warner have 12 years or more and have not sworn service to the lord King.'[135] No mention of being enrolled into tithings is made, but the reference to them being twelve years old suggests that this was the case. On this occasion the fines were paid by the servants themselves and were considerable. They each paid 12d.

Tradesmen who were employed to repair or construct buildings in the manor also employed servants, and other mentions of servants in the rolls are usually linked to petty crime such as assaults, thefts (of a fishing basket and a sheep) and playing tennis 'against the statute.'[136]

Debt and fraud

The manor court rolls provide many instances of debt, but this is not necessarily an indication of long-term financial problems, access to credit may sometimes be interpreted as an indicator of credit-worthiness.[137] In the early 1400s some animals in Willington were bought on credit, and on one occasion a tenant returned a bullock rather than pay for it.[138]

There were occasions when only one or two pleas of debt were brought to court, and there were no pleas of debt October 1397–October 1406, October 1416–May 1419 or October 1420–May 1449. There were, however, ongoing financial irregu-larities. In 1408: 'John Cartere recognises a debt to Simon Rysele of 14d. for 1 arrow and belt.'[139] In 1416, a new bailiff, Richard Marable, appears as the victim of fraud: 'And that John [6d] Goffe and Mariota his wife made illegal recovery from Richard Marable, the lord's bailiff. Therefore they are amerced.'[140] In 1421–22, the receiver's accounts reveal that William Rydere had built up substantial arrears and that two former Willington warreners, William Cook and William Warner, had left their posts while owing money to the lord's receiver.[141]

Officials were also implicated in fraud, and in 1421 there were two serious complaints against John Kempston, the woodward:

> And that John Kempston, Wodewarde of Shirehacche, is answerable for his account for the seventh year of the reign of Henry fifth for underwood cut down

---

[133] BARS, Box R212, Roll 3, October 1395; Roll 12, October 1410; Roll 14a, October 1411; Roll 31, October 1422.

[134] BARS, Box R212, Roll 14a, October 1411.

[135] BARS, Box R212, Roll 63, March 1522.

[136] BARS, Box R212, Roll 42a, October 1453; Roll 49b, October 1461; British Library, Add Ch. 26813/1, October 1463; Add Ch. 26813/3, October 1467; Add Ch. 26813/8, May 1470.

[137] Dyer, *Standards of Living,* p. 180.

[138] BARS, Box R212, Roll 13, April 1411.

[139] BARS, Box R212, Roll 10, October 1408. '*Canna et braccitectum*' the only reference to archery on the manor.

[140] BARS, Box R212, Roll 21, October 1416.

[141] Arundel Castle Archives, A1642.

and from the same John selling from the south part of Shirewood in a certain place called Beestonelesewe[142] of 11 acres and a half, 32 perches.[143] And afterwards it was accounted for by the Inquisition of John Boteler the understeward that the same John Kempston sold the same year from the same place 14 acres over and above. And so it has been concealed.

Also that the same John Kempston is answerable in the said accounts for 10 pairs of rabbits, sold from the Warren of Welyngton in the above year. And it was accounted in the inquisition of the aforesaid John Boteler that the said John on various days made sales of 20 pairs and so for various days and nights against orders until he worked to find pairs and concealed 50 pairs and more.[144]

As woodward, John Kempston was responsible for keeping the hedges in good repair, and in 1426 it was said that the enclosures round the wood were broken down; he was ordered to repair them or pay a fine of 100s.[145] It is surprising that Kempston was still employed.

After May 1453 pleas of debt ceased to be brought to the Willington manorial courts, and although in October 1463 the court attempted to ensure that cases for small amounts of debt were still handled there, it had no effect. 'It was ordained in Court, by the agreement of all the tenants, that no tenant henceforth shall prosecute another tenant, outside the demesne for debts, nor for trespass, unless they should exceed 40s., under penalty of 20s. forfeited to the lady.'[146]

Brewing, brewers and ale-tasters
Ale was plentiful and was probably brewed in a brew-house situated in the service buildings of the medieval manor house. This brew-house was mentioned in an inquisition of 1380 when the manor had been let rent-free on condition that the buildings were repaired, but the repairs to the manor house, the weir and the floodgates seem not to have been undertaken.[147] The manor's bakery, kitchen, chapel and closet were demolished 1384–85 and the materials sold, perhaps to pay for other repairs.[148]

At the end of the fourteenth century, large numbers of brewers and brewings are recorded.[149] Perhaps families on the manor brewed in rotation, sharing the brewings with friends and neighbours.[150] It was usual for two or three men, or their wives, to brew more regularly than the rest, and they may have supplied the ale-house. The first record of ale being sold dates from 1404 and is attributed to John Goffe.[151]

---

[142] Today this is outside the parish of Willington, on the southern facing slopes of the Greensand Ridge.
[143] The language used does not mean that he sold the land, but that he sold the crop of underwood, that is crops from the coppicing of trees, from an area of Sheerhatch Wood covering the area described.
[144] BARS, Box R212, Roll 30, April 1421.
[145] BARS, Box R212, Roll 36, September 1426.
[146] British Library, Add.Ch.26813/1 October 1463.
[147] Great Britain, Public Record Office, *Calendar of Inquisitions Miscellaneous (Chancery) Preserved in the Public Record Office*, vol. 4, no. 123 (H.M.S.O., 1957), pp.75–6.
[148] BARS, R8/62/2/3, and Thompson, *Bailiffs' Accounts for Willington*, BARS, CRT 130 Willington 11, p. 8.
[149] BARS, Box R212, Roll 2, October 1394; Roll 3, October 1395; Roll 4, May 1396. The roll for the view of frankpledge in 1396 is missing.
[150] Dyer, *Standards of Living*, p. 156; p. 158.
[151] BARS, Box R212, Roll 7, October 1404.

Matilda Yarwey may also have operated an ale-house as she owed 9s. 4d. in 1408 to Thomas Aylbrygt for ale.[152]

In 1416, John Goffe, who had sold ale by the bottle and the cup, was fined: 'And that the same John sold ale against the mandate of the tasters of ale and was fined four pence.'[153] John Goffe was soon in trouble again as a result of a defective malt-kiln which needed repair in 1417.[154] And in 1418 he had two other buildings needing repair and also:

> [he] sold old ale as he was ordered by the tasters of ale. And that the same John sold old ale and put a sign and afterwards it was withdrawn, therefore he was amerced two pence. And that the same John sold ale by the barrel and cup and was fined two pence. And the same John sold ale by measure without a seal and was amerced two pence.[155]

Two ale-tasters were elected by the manor court and their names often appeared in the views of frankpledge from 1407. William Rydere and Robert Myton were ale-tasters 1407–19, and other individuals with the same surname held important manorial roles such as those of reeve, bailiff, tithing men or jurors; though they are not named as constables. John and Robert Miton, or their sons, were ale-tasters throughout the period 1403–50 and continued to hold this office at intervals later in the century.[156] During this period the Mitons consistently shared this role with the office of assessor of fines.

After 1450 it became more usual for the role of ale-taster to be held for periods of up to four years by men who were villeins including members of the Bande, Bardolph, Baudewyn, Cook (or Coke, Cooke), Fesaunt, Flaundrys, Starlyng (or Sterlyng), Tayllour (or Taillour, Tailour, Taylor, Taylour), Totnam (or Cotnam) and Yarwey (or Yarewey, Yarewy, Yarway, Yerwey) families. John Gostwyk, from the village's most important free family, was ale-taster 1451–52; Henry Parker and John Warner, both thought to be free men, held the role in 1465.

Details of the role of ale-taster are incomplete, but it is evident that the ale-taster was responsible for seeing that everyone who brewed paid a fee to the lord, forming part of the lord's income. In 1394, 40% of householders paid fines for brewing.[157] When there were more than twenty brewers, as at the end of the fourteenth century, the role of ale-taster could have been a demanding one. In 1420 there were thirteen brewers and sixteen brewings. The numbers of brewers had reduced to six by 1425, and although the numbers fluctuated later in the fifteenth century, by 1475 they had reduced to three, and by 1537 there was only one. By this time the income to the lord for brewing was 2d., so that it had almost completely disappeared; there are no mentions in the rolls of ale-houses on the manor in this period.

At first the brewers were men; the wives may have done the work but were not named in the rolls. Cristiana Lyeghtfoot was one exception; she was named

[152] BARS, Box R212, Roll 8, October 1406.
[153] BARS, Box R212, Roll 21, October 1416.
[154] BARS, Box R212, Roll 22, May 1417.
[155] BARS, Box R212, Roll 25, October 1418.
[156] BARS, Box R212, Roll 9, October 1407.
[157] Twenty-three households of the recorded fifty-nine.

as a brewer in October 1394 when the numbers of brewers was near its height.[158] Other notable women brewers were Emma Skynner, 1451, who was expelled for running a bawdy house and Alicia Stoughton, 1453–67.

In 1448 John Beaumont and Katherine Neville experimented by combining the role of ale-taster with the role of constable; ale-tasters John Cook and John Myton held both roles and continued as ale-tasters for two further years. In 1451, John Redy became an ale-taster and John Stoughton a constant brewer, evidenced in the court roll where, for the only time, the names of three ale-tasters are recorded: 'John Yarwey the elder, John Gostwyk, John Redy tasters of ale present that John (6d.) Stoughton brewed constantly and broke the assize of ale, Emma (4d.) Skynner constantly, John (2d.) Tylere once, Robert (2d.) Taylour, Thomas (2d.) Myller once.'[159]

In 1454, John Yarwey and John Gostewyk were still ale-tasters, and Alicia Stoughton and John Redy were constant brewers both paying fines of 6d. each; unusually in that year the vicar also paid 12d. for one brewing.[160] The roll does not explain what the position of constant brewer entailed, but it became usual for there to be at least one person in this role and for him or her to pay 6d. for the privilege. It is possible that the constant brewer maintained the manor brew-house and was able to use it for as many brewings as required. The roll of 1454 suggests disagreement between the two constant brewers: 'John Redy has not brewed sufficiently so that the tenants will lack ale and that Alicia Stoughton did not wish to have a shortage of ale under the new brewings.'[161] He was fined 3d. and she was fined 2d. They must have reached an amicable agreement for he continued to brew alongside her for some years.

The roles of ale-taster and constable were once more combined 1461–62 and were undertaken by John Flaunders and John Starlyng. However, the joint appointments did not continue and the status quo resumed for some years. Ale-tasters were not named in 1474 or until October 1481 when Henry Parker and John Yarewey the younger were appointed, once more, to the joint roles. The combination of these manorial offices suggests that Katherine Neville and her council were attempting to simplify their management network and reduce costs.

Ale-tasters reported at every view of frankpledge or view with court held in late September or early October, and if found guilty of not doing their jobs properly were themselves fined – a not uncommon happening. John Miton and John Bande were fined in 1425:

> Brewing amercements 2s. 2d.
>
> Also that John (2d.) Miton and John (2d.) Bande the younger have not performed their offices as tasters, so they are amerced. Also that John (4d.) Rodland 2 times, John (2d.) Rider 1 time, John (2d.) Bande the elder 1 time, John (2d.) Gostwyk the younger 1 time, John (6d.) Goffe constantly, and Thomas (6d.) Starlyng constantly, brewed and sold ale against the assize and therefore they are amerced.[162]

[158] BARS, Box R212, Roll 2, October 1394.
[159] BARS, Box R212, Roll 40a, October 1451. At the top of the document the third taster of ale is named as John Yarwey the younger.
[160] BARS, Box R212, Roll 43a, October 1454.
[161] *Ibid.*
[162] BARS, Box R212, Roll 35, October 1425.

The ale-tasters also brought brewing crimes to the attention of the courts. In 1466, it was reported by the ale-tasters John Flaundrys and Randolph Baudewyn that: 'John Morborne does not want to sell ale by the gallon for one and a half pence and he buys a brewing for four shillings.'[163] For this he was fined 2d. And in 1469, it was reported that: 'John Warner and Robert Cooke, the Sworn Tasters there, present that William (6d.) Pares, John (6d.) Morborne, and John (6d.) Sterlyng were common brewers and broke the Assize by selling ale. Therefore they are amerced. And that Thomas Baylemonde is a common Seller of Ale.'[164] He was not fined.

The role of women

The written evidence for men is greater than that for women as women did not usually feature in the court rolls, although free women holding lands in their own name sometimes attended court and women were often named as brewers. Husbands took precedence over their wives, and the entries relating to men in the Willington rolls out-number the women by ten to one, but there are occasions when the control and influence exercised by women, whatever their status, can be glimpsed.

At marriage a woman, and any property that she owned, became the property of her husband unless a legal settlement had been agreed between the two families. Some husbands put lands which they acquired after marriage into joint names providing more security for their wives and children in the event of their death. The first example in the Willington court rolls of this procedure was in 1415, but the practice became more usual after the growth of copyhold tenure.[165] After being widowed women at all levels of society had greater freedom of choice and more control of their own estates and destiny.

Women's roles as brewers increased as the fifteenth century progressed, but their other involvement in the life of the manor is less visible. Their important home-making roles are not recorded. When married they managed the home, cared for the children and saw that everyone was fed. They, and their children, may have helped in the fields when required.

Life expectancy for women was sometimes longer than for men, and many widows continued to work their late-husband's holding. Those without family support or in poor health surrendered them after short periods of time, but others handled their own affairs for many years, possibly helped by sons or sons-in-law. The table below shows those known to have been granted holdings previously worked by their husbands, 1395–1418, when the population of the manor was at its lowest recorded level and lands not granted to widows may have been difficult to let. No grants of lands to widows appear after 1418.

163 BARS, Box R212, Roll 52b, October 1466.
164 British Library, Add.Ch.26813/7, October 1469.
165 BARS, Box R212, Roll 19, October 1415.

Women holding their late husbands' lands, 1395–1418

Date holding granted	Name	Date of death or surrender	Years held
1395	Joan Avenant	1396	1
1405	Matilda Yarwey	1410	5
1408	Joan Taylour	1423	15
1408	Alice Tele	After 1417	At least 9
1410	Agnes Thaxton	1412	2
1411	Felicia Prentys	1416	5
1414	Agnes Warner	1415	1
1416	Agnes Sterling	1418	2
1417	Joan Rider	Not known	Not known
1417	Joan Yarwey	After 1419	At least 2
1418	Matilda Gaubryel	1419	1

In the second half of the fifteenth century Lady Elizabeth Maryon was named as holding Coppyd Hall. The Maryon family had been tenants on the manor since 1395, and the family was described as holding Coppyd Hall in 1413. Lady Elizabeth played little part in the court process and was excused from attending seven times. On four occasions the jurors complained that she did not clear her ditches and watercourses. In 1465, tenants illegally took over some of her lands:

> It is ordered to everybody that they should provide certain land called Coppyd Hall, and later the quantity Nicholas [2d] Cruce has ploughed there, for the use of Elizabeth Maryon before the next [court] under penalty of 40d. And that the aforesaid Nicholas will put that right at the next cultivation under penalty of 12d. forfeited to the Lady.[166]

The matter is not mentioned in any of the following rolls, so it must be presumed that it was settled without further problems. Isabella Maryon is the last member of the family recorded in Willington and appears in the rolls 1474–75.[167]

Enclosures and the common lands
Enclosures of land are mentioned in the court roll of 1394, and it was usual for the tenants to have small enclosures on their land in which to keep their animals. In 1415 it was ordered that:

> Everyone whatsoever should keep their sheep and calves within their enclosures so that neither their sheep nor calves cause any damage in either the grain or the grass of their neighbours. Under penalties of 12d. paid to the lord and 12d. to the church.[168]

Most of these enclosures were surrounded by hedges and were either in the open fields or round the farm buildings.[169] Some were named: one was Le Mersshende

---

[166] BARS, Box R212, Roll 51b, April 1465. The lady of the manor was still Katherine Neville.
[167] BARS, Box R212, Roll 55a, October 1474; Roll 57a, October 1475.
[168] BARS, Box R212, Roll 18a, Michaelmas 1415.
[169] BARS, Box R212, Roll 5, October 1397; Roll 15, October 1413; Roll 46a, October 1457; Roll 47a

(Marsh End) pen[170] and another, Le Hoo.[171] Sheerhatch Wood was also enclosed and its hedges were repaired in 1426 and 1459.[172]

However, there is evidence that some tenants had attempted to add to their holdings by illegally ploughing strips of common land or lands belonging to their neighbours. Some tenants attempted to close or divert roads, footpaths and lanes across their lands or create illegal enclosures. John Pecke made an enclosure in 1413, and advice was taken about it from the lord's council; the decision was delayed until October 1416 when it was recorded that he had made:

> an enclosure of the lord's common in his wood, called the Hoo, with fences and a ditch and he put one of his granges there from ancient time. Therefore he is amerced. And he is ordered to make open the said enclosure before Easter under a penalty of half a mark [6s. 8d.].[173]

There is no evidence in the rolls that he paid the penalty, so he may have removed the enclosure.

The rules for management of life in the village, known as the custom of the manor, must originally have been handed down by word of mouth, and from before 1400 tenants were ordered to repair their ditches, boundaries and buildings, keep their animals under control and not trespass on land belonging to others. In 1411, shortly before Queen Joan handed Willington back to John Mowbray, a list of penalties for failure to keep animals under control and other offences was written in the court roll. Soon after John Mowbray gained control of his lands in 1413, it became usual for formal orders to be included in the court records. In 1415, five by-laws were passed and relatively heavy penalties were threatened. Interestingly, all five by-laws involve sharing some of the court's income from fines between the lord and the church. Sharing the fines with the church may have been a device to increase penalties without provoking undue resistance from the tenants and was used in Willington on rare occasions when the steward felt that serious misbehavior warranted heavy penalties.

> Orders:

> It was ordered by all the lord's tenants that everyone whatsoever who has any land in the common fields [illegible] is to make one drain on their land before the feast of St. Mark [perhaps 25 April] next in the future, so that the waters do not overflow the said fields but have been put in their watercourses outside the said fields, and that the said fields are not blackened by the aforesaid defective watercourses, under a penalty of 12d. paid and 12d. paid to the church.

> Also it was ordered by the same that everyone whatsoever should keep their sheep and calves within their enclosures so that neither their sheep nor calves

---

July 1459; Roll 51a, October 1464; Roll 51b, April 1465; Roll 52b, October 1466; Roll 53a, April 1467; Roll 56, April 1474.

[170] BARS, Box R212, Roll 2, October 1394; Roll 56, April 1474.
[171] BARS, Box R212, Roll 15, October 1413.
[172] BARS, Box R212, Roll 36, September 1426; Roll 47a, July 1459.
[173] BARS, Box R212, Roll 15, October 1413; Roll 21, October 1416.

cause any damage in either the grain or the grass of their neighbours. Under penalties of 12d. paid to the lord and 12d. to the church.

Also it was ordered by the same that everyone whatsoever who holds any pigs in the township, who puts the said pigs in the keeping of the community keeper of pigs, just as most of the community's pigs are put, if this does not happen, [they] must pay the lord 6d. and 6d. to the church. And anyone who always keeps his pigs in his own custody has paid the salary and stipend of the community keeper of pigs for his neighbours in the township.

Also it was ordered by the same that no-one is to tie any bullocks within the corn of their neighbours also that their foals make no damage. And if it should happen against this order he will pay 12d. to the lord and 12d. to the church.

Also it was ordered by the same that no bullocks are to be depastured or pastured for all the year in those fields in which horses are pastured. And if it should happen [he] will pay to the lord 12d. and 12d. to the church.[174]

After 1415 some customary tenants were fined for overstocking the common fields, and there were complaints about unfair use of these common resources. Further by-laws were passed to prevent pigs being kept unringed, or horses being put into fields with cows. Calves and colts were to be kept in enclosures so that they did not eat the grass of other tenants. Four members of the village elite disobeyed these orders:

Penalty incurred, that is to say 12d. penalty to be raised

Also they present that certain orders were made at the last Court that no head of tithing should permit any bullocks to run at large to destroy the corn of their neighbours. And that they are to be tied by cord and stake from the feast of St Bartholomew [24 August] until the feast of St Michael [29 September] under a penalty of 3d. paid to the lord and 3d. to the church. And now it was found by the aforesaid sworn men that John Yarwey, John Rodland, John Rydere, and John Palmer have made against the aforesaid orders, therefore they merit the aforesaid penalty and were ordered to raise the aforesaid penalty for the use of the lord.[175]

Higher penalties were paid in 1422, when the order that the tenants should not graze their animals in Fulwellfeld was ignored by Robert Myton, John Gaubryel and Walter Yarwey:

Penalty should be incurred 18d. to the lord, 18d. to the church

It was ordained by all the tenants that none shall graze beasts in a certain field called Fulwellefeld and the field sown with barley, nor in the meadows with others for one month after the feast of the Nativity of the Blessed Mary the Virgin [8 September] under a penalty of 6d. paid to the lord and 6d to the church. And now it was reckoned by the lord's tenants that Robert Myton, John Gaubryell [sic] and Walter Yarwey acted against this regulation. Therefore they have incurred the aforesaid penalty, that is to say, for each of them 6d. to the lord and the church equally.[176]

174   BARS, Box R212, Roll 18a, Michaelmas, 1415.
175   BARS, Box R212, Roll 19, October 1415.
176   BARS, Box R212, Roll 31, October 1422.

After 1449 the rolls make it clear that tenants were expected to keep their hedges in good repair.[177] William Couper was fined for breaking hedges and taking twigs from the warren 1457–66. He was the only tenant fined for doing so and it is likely he had fallen on hard times.[178] In October 1466 his holding was: 'almost derelict through the neglect of the aforesaid William, who has not sufficiently repaired it.'[179] John Maryon claimed that the lord had paid for repairs to his hedges in the past, and when they needed repair in 1451 the tenants were ordered to repair them under a penalty of 4d. each.[180] In 1454 the vicar was ordered to enclose the glebe lands: 'between the vicarage and the lord's holding in which John Clerk lives.'[181] This emphasis on the importance of hedges may have continued into the sixteenth century, as it did elsewhere in Bedfordshire, during a period of dramatic rise in population.[182]

The illegal ploughing of strips continued, and there were further attempts to destroy boundaries between fields, restrict entry to common lands and build illegal enclosures. Members of an established family of freemen, the Partrychs, were confident enough to close the common way over their lands in 1455–1456.[183] They encountered great opposition from the manor court.[184]

In 1465, when some tenants entered the lands of Elizabeth Maryon in order to cultivate them she appealed to the court to regain them.[185] In the previous year, a tenant called John Fage had ploughed her land illegally and made a drainage channel on it.[186] Instead of putting it right he was joined by Richard Hatley, and they both ploughed illegally in April 1468 and did not put the fields right for at least twelve months.[187] In October 1469, Richard Hatley also: 'enclosed the common belonging to the lady and her tenants in the field facing Castle Mill and has put one Pea-stack on it.' He was fined 6d. and: 'was ordered to compromise with the tenants of the lady under a penalty of 6s. 8d.'[188]

In 1467, John Warner was fined 2d. because he had: 'enclosed the common way by the township on the north side. Therefore he is amerced. And it is ordered that he should remove the enclosure before 8 days under a penalty of 12d.'[189] In the following year: 'it was ordered to all the tenants who possess hedges and make their Crofts to the north and south that they must remove them before 40 days under a penalty for each of 40d. so that each tenant should have access for their plough, except for Myllefelde which is only a footpath.'[190] There were also an unusually high number of illegal ploughings and a dispute about the use of a lane:

---

177 BARS, Box R212, Roll 38b, May 1449: Roll 41a, October 1452; Roll 42a October 1453; Roll 53b, October 1456.
178 BARS, Box R212, Roll 46a, October 1457; BL2, May 1464; Roll 51a, October 1464; Roll 51b, April 1465; Roll 52b, April 1466.
179 BARS, Box R212, Roll 53b, October 1466.
180 BARS, Box R212, Roll 39b, May 1451.
181 BARS, Box R212, Roll 43a, October 1454.
182 Godber, *History of Bedfordshire*, p.180n.
183 BARS, Box R212, Roll 43a, October 1454; Roll 44a, October 1455; Roll 45a, October 1456.
184 BARS, Box R212, Roll 44a, October 1455; Roll 45a, October 1456.
185 BARS, Box R212, Roll 51b, April 1465.
186 British Library, Add Ch.26813/2, May 1464.
187 British Library, Add Ch.26813/5, August 1468.
188 British Library, Add Ch.26813/7, October 1469.
189 British Library, Add Ch.26813/3, October 1467.
190 British Library, Add Ch.26813/4, May 1468.

The sworn men present that the lane that is the way to the turn next to the ~~pontem~~ M[illegible] of Robert Gostwyke as far as the Tenement of Richard Flowre and so to the wood called Sherehache [sic] is the lord's own land and the common way for the people of the lord King but pasture only for the use of the tenants of the lord and no others without permission, on which the lord will have all their goods confiscated if they do.[191]

Topographical details in the description of this lane suggest that it was a track from the ford in the north, situated west of the moated site now known as the Danish Camp, to Willington crossroads and south to Sheerhatch Wood. The order threatened outsiders with confiscation of their animals if they used it. As a result, outsiders were prevented access to the ford in the river and prevented from causing unwelcome damage to the surfaces of the lanes in Willington.

The court tried to control the use of the common fields and enclosures in 1468 when: 'it was ordered to all the tenants that henceforth none of them is to pasture any animals or cattle in any other individual pasture without agreement.'[192] In 1470: 'it was ordered that henceforth no commoners should make any footpath on Fulwell Headland which remains in the hand of Thomas Tayllour, under a penalty of 6d. for each of them.'[193] And that: 'following the agreement of all the tenants, that henceforth no commoners should pasture animals or their cattle in the pastures of the lady called Fulwell, Myttelmershe, Vyrtnell Furlong, Moutonswell Furlong, nor with their horses, before the feast of Saint Peter in Chains [1 August] under a penalty for each of them of 12d. for as many failings as are found.'[194] William Dyet, the keeper of the common in 1472, accused John Wodehyll of trespassing with his horses and plough beasts on the common, and John Cooke trespassed with his plough into Robert Partryche's fields in the same year.

Single by-laws covering the use of the fields and commons appeared at irregular intervals and became more frequent 1463–68 after the death of Katherine Neville's third husband, John Beaumont, when she held Willington in her own right, and then during and after her marriage to her fourth and last husband, John Woodville.

Although the evidence for enclosures, illegal ploughings and use of the commons suggests ambitions by some tenants to use land more profitably there is no evidence in the rolls of large-scale enclosure of the kind described at Burton Dassett, Warwickshire, in May 1497, where the lord of the manor leased all the closes of the township, and another field, to John Heritage for forty-one years for £21 a year.[195] At Willington, in 1520, when six tenants, Thomas Resse, William Yarwey, John Gostwyk, William Rolyt, John Myton and William Gostwyke made enclosures lying outside their tenements, 'on the north side' without the agreement of the other tenants, they were ordered to remove them under penalties of 3s. 4d. each.[196]

---

[191] This by-law is unique in the court rolls. It seems to say that any non-villagers who allowed their animals to graze on the verges of the village lanes would have had their goods and animals confiscated. Thus, the use of the ford across the Ouse and other passage of animals from outside the vill is effectively forbidden.

[192] British Library, Add Ch.26813/5, August 1468.

[193] British Library, Add Ch.26813/8, May 1470.

[194] Ibid.

[195] Dyer, Country Merchant, p. 34.

[196] BARS, Box R212, Roll 20, March 1520.

Engrossment

Engrossment began in Willington as early as 1382. Most tenants held single holdings, but there is evidence that some tenants held more than one. The bailiffs'
accounts 1382–97 record thirty-four holdings of half a virgate, formerly held in
bondage, but only twenty-eight of them with a messuage.[197]

In the early fifteenth century, evidence is provided by death records and records
of new incumbents of holdings. Between October 1395 and April 1421 eleven
tenants with more than one holding are recorded. Of them, Simon, Thomas and John
Tele each held two messuages and two half virgates from April 1409 and another
member of the same family, Robert Tele, described as the smith, surrendered two
cottages in October 1413.[198] The largest land holding was recorded on the death
of Henry Yarwey in 1423 when his wife, Joan, was granted his holdings. They
consisted of two messuages and two virgates, plus another messuage and virgate
with a toft, and a further half virgate.[199]

There is no clear evidence of an increase in engrossment in Willington in the
second half of the fifteenth century. Only eight tenants are listed with more than
one holding May 1451-May 1482.[200] They included William Launcelyn, who held
three holdings for short periods for no rent while he repaired the buildings;[201] and
Nicholas Cruce, John Norman, William Lorymer, John Church, Richard Myton,
John Yarwey and John Fraunceys and his wife Agnes.

Evidence of engrossment in the early sixteenth century is unreliable because so
few documents survive, but a damaged document of March 1522 seems to show
that Robert Cooper (or Cowper) was granted a large amount of land: a cottage; two
tofts with eighteen and a half acres of land and six roods of meadow with each one;
some lands in Bedford; a messuage; and another toft. But the tenants seem to still
be resisting large-scale engrossment and at that court they agreed: 'that no tenant
of the demesne lands should hold any further lands … [torn edge] … acres of land
in the Fallow Field on the fields of the common, under a penalty for each offence
of 20s.'[202]

Standards of living and leisure

All the buildings referred to in the documents 1382–1522 were built of wood, with
the possible exception of parts of the mill. A description of the medieval manorial
site in 1376 makes no mention of stone as a building material even in the foundations of: 'the third gate with a watch-tower at the entry to the motte and a drawbridge [which] is much ruined as regards timber, walls and roof.'[203] Most roofs were
of thatch, though occasionally there are references to the use of tile, but it is not
clear whether these were of stone or clay.

[197] BARS, R8/68/2/1–11, and Thompson, *Bailiffs' Accounts for Willington*, BARS, CRT 130 Willington
11, pp. 1, 4, 7, 11, 15, 20, 24, 28, 32, 38, 42.
[198] BARS, Box R212, Roll 15, October 1413.
[199] BARS, Box R212, Roll 23, October 1423.
[200] BARS, Box R212, Roll 39b, May 1451; Roll 40b, May 1452; Roll 41a, October 1452; Roll 46a,
October 1457; Roll 46b, July 1458; Roll 47, October 1458.
[201] BARS, Box R212, Roll 39b, May 1451; Roll 40b, May 1452; Roll 41a, October 1452.
[202] BARS, Box R212, Roll 63, March 1522.
[203] Bailey, *The English Manor*, p. 59.

The manor house would have been the largest domestic building on the manor, probably housing the manor court and acting as the centre of administration for a small group of manors. The names of some other larger houses and holdings first appear in 1394 when there is a reference to le Gostewykes.[204] In a later roll this was said to be at Coupulende.[205] Coppyd Hall was first mentioned in 1413 and was the home of the Maryon family.[206] John Roper's house, Pyke End, is mentioned in July and October 1458 and in July 1459.[207]

Evidence of different types of houses belonging to Willington's villein tenants, which included halls, halls with upper rooms called solars, and insethouses, is found in lists of domestic and agricultural buildings needing repair. Most hall-houses were of a single storey, approximately fifteen feet wide and three times as long and were divided into three spaces by screens, with the hall in the centre.[208] The hall, in which family and servants lived and slept, had a fire in the middle of the floor which filled the air with smoke before it found its way out through a hole in the roof. There were usually service rooms at one end of the building and family rooms at the other. A small number of halls in Willington are described as having solars or upper rooms, so having two floors; these would have belonged to more prosperous tenants.

In the years before 1426 the description 'hall' only appears twice in the documents; as Coppyd Hall, the home of the free Maryon family and when John Smith, a labourer, is said to have: 'a hall with defective foundation-beams and thatch.'[209] After the gap in the rolls 1426–48, William Launcelyn was said to hold the hall yard in 1449, but the context suggests that this was the medieval manor house; more halls held by villein tenants begin to appear in lists of ruined buildings from 1452.[210]

In May 1472 five halls were listed as needing repair, but the court roll implies that timber for repairs would not be provided: 'Therefore it was ordered that all the above tenants should make repairs to their aforesaid buildings before the next, under a penalty for each of 40d forfeited to the Lady.'[211] Engrossment may have been taking place, but it is possible that a group of tenants decided in May 1472 to resist demands by Katherine Neville's steward that they repair their buildings at their own expense. In 1522 twelve halls needed repair, and by then a greater number of buildings may have been neglected because of enclosure and engrossment, possibly leading to some reduction in population.

It has been suggested that insethouses were simple, single-storey buildings. There are very few details about the insethouses at Willington in the rolls, and the term insethouse only appears in conjunction with other farm buildings on five occasions: one room and an insethouse, and an insethouse and a grange, May 1416; one

[204] BARS, Box R212, Roll 2, October 1394.
[205] BARS, Box R212, Roll 9, October 1407. Cople End was probably adjacent to the church which stands very near to the parish boundary with Cople.
[206] BARS, Box R212, Roll 15, October 1413.
[207] BARS, Box R212, Roll 46b, July 1458; Roll 47, October 1458; 47a, July 1459.
[208] Christopher Dyer, 'English Peasant Buildings in the later Middle Ages', *Medieval Archaeology*, vol. 30 (1986), p. 24. These dimensions are given for buildings in the West Midlands, but elsewhere they may have been up to seventeen feet.
[209] BARS, Box R212, Roll 35, October 1425.
[210] BARS, Box R212, Roll 41a, October 1452.
[211] BARS, Box R212, Roll 54b, May 1472.

insethouse and a malt-kiln, September 1417; an insethouse and a room annexed to the same in October 1418; and a barn and insethouse in May 1452.[212]

There is evidence that before the mid-fourteenth century peasant buildings were single storey, and it is possible that this earlier type of building persisted in Willington until the middle of the fifteenth century and was called an inset-house.[213] At least two tenants extended their buildings by either adding a solar as an upper floor or adding another room at ground floor level.[214] Nineteen tenants in Willington were listed as holding insethouses which needed repair 1415–23,[215] but this type of building fell out of use later in the fifteenth century and was only later mentioned in May and October 1452, April and October 1456, October 1462 and May 1463.[216]

Unusually long lists of all sorts of defective buildings survive at intervals between 1418 and 1515. In October 1418 the list contained five granges, seven insethouses, two solars, one room, two messuages, two shippons, one malt-kiln, one cart house, one hay house and one cow barn.[217] No halls were included. Thomas Bekyngham ordered them to be repaired, and a detailed list of the timber to be supplied was written down.

The most detailed list of buildings in Willington was written in 1515, when the manor was held by Thomas Howard, Duke of Norfolk.[218] It is not a complete list as the buildings of the men with the largest land-holdings there at that time, John and William Gostwyk and the prior of Newnham, are not mentioned. The buildings of other freemen may also not have been included. The list included twelve bake-houses, sixteen barns, sixteen halls, two kitchens, one hay-house, one holding, one malt-house, six stables and one house. Not all were ruinous, some only required carpentry work, or repairs to the roofs. Significant changes had taken place in the manor for only five families seem to have survived in Willington from the fifteenth century; the Gostwykes, the Fischeres, the Riders, the Tayllours and the Yarweys. The large numbers of substantial buildings needing repair may indicate that the state of the manor had been neglected by the Duke of Norfolk. There is no mention of an insethouse in 1515, suggesting that standards of living had improved so that this type of rural living accommodation was no longer being used.

Protein foods formed a large part of the diet of wealthy tenants and visitors to the manor, as can be seen in the list of food provided for the steward and his party when they visited for the courts in April and September 1426:

[212] BARS, Box R212, Roll 20, May 1416; Roll 22, May 1417; Roll 25, October 1418; Roll 40b, July 1458.
[213] Mark Gardiner, 'Vernacular Buildings and the Development of the Later Medieval Domestic Plan in England', *Medieval Archaeology*, vol. 44 (2000), p. 162.
[214] BARS, Box R212, Roll 23, October 1417; Roll 25, October 1418.
[215] Robert Akyrman, John Bande, Richard Baudewene, William Day, Robert Fesound, John Gaubryel, John Goffe, Richard Lyghtfot, John Myton, John Rudland, John Rydere, Thomas Smith, Thomas Star-lyng, William Taylor, John Tele, Thomas Thresshere, John Wodeward, William Wryght and John Yarwey. BARS, Box R212, Roll 18a, Michaelmas 1415; Roll 19, October 1415; Roll 20, May 1416; Roll 22, May 1417; Roll 23, October 1417; Roll 24, April 1418; Roll 25, October 1418; Roll 31, October 1422; Roll 33, October 1423.
[216] BARS, Box R212, Rolls 40b, May 1452; Roll 41a, October 1452; Roll 44b, April 1456; Roll 45a, October 1456; Roll 50c, October 1462; Roll 50d, May 1463.
[217] BARS, Box R212, Roll 25, October 1418.
[218] BARS, Box R212, Roll 61, September 1515.

In bread 5d., ale 10d., in beef meat 5½d., in calf and piglet 12d., for 4 pullets 4d., 1 capon 3d., in pepper and saffron 1d., in supplies for the same 3d., and in parchment for the rolls and ink for writing 6d. Total 4s. 1½d.[219]

In bread 6d., beer 15d., various salt fish 4d., in fresh fish 11d., eels 3d., in flesh of castrated beef 14d., also 2 capons 8d., 1 goose 4d., 1 chicken 1d., in pepper and saffron 1d., 2 bushels of oats 6d. Total 6s. 4d.[220]

That larger numbers of visitors usually came to the courts in the autumn is suggested by the meal in September being more expensive. Presumably the oats were for the horses.

Details of the variety of protein foods consumed by the medieval lords and tenants of Willington can also be inferred from pieces of bone found during twentieth century excavations at the moated site in the east of the manor, thought to be the site of a manor house dating from the twelfth and thirteenth centuries. The bones were identified as being from cattle, sheep or goat, pig, goose, chicken, rabbit, deer and fish.[221] 'The animal bones indicate an economy typical of many southern English sites, with cattle, sheep and pig forming the bulk of the diet.'[222] There was a relatively high percentage of bird bones: 'which has parallels with other medieval sites such as Porchester Castle in Hampshire.'[223]

At Willington the percentages of bones from rabbits were unusually high; those from cattle and game and poultry were also high but those from sheep and horses were low when compared with other sites. While the variety and quantity of protein foods has been identified there is no evidence to show how frequently they formed part of the peasant diet. Later field name evidence shows that Willington warren was adjacent to the fisheries of the manor. The warrener may have lived there and enjoyed a varied diet, but the everyday diets of poorer tenants may have been very different.

For most country people of the time, the commonplace diet consisted of mutton, bread and ale, although a great variety of other food was available. Peas, beans, wheat, barley and oats were grown in the common fields at Willington as animal fodder and could be used to make pottage for the family when times were hard. Cottage gardens and orchards would provide fruit and vegetables and there was always poaching, a pursuit which also added variety and nutrition to the pot. In 1395: 'Richard [6d.] Starlyng killed one hare from within the lord's Warren without permission, therefore he is amerced. And that Simon [6d.] Tele killed 2 hares from within the Warren and that Nicholas [4d.] Wattes similarly one hare.'[224] A by-law, passed in April 1411, made some attempt to curtail such activities and seems to have been generally observed. It was ordered that: 'no tenant [should] at any time [have] hounds within the demesne of the lady under a penalty of half a mark, [6s. 8d.] neither any dogs to go down the lady's Warren under a penalty of half a

[219] BARS, Box R212, Roll 36a, April 1426.
[220] BARS, Box R212, Roll 36, September 1426.
[221] J. Hassall, 'Excavations in Willington, 1973', *Bedfordshire Archaeological Journal,* vol. 10 (1975), p.39, and G. Edmondson and A. Mudd, 'Medieval Occupation at Danish Camp Willington', *Bedfordshire Archaeology*, vol. 25 (2004), p. 220.
[222] Hassall, 'Excavations in Willington', p. 39.
[223] *Ibid.*
[224] BARS, Box R212, Roll 3, October 1395.

mark, [6s. 8d.].'[225] In 1451, John Couper took wild geese from the warren without permission and was fined 2d., but more serious poaching at Willington was done by outsiders.[226] The vicar of Aylesbury hunted in the warren and took at least twenty pairs of rabbits in 1423,[227] and the abbot of Warden was accused of fishing in the lord's waters in 1468.[228] In 1470, he and his servants drove a cart and horses on the meadow called the Burymede several times. They: 'trampled down and consumed the grass growing there making a heavy loss to the lady's tenants and they were ordered not to do it any more, under a penalty of 6s. 8d.'[229] In 1461: 'John Morborne the sworn Warrener there presents that John Fitz Geffrey esquire of Thirlye[230] in the county of Bedford, [had] this day at Court, for fishing within the head of water of the lady in the Wall[?] of the church's byn on the land of the mill and from there he took 2 small pikes without permission. Therefore a brief was presented against him.'[231]

The rolls provide little evidence of other leisure time activities. Spare time would have been in short supply during the summer, but on feast days and over the twelve days of Christmas there must have been some time to relax. It has been said that in medieval times men were expected to keep fit by practicing archery, but the only reference to archery in the Willington records was in 1408 when John Carter owed John Russell 2d. for an arrow and a belt.[232]

There is much more evidence of the brewing and drinking of ale and some evidence that it was sold, but brewing at the time of the church service was not tolerated. In 1450: 'John Stoughton and John John [sic] Redy brewed ale at service times at the church of Wylyton against the orders made therefrom. Therefore each of them has incurred the penalty of 40d. to the lord and to the church of Wylyton, divided equally.'[233]

Nor was there any tolerance for activities of a more amorous nature. In 1451, Emma Skynner, a new brewer, arrived with her husband or son John. He was involved in fights and she was accused of running a brothel. They were both immediately ordered off the manor: 'Also they present that Emma Skynner held a common brothel. Therefore the bailiff was ordered to put her outside the demesne.'[234]

Younger men may have played quoits or tennis although these games were forbidden. In October 1397 it was ordered that: 'no-one shall play the game called quoyte in the future, under a penalty of 12d.'[235] Seventy years later, in 1467, it was ordered that: 'henceforth none shall play at tennis at anytime of the year if they are more than 12 years old and that no-one shall play tennis at Christmas, under a penalty for each offence of 40d. and a punishment of imprisonment for one day and

[225] BARS, Box R212, Roll 13, April 1411.
[226] BARS, Box R212, Roll 39b, May 1451.
[227] BARS, Box R212, Roll 34, September 1423.
[228] British Library, Add.Ch.26813/4, May 1468.
[229] British Library, Add.Ch.26813/8, May 1470.
[230] Thurleigh.
[231] BARS, Box R212, Roll 49a, October 1461.
[232] BARS, Box R212, Roll 10, October 1408.
[233] BARS, Box R212, Roll 39a, October 1450.
[234] BARS, Box R212, Roll 40a, October 1451.
[235] BARS, Box R212, Roll 5, October 1397.

a night.'[236] In 1473 the second jury reported that: 'the tithing men and Constables presented well and faithfully and furthermore they said that Robert (4d.) Wareyn' [and] Thomas (4d.) Mores, servants of Nicholas (4d.) Cruce played tennis against the statute.'[237] The servants and their master were all fined. It is easy to imagine that timber-framed houses could be easily damaged by flying horseshoes and tennis balls, but the rolls do not contain any evidence of people being imprisoned.

Despite the simple peasant diet described above, the life-expectancy of men in Willington may have been greater than that of their lords, the Mowbrays. Many tenants lived to middle age and longer. It was usual for the elder son to be named after his father and there were many years when two generations of the same family, with the same names, served together on court juries: John Bande the elder and younger 1412–25; Walter Wryght the elder and younger 1416–25; John Yarwey the elder and younger served together or separately 1452–74; and three generations of men with this name served together or separately 1475–78. If the three men with the name John Yarwey represented three generations they would have been at least sixty, forty and twenty years old in 1475. There may have been other examples of fathers and sons with different first names serving together, but they cannot be identified. Someone named Walter Yarwey served as a juror for thirty-four years; the name could have represented two generations, or Walter could have lived into his late fifties.

The evidence for the lives of the tenants in Willington 1382–1522 is incomplete; some records have been lost and free tenants and gentry rarely appear in the court rolls. Nevertheless the manor can be seen to fit comfortably into the extensive Mowbray estates, with a settled pattern of mixed agriculture and good communication links with London and the rest of the country.

Supervision by the stewards appointed by the lords of the manor, the co-operation of the local bailiff and a community which was regulated by the custom of the manor and a system of tithings, was the basis of the tenants' life, but, in addition, the regular appointment of two juries of twelve men at the 'views' held in the autumn ensured that most households were represented in the court process. As a result there was little real violence, and no physical punishment was recorded in the court rolls.

Change took place slowly, and for much of the time Willington was under the stabilising influence of Katherine Neville and her husbands, resulting in a flexible pattern of control and co-operation in which the Mowbray stewards and surveyors, the manor bailiff and his cohort, and the local tenants all took part.

---

[236] British Library, Add.Ch.26813/3, October 1467. This is the only record of imprisonment in the Willington records 1382–1522.
[237] BARS, Box R212, Roll 54c, October 1473.

Chapter Five

The Mowbrays and their Management Networks

Willington manor was held by the Mowbrays from 1265 and managed through a council of close associates who in turn delegated responsibilities to a network, or affinity, of friends, blood relatives and in-laws who were to differing extents dependent on them for status, contacts, influence and income. It has not been possible to reconstruct the membership of these networks or affinities, partly because so many documents have not survived but also because of problems caused by the irregular spellings and abbreviations of names of people and places.

Further difficulties are caused by the occasional use of locative or occupational aliases as well as, or instead of, family names. The same man might appear under different names in the records. John Kempston and John Wodeward(e) were referred to ten times in Willington manor court rolls October 1418-September 1426.[1] In three of the rolls the phrases, 'John Kempston the wodeward', 'John Kempston wodewarde of Shirehatch' and 'John Wodewarde keeper of Shirehatch' were used, suggesting that Kempston was the family name and that wodewarde was an occupational alias.[2]

The surviving records show very clearly that the five men and one woman who were part of the Mowbray affinity, and who had the most influence over Willington manor in the late fourteenth and fifteenth centuries, were: Thomas Mowbray, first Duke of Norfolk, from 1383 until he was exiled to Venice in 1398; his brother John Mowbray (the fifth), who became second Duke of Norfolk, from 1413 to his death in 1432; John's head steward, Thomas Bekyngham, October 1417 to at least 1424; Katherine Neville, wife of John Mowbray and then dowager Duchess of Norfolk for fifty years, widowed 1432 and died c.1482; Katherine Neville's third husband, John Beaumont 1448–58; and Thomas Rokes, steward, 1457–74.

In the century after the Peasants' Revolt, Willington was not only part of the huge Mowbray estate but also part of smaller groupings of properties formed for convenience as the Mowbray's council divided up the lands according to the availability of receivers, stewards, accountants and auditors. Willington bailiffs, often members of the local Rider and Gostwyk families, formed the link between members of the council and the tenants. Other important, influential members of local families included Roger Hunte of Roxton, Robert de Wyllyton and William Launcelyn of Cople.

The loyalty of Mowbray council members or other officials was rewarded by benefits which included enhanced status from contact with their lord or lady and other members of their cohort, by gifts of land or money, or by opportunities to find

---

[1]   BARS, Box R212, Roll 25, October 1418; Roll 36, September 1426.
[2]   BARS, Box R212, Roll 27, October 1419; Roll 30, April 1421; Roll 33, October 1423.

suitable husbands or wives for their children. Punishments for being incompetent or disloyal could be dire; bands of the lord's men might attack a rebel's buildings or members of his household including his family. On three occasions it was reported that John de Mowbray's men broke into Willington manor while it was held by his mother's second husband. In 1329 they drove away animals worth £300 and took other goods; in 1332 they carried off crops; and later in 1332 they took horses and other animals worth 500 marks (just over £330) as well as: 'some writs of the king and trampled them underfoot.' There were further family arguments in the 1360s.[3]

The Mowbrays have been described as one of England's great medieval families.[4] At least three members of the family were with William the Conqueror at the Battle of Hastings in 1066. A William Mowbray was one of the barons charged with arranging the implementation of Magna Carta in the early thirteenth century, and in 1295 a Roger Mowbray was summoned to the Model Parliament of Edward I. By the fourteenth century they belonged to an elite group of magnates, earls and dukes, fifteen or twenty strong, who were distinguished from other peers and gentry by their landed wealth.[5] Despite their great estates and advantageous marriages they suffered a series of reverses at the end of the fourteenth century when they were lords of the manor of Willington and the Willington bailiffs' accounts and the earliest surviving manor court rolls were being written. Their ambitions may then have been greater than their means.[6]

During the period 1286–1476 the elder sons of the Mowbray family were usually named John and died young; during the fourteenth century only one heir was of age at the time of his father's death. Although the Mowbrays demonstrated fairly consistent service to the Crown, and were rewarded by royal favour, periods of political miscalculation led to the execution of the first John de Mowbray in 1322, to Thomas Mowbray being exiled for life in 1398 and his elder son, also called Thomas, being beheaded in 1405.

The fourth John de Mowbray was named as the lord of Willington in the bailiff's account 1382–83, but he died unmarried in 1383, aged 22, and was succeeded by his younger brother Thomas. It appears that Thomas was an able man, and that at first he was a favourite of Richard II. He became Earl Marshal of England in 1385 and was then created first Duke of Norfolk in September 1397, although he was disgraced and banished to Venice in October 1398, just over a year later.[7] He died there of plague in 1399 and the family's lands and titles were confiscated, but the Willington bailiffs' accounts and the earliest manor court rolls give no hint of his tumultuous life 1382–99. His son and heir, another Thomas Mowbray, still a minor at the time of his father's death, was later involved in a rebellion against the Crown and was executed at York in 1405 shortly before his twentieth birthday.[8]

---

3   VCH, vol. 3, p. 263.
4   Roberts, *Mowbray Legacy*, pp. 65–123.
5   G. A Holmes, *The Estates of the Higher Nobility in Fourteenth Century England* (Cambridge, 1957), p. 39.
6   R. E Archer, *The Mowbrays, Earls of Nottingham and Dukes of Norfolk, to 1432* (unpublished PhD thesis, 1984), University of Oxford.
7   The Earl Marshal was head of the armed forces.
8   The Mowbray family has been described as: 'A shady bunch, the first duke and his elder son dabbling in treason, the third and fourth dukes ruthlessly hiring gangs of hired bullies to intimidate their neighbours and ride rough-shod over their property rights. Only the second duke's reputation is fairly

After the disgrace and death of Thomas Mowbray, Willington may have passed into the hands of Sir Thomas de Rempston, but although two rolls survive dated October 1403 and October 1404 his name does not appear in the headings.[9] The heading of the next view with court, 26 October 1406, describes Queen Joan, second wife of Henry IV, as: 'keeper of all the lands and tenements in common lately belonging to Thomas Mowbray. Rendered into the hands of the lady being Queen during the minority of John Mowbray.'[10]

Willington custodians 1380–1483[11]

Custodian	Date of lordship	Relationship with the Mowbrays	Crown influence
John Mowbray, Earl of Nottingham	c.1380–1383		Royal ward while a minor. Created Earl at the coronation of Richard II, 1377.
Thomas Mowbray, Earl of Nottingham. Later Earl Marshall and Duke of Norfolk. Exiled 1398.	1383–1399	Inherited	Granted estates while still a minor. His betrothed wife, Elizabeth Lestrange died and his estates went back to the Crown. He married in 1384, but did not gain control of all his estates until 1389.
King Richard II	1398–1399	None	Estates seized by the Crown on Mowbray's disgrace.
Sir Thomas de Rempston	1399–1406?	Not known	The Mowbray heir was a minor and a ward in the Queen's household.
Queen Joan	1406–1412/13	None	Second wife of Henry IV.
John Mowbray. Later second Duke of Norfolk	1412/13–1432	Inherited. Lands restored on his majority.	
Katherine Neville, Dowager Duchess of Norfolk with her three husbands - Thomas Strangeways, John Beaumont, first Viscount Beaumont, and Sir John Woodville	1432–c.1483	John Mowbray's widow. Willington was part of her dower lands.	

---

clear, largely because he spent much of his life in France.' L. E. Moye, *The Estates and Finances of the Mowbray Family, Earls Marshall and Dukes of Norfolk, 1401–1476* (unpublished PhD thesis, 1985), Duke University, p. 2.

[9]   BARS, Box R212, Roll 6, October 1403; Roll 7, October 1404. The link between Sir Thomas de Rempston (or Kempston) and Willington is stated in VCH, vol. 3, p. 263.

[10]   BARS, Box R212, Roll 8, October 1406.

[11]   The information in this table has been collected from several sources, including from R. E. Archer, 'Rich Old Ladies and the Problem of Late Medieval Dowagers' in A. J. Pollard, ed., *Property and Politics: Essays in Later Medieval History* (Gloucester, 1984), pp. 15–35.

John Mowbray (the fifth), later the second Duke of Norfolk, reclaimed the Mowbray lands and titles 1412/13, about the time that he married the twelve year old Katherine Neville and after the death of Henry IV and the accession of Henry V. His name and titles first appear in the heading of the Willington court rolls in 1413.[12] The exact date of his birth is unclear, but it is usually given as 1392; the title Duke of Norfolk was restored to him in 1425.

After John Mowbray's death in 1432 Katherine Neville and her later husbands controlled about a third of the Mowbray estates. John Mowbray (the sixth), 1415–61, later third Duke of Norfolk, Earl of Norfolk, Earl of Nottingham and Earl Marshall, did not became lord of the manor of Willington. He had a long military career and supported the Yorkists in the Wars of the Roses, dying in the battle of Towton.[13] Although a Yorkist, he had close family links with the Lancastrians through his brother-in-law Lord Buckingham and step-father John Beaumont.

After the third Duke's death in 1461, the fourth Duke of Norfolk was encumbered with an additional dower for Eleanor Bouchier, who died in 1474.[14] Katherine and Eleanor between them held about two-thirds of the inheritance and he was said to have: 'spent most of his short life making property arrangements and attempting to deal with steadily worsening financial difficulties.'[15]

When the fourth Duke of Norfolk died suddenly at Framlingham Castle in 1476, aged thirty-one, the dukedom of Norfolk, and the earldoms he held became extinct.[16] There was no male heir and the Mowbray estates, apart from those held by the two dowager duchesses, found their way into the Crown's hands in 1478, when the little Mowbray heiress, Anne, Countess of Norfolk aged five or six, married Prince Richard, Duke of York. He became one of the ill-fated Princes in the Tower, and after Anne's early death in 1481 her estates went to her co-heirs, Lord William Berkeley and Lord John Howard.[17]

Central administration and the council

It was usual for the councils of noble families to be made up of prominent neighbouring magnates; lawyers; a judge or a king's official; estate and household officials, including the chief or head steward; the receiver general; and the head of household. There would also be an inner group of the most trusted officials and associates. The council was given: 'broad authority over the administration of the estate and a wide range of activities in other areas.'[18] A much larger network of associates was called upon when needed, but these associates may not necessarily have been members of the council.

The council is mentioned sixteen times in the manor court rolls 1394–1425, but evidence of decisions being taken is often missing. In 1407 an entry reads:

[12]   'View of Frankpledge with Court of John Mowbray, Earl of Nottingham and Marshall of England, held there on Wednesday next after the feast of St Michael the Archangel [29 September] in the first year of the reign of Henry the fifth after the conquest [4 October 1413]', BARS, Box R212, Roll 15, October 1413.
[13]   Roberts, *Mowbray Legacy*, pp. 100–7.
[14]   Roberts, *Mowbray Legacy,* p.109.
[15]   Moye, *The Estates and Finances of the Mowbray Family*, p. 26.
[16]   Roberts, *Mowbray Legacy*, pp. 109–13.
[17]   Roberts, *Mowbray Legacy*, pp. 113–16.
[18]   Moye, *The Estates and Finances of the Mowbray Family*, p. 62.

And that the lady is to have a common way in the hoodych from the feast of the Apostle Saint Peter in Chains [1 August] until the feast of the purification of the Blessed Mary [2 February] which certain way and common have been blocked and obstructed by Richard Pecke. Therefore he should consult [illegible] with the lady's council.[19]

A note was added in the margin of the roll, in darker ink, saying, 'Council in consultation with the lady Queen', but there is no reference to a decision in the following rolls. Richard Pecke, who had obstructed the common way, does not appear again in the records. However, in 1413, there is a note regarding another member of the Pecke family, John Pecke, in relation to the lord's council:

Consulting note well – [written in darker ink and a different hand]

Also they present that John Pecke has one enclosure called le hoo in which the Lord of this lordship should have common pasture for his livestock from the feast of St. Peter in Chains [1 August] until the Feast of the Purification of the Blessed Mary the Virgin [2 February] that the said John enclosed with hedges and ditches so that the lord cannot have the aforesaid common at a great loss to the lord. Therefore advice would be taken from the lord's council.[20]

Again there is no evidence in the records of any decision being taken; John Pecke went on to trespass in the woods and put a barn in his enclosure in later years.

In May 1417 the council ordered the bailiff to deal with the issue of a large poplar that had been cut down by the tenants without permission and sold, instead of being used to repair buildings. The bailiff was required: 'to sell it and be responsible to the lord for the true value.'[21] Later, in 1425, the council was involved in negotiations about whether or not three tenants were entitled to have dovecotes on their lands and: 'the said dovecots were placed in respite [i.e. confiscated] until Roger Hunte [the steward] shall have spoken with the lord's council.'[22] The following two rolls, for April and September 1426, still exist, but the dovecotes are not mentioned and no evidence of the decisions made about them by the council has survived.

In the period 1382–97 there were three head or chief stewards, three receiver generals and three men who were receivers of Bedfordshire or Mowbray lands elsewhere, suggesting a large and diverse pool of available members of the Mowbray affinity. The frequent changes suggest a flexible, pragmatic approach, but the posts may have been demanding and candidates may soon have proved unsuitable.[23] Many of the men would have been members of the Mowbray councils before 1400. The names of fewer administrators from the fifteenth century have been found because fewer accounts have survived.

19 BARS, Box R212, Roll 9, October 1407.
20 BARS, Box R212, Roll 15, October 1413.
21 BARS, Box R212, Roll 22, May 1417.
22 BARS, Box R212, Roll 35, October 1425
23 Lucy Moye argued that the Mowbray administration lacked the stability of its counterparts on other noble estates such as those of the Staffords and the Duchy of Lancaster with whom they had family ties. She considered that its approach was pragmatic rather than structural and that its distinguishing features were its flexibility both in personnel and function. She observed that: 'continuity over the century was confined to the lowest and highest levels of the administration.' Moye, *The Estates and Finances of the Mowbray Family*, p. 62, pp. 52–3.

When the Mowbray estates were returned to John Mowbray, in 1413, he retained the services of John Boteler who had been Queen Joan's steward for Willington, although he later demoted him. John Lancaster of Bressingham, Norfolk, who may have been chief steward after 1397, remained as a senior member of John Mowbray's council, and he, with the Mowbray's chamberlain Richard Stereacre and auditor Nicholas Blaxhale, acted for the second Duke of Norfolk when he was in France 1414–15, 1420–21 and 1422–23.[24] These men stayed in England to handle the Duke's affairs, authorise expenditure and deal with legal matters, communicating by sending frequent letters and using messengers. From the spring of 1420 John Mowbray's young son lived with John Lancaster while both his parents were in France.[25]

John Lewys was receiver general to the Mowbrays 1401–5 although he was not thought to have been a member of the council;[26] from 1412–26/27 the post was held by Robert Southwell, a prominent and much trusted councillor.[27] Five accounts kept by the Mowbrays' receiver generals have survived 1401–23, only two of them are complete.[28]

A single receiver's account for Willington forms part of the accounts 1421–22.[29] It shows a difficult period in the history of Willington manor, after which there were large numbers of vacant holdings and a long list of buildings needing repair. Arrears from the bailiff of £30 had been paid to William Gillow, bailiff of the manor of Fennystanton, and receipt was acknowledged by his seal. William Gillow does not appear in any of the manor court rolls, and it must be assumed that for some reason he had been given responsibility that year for collecting payments from the manor.

Later, the second Duke's receiver general was Richard Walys. After the Duke died in 1432, Richard continued to work for Katherine Neville in the same role. How long he worked for her, and whether he performed the same role for her son, John Mowbray the sixth, later the third Duke, is not clear. This John Mowbray was still a minor, about seventeen, at the time of his father's death. He later distinguished himself as warden of the Scottish borders and captain of Berwick in 1437, when aged twenty-two, and in 1443 he was instrumental in putting down riots in Norwich, after which the title of Duke of Norfolk was restored him in 1445.[30]

The third Duke then made the mistake of appointing, as his receiver general, a man with a reputation as a trouble-maker, Sir Robert Wingfield.[31] The receiver general had personal responsibility for the collection of revenue throughout the Mowbray estates and might be expected to be stable, professional, devoted to the

---

24   John Lancaster is not mentioned in the Willington bailiffs' accounts or the manor court rolls, but he is mentioned once in the Mowbray's receiver's account of 1421–22, which refers to the receiver receiving money from Newnham, 'outside John Lancaster's house' but does not indicate where that was.

25   Moye, *The Estates and Finances of the Mowbray Family*, pp. 55, 57, 58, 61, 399.

26   Moye, *The Estates and Finances of the Mowbray Family*, p. 69.

27   Moye, *The Estates and Finances of the Mowbray Family*, p. 80.

28   Moye, *The Estates and Finances of the Mowbray Family*, p. 29.

29   Arundel Castle Archives, A1642. The figures pencilled in by the auditors do not match those in the document exactly. Their notes in the margin indicate that receipts of £123 4s. 1 ¾ d. had been proved, slightly more than the total written in the accounts, which was £122 19s. 8½d.

30   Roberts, *Mowbray Legacy*, p.100.

31   Moye, *The Estates and Finances of the Mowbray Family*, p. 80.

lord and his interests and unquestioningly loyal.[32] Unfortunately Robert Wingfield appears to have been none of these things. No accounts survive 1446–47 and they may never have been prepared. Violent disagreements between the Duke and Wingfield led to both men spending time in prison and the Duke being ordered to pay Wingfield 3,500 marks (more than £2,300) in compensation for damage caused to the latter's house and park.[33] After 1448 the post of receiver general disappeared, and the third and fourth Dukes of Norfolk no longer allowed one man to control their financial affairs. Responsibility was shared between different individuals.[34]

The details in the Willington bailiffs' and receivers' accounts and manor court rolls 1432–83 relate only to that part of the Mowbray estates which were the dower of Katherine Neville; the links between the councils of her son and grandson and her, and her later husbands are unclear.

Katherine Neville's dower and its management

Katherine Neville was a member of the extended royal house of Lancaster, being the eldest daughter of Ralph Neville, Earl of Westmorland, and a Lancastrian. She was a legitimised grand-daughter of John O'Gaunt, and her mother was half-sister to Henry IV. The north-country Neville family produced several powerful men and women in the fifteenth century. These included Katherine and her two sisters, who all outlived their first husbands by long periods.

Ralph Neville paid 3,000 marks (about £2,000) to Henry IV for the wardship and marriage of young John Mowbray (the fifth) to Katherine and also promised John Mowbray 750 marks (£500).[35] The couple were married in 1412, and Katherine lived much of her life in Epworth, on the Isle of Axholme, near Scunthorpe. There is no evidence that her father ever paid the full dowry to John Mowbray, and when he asked for the final instalment of 700 marks (about £470) in 1415 to help fund the costs of his preparations for the wars in France his father-in-law gave him just £40.[36] John borrowed the extra £1,000 that he needed from an uncle.[37]

In preparation for the period when he would be away John Mowbray appointed Thomas Bekyngham as steward and demoted John Boteler to under-steward. Although the court rolls show that Bekyngham was determined to keep the buildings on the manor in good repair, by 1423, soon after John Mowbray returned, many holdings were vacant and the list of ruined buildings was very long.

Katherine Neville's association with Willington manor dated from her marriage to John Mowbray in 1412 until her death in about 1483, and ensured stability at the highest level. Continuity of management was achieved by her longevity; for fifty years she shared the lordship with three further husbands. Control by her husbands, stewards and manorial officers gave her administration resilience and cohesion so that, despite changes in personnel, the pattern of administration remained consistent.

After the death of her first husband in 1432, as Dowager Duchess of Norfolk, Katherine received the Mowbray family home, Vine Garth in Epworth, and a large

---

32   *Ibid*, p. 68.
33   *Ibid*, p. 89.
34   *Ibid*, p. 91.
35   *Ibid*, p. 151.
36   Archer, 'Rich Old Ladies: the Problem of late Medieval Dowagers', p. 24.
37   *Ibid*, n.81, p. 29.

part of the estate – at least a third – as her dower.[38] It included Bedford Castle, Bromham, Haynes, parts of Stotfold and Cople, and Willington in Bedfordshire, and further lands in Buckinghamshire, Essex, Gloucestershire and the March, Leicestershire, Norfolk and Surrey. The value of her dower has been estimated at £617 7s. 8d., about a third of the total value of the Mowbray estates in the mid-fifteenth century. Her most valuable lands were in Norfolk (£220 13s. 11d.), Gloucestershire (£107 10s. 7d.) and Essex (£102 10s. 9d). Willington's value was £32 17s., from the Bedfordshire total of £751 5s.[39]

Katherine then married Thomas Strangeways, previously one of her husband's staff, but was widowed once again sometime before 1443. The only roll surviving from this period is dated 22 April 1440 and contains details of the costs of a new barn and repairs to other buildings, which she paid for.[40] Her two later husbands took precedence over her in the headings of the court rolls for Willington and elsewhere, despite their lower social status, but there is no reason to suppose that she did not participate in the work of the council that governed her estates; she governed the estates effectively herself in the years when she was a widow. The influence of Katherine Neville, her husbands, their councils, associates and employees would have been felt by the bailiffs, the manorial officers and the tenants through her paid representatives, the receivers, stewards or under-stewards, ensuring continuity at local level.

Her third husband was John Beaumont, an experienced courtier and landowner from East Anglia. The evidence from the rolls shows that he was an able administrator and that the manor was well-run under his supervision. When the series of rolls begins again in 1448, the heading shows that he took precedence over the dowager duchess:

> View of frankpledge with court of lord John, the viscount of Beaumont and Katherine duchess of Norfolk, held there on the Monday next after the feast of the translation of Saint Hugh the bishop, in the 27th year of the reign of King Henry 6th after the conquest [14 October 1448].

A complete series of rolls from 1448 until June or July 1459 is still extant. The last roll to contain John Beaumont's name was dated October 1458.[41]

Several references to the lord's council are to be found during the ten years between October 1448 and the appointment of a new steward, Thomas Rokes, in April 1457.[42] The only names of officials to appear in the Willington records later in the fifteenth century are John Rammesbury, receiver in the Willington bailiff's account 1457–58, and John Sapcote, esquire, named as the lady's receiver in the bailiff's account 1481–82. In that account William Paryssh is described as bailiff and reeve of Willington, and named as collector of payments for Bedford Castle and bailiff and rent collector for Bromham.

---

38   Roberts, *Mowbray Legacy*, pp. 97–100.
39   Moye, *The Estates and Finances of the Mowbray Family*, p. 156.
40   BARS, Box R212, Roll 37, April 1440.
41   BARS, Box R212, Roll 47, October 1458.
42   Views of frankpledge, BARS, Box R212, Roll 38a, October 1448; Roll 42a, October 1453; Roll 44a, October 1455; Roll 45a, October 1456. Halmoots, BARS, Box R212, Roll 38b, May 1449; Roll 39b, May 1451; Roll 40b, May 1452; Roll 42b, May 1454; Roll 43b, May 1455; Roll 45b, April 1457.

During the period 1448–57 there were consultations with the council when tenants were required to repair buildings, and there were disagreements about whether the council or the lord should pay for them. Robert Rydere appealed to the council for help when he was required to repair a malt-kiln that had burned down in October 1448, but there was no response.[43] In May 1449, the council made an order about the keeping of animals in the fields and pigs on the manor and ordered allowances of oaks to repair the mill. In May 1451 at least four holdings were without tenants and in ruinous states, and although the council was involved in some negotiations several holdings continued to need repairs.[44]

Three men from Blunham were accused of stealing oak trees from Willington Grove and Sheerhatch Wood in October 1450 but: 'the keeper of the woodland came there and carried them away to his house to the profit of the lord.'[45] The three men were each fined 40d. In May 1452 they all appeared in court, on the orders of the lord's council, accused of felling and removing these trees.[46] Four respected Willington tenants had acted as surveyors for the receiver who was expected to visit Willington, but there is no mention of the trees in the roll of May 1453, though it seems that the receiver was still expected.[47] At the same court Thomas Maryon was found guilty of having dug in the common. He was ordered to put it right but pleaded that a decision should be postponed until, 'Benet the Receiver came'; Benet is not mentioned in any of the later rolls.

The council continued to take a hard line on requests for help with repairs. In October 1455:

> …that the tenement in which Robert Partrych stays is ruined and the bailiff says that the receiver general of the council says the same Robert should pay 40s. for making the aforesaid repairs, 20s. for this year and 20s. next year. That thereafter it is to be always provided by the plaintiff, and he should provide sufficient security for payment. And now the bailiff presents that he has not provided security. Therefore the bailiff was ordered to take possession of all his goods and chattels whatsoever, being within the demesne, to provide sufficient maintenance for making the aforesaid repairs or willows as payment as permitted.[48]

The above is the last reference to a receiver general in John Beaumont's and Katherine Neville's council. The next year, in October 1456, a tenant was accused of not using twenty laths which had been allowed to him for repairs and was threatened with a penalty of 40d. if he did not use them in the next few months.[49] He was also

---

[43] BARS, Box R212, Roll 38a, October 1448. Later rolls note that he paid 20s. to William Launcelyn to repair it, but no repairs were carried out. There must have been a dispute over who should provide the timber to repair the kiln. Perhaps both men thought that the steward would provide some from the lord's woods, but this did not happen. In May 1452 the halmoot roll records that: 'the aforesaid Robert will provide the timber for the aforesaid William to repair it', though it had still not been repaired, BARS, Box R212, Roll 40b, May 1452. It had not been repaired in October 1452 either, and there are no further mentions of it in the rolls.

[44] BARS, Box R212, Roll 39b, May 1451.

[45] BARS, Box R212, Roll 39a, October 1450.

[46] BARS, Box R212, Roll 40b, May 1452.

[47] BARS, Box R212, Roll 41b, May 1453.

[48] BARS, Box R212, Roll 44a, October 1455.

[49] BARS, Box R212, Roll 45a, October 1456.

accused of not using some reeds that he had been given and was ordered to undertake repairs before the next court or pay a penalty to the council.

A new steward, Thomas Rokes, is first mentioned in the halmoot, April 1457. At that court, 'the sworn men present that the lord obliged the tenants to make a building on the holding which John Stones held, a plea in respect of which was with the lord's Council.'[50] The new steward began by recycling timber from an old building and by ordering the bailiff to collect in timber given to tenants for repairs and not used. At the next court, after consulting with the council, he answered John Stones' request by stating that: 'the Lord required the tenants to repair the malt-kiln in the holding of John Stones.'[51] The lord's council is not mentioned after this date for as long as Katherine Neville was alive, suggesting that a layer of management had been removed and that more responsibility was given to the steward and the bailiff. Although on many estates: 'by the fifteenth century the steward's responsibility for supervising local officials closely had diminished, and control of them was exercised principally through the annual audit of the account instead' this was not the case on Katherine Neville's dower.[52] She and John Beaumont invested responsibility in Thomas Rokes, a man who must have been an able administrator.

Continuity was maintained by Katherine Neville after John Beaumont's death by retaining the services of their steward, Thomas Rokes, through the years when she was a widow for the third time, and through the lordship of her fourth husband. Documents which survive, and are related to the beginning of Rokes' stewardship, include Willington bailiff's account 1457–58, four short rolls for Cardington (the only Cardington rolls to survive),[53] and all the Willington rolls currently held in the British Library.[54]

In 1465 Katherine Neville was married for the fourth time, to John Woodville, brother of Elizabeth Woodville, the king's wife. A complete series of rolls exists from October 1462–May 1470 and three rolls from this fourth marriage are dated October 1465, April and October 1466.[55] John Woodville was said to be about twenty years old at the time of his marriage and Katherine must have been over sixty. Her contemporaries described the match as a *maritagium diabolicum*.[56] It is impossible to know what her motives were, no doubt being close to the king's wife's family would have been advantageous for her children, or she may have been using marriage as a way to fund the Yorkist cause in the Wars of the Roses. After John Woodville was executed by the Lancastrians in 1469 she did not remarry.[57]

The series of rolls after 1470 is less complete and rolls are missing for autumn 1470 and spring 1471. Katherine Neville was getting older and her grandson, the fourth Duke of Norfolk, instead of being able to support her, was involved in serious

[50] BARS, Box R212, Roll 45b, April 1457.
[51] BARS, Box R212, Roll 46a, October 1457.
[52] Bailey, *The English Manor*, p. 100.
[53] BARS, Box R212, Roll 48, June or July 1459; Roll 49b, October 1461; Roll 50a, October 1462; Roll 50b, May 1463.
[54] British Library, Add Ch.26813/1–8.
[55] BARS, Box R212, Roll 52a, October 1465; Roll 52b, April 1466; Roll 53b, October 1466.
[56] Archer, 'Rich Old Ladies: the Problem of late Medieval Dowagers', p. 24.
[57] Roberts, *Mowbray Legacy*, p. 100.

problems of his own from before and after the Battle of Tewksbury in 1471 until the end of his life in 1476.[58]

The roll for autumn 1471 suggests a change of clerk as there is a change in the layout of the document; it is the only Willington court roll which names the two constables immediately after the heading. It is possible that no courts were held at Willington in autumn 1472, spring 1473, autumn 1476, spring 1477, and spring 1479-spring 1481, as these rolls are missing. However the detail in the rolls which do survive does not indicate a back-log of business, which might have been expected after breaks in the court schedule.[59] From spring 1475 the rolls contain less detail and are shorter. It seems that, as elsewhere, the importance of the steward had declined and control over local officials was exercised by the auditors through the processes of auditing the accounts.[60]

In the years between the death of her third husband, John Beaumont, and 1465 when she married John Woodville, and after his death in 1469, Katherine Neville held the manor alone with the assistance of her council. The rolls suggest that she and her last two husbands were efficient administrators and that the manor had stability under the supervision of sensible local bailiffs during these periods. There is however a possibility that, like her grandson, she needed to rationalise her estates; she sold lands in Chepstow, Tidenham and in Gloucestershire and the March in 1468. She surrendered Dovercourt, Great Chesterford and Harwich in Essex, and Earsham and Lopham in Norfolk in 1474.[61] On 1 March 1477, Lopham, Dovercourt, Great Chesterford and Harwich became the property of her great-grand-daughter Anne.[62] Katherine Neville's name last appeared in the Willington court rolls in October 1481.

Role of the steward and other officials

Originally a steward would have been responsible for a number of manors, usually visiting them twice a year to take the manor courts. He would have supervised the larger building projects, sanctioned unusually large expenditure on repairs or improvements and negotiated with the tenants on major, sensitive issues. He did not act as judge in the manor court as this responsibility rested with the bailiff and the members of the jury.[63] The head steward was answerable to the lord or lady of the manor and to the council in which he played an active part. When there was a change of lordship the stewards were not immediately replaced, although there may have been other changes in administration.

Until the middle of the fifteenth century the Mowbray's manors were grouped into territorial divisions each with its own steward, who worked with local bailiffs and exercised personal control from above. These groupings changed according to the management policy of the lord of the time. In the only surviving receiver's account for Willington 1421–22, when it was part of the estates of John Mowbray the fifth, the second Duke of Norfolk, the manor was part of a group of properties which also

58   Roberts, *Mowbray Legacy*, pp. 112–13.
59   BARS, Box R212, Roll 58a, October 1477; Roll 60a, October 1481.
60   Bailey, *The English Manor*, p. 100.
61   Moye, *The Estates and Finances of the Mowbray Family*, p. 156.
62   Moye, *The Estates and Finances of the Mowbray Family*, p. 226.
63   Bailey, *The English Manor*, p.100 and p. 172.

included Bedford Castle, Newnham, Bromham, Linslade, Wing and Seagrave.[64] In the Willington bailiff's account 1457–58, when the manor was part of Katherine Neville's dower at the end of the life of her third husband John Beaumont, it was part of a group which included Bedford Castle, Bromham, and lands in Barford, Cople, Cardington, Ickwell, Renhold (Salph) and Southill.[65] The ministers' accounts of Thomas, Earl of Surrey, show that Willington had become part of a group of properties which included Framlingham at the Castle, Kettleburgh, Hacheston, Peasenhall and Kelsale by the end of the fifteenth century.[66]

After the mid-fifteenth century the administration of the Mowbray estates not managed by Katherine Neville and her husbands followed a pattern similar to that used by the Crown's administrators. Manors continued to be grouped into territorial divisions and the role of the steward became less important. As was usual on other large estates the manors were managed by a hierarchy of supervisors, the structure of which varied but included stewards, under-stewards, receivers and other servants including the bailiffs, who often had responsibility for a small group of manors. This hierarchy gradually reduced and eventually the individual manors were scrutinised by the lord's auditors once or twice a year and were managed by the local bailiff.[67]

The pattern of management was different for manors in Katherine Neville's dower where the steward continued to play an important role almost until her death. The evidence in the Willington manor court rolls and accounts shows that the steward remained part of the management structure of Katherine Neville and her husbands throughout most of the fifteenth century.

The stewards made adjustments to their management strategies for their distant properties in Bedfordshire from the late fourteenth century, leading to the empowerment of some villein tenants, especially members of the Rider family one of whom, William, appears at least thirty-one times in the records 1394–1426 (but may have been a father and son). In the early fifteenth century a second jury was introduced to the court process to verify the presentments made by the manorial officers in the views of frankpledge.[68] It is not clear whether the steward intended that the local bailiff and the second jury would control the growing independence of the tenant elite or whether he hoped to encourage all the tenants to conform by using these methods.

The seven earliest surviving Willington court rolls 1394–1404, contain just two references to the steward, in October 1397 and October 1404.[69] From 1406 onwards there are more regular references, and, until the late 1460s, almost all the records show that the steward was accompanied by other Mowbray servants.

64 Arundel Castle Archives, A1642.
65 British Library, Add Ch. 657.
66 *Compoti of all the Ministers of Thomas, Earl of Surrey, for Manors of Framlingham at the Castle, Kettleburgh, Hacheston, Peasenhall, Kelsale and Willington (Bd)*, Suffolk Record Office, Iveagh Collection, HD1538/225/2,4,5.
67 Harvey, *Manorial Records*, p. 6.
68 BARS, Box R212, Roll 7, October 1404.
69 'At this Court it was ordered by the Steward that no-one shall play the game called Qoyte in the future under a penalty of 12d', BARS, Box R212, Roll 5, October 1397. Adam: 'justly called the hue on Richard [2d] Heyne by the pledge of the Constable and that the same [2d] Richard contradicted the presentment in the presence of the steward and [is] in contempt of Court and is amerced', BARS, Box R212, Roll 7, October 1404.

These servants were never named and are regularly referred to as 'others'. Some-times they are described as surveyors, supervisors, tenants, visitors, officials or clerks, or combinations of these.

For several years before 1416 the Mowbray's steward had been John Boteler, who had been steward for the manor when it was held by Queen Joan. He was demoted and Thomas Bekyngham took control in May 1416.[70] In October 1417 Bekyngham was referred to as head steward.[71] He continued to be referred to as head steward until May 1420 and may have been in post later as his name still appears at the beginning of the roll for September or October 1423, and there are references to the work of the head steward and the chief steward in the text.

A new steward, Roger Hunte, is mentioned in October 1425,[72] and Thomas Bekyngham is referred to as 'formerly steward' in April 1426.[73] One of Roger Hunte's first tasks was to settle a dispute between the lord and three tenants over whether they were entitled to have dovecotes on their land or not. The result of this dispute has been lost.

In the second half of the fifteenth century stewards continued to take an active roll at Willington. During the years when the manor was under the care of John Beaumont and Katherine Neville 1448–58, some of the tenants negotiated lower rents with the steward and the income from the manor reduced as they did so. In April 1457, the steward was mentioned twice at the end of the roll when he ordered the bailiff to provide for making some repairs to the malt-kiln before the next court and granted 40d. to Nicholas Crewce for making repairs to the thatch on his ruined hall.[74]

In May 1464 John Yarwey, the bailiff: 'delivered six pieces of timber for the repair of one door of Bedford Castle, on the order of the steward.'[75] He also delivered fourteen large pieces of large timber and twenty-two laths, through the order of the steward, for making a barn at Bromham in the holding of Robert Lumpney, 'that was exceedingly ruined' and twenty-nine large pieces of timber for the mill of Willington, through the order of the steward.

In two short periods 1466–71 and 1475–79, towards the end of Katherine Neville's life, the rolls show that a steward attended the court, but there is no evidence that he was accompanied. This omission might indicate a change of clerk or may indicate that Katherine Neville and her stewards were taking action to control their costs. Steward's expenses had been high immediately following the appointment of Thomas Rokes in 1457, averaging over 7s. for three courts although they then reduced so that they hovered at about half that figure.[76] They rose again in 1471 to 5s. 4d. when extra surveyors would perhaps have been required to advise on repairs to the mill dam and plans to take: 'from Sherehache 10 perches of withies to make wattled hurdles to turn the water in the river.'[77] It is not clear why costs increased

[70] BARS, Box R212, Roll 20, May 1416.
[71] BARS, Box R212, Roll 23, October 1417.
[72] BARS, Box R212, Roll 35, October 1425.
[73] BARS, Box R212, Roll 36a, April 1426.
[74] BARS, Box R212, Roll 45b, April 1457.
[75] British Library, Add Ch.2613/2, May 1464.
[76] BARS, Box R212, Roll 45b, April 1457; Roll 46a, October 1457; Roll 46b, July 1458.
[77] BARS, Box R212, Roll 54a, October 1471.

to 5s. in 1477 though the roll says: 'In expenses of the Steward with [or for] the court rolls 5s.'[78] This phrase does not appear elsewhere in the Willington documents though the payment of a few pence for ink, paper and parchment is regularly included with the stewards' expenses and written at the end of the rolls.[79] Very occasionally these costs amount to 12d. The higher fees for stewards' expenses in 1481 (6s. 8d.) and 1482 (5s.) may have been due to the death, or impending death, of Katherine Neville.[80]

The language used in the five rolls 1474–76 suggests changes in the steward's role as he attempted to make adjustments to the granting of lands to tenants for which he provided pledges or guarantees, on several occasions.[81] In April 1474 he pledged for the granting of a cottage to Richard Myton and his family, for nine acres of land to Richard Yarwey and for a messuage and nine acres to George Claydon.[82] These three holdings were each said to be transferred, 'with the right to be devised or bequeathed', and the steward also granted seisin, that is, he agreed to the tenants holding the land. No mention of copyhold is written into these documents, but these tenants, at least, were granted customary holdings under terms similar to free holdings. The steward was again involved in March 1475 as he tried to extend the length of the leases for some manorial assets.[83] Thomas Passewater leased the fishing waters, the rabbit warren and the waters of the mill for forty years. They were granted to him by the lady, through the pledge of the steward, but just over a year later, he surrendered the watermill into the hand of the steward, and it was granted to Henry Parker for forty years under different terms, again 'through the pledge of the steward.'[84]

There is no documentary evidence of the exploitation of tenants by the lord, or of overt antipathy by the tenants towards the stewards, but there were some instances of assaults and petty crime which may have had their roots in resentment to control. The recorded levels of crime were generally low; a system of standard fines was used to punish offenders and there is no record of physical punishment. However, it became increasingly difficult for the steward and the council to control events in the manor in the second half of the fifteenth century. By-laws imposed on the tenants through the manor court suggest that earlier customs and statutes were being ignored.

The role of the bailiff

Bailiffs were usually appointed from outside the manors for which they were responsible, and in the fourteenth century, before lords began to lease out their demesne lands, both a bailiff and a reeve might be appointed. In some manors

---

78   BARS, Box R212, Roll 58a, October 1477.
79   BARS, Box R212, Roll 7, October 1404, (3d.); Roll 24, April 1418, (2d.); Roll 26, May 1419, (2d.); Roll 36a, April 1426, (6d.). For Willington and Cardington Roll 38b, May 1449 (4d.); Roll 39b, May 1451, (4d.); Roll 40b, May 1452, (4d.); Roll 41b, May 1453, (4d.); Roll 42b, May 1454, (4d.); Roll 54c, October 1473, (4d.); Roll 60b, May 1482, (4d.). For Willington, Cardington and Bromham, BARS, Box R212, Roll 45b, April 1457, (12d.).
80   BARS, Box R212, Roll 60a, October 1481; Roll 60b, May 1482.
81   BARS, Box R212, Roll 55a, March 1474; Roll 55b, March 1475; Roll 56, April 1474; Roll 57a, October 1475; Roll 57b, April or May 1476.
82   BARS, Box R212, Roll 56, April 1474.
83   BARS, Box R212, Roll 55b, March 1475.
84   BARS, Box R212, Roll 57b, April or May 1476.

adverse conditions caused some lords to discontinue the employment of a bailiff and a reeve; at Willington the bailiff combined both roles and was occasionally referred to as the reeve. He was usually appointed from a Willington family that had lived on the manor at least since the early fourteenth century.[85] The appointment of a local bailiff and the introduction of a second jury into the manor court involved large numbers of tenants in the court procedures and led to the development of a powerful manor elite.

The bailiff was the local link between the Mowbrays' councils, their officials and the Willington tenants. He was a paid professional, answerable to the head steward or one of the under stewards and worked with members of the village elite - of which he was one – such as the heads of tithings or the holders of offices such as constable, ale-taster or assessor of fines. He was responsible for day to day management of the lord's assets, was a key person in the administration and control of the manor and influenced the lives of free and customary tenants. As on many other Mowbray manors, the bailiff combined the collection of rents from Willington and other neighbouring properties with preparing the accounts.[86] He may have purchased the supplies of paper, parchment and ink for the court rolls.[87] His annual accounts were audited by a member of the lord's council. The first bailiff recorded in the Willington bailiffs' accounts was Robert Gostwyk.

The bailiffs' duties also included the supervision of the customary tenants, their holdings, rents and buildings; the mill; woodlands; warrens; fisheries; dovecotes; stray animals and swarms of bees. The views of frankpledge record that swarms of bees entered the manor eleven times 1394–1425 and that they were sold to tenants for a few pence: for example, to Thomas Herynge for 2d. in 1403 and to Henry Yarwey for 6d. in 1413. In 1425 John Taillour paid 12d. for three swarms and John Kempston paid 6d. for one other. No swarms were recorded after that date.[88] A wide variety of stray animals entered the manor 1394–1471. They were held temporarily for up to a year and a day by one of the tenants. A proclamation was made so giving the owner enough time to reclaim his property; if unclaimed the strays were sold to tenants on the manor. The only record of strays being claimed is in October 1453:

> And that a certain heifer aged one year, worth [blank] came as a stray, which is in the keeping of John Flaunders. He was ordered to make a proclamation. And afterwards Reginald Bonn came and claimed the aforesaid heifer and on this day [came] to prove it and it was proved. And she was handed over to him. ... And that two oxen arrived as strays and were not proclaimed. And the bailiff was ordered to proclaim them. And afterwards a certain Richard Okham came and claimed and [it was] sufficiently proved. And they were handed over to him.[89]

There are no details of how the proclamation was made, nor are there details of how the income for the lord which the strays generated was calculated. It became part of the perquisites of court and may have been calculated by the assessors of fines.

---

85 BARS, R8/62/2/1–11, and Thompson, *Bailiffs' Accounts for Willington*, BARS, CRT 130 Willington 11.
86 British Library, Add Ch.657.
87 BARS, Box R212, Roll 45b, April 1457.
88 BARS, Box R212, Roll 2, October 1394; Roll 6, October 1403; Roll 15, October 1413; Roll 19, October 1415; Roll 23, October 1417; Roll 35, October 1425.
89 BARS, Box R212, Roll 42a, October 1453.

People were surprisingly mobile in the Middle Ages. The Mowbrays travelled all round the British Isles and France in the service of the king, and their officials travelled once or twice a year from the family's power base in Lincolnshire to visit outlying manors like Willington, Haynes, Linslade and Wing, which all feature in the Willington bailiffs' accounts and the manor court records. The Willington bailiff travelled too, as he delivered the money he had collected to the Mowbray's receivers or receiver generals who were based in Bedfordshire and nearby counties or in London.

Eleven bailiffs' accounts for Willington, and nine for Haynes, plus single records for Wing and Linslade, survive from the years 1382–97. In these years there were at least sixty-five occasions when the local bailiff met officials from the lord's management network, an average of just over three times for each account. Eleven of these meetings took place in London. On other occasions meetings took place at Alconbury (Hunts), Hynton (Cambs), Epworth (Lincs), Irthlingborough (Northants) Shefford and Wardon. No venue is given for the other two-thirds of meetings, so presumably on these occasions the lord's officials travelled to Bedfordshire to collect payments from Willington, Haynes or Bedford.

No mention of a new bailiff can be found in the court rolls after 1472, but a draft of the Willington bailiff's account 1486–87 shows that William Otley, from outside the manor, was the bailiff and William Gostwyk his deputy in that year.[90]

The bailiff's cohorts

The bailiff's closest associates included the manor's constables, ale-tasters, heads of tithings, warreners, woodwards, rent collectors and other neighbours, friends and relatives who formed the juries at the manor courts. Prosperous widows, other women and children, poor cottagers, labourers and servants seldom appear in the court rolls and were less influential.

Two men are named as rent collectors. Simon Pynell helped bailiff Robert Gostwyk by collecting rents from Cardington, Cople and Barford, 1390–95, and from Bromham, 1394–95. He had links with Bedford Castle, 1394–95, and is recorded as: 'farmer of the lord in Cardington, Cople and Barford' in 1396–97.[91] The other rent collector was William Pecke who collected rents, 1392–93.[92]

A core of families holding manorial offices emerges from analysis of the court rolls. Generations of Mitons served as assessors of fines almost continuously 1395–1451, members of the Partrych family were often jurors and constables 1396–1426.

It seems very likely that the villein bailiffs William Ridere and John Yarwey, and some of the influential free Miton, Partrych and Gostwyk families, were able to read and write.[93] There is no evidence of a school in Willington in the fifteenth century although canon law required every rural parish to have a clerk to attend the priest, look after the church and 'keep a school for the children.'[94]

90 Suffolk Record Office, HD1538/225/2-6.
91 BARS, R8/62/2/8, 9, 10, 11, and Thompson, *Bailiffs' Accounts for Willington*, BARS, CRT 130 Willington 11, pp. 30, 34, 40, 43–4. 'Farmer' in this context indicates a person who pays rents.
92 BARS, R8/62/2/9, 10, and Thompson, *Bailiffs' Accounts for Willington*, BARS, CRT 130 Willington 11, pp. 32–6, 41.
93 British Library, Add Ch.657.
94 W. W. Capes, *The English Church in the Fourteenth and Fifteenth Centuries* (London, 1920), p. 334.

Several men served as jurors and may have held manorial office for periods of twenty or thirty years 1394–1426: a William Ridere was a juror for five years, and bailiff for more than twenty years and ale-taster,1411–19; John Rider was a juror for more than twenty years, 1394–1417; Thomas Rider served for nineteen years and was assessor of fines, 1395–1415; John Treket served as juror for twenty-nine years, 1406–26; John Bande the elder for thirty years, 1394–1423; John Yarwey also for thirty years 1394–1423; John Miton, served as a juror for thirty-three years, 1395–1426, and members of his family were ale-tasters 1416–25 and often assessors of fines; Robert Miton was assessor of fines over a period of eighteen years, 1403–22; a further eleven men served on the main jury for periods of between eleven and twenty years.

Ten free men of the manor are listed in the bailiff's account 1457–58 as John Norman, John Abel, Robert Partriche, Robert Miton, Robert Warner, John Cawde, John Miton, Thomas Stoughton, the prior of Newnham, John Gostewik the elder.[95] Free men are seldom named in the court rolls, but their enhanced social status did not prevent them from being obliged to repair their buildings, clear their ditches, conform to the custom of the manor and submit to the control exercised by the bailiff.

The manorial records show a number of families, or one very large extended family, with the name Warner (or Wareyn, Warrener, Waryner). These surnames may have been used for the families of villein men who worked as warrener on the manor. The last John Warner to be warrener in Willington held the office until shortly before 1417.[96] In 1419 Robert de Wyllyton, who was almost certainly a free man, was appointed keeper of the warren of Willington and of the wood of Sheerhatch for life. This seems to have been a management post, or a sinecure in payment for his service to the Duke of Norfolk as surgeon, but he may have supervised the work of the woodward, John Kempston, whose concealment of sales of rabbits and other offences were eventually punished.[97]

The most important member of the bailiff's cohort was the constable, and at the end of the fourteenth century it was usual for just one to be appointed and to serve for several years. There is no evidence to suggest that tenants were paid for performing this role, and on several occasions constables did not perform their offices as required. After the appointment of the unsuitable Adam Warde in 1404 and the return of the Mowbray estates to John Mowbray in 1413, the steward appointed two constables from experienced members of the court juries who served for periods of nine or ten years. Later in the century constables were usually appointed for periods of two years. The role was sometimes combined with that of ale-taster. The men appointed to the role of ale-taster were part of the manor elite, of either free or villein status, and served for different lengths of time; the post was sometimes passed down from father to son or held by different members of the same family.

All the men listed above as manorial officers also served as jurors in the manor court. Different clerks used different terms to describe them – 'the homage', 'sworn men' or 'tithing men' – though the size and number of tithings at Willington is

95   British Library, Add Ch. 657.
96   BARS, Box R212, Roll 23, October 1417.
97   BARS, Box R212, Roll 30, April 1421.

unclear. They would have been responsible for the appointment of the manorial officers although no details of the electoral process were given.

Stability among the manor elite

The manor elite used the courts to influence decisions, maintain the custom of the manor, enforce agricultural practice and keep law and order. There was a reciprocal relationship between the manor elite and the lord's officials and an acceptance that they depended on each other.

Despite evidence of families moving in and out of the manor in the fifteenth century, eight family names survived for 100–150 years. Some continued even longer, the Partrych family survived for 172 years and the Carter, Gostwyk, Pecke, Rider and Yarwey family names survived for at least 200 years. In Willington, even after the mid-fifteenth century, the difference in status of tenants was still noted although some families had lived on the manor for long periods. Many of the villein families left the manor after Katherine Neville's death and most of the active families who remained were free: the Warners, who may have been two families; the Fischeres (or Fisshe, Fysshere); the Mitons; the Peckes, who may have been gentry; and the Gostwyks. The Yarweys too survived; they may have started out as villeins but were very well established during the fifteenth century. The conclusion may be drawn that although mentions of serfdom and its disadvantages disappear from the records in the fifteenth century the disadvantages lingered on. All but one of the tenants who survived into the sixteenth century was free.

The family histories of the six families whose residence in Willington lasted for the longest periods are very different. The Partrych family were active on the manor until 1481 but do not appear afterwards; the Riders were very active before 1426, but their influence reduced dramatically until they only appeared once after 1481; the Yarwey family were almost as active as the Riders until 1426 and continued active until 1481, with eight mentions in the rolls between that date and 1522; Adam and John Carter both appear regularly as jurors before 1404, and the family appears in the rolls thirty-three times before 1426 but disappears after that date although an Edmund Carter surrendered a cottage in March 1522;[98] the Pecke family appeared seventeen times before 1426 and continue to be mentioned occasionally after that; the Gostwyk family, although free, appeared regularly in the court rolls 1309–1540.

Members of the free Partrych family were often jurors and constables 1396–1426. Over the years the prosperity of the Partrych family seems to have declined. Agnes Partrych stole two pairs of stockings from Robert Cook in 1457.[99] She and other members of her family were in conflict with other tenants during the 1450s as they sought to enclose their holding and exclude others. They allowed willows to grow over the common way alongside their holding, and later closed it altogether, but it is unclear whether they wished to exclude other tenants from their lands, whether they were protesting at the control exercised by John Beaumont, or whether they were experiencing financial or personal difficulties.[100] They also refused to repair their ruined buildings.

98   BARS, Box R212, Roll 63, March 1522.
99   BARS, Box R212, Roll 45a, October 1456.
100 BARS, Box R212, Roll 39a, October 1450.

Long-term survival of some family names in Willington[101]

Family name	Status in 1457–8[102]	First appears manorial records	No. of entries	Last appears in manorial records	Minimum years in the manor
Passewater	Villein	1408	23	1507	100
Fesound/Fesaunt	Villein	1394	65	1507	111
Wright	Villein	1395	42	1515	120
Chamberleyn	Villein?	1404	9	1522	133
Tayllour/Taillour/ Taylor/Taylour	Villein	1391?	121	1522	131
Warner/ Wareyn/ Warrener/Waryner	Free	1394	145	1522	146
Fischere/Fisshe/ Fysshere	Free?	1394	7	1522	146
Miton/Myton	Free	1394	142	1522	146
Partrych/Partriche/ Partryche	Free	1309	65	1481	172
Rider/Ridere/Ryder/ Rydere	Villein	1309	116	1515	206
Yarwey/Yarewy/ Yarewy/Yarway/ Yerwey	Villein	1332	151	1522	208
Carter/Cartere	Villein	1309	36	1522	213
Pecke	Free	1309	25	1522	213
Gostwyk/ Gorstwyk/ Gostewik/ Gostwick/ Gostwyke	Free	1309 or before	67	1540	231 and more

The Rider family first appeared in the subsidy roll of 1309, and after William Ridere was appointed bailiff in 1394 he and his relatives dominated the manor for over twenty years. They were regularly ale-tasters, assessors of fines and jurors at the manor court. Some of them were capable of using force.[103]

The Yarweys were villeins and served on juries alongside the Riders 1394–1426. After the Rider demise, in the second half of the fifteenth century, the Yarweys dominated the manor courts. Between 1448–83 the name John Yarwey appears sixty-one times on the jury lists, with father and son often serving at the same time and occasionally three generations of the family sitting on the same jury.[104] John Yarwey was very often named as the first sworn man, and a John Yarwey was bailiff 1462–69 or longer. A John Yarwey was said to be the clerk in 1473 and there are records of fights between members of his family and members of the Miton family

[101] Members of the Miton and Yarwey families still lived in Willington in the sixteenth century, but by the time that the parish registers begin, in 1602, they and the Partrych, Rider and Warner families, have died out or left the manor.

[102] British Library, Add Ch. 657. This account names the ten free men of the manor who paid rents of assize. They were John Norman, John Abel, Robert Partriche, Robert Miton, Robert Warner, John Cawde, John Miton, Thomas Stoughton, the prior of Newnham and John Gostewik the elder. The other tenants are presumed to be villeins.

[103] BARS, Box R212, Roll 3, October 1395; Roll 26, May 1419.

[104] BARS, Box R212, Roll 55a, March 1474; Roll 55b, March 1475.

about the same time. In October 1481 three men named John Yarwey were jurors and served as constable, ale-taster or assessor of fines.[105] It is not clear whether these posts were held by the same man or by men from two or three generations. One Walter Yarwey was a juror on thirty-five occasions but never held any other manorial office.

Willington village life during the hundred years after the Peasants' Revolt was more likely to be affected by weather and disease than by political and military events. The villein status of many tenants continued to be of importance to the lord and his stewards in the early years, but as the fifteenth century progressed overt references to villein status ceased although some customary practices continued. As Katherine Neville approached the end of her life the court rolls became significantly shorter, especially those of the halmoots in the spring, and the court rolls 1475–79 indicate less diligence in the preparation of the records. During the years after her death, as the Tudors came to the throne, ownership of Willington manor passed to the Howards, based not in East Anglia but on the south coast at Arundel Castle. Documents from the period 1482–1529, when the manor was sold to John Gostwyk and his wife Joan, are infrequent, but the Newnham Priory Terrier of 1507 and the manor court rolls 1515–22 indicate some continuity.

In the few rolls surviving from the early sixteenth century, that is for autumn 1515, spring 1519 or 1520, spring and December 1522, no stewards expenses are mentioned, nor is it recorded that the stewards took an active part in the courts, but it appears that they attended at least once as in March 1520 the tenants were ordered: 'to show in this court before the steward at the next court what acres of land and meadowland [they hold].[106] Willington had become unprofitable, and it seems that the Duke of Norfolk was making preparations to sell. John and Joan Gostwyk presided over a huge building programme on the manor during the 1530s and 1540s. They, and their heirs, were resident lords and ladies of the manor until the early eighteenth century.

[105] BARS, Box R212, Roll 60a, October 1481.
[106] The edge of the roll is torn so that the final part of this text is missing.

Chapter Six

Finances and Assets

After the Peasants' Revolt the Mowbrays' plans for their estates were straightforward. They sought to maximise income from their lands and maintain the value of their assets, despite the period 1380–1530 being one of general agricultural depression.[1] The period 1440–80 was particularly difficult for them.

The Mowbrays strove to maintain a ducal lifestyle and support expensive military campaigns, but it became increasingly difficult for them to live within their means. Referencing twenty-nine Mowbray manors, 1447–48 and 1472–73, Moye demonstrates that just twelve increased their income, although in some cases this was only by a very small amount.[2] The seventeen manors from which income reduced included four medium to large manors. The reduction, however, was less than £1 in these manors, and there is no clear evidence of a direct link between manor size and loss of income. Three of the four Norfolk manors showed losses, as did five of the six manors in Suffolk. Location, or a different management style, may have been important factors, as seven of the thirteen manors in Sussex showed increases in income.[3]

John Mowbray, the third Duke of Norfolk, suffered from an incompetent and unscrupulous receiver general in the 1440s, and the role of receiver general was subsequently abolished. However, by 1461 the family was heavily in debt despite the third and fourth dukes struggling to economise by occasionally suspending the payment of wages, fees and annuities to members of staff as well as other measures.[4]

The incomes of the dukes of Norfolk suffered because they were required to support three dowagers: Elizabeth Fitzalan, wife of Thomas Mowbray, who lived until 1425;[5] Constance Holland, who held Mowbray lands until 1437;[6] and Katherine Neville, who received about one third of the Mowbray estates as her dower after the death of her first husband, John Mowbray, in 1432.[7] When John Mowbray, the fourth Duke of Norfolk, died in 1476 the Mowbray dukedom came to an end, and he left another dowager, Elizabeth Talbot, daughter of the Earl of Shrewsbury.

The manor court proceedings and the bailiffs' accounts were important parts of the Mowbray administrative machine and enabled the lord, through the steward

---

1   Bailey, *The English Manor*, p. 108.
2   Moye, *The Estates and Finances of the Mowbray Family*, p. 125.
3   The manor which demonstrated the largest increase in income was Fen Stanton in Cambridgeshire (6½%).
4   Moye, *The Estates and Finances of the Mowbray Family*, p. 28.
5   Roberts, *Mowbray Legacy*, p. 86 and Moye, *The Estates and Finances of the Mowbray Family*, p. 142.
6   Moye, *The Estates and Finances of the Mowbray Family*, pp. 148–150.
7   Moye, *The Estates and Finances of the Mowbray Family*, pp. 151–156.

and other council members, to find ways of protecting their income and maintaining the value of their assets. Katherine Neville might display enlightened self-interest, as when a new barn was built for Thomas Wyltshyre in 1440,[8] but the tenants were expected to build a barn for John Stones in 1457.[9] Relationships with the tenants were business ones delivered within a social context, which included a meal for the steward, the officials who accompanied him and some of the tenants after each court.

Bailiffs' accounts, which provide considerable information about the financial arrangements for the manor of Willington, divide into three phases. The first, 1382–97, when most of the accounts are still extant, provides evidence of declining income and increasing costs for the Mowbrays. During this period they continued to attempt to maintain the value of their woodlands and buildings while encouraging their estate officials to manage the rent-rolls and tenants more actively.

The second period, 1400–26, during which very few accounts for Willington survive, was a more disturbed phase in the history of the family. Lands were held by a Crown nominee and then by Queen Joan before being returned to John Mowbray in 1413. The third and final period, 1448–83, is when Katherine Neville and her third and fourth husbands held her dower separate from the rest of the Mowbray estates. Manors in her dower did not therefore suffer from the desperate attempts made by her son and grandson to maintain their ducal status during the later fifteenth century.

Bailiffs' Accounts for Willington and Haynes, 1382–97

Like those of most other estates, the Mowbrays' accounts for Willington were prepared annually at Michaelmas (25 September). They were of the charge and discharge form and usually subjected to three levels of responsibility.[10] A bailiff or a lessee would draw up the accounts locally; a local receiver would collect the money from him; and a receiver general would transfer the money, and the records, to the lord's household or to his council. The 'charges' include income from rents, arrears, fines, sales of wood and other building materials, income from sheriff's aid and a sum total. The 'discharges', or expenses, include payments to the Bedford sheriff for hideage and shirreveshot, the assize of bread and ale, tithes, steward's expenses, wages, costs of repairs and money payments. The total of the discharges is subtracted from the sum total of the charges to show the amount still owing, which becomes the arrears in the next account.

Eleven bailiffs' accounts for Willington, 1382–97, and nine for Haynes, 1384–97, survive, written on eleven membranes of parchment, each about one foot in width and up to four feet in length.[11] Haynes accounts 1387–88, 1391–92, 1393–94 and 1395–96 are missing, as are the accounts for Willington 1383–84, 1391–92, 1393–94 and 1395–96. The accounts belong to what has been described as the third phase of manorial accounts: 'dating from the mid-fourteenth century

8   BARS, Box R212, Roll 37, April 1440.
9   BARS, Box R212, Roll 45b, April 1457.
10   Harvey, *Manorial Records*, p. 36.
11   They are sewn together with a single leather stitch and small flaps of parchment, containing extra information, have been sewn on to the main document with small stitches.

onwards, when leasing manors was becoming once again the usual way of running an estate.'[12]

The importance of the bailiffs' accounts is evident from the good quality of the parchment on which they are written and the spacious layout. The eleven membranes each contain a Willington account on the front and Haynes, or other accounts, on the dorse. They are sewn together at the top and have two small pieces of parchment attached. The first parchment is fastened to the Willington account 1386–87 and is written in French. It refers to an order to Robert Gostwyk by Lord Mowbray about repairs to the mill. The second parchment is a list of pigs that grazed in Haynes Park, 1392–93.[13] There is evidence that medieval scribes sometimes made mistakes in the accounts as when the demesne lands were misrecorded 1382–83.[14] The error was not rectified until 1388–89.[15]

Most of the surviving bailiffs' accounts for Willington begin with the name of the manor and the bailiff, followed by the name and title of the lord, with the date in regnal years and saints' days. The anticipated income was listed variously under the following headings: arrears from the previous year; rents of free tenants; rents of half-virgates formerly held in bondage; rents of acremen and cottars; rent in Barford; rents in kind; rents for demesne land; sale of underwood; proceeds of the manor; perquisites of view with court; sheriff's aid. The income was followed by the sum total of receipts with arrears.

The sum total was followed by payments for expenses such as customary payments to the Bedford sheriff, tithes to the prior of Newnham, repairs to the mill, costs of the steward attending the court and wages. These were followed by a list of allowances, including payments for miscellaneous repairs; wages for workmen and rent collectors; and reductions, adjustments or non-payments of rent. A total of allowances and payments was arrived at, although at the end of the fourteenth century no allowances for Willington were entered at this point. The allowances and payments were deducted from the receipts with arrears to give the money still outstanding, which was then written as arrears in the account for the coming year.

The accounts seem to have been written up beforehand, with the arrears calculated before all the information had reached the accountant, for the arrears figure was often adjusted as more money was handed over to the receiver and allowances of payment from different sources were deducted. The information often seems confusing but must have satisfied late-medieval accountants and auditors at the time.

The heading of the first surviving account, 1382–83, names the bailiff as Robert Gostwyk and documents the change of lordship from:

---

12   Harvey, *Manorial Records*, p. 35.
13   BARS, R8/68/1/7, and Thompson, *Bailiffs' Accounts for Willington*, BARS, CRT 130 Willington 11, p. 36.
14   BARS, R8/62/2/1, and Thompson, *Bailiffs' Accounts for Willington*, BARS, CRT 130 Willington 11, p. 1.
15   BARS, R8/62/2/6, and Thompson, *Bailiffs' Accounts for Willington*, BARS, CRT 130 Willington 11, p. 20.

Lord John of Mountbray, Earl of Notynghame, the lord there, from the feast of Michaelmas in the 6th year of the reign of king Richard 11 [1382] up to 11 February next following, on which day the same Earl died ... to 'Lord Thomas of Mounbray, now Earl of Notynghame, the lord there, the brother and heir of the former Earl.[16]

The existence of previous accounts, now lost, is indicated in this first account by the statement that the bailiff, Robert Gostwyk, owed £6: 'for arrears for his last account there in the preceding year, as appears in the extract of John Leye, formerly auditor.'[17] The amounts of arrears in these early accounts fluctuate dramatically: £6, 1382–83; £49 6s. 7½d., 1384–85; £36 19s. 2¾d., 1385–86; £22 9s. 5d., 1386–87; £45 12s. 6d., 1387–98. They reduced to £6 11s., 1396–97. The accounts 1382–83 and 1394–95 were complicated by Robert Gostwyk's grant of rent reductions of 32s. for over ten years to the tenants of the former demesne land because they claimed to have been over charged.

Willington bailiff Robert Gostwyk retired or died in August 1393 and was replaced by William Pecke. The next bailiff's account is missing, but by Michaelmas 1394 William Pecke had already been replaced by William Ridere. There had also been a change in the wardenship of Sheerhatch Wood. Wages of 60s. 8d. a year (2d. a day) had been paid to John Disworth (or Dysworth) from when he was first described as forester, 1382–83, then as, 'forester and warden of Shirehache', 1389–94. Entries in the account 1394–95 show that he had been replaced by John Tunstall and so was only paid for half a year's work. Changes in accounting practice seem to have resulted from the change of warden. The account 1396–97 does not include wages for John Tunstall, and the entry is ambiguous: 'and paid to John Tunstall, warden of Shirehach wood, as in the rent of the dovecot and the warren, leased to him by William Rees, head steward of the lord's land, as above without tally, 13s. 4d.'[18] A partial bailiff's account, headed 'The account of John Tunstall, warden of the lord's warren and wood at Shirehatch', written in a large and very distinctive script and dated: 'from Michaelmas in the 20th year of King Richard II up to the morrow of Michaelmas in the 21st year of the aforesaid king, for one whole year, from which Michaelmas in the 21st year the same John will then make another reckoning' shows that John Tunstall sold underwood and wood to the value of 119s. 8½d. 1396–97 and that he was paid a fee and annuity from the receipts. None of his later accounts survive, but he continued to work on the manor until 1412.[19]

The arrears are followed by details of the rents expected from the tenants of the different types of holdings. Details of the lands held by free tenants are not included. They paid very small rents, referred to as fixed rents or rents of assize, rather as leaseholders often pay ground rents today. During the years 1382–97 the bailiffs' accounts consistently record that the rents paid by the free tenants of Willington were a small part of the receipts, just 6s.½d. These rents

---

[16] BARS, R8/62/2/1, and Thompson, *Bailiffs' Accounts for Willington*, BARS, CRT 130 Willington 11, p. 1.
[17] *Ibid.*
[18] BARS, R8/62/2/11, and Thompson, *Bailiffs' Accounts for Willington*, BARS, CRT 130 Willington 11, pp. 42–45.
[19] BARS, Box R212, Roll 14b, May 1412.

had only increased to 6s. 10½d. 1457–58.[20] The accounts 1480–81 show the same amount generated from the ten free tenants that year.[21] At the end of the fourteenth century the Willington accounts also included rents from the free tenants of Cople and Cardington.

The rents from standard-sized customary lands follow. They had formerly been held in bondage by serfs, described as acremen or molemen, but by the 1380s the unfree tenants were usually referred to as villeins. There were twenty-eight messuages with thirty-four standard-sized holdings of half a virgate, about ten acres, with standard-sized rents of 13s. 4d., and in 1382–83 the account describes them as the: 'Rents of half virgates formerly held in bondage now leased to various tenants of the lord to hold freely, as appears in the new extent.'[22] A copy of the 'new extent' does not now exist, but it was referenced until 1397. The new extent may have been produced as a result of the Peasants' Revolt of 1381. Tenants, who were formerly acremen or molemen, also held a variety of non-standard holdings, eight messuages with land and a variety of smaller pieces of land. There was income from a piece of land in Barford, and five tenants of Willington and Cardington paid their rents in kind.

Patterns of management on the nearby manors of Willington and Haynes are very different and make it clear that the Mowbrays managed their lands flexibly and in individual ways depending on the history, the assets and the human resources of each. In 1382 the Willington bailiff prepared the accounts, but the accounts for Haynes 1384–93 were prepared by two men, the lessee who held the manor as a whole, Roger Tunstall, described as 'farmer',[23] and Roger of Shefford, the park-keeper.[24] After February 1393, John Edward, described as, 'warden of the park there' prepared the accounts, but within a few months he was replaced by William Mareschall who continued in post until Michaelmas 1397 or later.

The name 'Roger' appears four times in the first Haynes account. The men were Roger Tunstall, the man who leased the manor for £22 a year; Roger of Shefford; Roger Parker of Shefford; and Roger Rulle, who paid 20s. for underwood.[25] It seems likely that Roger of Shefford and Roger Parker of Shefford were the same man using both an occupational and a locative alias. In the bailiff's account 1388–89, Roger of Shefford was appointed warden of Haynes Park for life at 2d. a day (60s. 8d. a year) and referred to as receiver for Bedfordshire.[26] In the Willington account 1392–93 Roger Shefford is referred to as: 'Receiver of the lord's money in the aforesaid county at the beginning of the year', and

[20]   British Library, Add Ch. 657.
[21]   Arundel Castle Archives, A1328.
[22]   BARS, R8/62/2/1, and Thompson, *Bailiffs' Accounts for Willington*, BARS, CRT 130 Willington 11, p. 2. It would have been more correct for the word 'granted' to be used instead of 'leased' which implies a formal agreement for a period of years. These tenants were later all described as being 'tenants at will' so did not have secure tenure.
[23]   In this context, this means the person who pays 'the farm' or rent.
[24]   He was said at first to be deputy of William Burton, park-keeper of Lord Thomas of Montbray, Earl of Nottingham and was named in the headings of the seven Haynes accounts, 1384–91.
[25]   BARS, R8/68/1/1, and Thompson, *Bailiffs' Accounts for Willington*, BARS, CRT 130 Willington 11, p. 6.
[26]   BARS, R8/68/1/4, and Thompson, *Bailiffs' Accounts for Willington*, BARS, CRT 130 Willington 11, pp. 22–4.

Roger Tunstall as: 'Receiver of the lord's money in the country of Bedford and elsewhere through the hands of Sir Thomas Yokflete, Receiver General of the lord's money…'[27]

The nine late-fourteenth century bailiffs' accounts which survive for Haynes concentrate on the income and expenditure of the park with few references to other manorial business, although in 1389–90 there is a note that there were no sales of: 'underwood under oak or old hedges [because of] a plague running through the district.'[28] Minor forest courts, which were described as attachments, were held at the end of the fourteenth century and were referred to in the accounts 1396–97, but none of the records have survived. Receipts were recorded under six headings: arrears; rent of the manor farm; grazing in the park; rent of the mill; and external receipts, which included sales of underwood and other items. Costs of the park included wages and other expenditure such as the provision and repair of hedges and maintenance of the warren. The charges and discharges were each totalled and then compared. Money payments to the receiver for Bedfordshire were listed and the amount still owed by the lessee was calculated.

Reductions in the Mowbrays' income from Haynes had begun by the end of the fourteenth century. A calculation of their income shows that it was almost £40, 1384–85, but that by the end of the surviving accounts, 1392–93 and 1394–95, it had reduced to less than £19.[29] However, in the account of 1384–85 Roger Tunstall owed £11 11s. in arrears, and by 1392–95 no arrears were recorded. The manor was at first leased to him for £22 a year and then, for ten years 1389–90 onwards, for £20 a year.[30] He had the use of all the farm buildings and equipment, but he was not entitled to any income from the: 'knight's fee, advowsons of churches, wards, marriages, reliefs, escheats, forfeitures, the park, warren, mill and wood.'[31]

In 1388–89 Roger of Shefford was unable to collect all of the rents from Haynes, but this was unusual.[32] The rent of the windmill had become impossible to collect; at first 10s. a year had been paid by Hugh Milleward, but no payments of rent were recorded 1386–91 because the building needed repairs.[33] In 1392–93, 11s. 8d. was paid when the mill was held for half a year by William Mellor for 6s. 8d., and then by William Milleward for 5s.[34] The records do not make it clear whether these were two different men, or whether William Mellor had negotiated a reduction in rent for the second half of the year and Milleward was an occupa-

[27]   BARS, R8/62/2/9, and Thompson, *Bailiffs' Accounts for Willington*, BARS, CRT 130 Willington 11, p. 35.
[28]   BARS, R8/68/1/5, and Thompson, *Bailiffs' Accounts for Willington*, BARS, CRT 130 Willington 11, p. 27.
[29]   D. Jamieson, *Willington: Manor and the Honour of Mowbray* (unpublished dissertation for the Advanced Research Diploma in Local History, 1999) University of Cambridge, Table 7.
[30]   BARS, R8/68/1/5, and Thompson, *Bailiffs' Accounts for Willington*, BARS, CRT 130 Willington 11, p. 27.
[31]   *Ibid.*
[32]   BARS, R8/68/1/4, and Thompson, *Bailiffs' Accounts for Willington*, BARS, CRT 130 Willington 11, p. 23.
[33]   BARS, R8/68/1/1, and Thompson, *Bailiffs' Accounts for Willington*, BARS, CRT 130 Willington 11, p. 6.
[34]   BARS, R8/68/1/7, and Thompson, *Bailiffs' Accounts for Willington*, BARS, CRT 130 Willington 11, p. 37.

tional alias. However, the mill was, 'overwhelmed with thunder and destroyed by lightning' 1394–95 and no further payments were received.[35]

At Haynes, as at Willington, timber from old buildings and the woodland was sold in some years. Income from this source was greatest at Haynes 1384–85 and 1386–87 when it amounted to £11 4s. 9d. for underwood from the park and an, 'old dry oak sold to John Cauley.'[36] Later sales amounted to less than 45s.

The Haynes accounts share some features with the accounts for Willington: the renegotiation of rents; the reducing viability of the mill, with a total loss of income from this source in Haynes; and reductions in total income at the end of the fourteenth century. No lists of stock or yields of grain or other crops which belonged to the lord of the manor were included from either manor because the Mowbrays no longer farmed the lands directly. But they continued to take careful note of sales of timber and underwood from both manors to nearby landowners or granted to Willington tenants to repair buildings.[37] At Haynes, as at Willington, building materials from old buildings were recycled and sold. This included material from an old lodge by the gate of the park[38] and 'a certain old kitchen' sold to parishioners of Cople 1390–91.[39]

Protecting the Mowbrays' assets

Rents

The Mowbrays took steps to maintain the value of their assets in Willington which included their woodlands; the farmhouses and buildings; the mill, warrens, fisheries and dovecote. But their most important assets were their tenants - without enough good, reliable tenants incomes would reduce. The Mowbrays would be unable to make gifts to Newnham Priory and other religious organisations, or pay grants or annuities to former employees; their buildings, hedges, waterways and woodlands would be neglected and the manor courts would not function properly. The family needed to let as many of their holdings as possible to ensure maximum profit from the manor, and this was not always easy.

One such example was the holding of Felicity Prentys who held it from the death of her husband in 1411 until its surrender in May 1416.[40] The holding was then without a tenant for a few months and the bailiff, in October 1416, asked other tenants to enquire whether: 'there is anyone native or other within the demesne of the lord that could hold and occupy the said tenement.'[41] A new tenant was found by May 1417, but he left the manor within a few months.[42] The fields in this

35 BARS, R8/68/1/8, and Thompson, *Bailiffs' Accounts for Willington*, BARS, CRT 130 Willington 11, p. 41.
36 BARS, R8/68/1/3, and Thompson, *Bailiffs' Accounts for Willington*, BARS, CRT 130 Willington 11, p. 14.
37 Jamieson, *Willington Manor and the Honour of Mowbray*, Table 3 and 5.
38 BARS, R8/68/1/5, and Thompson, *Bailiffs' Accounts for Willington*, BARS, CRT 130 Willington 11, p. 27.
39 BARS, R8/68/1/6, and Thompson, *Bailiffs' Accounts for Willington*, BARS, CRT 130 Willington 11, p. 32.
40 BARS, Box R212, Roll 20, May 1416.
41 BARS, Box R212, Roll 21, October 1416.
42 BARS, Box R212, Roll 22, May 1417.

holding were subsequently let for short periods and the buildings fell into disrepair. There were no reports of it being let as a whole until much later, in 1478, when William Partryche and his wife Agnes took it and another messuage called Myton, which had also been difficult to let in the past,[43] 'for the term of their lives at the will of the Lady.'[44]

Leasing out the demesne lands immediately after the Peasants' Revolt began a series of reductions in rent which lasted until the second half of the fifteenth century. The lands were first granted to various bondsmen tenants and certain tenants at will in 1382 at a total rent of £25 6s. 8d. which increased the next year to £27 6s. 9d. The tenants refused to pay the full amount because they claimed that the rent they had paid previously included the rents of four messuages and thirty-two acres of land for which they were now being charged an additional 32s. The bailiff, Robert Gostwyk, allowed debts of 32s. a year to accumulate until August 1393, by which time the tenants owed £17 12s. He was then replaced, and the lord's council made an enquiry. Although no copy of the accounts, 1393–94, survives there was no mention of any reductions in the account of 1394–95; rents of 32s. for the four messuages and thirty-two acres of land were paid and the rent of £27 6s. 8d. continued to be charged for the former demesne lands, but the tenants' debts had been cancelled.

One of the original farmers of the demesne land, Richard Yarwey, died in 1404.[45] A heriot of one bullock worth 8s. was paid, and the holding was transferred to his wife for her life.[46] But when, in 1417, Richard Bawdewene surrendered one quarter of assarted demesne land into the hand of the lord, for which he paid 8s. a year, a new tenant could not be found and the bailiff was ordered to be answerable for the profits.[47] It appears that some way of persuading Richard to continue in his holding was found, but in May 1420 he finally surrendered the land: 'because he was a poor man [and] was incapable of holding the said holding.'[48] In April 1421 it was still vacant, as was another piece of the demesne lands.[49] The attempts made by the steward to keep this tenant reinforce the impression that the Mowbrays were experiencing difficulties in letting their lands. Although the steward, Thomas Bekyngham, and others stayed overnight on 17 June 1421 to agree the rents of the demesne land with the tenants, Richard Bawdewene's former holding was still without a tenant in October 1423.[50]

No further details of demesne holdings survive until 1449 when they were divided into eleven lots of differing sizes and were leased to twelve tenants, including William Launcelyn who: 'holds the hall yard and le Orcharde and half of Thalde Well as divided by the ditch there and renders 20s. a year, which certain 20s. are part of the aforesaid £18 to be paid in the future.'[51] The tenants agreed to pay £18 a year between them for three years, with the following benefits: 'And also the lord

43   BARS, Box R212, Roll 42b, April 1457. Mytons had been without a tenant for seven years by 1457.
44   BARS, Box R212, Roll 59a, November 1478.
45   'farmer' is used here in its medieval sense, that is, meaning someone who pays a rent or a 'farm.'
46   BARS, Box R212, Roll 7, October 1404.
47   This is the only reference in the rolls to the demesne being assarted land, that is, land which has been cleared from woodland.
48   BARS, Box R212, Roll 28, May 1420.
49   BARS, Box R212, Roll 30, April 1421.
50   BARS, Box R212, Roll 33, October 1423.
51   BARS, Box R212, Roll 38b, May 1449.

granted to the same tenants 8s. a year for ploughbote. And the lord will allow the benefit, in the third year of the aforesaid term, for them to enter upon the Fallow pasture and meadow land at the feast of the annunciation of the blessed Mary.'[52]

The demesne lands were again surrendered in 1454;[53] the following court rolls do not show how long they remained in the lord's hands, but by 1457–58 it seems that the new steward, Thomas Rokes, had found fresh tenants: 'And for £18 as rent of various lands of Wilyngton so handed over to tenants of the same vill by the steward this year as appears through the roll [torn edge illegible][54] £17 and lately £20. Sum total £18.'[55] During the next twenty years fewer grants of lands, including the demesne lands, were recorded, and holdings were increasingly let for two or three lives, or leased for longer periods; there are no further records of the demesne lands being distributed.

The rents for lands held by former acremen for the former demesne had all reduced substantially before 1457–58. The next surviving account, 1481–82, shows that rents payable for lands in Barford had ceased, and although the rents of free tenants had increased slightly and the levels of rents for the half-virgates, the fisheries and the warren were maintained, there were other unspecified reductions of rents: 'And in the reductions of rent for various lands and tenements in Wyllyngton as ordered above rendered of old that is to say in Title, fixed rents, rents in kind, rents of half virgates of land, and rents of acremen ... in reductions this year £7 22d.'[56]

Not all the Midland manors belonging to the Mowbrays showed such a decline in revenues, but the bailiff's accounts for the nearby Mowbray manors 1480–81 make depressing reading.[57] In Haynes there were reductions of rent for two holdings and a loss of income because the rabbit warren was without a tenant; there was no tenant for the fisheries at Bedford Castle; and at Bromham reductions in the rents from cottages and tenements amounted to 17s. 8d.[58]

The mill, fisheries, dovecote and warren
The lord sought to raise income from various capital assets on the manor including the mill, fisheries, dovecote and warren. This was not, however, without its difficulties.

The mill was leased for periods of years to men of substance who usually came from outside the manor. The lord initially paid for mill repairs but later attempted to keep it in good condition by tightening the provisions under which it was leased and attempting to make it clear which repairs were the responsibility of the miller.

Just before the Peasants' Revolt, in 1376, the building was said to be: 'sufficient, but repairs are greatly needed to the wheel and the necessary working parts in the water, and to the floodgates, weir and foundation of the mill.'[59] The accounts of

---

52   *Ibid.*
53   BARS, Box R212, Roll 42b, May 1454.
54   The original document appears to read *cum ro* but some text is missing. It may be interpreted as 'formerly.'
55   British Library, Add Ch. 657. The discrepancy in the amounts paid has been checked with the original in the British Library.
56   Arundel Castle Archive, A1328.
57   Moye, *The Estates and Finances of the Mowbray Family*, pp.109–10.
58   Arundel Castle Archives, A1328.
59   Bailey, *The English Manor*, p. 59.

Robert Gostwyk, 1382–83, show that 21s. 8d. was paid by the lord: 'on account of various defects of the dams, the pond of the watermill was carried away by a certain flood of water coming this year about Christmas; for several men to repair the channel several times, according as it was inspected.'[60] Repairs continued to be needed after more floods in December 1384.[61]

There was a new lease of the mill of £5 6s. 8d. in 1382–83, but in 1384–85 the rent was raised to £6 'and no more' because of the aforementioned flood: 'the pool of the same mill was carried away by a flood of water ... and it remained under repair from the same month up to Lady day next following, for one quarter.'[62] These repairs cost £4 3s. 4d.[63] The rent was still fixed at £6 when John Phille secured a new lease, 1386–87.[64] The following year he renegotiated the lease for seven years and the rent returned to its 1382–83 level.

> And for 106s. 8d. for the rent of one watermill there, thus leased to John Phille for a term of seven years, this year the first, as appears in the court roll. Then it used to be leased for £6. And the same John maintaining the said mill and the pond of the same all at his own expense, besides which he will have timber from the lord, and moreover he will maintain 'les bayes' and the gates and the house during the aforesaid term.[65]

All went well at first, and John Phille renewed his lease. The mill pond was reported to be in need of repair in May 1408 when he was ordered to repair it, and again in October 1410, when he was allowed twenty trees for piles and other timber to make the repairs.[66] The repairs were not considered good enough however, and in April 1411 he was threatened with a penalty of 40s. if they were not done properly.[67] The threat was repeated in October that year.[68]

In October 1413 the mill was leased to John Usshere for nine years at the same rent. The contract was even more detailed and precise:

> The said John and his assigns will provide for millstones and all of the Machinery[69] pertaining to the said mill during their aforesaid term at the mill. And they will sufficiently sustain or sufficiently repair the mill Dams and the holding and will put them right at their own expense taking timber as necessary from the Lord for repairing the aforesaid mill and Dam as is found necessary by the assigns and lord's officials handing over who have been instructed to deputise for him for the custom and expense of the said John. And they will provide one limb for the same John to repair and put right the said Dam during the

---

[60]   BARS, R8/62/2/1, and Thompson, *Bailiffs' Accounts for Willington*, BARS, CRT 130 Willington 11, p. 2.

[61]   BARS, R8/62/2/2, and Thompson, *Bailiffs' Accounts for Willington*, BARS, CRT 130 Willington 11, p. 6.

[62]   That is the 25 March.

[63]   BARS, R8/62/2/2, and Thompson, *Bailiffs' Accounts for Willington*, BARS, CRT 130 Willington 11, p. 4.

[64]   BARS, R8/62/2/4, and Thompson, *Bailiffs' Accounts for Willington*, BARS, CRT 130 Willington 11, p. 11.

[65]   BARS, R6/62/2/8, and Thompson, *Bailiffs' Accounts for Willington*, BARS, CRT 130 Willington 11, p. 16.

[66]   BARS, Box R212, Roll 9b, May 1408; Roll 12, October 1410.

[67]   BARS, Box R212, Roll 13, April 1411.

[68]   BARS, Box R212, Roll 14, October 1411.

[69]   Described as *Goyngere*.

aforesaid term. And the said John and his assigns will hand over the said mill, the stones for milling and all the Machinery pertaining to the said mill and the mill Dams at the end of the term of the tenancy well and sufficiently repaired. Agreeing that the same shall be well and faithfully observed and be held by the same John Usshere and at the end his obligations obliged by his heirs and his executors. And he provided twenty pounds in sterling silver, as above, as obliged and fully complete in the above script. Which certain deed remains in the bag of rolls of Bedford.[70]

For eight years John Usshere repaired the mill regularly; he was allowed twelve trees for the dam in April 1414, two crab trees for the workings in April 1415 and four trees for the cogs in October 1416, but by June 1423 major repairs were necessary and it was put into the hands of the steward, John Boteler, and a certain John Woketon, who does not appear elsewhere in the records. Together they arranged that local carpenter Richard Lygtfot should: 'make and repair all the defects in the buildings pertaining to the same mill, the foundation beams and studs for the walls and roof to be repaired by the aforesaid carpenter. Also taking the laths from the lord.'[71] The total cost was 26s. 8d. John Usshere's share of the costs was 7s. 6d., although by that time he may have been replaced by Thomas Stoughton who was fined 6d. for taking: 'unjust and excessive toll by unlawful measure without seal' in October 1425.[72]

In May 1449 the lord's council allowed twenty oak trees, twenty piles and six large elms for repairs.[73] In May 1452 the mill was leased to Thomas Myller, for six years, at a lower rent of £3 13s. 4d. Thomas named three men as guarantors for repairs and rent, and the conditions of the contract he negotiated stated that:

> The lord will provide and allow for the aforesaid mill all the stuffs for the repairs of the mill as and when they are [repaired]. And the aforesaid Thomas will provide all the Carpentry works and iron for the working parts for the belt mechanisms and stones. And at the end of his term the aforesaid will well and sufficiently repair the aforesaid mill with stones and all other necessaries, and hand it back as it was received. And the lord will find everything for the repairs of the building of the said mill and the dam, to be made as and when [needed] during the aforesaid term. And the aforesaid Thomas will quarry the Gravel near the mill once in the aforesaid principal term. And the aforesaid will have the fisheries in Les Fletzates[74] and heads of willows round the mill and all the underwood on the dam with the reeds and ozier beds and other profits pertaining and he makes limewash there when he is able.[75]

In 1455 the mill rent was reduced as it needed repairs and was out of action for nine weeks.[76] Thomas Myller is recorded as paying rent until 1458 by which time the rent had returned to its May 1452 level of 73s. 4d.[77] In 1459 there were major repairs under the supervision of John Gostwyk:

[70]   BARS, Box R212, Roll 15, October 1413.
[71]   BARS, Box R212, Roll 32, June 1423.
[72]   BARS, Box R212, Roll 35, October 1425.
[73]   BARS, Box R212, Roll 38b, May 1449.
[74]   Possibly the flood gates.
[75]   BARS, Box R212, Roll 40b, May 1452.
[76]   BARS, Box R212, Roll 44a, October 1455.
[77]   British Library, Add Ch. 657.

3s. paid to John Stone, workman, for supervising the improvements to the Dam next to the lord's mill for 9 days at 4d. a day

And for 2s. paid to John Roper for carrying clay for making the Dam for 2 days at 12d. a day

And for 7d. paid to the same John Roper for cutting and carrying one cart of Underwood from Schyrehatch to the mill

And for 3s. 2d. paid to John Goddard for one Brace bought by himself for the lords mill

For 2s. 1¼d. paid to John Farthyng for 33 pieces of ironwork bought by himself, one with iron machinery bought for putting right one Spindle for the said mill.

And to 4s. 4d. paid to Simon Usshere in part payment of 30s for making [illegible] part of the rape[78] of the mill at the west end from the start, in full[79]

And in 16d. paid to Thomas Ovveystond and his servant for trimming one quarter and sawing 140 feet of the table of the said quarter for the use of the miller from beginning to end, in full

And for 5d. paid to John Roper for the carriage of the said quarter etc.[80]

Simon Usshere appears to have taken on the mill by 1458 and remained in post until 1462.[81] In October of that year he was fined 2d. for taking excessive toll. An illegible passage at the end of the October 1462 roll seems to indicate that a new miller, Thomas Gybon, paid the rent that year.[82] Thomas Gybon (or Cebon) is described as the miller in 1463 and there were repairs to the mill, the dam and the causeway, and wicker hurdles were made, 'for turning the river' in 1464.[83] Twenty-nine large pieces of timber for further repairs were granted at the next court,[84] and there were further repairs to the dam in May 1468.[85] William Watt was established as miller by April 1469, and in the next few years there were more repairs.[86]

Maintenance of the mill had become very expensive, and in March 1475 Thomas Passewater embarked on an ambitious experiment. He was granted the mill and its waters and the fisheries and rabbit warren on forty-year leases, at 40s. a year and 26s. 8d. a year respectively. It was agreed that:

The Lady through the pledge of the Steward, granted to Thomas Passewater her several fishing waters in Welyngton with 2 islands and the Rabbit Warren and the game of the Warren within all the demesne of Welyngton with all of them

[78] *Rape* – meaning unknown.
[79] This may mean that this is the final payment.
[80] BARS, Box R212, Roll 47a, June 1459. John Goddard and Thomas Ovveystond were not village tenants as their names do not reappear in the documents. The other men in this list were probably local to Willington.
[81] He was described as being the miller of two years in 1461. BARS, Box R212, Roll 49a, October 1461.
[82] BARS, Box R212, Roll 50c, October 1462.
[83] British Library, Add Ch. 26813/1, October 1463. The meaning of *Flekys*, is not clear, but they are assumed to be basket-work panels.
[84] British Library, Add Ch. 26813/2, May 1464.
[85] British Library, Add Ch. 26813/4, May 1468.
[86] British Library, Add Ch. 26813/6, April 1469.

properly pertaining and the Dead Trees and the toppe and loppe[87] as placed upon the wild Rabbits. To have and to hold for the term of 40 years next following, rendering therefrom 26s. 8d. a year to the Lady as written within.

The Lady granted, through the Steward, to the said Thomas the waters of the Mill in the said Township with all of the appurtenances of the same. The said Thomas will provide for the weir above, and the lady will provide the large timber pertaining to the warren. And the said Thomas will make repairs of the Dam; to have and to hold for the said term of 40 years rendering therefrom 40s. a year.[88]

However, the forty year lease was too ambitious, and in April 1476 Thomas Passewater surrendered the watermill for the use of Henry Parker, who agreed to another forty-year lease at 40s. a year.

Thomas Passewater came to this court and surrendered the Welyngton Watermill into the hand of the Steward, for the use of Henry Parker who was granted seisin by the Lady, through the pledge of the Steward. To have and to hold himself for the term of 40 years, rendering 40s. therefrom annually to the lady and suit of Court. And the said Henry will sustain and sufficiently repair the Dam and maintain all the Moving Parts pertaining to the said mill, that is to say, the stones for Milling, the Hoops and Spindles and Cogs and Wheels[89] and blades for two wheels, that is to say, the water wheel and cog wheel pertaining. The lady will provide him with large timber and pertinences as needed.[90]

This experiment did not work either, and the rent for the mill was reduced to 53s. 4d. when it was leased for twelve years to John German, 1478–79.[91] It was agreed then that: 'the said John will repair the said mill and all parts of the building at his own cost and expense during the aforesaid term.'[92] This rent was only half the value of that of 1382–83.[93] It reduced yet again to £2, 1480–81.[94] There are no further details of the mill until a Richard Smalwood is recorded as miller in December 1522 and was fined 2d. for taking excessive toll.[95]

The significant fall in the rent of the mill may suggest poverty on the manor, but the evidence is not conclusive. It may equally indicate significant changes in agriculture as tenants adjusted to changing eating patterns and markets. A reduced demand for grain and an increase of animal protein in most peoples' diets, or increased profits from keeping sheep, may have meant that the percentage of land under the plough reduced and less corn was ground by the mill so that it became less profitable.[96]

The lord gained a small extra income from the fines paid by the millers for charging the tenants unfair tolls for the grain which they ground for them. John

[87]   Presumably the prunings from trees.
[88]   BARS, Box R212, Roll 55b, March 1475.
[89]   This term is written as *rowns*, so the translation 'wheels' has been assumed.
[90]   BARS, Box R212, Roll 57b, April 1476.
[91]   Arundel Castle Archives, A1328. In this account, 1480–81 is said to be the third year of John German's lease.
[92]   Arundel Castle Archives, A1328.
[93]   Arundel Castle Archives, A1328.
[94]   Moye, *The Estates and Finances of the Mowbray Family*, p. 109.
[95]   BARS, Box R212, Roll 64, December 1522.
[96]   Britnell, 'Markets and Incentives: Common Themes and Regional Variations', p. 16.

Phille paid fines in October 1394, October 1395 and 1410. No fines were paid while Queen Joan held the manor, but John Usshere paid them on nine occasions after 1414. There are records that millers paid fines for unfair tolls in the views of frankpledge with courts in 1425, 1455, 1458, 1461, 1462, 1472 and 1522.[97]

As with the mill, the Mowbrays hoped to receive an income from their fisheries, dovecote and warren. The fisheries and warren were situated on a strip of land of mixed quality, consisting of sandy soils and beds of gravel with patches of heavy clay, near the river. The dovecote was probably situated near to the medieval manor site, believed to have been just north of the church, near the where the Tudor dovecote and stables stand today.

In the late fourteenth century the accounts describe: 'private fishing water of the Ouse at Willington, with the holme there', which by 1467 was described as, 'several fisheries in Wyllyngton with 2 islands.'[98] There are two islands at the Danish Camp site today. There may have been eels in the millpond and bream, perch, pike, roach and tench may have restocked naturally in the river. No evidence of commercial fish production or sale has been found, but lessees of the fisheries may have sold their catch to fishmongers in the markets at Bedford, Potton or Cambridge and also used the ponds to rear ducks, geese or swans for the table.

Dovecotes represented the lord's domination of the manor and must have been resented by the tenants; the pigeons fed on their fields reducing their crop yields. By 1425 three tenants had dovecotes on their Willington holdings and were required to explain how this had come about.[99] Although the matter was referred to the lord's council it is not clear how it was resolved. The solution is not mentioned in the two rolls of 1426 and must have taken place in the years for which no rolls survive.

The rabbit warren had mixed success. Rabbits were luxury items, valued for food and for their skins, but often vulnerable to the cold and damp in winter.[100] The Mowbrays founded warrens in east Suffolk at the end of the fourteenth century, and rabbit warrens were established on the free-draining soil south of the river in Willington and in the nearby manor of Haynes about this time.[101] There are no descriptions of the warren at Willington, but the one at Haynes was enclosed by a ditch with hedges on the top and was secured by a locked gate.[102] Some warrens in East Anglia were protected by look-out towers to discourage poachers and natural predators, but there is no evidence of such buildings at Haynes or Willington where brambles were used to protect the rabbit holes, unlike parts of East Anglia where gorse was used.[103]

In 1423 the vicar of Aylesbury was accused of taking rabbits from the warren in 1419:

---

[97] BARS, Box R212, Roll 35, October 1425; Roll 44a, October 1455; Roll 47, October 1458; Roll 49a, October 1461; Roll 50c, October 1462; Roll 54b, May 1472; Roll 64, December 1522.
[98] BARS, Box R212, Roll 53a, April 1467.
[99] BARS, Box R212, Roll 35, October 1425.
[100] M. Bailey, 'The Rabbit and the Medieval East Anglian Economy', *Agricultural History Review,* vol. 36 (1998), p. 4.
[101] Bailey, 'The Rabbit and the Medieval East Anglian Economy', pp. 1–2.
[102] BARS, Box R214, m. 123 dorse.
[103] The use of brambles was recorded in the lease of the warrens in BARS, Box R212, Roll 53a, April 1467 and Roll 57b, April 1476.

They present that Thomas Roger, vicar of the church at Aylesbury in the County of Buckinghamshire, on the Tuesday next after the feast of the Nativity of our Lord in the 7th year of the reign of Henry V [26 December 1419] came within the warren of the lord at Welyngton in the county of Bedford and hunted in the aforesaid warren and took at least 20 pairs of rabbits. Therefore a writ is prosecuted against the said Thomas etc.[104]

During the fifteenth century rabbits continued to be given as gifts to friends and their pelts were valued as trimmings for garments. Thomas Cramfeld built a rabbit warren in Michaelmas Field, but in 1474 he was ordered not to use it under a penalty of 6s. 8d.[105] The lady of the manor was protecting her right of free warren and in doing so she also protected the tenants' crops from devastation. In 1497, Thomas Howard, Earl of Surrey, leased the rabbit warren with the fisheries to John and William Gostwyk, who may have hoped to produce rabbits commercially.[106]

The income from the dovecote and warren remained irregular. The dovecote yielded 3s. 4d. 1387–88 and 1388–89, but there was nothing from the warren as, 'the rabbits were used in the lord's household.'[107] In 1389–90 and 1390–91 there was no income from the warren because it was being restocked, and there were few rabbits 1392–93 or 1394–95.[108] Richard Pullet paid a rent of 13s. 4d. for the dovecote 1389–90. When it was re-roofed in 1390–91 the costs included 17s. for 1000 tiles from Cople, two quarters four bushels of fired lime from Bedford and twelve days wages for a tiler and his servant.[109] In 1396–97 the head steward leased the dovecot and the warren to John Tunstall for 13s. 4d. Much later, in 1487 and 1504, the warren was included in the rent of the fisheries.[110] At that time no mention was made of the dovecote.

Woodlands and timber

Timber and woodlands were important as long-term investments and as status symbols. They were also a useful source of revenue in difficult times, providing renewable sources of building material and fuel.

Evidence that the use of timber from the woodlands for the repair of tenants' buildings was controlled begins to appear from April 1407.[111] In October 1407, when Robert Partryche was granted a messuage with half a virgate of land, it was agreed that: 'he will take large timber from the lady according to the custom.'[112] No earlier reference to allowances of timber has been found, so it is not known under what conditions timber had previously been allocated.

[104] BARS, Box R212, Roll 34, September 1423.
[105] BARS, Box R212, Roll 55a, March 1474.
[106] Finberg, 'Gostwicks of Willington', p. 53.
[107] BARS, R6/62/2/8, and Thompson, *Bailiffs' Accounts for Willington*, BARS, CRT 130 Willington 11, pp. 16–20.
[108] BARS, R6/62/2/8, and Thompson, *Bailiffs' Accounts for Willington*, BARS, CRT 130 Willington 11, pp. 25, 29, 33, 39.
[109] BARS, R6/62/2/8, and Thompson, *Bailiffs' Accounts for Willington*, BARS, CRT 130 Willington 11, p. 30. The transcription says that the roofing materials were slates, but because of the extensive clay available they were probably tiles.
[110] *Compoti of all the Ministers of Thomas, Earl of Surrey, for Manors of Framlingham at the Castle, Kettleburgh, Hacheston, Peasenhall, Kelsale and Willington (Bd)*, HD1538/225/5-6.
[111] BARS, Box R212, Roll 8a, April 1407.
[112] BARS, Box R212, Roll 9, October 1407.

Maintenance of the hedges was also important, and in 1391 Henry Plasshe was paid 3s. 4d. for ten days work in May, June and July to close the gaps in the hedge round Sheerhatch Wood.[113] By 1426 the hedges were again broken down, and John Kempston was ordered to repair them before the next Easter or pay a penalty of 100s.[114] When he failed to do so he was given another year to complete the task, but no evidence has survived to indicate whether he ever did.

In 1384–85 timber from the bakery, kitchen and chapel of the manor house, 'with lead of one closet from the same' was recycled and sold for £7 6s. 8d.[115] Later, in 1455–57, it was again accepted that some buildings were redundant or not worth renewing and more surplus timber and building materials were recycled.[116] The items were valued before being sold or were distributed to tenants free of charge. Thomas Rokes, the new steward in charge of the distribution, undertook this carefully:

> And of the old timber found in the tenement which Nicholas Waryn held, lately in the holding of Robert Partrych, the aforesaid timber was allowed to various tenants to make their repairs under the supervision of the bailiff. Therefrom 3 spars are to be allowed to John Yarwey the elder, and to Nicholas Crewce 1 spar, also to John Ferthyng 1 spar, also to John Roper 3 spars, to John Clerk 3 spars, whatsoever timber was allowed on the day of payment on condition that the lord had right of possession, were customarily allowed by the lord and [were] all good trees as were previously had and were received on the above day.

> Also to John Salt 25 spars. Also there were certain granted by the bailiff for repairs in the same holding. That is to say for the above Stable 3 foundation beams, also 4 studs for one hood[117] and 3 in another hood. Also one Sydrafter for the Forge, with one spar.[118] Also for the Pig sty, 2 spars. Also for on the bakehouse there 5 spars, 6 studs, one horizontal beam. Also for on the hall, two Spars. Also to John Redy 1 foundation beam. And there remain there 4 spars which have no value for they were lying at some time in the water and at some time in air. And it is known that 2 wall-plates are lying there, with all the roof and they have no value.

> And they were ordered by the bailiff to hand over all the aforesaid timber for use of the lord and to repair the same [illegible] and he should make delivery to the tenement of Nicholas Waryn of sufficient timber for him to make repairs to his tenement. And the aforesaid Nicholas Waryn agreed in full Court to make the aforesaid to the building. Also that the lord will pay 20s. And the Steward has agreed.[119]

Sheerhatch Wood and Conduit Grove were, and still are, situated on the heavy clays which cover the greensand ridge in the south of the manor. The manual tasks of

---

[113] BARS, R6/62/2/8, and Thompson, *Bailiffs' Accounts for Willington*, BARS, CRT 130 Willington 11, p. 30.

[114] BARS, Box R212, Roll 36a, April 1426; Roll 36, September 1426.

[115] BARS, R6/62/2/2, and Thompson, *Bailiffs' Accounts for Willington*, BARS, CRT 130 Willington 11, p. 5.

[116] BARS, Box R212, Roll 43b, May 1455; Roll 44a, October 1455; Roll 44b, April 1456; Roll 45b, April 1457; Roll 46a, October 1457.

[117] *Capite.* The meaning is not clear, but the context suggests that this was a cover to protect the entrance, not part of the main structure.

[118] Side-rafter.

[119] BARS, Box R212, Roll 45b, April 1457.

clearing and cutting wood and repairing fences and gates were the responsibility of the woodward, working under the supervision of the keeper of Sheerhatch, usually a member of the gentry, or the bailiff. The bailiffs' accounts 1382–97 show that twelve-year cropping cycles for underwood were used; the eastern part of the wood was cropped for underwood 1384–85 and 1385–86 and was not cropped again until 1396–97. Underwood was sold at 6s. 8d. an acre in most years, and the cropping locations were usually given. The accounts show that the wood was divided into at least seven sections described as Sheerhatch itself; the eastern part of the same; the middle quarter; Sheerhache next Bynlegh quarter; next Coppynhamgate; the southern part of the wood; and Sheerhatch wood next Willington.[120] At Willington, croppings of willow and oak cuttings were sometimes sold; a maple blown down in the wind was sold for 3s. 1389–90,[121] and large wood was sold for 40s. an acre 1392–93.[122] At Haynes John Caule (or Cauley) bought old dry oaks on three occasions for 3s. each, 1385–86, 1386–87 and 1390–91.[123] This seasoned, expensive timber was unlikely to have been used for buildings, farm carts or other implements, but the documents give no clues about what was made from it. Underwood with an estimated value of 100s. was donated from Haynes to the, 'hospice of our lady at Newenham', 1396–97.[124]

The survival of Sheerhatch Wood to the present day is surprising. Although: 'the survival of almost any large tract of woodland suggests that there has been an industry to protect it against the claims of farmers' this was not the case in Willington where, although timber was used for building, brewing, baking and possibly small-scale brick making, there is no evidence of other industrial use.[125]

Building maintenance
The Mowbrays took steps to maintain the value of their building stock. The steward might agree to the delivery of timber to repair buildings and occasionally sanction payment for repairs, but instances of both were kept to a minimum and avoided where possible. Tenants therefore often delayed making the required repairs and occasionally avoided them altogether even though they were expected to renovate buildings and to hand them back in good condition at the end of a tenancy. Regular inspections were made of the state of all the buildings on the manor, and a variety of techniques were used to attempt to force the tenants to maintain them.

The first roll, dated April 1394, granted three new tenancies on condition that each tenant paid the same rent and performed the same services as the previous tenants, but these were not specified. A later entry in the same court roll, however,

[120] The locations of Bynlegh and Coppynhamgate are not known, and there are no other references to them in surviving documents.
[121] BARS, R8/62/2/7, and Thompson, *Bailiffs' Accounts for Willington*, BARS, CRT 130 Willington 11, p. 25.
[122] BARS, R8/62/2/9, and Thompson, *Bailiffs' Accounts for Willington*, BARS, CRT 130 Willington 11, p. 34.
[123] BARS, R8/68/2, 3, 6 and Thompson, *Bailiffs' Accounts for Willington*, BARS, CRT 130 Willington 11, pp. 10, 14, 31.
[124] BARS, R8/68/2/9, and Thompson, *Bailiffs' Accounts for Willington*, BARS, CRT 130 Willington 11, p. 46
[125] O. Rackham, *Trees and Woodland in the British Landscape* (London, 1973), p. 73.

makes it clear that keeping buildings in good repair was a condition of tenancy; four tenants, Thomas Taillour, Edward Taillour, John Berde and John Wattes, who formerly held tenancies from the lord in bondage, had, 'ruined and defective houses' and were ordered to, 'repair and mend these under penalty of forfeiture.' On this occasion these tenants were not fined for having ruined buildings, but in the next roll eight tenants were each fined 2d. and threatened with penalties of 10s. if their buildings were not repaired by the next court.

The most important building on the manor was the manor house with its complex of farm buildings.[126] A detailed list of these buildings in 1376 includes: 'a hall of ancient fashion with a pantry, a buttery, a passage and a kitchen annexed ... a bake-house, a chamber called Knights' chamber, a building called 'la Nuricierie',[127] a chapel and a building called the Garret which used to be used as a wardrobe for clothes.'[128] It was estimated that the cost of the necessary repairs would be £100. There is evidence of alterations to the manor house 1384–85.[129] In this year the bailiff's account begins with huge arrears of almost £50 but includes details of the sale of timber from a bakery, a kitchen and a chapel from the manor, and of lead from a closet, which was arranged by Thomas Tuttebury, the lord's receiver general. No mention of other, later repairs to the manorial complex have been found. The manor court may have been held in the hall of the medieval manor house before it was demolished, and the moat filled in, during the 1530s, when it was replaced by a Tudor building.[130]

Damage to buildings, caused by bad weather, neglect by the tenants or other factors, would have been an ongoing state of affairs, but unusually large numbers of buildings needing repair are recorded in anticipation of changes in lordship or stewardship when the surveys would have been more rigorous. In April 1409 five tenants were offered timber to repair the buildings on their holdings:

> And that Simon Tele has two still has a day inset houses that have fallen down. Therefore he was ordered that he should repair them fully before the next [court] under a penalty of 40d. And that John mended Goffe has one shippon, Adam mended Warde one grange, William Webbe one grange and one room ruined and deficient. Therefore they are ordered to repair them before the next [court] under a penalty for each of 40d. And that William [1d] Webbe had 5 trees to repair his buildings of which 3 were not put in repairs he made, as above. Therefore he was amerced and he was ordered to put the aforesaid trees in the repairs of his buildings before the next [court] under a penalty of 2s. And that Nicholas [2d] Shaxton had 8 trees as before and still has not put them in the repairs of the buildings. Therefore he was amerced. And he was ordered to put the trees in the repairs of his buildings before the next [court] under a penalty of 40d. [131]

---

[126] Described as the 'capital messuage' in Bailey, *The English Manor*, p. 58.
[127] This was either a nursery for the children, or somewhere for the care of the sick.
[128] Bailey, *The English Manor*, p. 59.
[129] BARS, R8/62/2/2, and Thompson, *Bailiffs' Accounts for Willington*, BARS, CRT 130 Willington 11, p. 5.
[130] Finberg, 'Gostwicks of Willington', p. 60.
[131] BARS, Box R212, Roll 11, April 1409.The superscript words in the original document suggest that it was written out before the court and that they were later additions. 'still has a day' implies that Simon Tele was being given time to complete his repairs.

In addition, John Tunstall, keeper of the Sheerhatch wood, was ordered to hand over more than 150 trees to fourteen other tenants,[132] who were ordered to use them to repair their buildings before Michaelmas (29 September) or pay a penalty for each of 40d.[133] Queen Joan appears to have been making a determined effort to hand Willington and its buildings over to John Mowbray in good condition when he reached his majority, although his stock of timber must have been depleted.

The Queen appointed a new steward, John Boteler, in 1410, and he demonstrated a robust approach to management, making strenuous efforts to find tenants for vacant holdings despite more than the usual deaths and surrenders at that time. In 1410 three members of the manor elite, William Pecke, John Gostwyk and John Myton, took over lands without permission, but the changes were recognised by the court and they later swore fealty.[134]

In April 1411 Queen Joan agreed that a new tenant of a ruined holding should be given 6s. 8d. towards repairs, but she soon reinforced the requirement that tenants were responsible for the repair of their buildings.[135] John Akyrman was ordered to: 'maintain, sustain, repair and put right the said holding at his own expense, except taking large timber from the lady.'[136] Thomas Smythe, Richard Baudewyne, John Rodland and Robert Dolt were each granted holdings for the terms of their lives on agreement that: 'the said holding will be well and sufficiently repaired when handed over at the end of his term.'[137] Two tenants were deprived of their holdings in May 1412 because they were no longer capable of caring for them properly.[138]

In the first two courts after John Mowbray was granted his estates in 1413 his steward ordered nineteen buildings to be repaired.[139] In May 1416, when the manor's population was at its lowest point, shortage of straw was given as the reason why several tenants were unable to repair their roofs.[140] The only other reference to straw in the records is from the court roll of April 1440, when it is an item in the list of costs for building a new barn.[141] John Mowbray began a five-year period of fighting in France in 1417, having appointed Thomas Bekyngham as steward while he was away, and between twelve and sixteen buildings needing repair were listed in each of the four rolls October 1418–May 1420.[142]

In 1420, John Wodeward, William Wryght the younger, John Yarwey and Richard Baudewene appealed to the lord's council, saying that they could not afford to make the required repairs to their buildings, but the unsympathetic response was that:

[132] *Ibid.* '… to William Rydere to repair his buildings eight trees, to Thomas Shireborn ten, John Bande seven, John Myton twelve, Robert Partryche twelve, Adam Warde three, Henry Yarwey ten, and John Grace seven, Alec Tele ten, John Rydere forty, Robert Chaumbrileyn twelve, John Treket ten, John Pelle four, and Robert Myton eight, for repairs.'

[133] *Ibid.*

[134] BARS, Box R212, Roll 12, October 1410.

[135] BARS, Box R212, Roll 13, April 1411.

[136] BARS, Box R212, Roll 14, October 1411.

[137] BARS, Box R212, Roll 14b, May 1412.

[138] *Ibid.*

[139] BARS, Box R212, Roll 15, October 1413, Roll 16, April 1414.

[140] BARS, Box R212, Roll 20, May 1416.

[141] BARS, Box R212, Roll 37, April 1440.

[142] BARS, Box R212, Roll 25, October 1418; Roll 26, May 1419; Roll 27, October 1419; Roll 28, May 1420.

'because the said tenants are paupers and in the greatest penury between them, then let them help one another.'[143]

John Mowbray's tour of duty in France came to an end in 1422. The view of frankpledge of September 1423 and the extra court of October the same year show that Willington had been neglected in his absence.[144] In October 1423 three holdings were vacant after the death of two widows and seven messuages were without tenants. More than twenty buildings needed repair, although half seem to have been repaired very promptly. Roger Hunte had been appointed steward by October 1425, and there are more long lists of ruined buildings in the three court rolls from his stewardship.[145] Twenty men are listed in October 1425 as having been given timber for repairs, seven of whom planned to repair buildings on their sons' holdings, and one tenant had demolished a dwelling without permission and was fined 20d. In April 1426 five holdings were vacant and two holdings were granted rent-free, but no timber was supplied to tenants.[146] The head steward granted one messuage and half a virgate to John Kempston, the woodward, for two years without rent, that is, 'for nothing so that he might repair the said messuage.'[147] The effectiveness of this arrangement is not known. In September 1426 ten tenants were given timber for repairs.[148]

In the single roll surviving after September 1426 and before October 1448 Katherine Neville's steward listed ten buildings and a barn needing repair. The importance of the cereal harvest at that time is implied by the building in 1440 of a large barn for Thomas Wyltshyre costing £8 4s., including 33s. 4d. for straw for the roof.[149] In addition to paying for a new barn for Thomas Wyltshyre, in 1440, Katherine Neville paid for buildings held by Robert Tayllour, alias Clerk, costing £4 6s. 6d., and for works round the mill pond. These building accounts show that temporary workers in Willington were paid a fee for a fixed task or were paid by the day.[150] The usual day rate was 3d., although 4d. a day was paid for good carpenters and other skilled workers. The names of all the workmen involved were given, but the Mowbray receivers or stewards are not named. The roll ends with the costs for, 'accounting for the fee itself 30 shillings and 4 pence.'

In the second half of the fifteenth century Katherine Neville and her later husbands needed to be flexible in order to find, and keep, good tenants. Fewer land transfers were recorded because it became the norm to grant holdings for three lives, usually the man, his wife and one following, and copyhold tenancies also developed. Tenants were still required to repair the buildings on their holdings and there are references to small numbers of buildings in need of repair in every court roll extant April 1457–April 1467 during which period John Beaumont died. No buildings needing repair are listed in the three rolls shortly after the execution of Katherine Neville's fourth husband, John Woodville,[151] or in seven rolls during the last eight

143 BARS, Box R212, Roll 29, October 1420.
144 BARS, Box R212, Roll 34, September 1423 and Roll 33, October 1423, respectively.
145 BARS, Box R212, Roll 35, October 1425.
146 BARS, Box R212, Roll 36a, April 1426.
147 BARS, Box R212, Roll 36a, April 1426.
148 BARS, Box R212, Roll 36, September 1426.
149 BARS, Box R212, Roll 37, April 1440.
150 *Ibid.*
151 British Library, Add. Ch. 26813/3, October 1467; 26813/4, May 1468.

years of her life, suggesting that she and her steward had abandoned the requirement for tenants to repair all their buildings.[152]

Perquisites of court, common fines and sheriff's aid

Income from perquisites of court was greater from the views of frankpledge in the autumn than from the halmoots in the spring, and at its highest was 66s. 7d., 1384–85, from heriots and amercements.[153] Income was also high 1417–18. In October 1417, 42s. 9d., less steward's expenses, was raised when there were three heriots with a value of 25s. 4d;[154] and an income of 3s. 2d was raised in April 1418, making a gross annual total of at least 45s. 2d. After 1448 it became usual for the income from the halmoots to be insufficient to pay the cost of the stewards' expenses; in 1466, 1470, 1474, 1475 and 1479 there was no income from perquisites of court, although there were some wood sales in 1466, 1474 and 1475.[155]

Common fines were paid at the view of frankpledge each autumn so becoming part of the perquisites of court. They amounted to about 12s. a year, 1394–1425, although there were no details as to how they may have been calculated until nearly two hundred years later.[156] Common fines had reduced to 7s. 2d. by October 1448, and to 6s. 11d. in 1452, before rising to 7s. 9d. in 1457.[157] They continued to fluctuate, and these fluctuations suggest changes in types of tenancies in Willington 1448–81, but the extant records do not contain firm evidence of this.

From 1537 these common fines began to be referred to as land-silver, usually bringing in an income of 5s. 4d.–5s. 8d. a year, and head-silver, realising an income of between 16d.–24d. a year.[158] At the start of the seventeenth century one roll, for October 1609, has survived with explanatory information: 'the residents and Inhabitants within the aforesaid view gave 8s. 11d. to the lord as Common fine for Land-silver and Head-silver, on this day following the ancient Custom usual there.'[159] In that year twenty-seven tenants kept 913 sheep on the commons. One penny entitled a tenant to keep five or six sheep and two beasts or bullocks on the commons; 15d. allowed a tenant to keep 180 sheep, eight horses and twenty-four beasts or bullocks on the commons. The common fines came to a total of 8s. 11d., described as head-silver and land-silver but not explaining how each was calculated. The roll also contains a long list of rules governing the use of the commons, one of which made it clear that the commons were only for the use of Willington tenants and gave the penalties for rule breaking.

The manor received 21s. 3d. a year for sheriff's aid (known as sherevesshot), 1382–97. It was paid in three instalments: 9s. 2½d. in the autumn and at midsummer, and 2s. 10d. at Easter. At the same time the manor paid the Bedford sheriff 32s.

[152] BARS, Box R212, Roll 55b, March 1475; Roll 58a, October 1477; Roll 59a, November 1478; Roll 60b, May 1482.
[153] Including a common fine of 12s.
[154] BARS, Box R212, Roll 23, October 1417.
[155] British Library, Add Ch.26813/8, and BARS, Box R212, Roll 52b, April 1466; Roll 56, April 1474; Roll 55b, March 1475; Roll 59b, November 1479.
[156] BARS, Box R212, Roll 74, October 1599.
[157] BARS, Box R212, Roll 38a, October 1448; Roll 46a, October 1457.
[158] BARS, Box R212, Roll 65, October 1537; Roll 66, October 1538; Roll 67, October 1539; Roll 68, November 1540.
[159] BARS, Box R212, Roll 77, October 1609.

for hideage and sherevesshot, in two equal instalments, at autumn and midsummer. Hideage was based on the size of the manor, and sheriff's aid paid for the administration of the regulation of the assize of bread and ale and other unspecified services. The manor made payments to the Bedford sheriff, 'for the assize of ale from ancient custom' at midsummer until at least 1481.

Vacant holdings

At the end of the fourteenth century holdings without tenants were usually let by the time of the next court, thus minimising loss of income. During the early fifteenth century, when the recorded level of population was at its lowest, the number of vacant holdings grew so that by 1421 there were six holdings without tenants, and eight in 1426.[160] There were also large numbers of vacant holdings 1448–56; five in 1448; seven in 1450 51; and two holdings said to have been vacant for a long time in 1454.[161] In response to these vacancies parts of a holding without a tenant were let in April 1456 to other tenants.[162] It became part of the bailiff's responsibility to arrange short term lets where possible, as the following entry makes clear:

> And for one tenement lately in the holding of William Shakston at 10s. a year now in the lord's hands, the bailiff is answerable for 20d. raised this year from meadow. And for 2s. for three acres of land demised to William Taylour. And 3d. for one croft demised to him. And for 2d. for one rood demised to John Gostwyk. And for 8d. for one acre thus demised to William Shakston.[163]

In October 1463 and 1464 temporary allowances of 20s. each year were given, 'to the tenants who hold the Ovryland, from their rent.' No reason is given for these allowances, but it was presumably to encourage the tenants not to surrender their holdings.[164] This piece of land is not mentioned again in the documents.

Although substantial depopulation has been suggested as the cause of falling rents for the demesne lands and other holdings in Willington, the surname evidence suggests that, after being at its lowest level in about 1414, there was a gradual rise in population until the 1460s, then an apparent fall in the 1470s, followed by further rises.[165] Falling rents, vacant holdings and buildings needing repair were signs of manorial decay when seen from the perspective of the lord, but the evidence from the manor court rolls suggests that, far from being depopulated, the size of the population of Willington seems to have remained between 170–200 persons after the early fifteenth century, rising above that in the years 1461 and 1481. In addition, temporary workers were attracted into the manor in most years. However, these estimates of the population are dependent on the detail contained in the individual court rolls and need to be treated with caution.

Although life for Willington tenants may have been difficult in the first quarter of the fifteenth century as a result of agricultural depression, John Beaumont

---

[160] BARS, Box R212, Roll 30, April 1421; Roll 30a, April 1426.
[161] BARS, Box R212, Roll 38a, October 1448; Roll 39a, October 1450; Roll 40a, October 1451; Roll 43a, October 1454.
[162] BARS, Box R212, Roll 44b, April 1456.
[163] *Ibid.*
[164] British Library Add.Ch.26813/1, October 1463; BARS, Box R212, Roll 51a, October 1464.
[165] Moye, *The Estates and Finances of the Mowbray Family*, p. 111.

and Katherine Neville were able to attract new tenants for their vacant holdings 1448–54 and to retain most of them from 1457, after the appointment of Thomas Rokes as steward.

Necessary expenditure

Stewards' expenses
The differences in the amounts allowed for stewards' expenses for individual courts suggest that the size of the stewards' parties rose when major events were taking place. When the manor was in the temporary lordship of Queen Joan, 1405–11, they remained at levels similar to those of the previous century. Expenses rose 1416–20, soon after the manor and the other Mowbray estates were restored to John Mowbray. When the head steward Thomas Bekyngham held the manor courts, in April 1421, the steward's expenses were 3s. 3d., but he, and others, paid an extra visit in June: 'for one day and one night to agree with the lord's tenants the rents of the demesne land there' for which the expenses were 4s.1d., making a total of 7s. 4d. for the two visits.[166]

Two courts are recorded as being held in September and October 1423, and the steward's expenses for these two courts amounted to 6s. 6d.[167] Steward's expenses were also high in 1440 when the new barn for Thomas Wyltshyre and other buildings were constructed, suggesting that more of the lady's officials visited that year to oversee the buildings. They were also high, at 7s. 2d. in October 1455, two years before the appointment of Thomas Rokes, when: 'the tenement in which Robert Partrych stays is ruined and the bailiff says that the Receiver General of the Council says the same Robert should pay 40s. for making the aforesaid repairs, 20s. for this year and 20s. next year.'[168] His goods and chattels were seized. Old timber 'fallen down' from elsewhere on the manor was given to four tenants to repair two pigsties, a stable, and make repairs to a barn.

The steward and other officials stayed over, presumably in the Willington manor house, in October 1461 and October 1462, taking courts in Cardington the day after the court in Willington. On 8 October 1461 the steward's expenses for Willington were 7s. 8d., and the income from the court was 13s. 4d.[169] The next day in Cardington the expenses were 4s. 3d. and the income 10s. 2d.[170] The evidence suggests that a much smaller number of officials stayed over the next year, when both the expenses and income were significantly less. The steward's expenses for Willington were 2s. 2d., and the income from the court was 9s. 6d .[171] The next day in Cardington the expenses were 12d. with an income of 2s. 2d. [172]

---

[166] BARS, Box R212, Roll 30, April 1421.
[167] BARS, Box R212, Rolls 33, October 1423; Roll 34, September 1423. It was unusual for two courts to be held so close together so it is possible that the medieval scribe made an error with one of these dates.
[168] BARS, Box R212, Roll 44a, October 1455.
[169] BARS, Box R212, Roll 49a, October 1461.
[170] BARS, Box R212, Roll 49b, October 1461 (Cardington).
[171] BARS, Box R212, Roll 50c, October 1462.
[172] BARS, Box R212, Roll 50a, October 1462 (Cardington).

Grants, pensions and benefactions

The income from the manor was reduced by a variety of grants and payments: for repairs to the buildings at Willington; the costs of the maintenance of hedges; and by providing materials for use elsewhere on the Mowbray estates. Grants were also paid from the Willington manor accounts to members of the Mowbray affinity: Joan Caule, from May 1388, who was presumably a pensioner, or widow of an employee; John Tunstall, from 1394 for at least ten years, a forester and keeper of Sheerhatch; John Inglethorpe, from 1396 for two or three years, a knight; William Rees, 1397–1410, head steward; John Lancastre, from 1398 for several years, a senior member of the Mowbray council; Robert Goushill, from 1398 for five or six years, third husband of Elizabeth Fitzalan after the death of her second husband Thomas Mowbray, lord of Willington during the period that the bailiffs' accounts were written; William Bachiler, 1416–21, esquire; Robert Williton, from 1419 to after 1432, warrener; and Roger Hunt, June 1427 to after 1432, former steward.[173] These grants may have been rewards for good service, but for Joan Caule and William Bachiler they appear to have been pensions.

Joan Caule's annuity of £6 13s. 4d. was a considerable sum, probably worth about £35,000 today and much larger than the wages paid to manorial officers such as the bailiff, the warreners and the foresters, who were paid 2d. a day for working 364 days a year, amounting to 60s. 8d. a year.[174] The officers' incomes may have been supplemented by sales and transactions which do not appear in the surviving documents or may have been deliberately concealed. The bailiff was paid 20s. a year, but this had risen to 30s. 4d. by 1480–81. As bailiff-accountant he may have received other fees from nearby local manors, and part of his income may have been received as payments in kind. It is possible that he lived in the medieval manor house and received additional income from other land-holdings.

Other discharges from the manor included rents paid for land belonging to the abbot of Warden and to the prior of Newnham Priory for twelve months, 1387–88;[175] the cost of sending oats, rabbits and partridges to the lord's house at Hynton, 1388–89 and to repairs to the grange there;[176] and for making a gate for Bedford Castle, 1457–58.[177]

The Mowbrays also had a tradition of benefactions to religious houses. 'By the fifteenth century, the favoured houses of their Mowbray ancestors in Yorkshire, among them the foundations of Newburgh and Byland, had largely been replaced as objects of the family's charity by others, including Newnham Priory near Bedford, a Beauchamp of Bedford foundation.'[178]

---

173 Moye, *The Estates and Finances of the Mowbray Family*, p. 425.
174 BARS, R8/62/2/6, and Thompson, *Bailiffs' Accounts for Willington*, BARS, CRT 130 Willington 11, p. 21.
175 BARS, R8/62/2/5, and Thompson, *Bailiffs' Accounts for Willington*, BARS, CRT 130 Willington 11, p. 17.
176 BARS, R8/62/2/6, and Thompson, *Bailiffs' Accounts for Willington*, BARS, CRT 130 Willington 11, p. 22, p. 26.
177 British Library, Add Ch. 26813/1–8.
178 Moye *The Estates and Finances of the Mowbray Family*, pp.187–8.

Management under the Howards, Dukes of Norfolk

The plans of the prestigious and powerful Mowbray family collapsed when John Mowbray, the fourth Duke of Norfolk, died suddenly in 1476 without a male heir.[179] His daughter, Anne, was only four when she became Countess of Norfolk. She was betrothed and married two years later to the younger son of Edward IV, the Duke of York, but died in November 1481.[180] Her Mowbray estates were absorbed into the Crown lands before he became one of the Princes in the Tower and disappeared.

Willington and other lands in Bedfordshire, Buckinghamshire, Essex, Gloucestershire and the March, Leicestershire, Norfolk and Surrey from Katherine Neville's dower were inherited by the Howard family.[181] Thomas Howard was created Duke of Norfolk in 1514.[182]

Only four court rolls survive from the period when Willington was held by the Howards. They are all headed as views of frankpledge but were held at irregular intervals in September, March and December, suggesting that administration in this period was less regular and therefore less costly.[183] Assessors of fines were named in all four rolls, and both rolls dated 1522 showed that men were still being enrolled into tithings. The sixteenth century bailiff was not named and nor were any of the other manorial officers, with the exception of the constables in December 1522: 'William Yarwey, John Myton sworn men, in place of John Warner, Edmund Totnam.'[184] New constables may have been needed that year as the court roll contains the only evidence of violence on the manor while it was held by the Howards: 'John Gostwyke, Thomas Myton, William Dyk, Thomas Warner and Robert Dutton assaulted others' and were fined 2d. each.

Excuses for non-attendance at court were given in March and December 1522, and some tenants were fined for default. The number of tenants sworn in as members of the jury increased; there were twelve in 1515, thirteen in 1520, and fifteen and fourteen in the courts of 1522. There is no mention of a second jury. The figures might suggest greater independence by the tenants, or a greater willingness on the part of the Howards to involve the locals in the management of the manor, but no further evidence is available from the documents to support these hypotheses.

In 1520 the tenants were all ordered to bring the evidence of how they held their land to the next court, but the roll for the following court has not survived. There is no evidence of a transfer of lands in 1520, and the record for March 1522 is damaged, but some cottages and messuages were transferred then:

---

[179] Roberts. *Mowbray Legacy*, p. 113.

[180] Roberts. *Mowbray Legacy*, p. 113–18.

[181] Moye, *The Estates and Finances of the Mowbray Family*, p.156, gives an estimated value of £617 7s. 8d.

[182] VCH, vol. 3, p. 263. This account of Willington manor may correctly describe the titles of Thomas Howard, but is not correct when it states that Willington became part of the estates of the son of John Mowbray, third Duke of Norfolk in 1461. Willington was not part of the main Mowbray estates after 1432, when it became part of the dower of Katherine Neville, the widow of John Mowbray, second Duke of Norfolk.

[183] BARS, Box R212, Roll 61, September 1515; Roll 62, March 1520; Roll 63, March 1522; Roll 64, December 1522.

[184] BARS, Box R212, Roll 64, December 1522.

William Gostwyke died after the last Court and he held on the day of his death certain lands and tenements within the demesne of that fee by what service is not known. And that John D Goswyke is his son and his heir following and is aged 26 years and more. And he has a day to swear the aforesaid at a better Inquiry of the aforesaid lands and tenements before the next court.[185]

This was not John Gostwyk who bought the manor in 1529, whose father died in 1507, but his cousin and namesake of a similar age. There is evidence that in later years this John Gostwyk's relationships with his family were disturbed; perhaps feelings of resentment grew after his cousin bought the manor and became his land-lord.

The rolls continued to contain some information about farming on the manor. Two geldings, a sheep and a lamb were reported as strays in 1515, and orders about the keeping of pigs were made in that year and in December 1522. Tenants continued to be ordered to scour their ditches, and in 1520 it: 'was agreed by all the tenants that Thomas Resse, William Yarwey, John Gostwyke, William Rolyt, John Myton, William Gostwyke made enclosures lying outside their tenements on the north side, without their agreement.'[186] They were ordered to remove them or pay penalties of 3s. 4d. for each enclosure.

In 1515 the Howards made a determined effort to oblige the tenants to repair their buildings. More than twenty tenants were listed who between them held more than sixty buildings needing a variety of repairs.[187] Penalties for non-compliance were threatened but the amounts were not given. At this time there were at least eighteen houses on the manor which had a hall, a large space where family and servants all slept, usually with service rooms at one end separated from it by a screen and a passage. The list of buildings needing repair did not include those belonging to the Gostwyks and the Mitons or buildings on holdings held by people from outside the manor such as the prior of Newnham. Half of the names of tenants ordered to undertake repairs do not reappear in any later court records so the survey may have been intended to drive out those who were too poor, or were unwilling, to adequately maintain their buildings.

The Howards continued to order repairs but no other detailed lists survive, and in December 1522 only one house was reported as being: 'very ruined both in roofing with timber and in walls.'[188] It was arranged that the former tenant would pay 2s. 9d. towards the repairs and that the current tenant would do the repairs before the next court or pay a penalty of 10s.

The rolls continued to be important documents for the Howards although the courts no longer provided a substantial income for them. The only roll in which an income from the court is recorded is that of 1520, but this was only 12d. Willington was about a hundred miles from Framlingham, and even further away from Arundel Castle, the two most important administrative centres of the Howard family. Willington's distance from these centres must have contributed to Thomas Howard's decision to sell the manor in the sixteenth century.

---

185 BARS, Box R212, Roll 63, March 1522.
186 That is, without the tenants' agreement. BARS, Box R212, Roll 62, March 1520.
187 BARS, Box R212, Roll 61, September 1515.
188 BARS, Box R212, Roll 64, December 1522.

Chapter Seven

Newnham Priory

There are few surviving documents from the fourteenth and fifteenth centuries linking Willington manor and Newnham Priory. However, the extant documents, when taken together, provide some insight into the relationships between the two bodies.

The Willington *Domesday Book* entry of 1086 does not mention a church, but one had been built by 1166 when it was named in the first charter of Newnham Priory. The priory had been founded by Simon de Beauchamp, Baron of Bedford, in that year.[1] The Augustinian prior and canons of Newnham Priory became patrons and rectors of Willington church, holding the advowson from 1229, or before, when the first recorded chaplain or vicar was Nicholas de Wileton.[2]

Simon de Beauchamp endowed Willington church, the tithe from Willington mill, certain rents from the manor and wood sales to Newnham Priory. Furthermore, the priory owned glebe land in Willington amounting to about ten acres, and other lands were granted by Willington parishioners in the early thirteenth century, including a capital messuage and land.[3]

When the Beauchamp's barony of Bedford came to an end, with the death of the last baron in 1265, the patronage of the priory passed to the Mowbrays as part of the Beauchamp estate inherited by the late baron's sister, Maud, who had married Sir Roger de Mowbray (believed to have died 1266).[4]

Willington, the Mowbrays and Newnham Priory

In 1385 Richard II had made a grant of free warren to Newnham Priory for lands in fourteen parishes which had links to the priory and the Mowbrays: Barford, Bedford, Biddenham, Cardington and Cotes, Goldington, Newnham, Ravensden, Renhold, Sharnbrook, Stagsden, Stotfold, Willington and Wootton. The grant recorded the right of the prior, the convent of Newnham and their successors to:

> hold forever free warren in all their demesne lands … [and that] … none shall enter those lands for the purpose of hunting or capturing anything which belongs to the warren without the permission and will of the aforesaid prior and convent or their successors, upon forfeiture to us of £10.[5]

---

[1] Godber, *History of Bedfordshire*, p. 41.
[2] Gordon Vowles, *The Parish of St Lawrence, Willington, its Church and Vicars* (Willington, 2016), p. 19.
[3] Joyce Godber, ed., *Cartulary of Newnham Priory*, BHRS, vol. 43 (Luton, 1963), pp. 329–32.
[4] V.C.H., vol. 1, p.379 and Marilyn Roberts, *The Mowbray Legacy*, p. 46.
[5] J. Hamson, 'Grant of Free Warren to Newnham Priory', in *Publications of Bedfordshire Historical Record Society*, vol. 5 (Aspley Guise, 1920), pp. 97–100.

Among the witnesses was Thomas de Mowbray, Earl of Nottingham. The other witnesses were a very distinguished group. They included the Archbishop of Canterbury; the Archbishop of York; John, King of Castile and Leon; John O'Gaunt, the Duke of Lancaster; Edmund, Duke of York; Thomas, Duke of Lancaster; Michael de la Pole, Richard II's chancellor; Hugh de Seagrave, the King's treasurer; Master Walter de Stirlowe, bishop elect of Coventry and Lichfield and keeper of the privy seal; and John de Montacute, keeper of the royal household. The King attached his seal.

The privilege of free warren was probably a reciprocal arrangement. It allowed the prior and his canons to take hares, rabbits, partridges and pheasants from the permitted areas without being prosecuted for poaching. And Thomas de Mowbray may have been pleased for free warren to be granted to provide sport and extra food for the priory in return for prayers for his soul and the protection of game from poachers.

This link with Newnham Priory did not, however, prevent a neighbouring religious house from trespassing on the manor. It seems that the abbot of Wardon, or his servants, trespassed in Willington manor in 1468. In May that year the court roll records that: 'The homage has a day until the next [court] to present whether the Abbot of Wardon has fished in the several waters of the lord or not.'[6] In 1470 it was reported that: 'The servants of the abbot of Warden have driven one cart on the separate meadows of the lady called the Burymede, several times, with their horses and have trampled down and consumed the grass growing there making a heavy loss to the lady's tenants and they were ordered not to do it any more, under a penalty of 6s. 8d.'[7]

When the Mowbrays' management style changed, about the time of the Peasants' Revolt, the demesne lands were let at first to, 'various bondsmen tenants and certain tenants at will.'[8] Then, in 1449, they were divided between thirteen tenants.[9] As a result of this fragmentation tithes may have been more difficult to collect. The early Willington court rolls and accounts show tithes of a tenth being paid irregularly to the prior of Newnham Priory, as rector of Willington church, on sales of underwood, which was the growth from coppiced trees in Sheerhatch Wood. They are recorded in the bailiffs' accounts as having been paid five times 1382–97. Payments of tithes are also referred to in the bailiff's account 1457–58,[10] and in the manor court roll of 1459 and most halmoots or courts baron 1463–75 when John Gostwyk and John Yerwey were the bailiffs, and tithes amounting to ten percent of the sales of underwood were paid in cash or in deliveries of the underwood from parts of Sheerhatch Wood.[11]

The Mowbrays' patronage of the priory also took another form. In 1420–21, the second Duke of Norfolk, John Mowbray, granted £20 for the great east window in

6   British Library, Add.Ch.26813/4, May 1468.
7   British Library, Add.Ch.26813/8, May 1470.
8   BARS, R8/62/2/6 and Thompson, *Bailiffs' Accounts for Willington*, BARS, CRT 130 Willington 11, pp. 19–22.
9   BARS, Box R212, Roll 38b, May 1449.
10   British Library, Add. Ch. 657.
11   BARS, Box R212, Roll 47a, June or July 1459; Roll 50d, May 1463; British Library, Add. Ch.26813/2, May 1464; Roll 51b, April 1465; Roll 52b, April 1466; British Library, Add.Ch.26813/4, May 1468; British Library, Add.Ch.26813/6, April 1469; British Library, Add.Ch.26813/8, May 1470; Roll 54b, May 1472; Roll 55b, March 1475.

the priory church, payable in three instalments of £6 13s. 4d.[12] No other evidence of the Mowbray's patronage has been found.

The Willington incumbents
There is no evidence that the vicar, who was appointed by Newnham Priory, greatly influenced events in Willington. During the years 1275–1400 there were nine changes in incumbent, an average tenure of fourteen years for each post holder. But during the fifteenth century the length of the incumbencies varied widely and many were very short. They were shorter in Willington than in any of the other churches which formed part of the Beauchamp endowment.

Changes of incumbency in the fifteenth century in the group of churches which formed part of the endowment of Simon de Beauchamp to Newnham Priory in 1166[13]

Manor church	Number of changes in incumbents	Average length of incumbency	Longest incumbency	
Cardington	13	8 years	23 years 1415–38	Referred to as chaplains or priests. Two vacant periods, c.1411 and 1455–57.
Goldington	14	7 years	14 years 1461–75	Referred to as chaplains, priests or vicars. Two vacant periods, c.1441 and sometime after 1461 and before 1475.
Great Barford	13	8 years	36 years 1468–1504	Referred to as chaplains, priests or vicars. At least one vacant. c. 1401, list incomplete.
Ravensden	15	6.6 years	27 years 1439–66	Referred to as chaplains, priests or vicars. No vacant periods recorded.
Renhold	7	14 years	39 years 1489–28	Referred to as chaplains or priests. No vacant periods recorded.
Southill[14]	9	11 years	48 years 1485–1533	Referred to as chaplains or priests. No vacant periods recorded.
Stagsden	10 or 11	9 or 10 years	26 years 1446–72?	Referred to as chaplains or priests. No vacant periods recorded.
Willington	20	5 years	17 years 1432–49	Referred to as chaplains, priests or vicars. Four vacant periods, 1401, 1448–49, 1452 and 1457.
Wootton	8	12.5 years	33 years 1457–90	Referred to as chaplains or priests.

The problems of appointing incumbents to Willington were especially acute during the period when the Mowbray family was in disgrace, at the beginning of

12   Moye, *The Estates and Finances of the Mowbray Family*, p.187.
13   Information in this table is extracted from BARS database BARS.adlibsoft.com. Aspley Guise and Cockayne Hatley have not been included as they were claimed by Dunstable Priory and the Port family respectively. Also from, Godber, *Cartulary of Newnham Priory*, p. xiii.
14   It is unclear whether Newnham Priory continued to hold this church.

the fifteenth century, and in 1457 when a new steward was appointed and when Katherine Neville's third husband was nearing the end of his life.

The bailiff's account 1382–83 names John Dowe as vicar. He had taken a ten-year lease of the private fishing water in the River Great Ouse and the island there, for which he paid 13s. 4d.[15] He held the fishery until 1390–91, when it was leased to John Fisher of Fenlake for an increased fee.[16] John Dowe resigned from the living in August 1401, and during the years 1401–1500 there were twenty-one changes of incumbent each serving an average of less than five years.[17] During the sixteenth century there were seven changes of incumbent, each serving an average of about fourteen years. The difference between the number of changes in the fifteenth century from the preceding and following centuries is surprising, but there is insufficient evidence to draw firm conclusions about the causes. Changes within the Mowbray family may have contributed, but there could have been other reasons; Newnham Priory may have had some problems in finding good clerics at the time or the value of the living may have influenced the rapid turnover.

Willington incumbents 1381–1522

Name	Date	Lord of the manor	Bailiff	Vicars entries in rolls/accounts
John Dowe/ Douve	1381	John de Mountbray, Earl of Nottingham	Robert Gostwyk	1385, ten year lease of fisheries, from 1383[18]
Richard Knyghton	1385	Thomas, Earl of Nottingham, Lord of Montbray and Seagrave and Marshall of England[19]	Robert Gostwyk	Stayed one month and then moved to Wootton[20]
Ralph Lokyn	1401	Possibly Sir Thomas de Rempston[21]	Not named	Temporary chaplain, stayed two months[22]
John Moysond	1401	Possibly Sir Thomas de Rempston	Not named	Exchanged with William Tooee[23]
William Tooee	1404	Not named	Not named	None known

---

[15] BARS, R8/62/2/1. His surname is written as 'Downe' in the *Fasti Ecclesiae Bedfordiensis* used in Vowles, *The Parish of St Lawrence, Willington,* p. 65.
[16] BARS, R8/62/2/6 and Thompson, *Bailiffs' Accounts for Willington*, BARS, CRT 130 Willington 11, p. 29.
[17] The names and dates of Willington vicars are taken mostly from *Fasti Ecclesiae Bedfordiensis*, as listed in Vowles, *The Parish of St Lawrence, Willington,* p. 65.
[18] BARS, R8/62/2/6 and Thompson, *Bailiffs' Accounts for Willington*, BARS, CRT 130 Willington 11, pp. 19–22.
[19] The two different spellings of Mowbray are as they appeared in documents at that time. One of the difficulties in the transcription and translation of medieval Latin texts is the use of minims, that is short vertical strokes, to represent the letters u, v, w, n, and m, and irregularities in the numbers of minims used. In 1382 four minims have been interpreted as 'un' not 'nn,' 'im,' or 'iw. In 1385 two minims have been interpreted as 'n' but could have represented 'u.'
[20] Vowles, *The Parish of St Lawrence, Willington,* p. 22.
[21] VCH, vol. 3, p. 263.
[22] Vowles, *The Parish of St Lawrence, Willington,* p. 22.
[23] *Ibid.*

Bartholomew Fermour	1405	Not named	William Ridere	Stayed until his death in 1420[24]
John Clandon	1420	John Mowbray	William Ridere	None known
Robert Calyser	1421	John Mowbray	William Ridere	None known
Robert Chapman	–	John Mowbray	William Ridere	Had a dovecote, made by the parishioners in 1411–12 [25]
Hugh Chapman	1432	John Mowbray, died October 1432	Not named	Longest surviving vicar of fifteenth century
William Hoveden	1449	John Beaumont (and Katherine Neville)	Not named	1448, the prior of Newnham holds a certain wall to repair, between the vicarage and the lord's holding [26]
Richard Whythove	1452	John Beaumont (and Katherine Neville)	Not named	1453, Richard Whythove, clerk, is involved in a plea of debt [27] 1454, Richard Whythove, clerk, to enclose the glebe lands and has made one large brewing [28]
Richard Newton	1457	John Beaumont (and Katherine Neville)	John Gostwyk	None known
William Gibbison	1457	John Beaumont (and Katherine Neville)	John Gostwyk	None known
Richard Dalby	1458	John Beaumont (and Katherine Neville)	John Gostwyk	None known
Thomas Marchall	1463	Katherine Neville	John Gostwyk then John Yerwey	None known
John Wirlett	1463	Katherine Neville	John Yerwey	None known
William Hammond	1471	Katherine Neville	John Yerwey	None known
John Wilkyns	1473	Katherine Neville	Not named	None known
Robert Pecher	1489	Probably Thomas Howard, Duke of Norfolk	Not named	None known
William Fissher	–	Probably Thomas Howard, Duke of Norfolk	Not named	None known
Robert Reve	1508	Probably Thomas Howard, Duke of Norfolk	Not named	None known

24   *Ibid.*
25   BARS, Box R212, Roll 35, October 1425.
26   BARS, Box R212, Roll 38a, October 1448.
27   BARS, Box R212, Roll 42a, October 1453.
28   BARS, Box R212, Roll 43a, October 1454.

Management of Newnham Priory

Although the *Victoria County History* says that the priory had a good reputation at all times, examination of the visitations by the bishops of Lincoln suggests that this was not always the case. There was a dispute with Cauldwell Priory at the beginning of the fifteenth century,[29] and when Bishop Grey visited in about 1420 he found that the prior had grown old and feeble and that William Bedford and John Bromham, the sub-prior and third prior, were doing his work. There were complaints about lax management by the prior and consequent problems with discipline and with the accounts.[30] The cook and the butler were: 'not only useless, but rather harmful to the Priory in their offices.'[31] In 1435, near the end of the forty year term of office of the aged prior William Wootton, there was: 'forcible shedding of blood by brothers John Rothewelle and William Thorneham, canons of the said priory.'[32]

When William Alnwick visited Newnham Priory on 18 January 1442 he found that the number of canons had fallen from twenty-one to thirteen.[33] This was not unusual as many ecclesiastical establishments at this time found it difficult to make ends meet and were reducing recruitment as a way of controlling costs.[34] In his report the bishop expressed concerns about the management of the priory by the prior, non-observance of religious practices, lack of reverence by the younger canons, inappropriate relationships with secular people, lack of a teacher for both the canons and the four teachable boys, poor quality food and the absence of alms for the poor. One brother had been elected to be third prior and had refused.[35] The prior was: 'remiss or excessively careless in correcting the brethren.' There was a long list of complaints followed by instructions showing how he should improve, with punishments, including in some cases excommunication.[36]

John Kempston, whose namesake was the woodward of Willington 1418–26, was singled out for special criticism in the visitation. He was one of three canons accused of having mistresses, although, of course, they denied the charge.[37] He was accused of going into the priory kitchen for something to eat in the early morning, instead of attending prayers, and: 'having more care for his belly than divine service.'[38] It was said that he was: 'almost unlettered and he understands not what he reads. Nor does he work to acquire knowledge.'[39]

---

29   VCH Bedfordshire, vol. 1, p.379, and A. Hamilton-Thompson, ed., *Visitations of Religious Houses in the Diocese of Lincoln*, vol. 1.: *Injunctions and other Documents from the Registers of Richard Flemyng and William Grey, Bishops of Lincoln, A.D. 1420 to A.D. 1436*, Canterbury and York Society (Horncastle, 1914), pp. 91–2.
30   Hamilton-Thompson, *Visitations of Religious Houses*, vol. 1, p. 91.
31   Hamilton-Thompson, *Visitations of Religious Houses*, vol. 1, p. 90.
32   Hamilton-Thompson, *Visitations of Religious Houses*, vol. 1, p. 91–2.
33   A. Hamilton-Thompson, ed., *Visitations of Religious Houses in the Diocese of Lincoln*, vol. 3: *Visitations of Religious Houses (concluded) by Bishops Atwater and Longland and by their Commissaries, 1517–1531*, Lincoln Record Society (Hereford, 1940–47), p. 233.
34   C. Dyer, *Standards of Living in the Later Middle Ages: Social Change in England c1200 – 1500* (Cambridge, 1989), p. 98.
35   Hamilton-Thompson, *Visitations of Religious Houses*, vol. 3, p. 233.
36   Hamilton-Thompson, *Visitations of Religious Houses*, vol. 3, p. 235.
37   Hamilton-Thompson, *Visitations of Religious Houses*, vol. 3, p. 232.
38   BARS, Box R212, Roll 30, April 1421.
39   Godber, *History of Bedfordshire*, p.150, and Hamilton-Thompson, *Visitations of Religious Houses*, vol. 3, p. 273.

Valuations of local vicarages are included in the cartulary of Newnham Priory, though the dates of the valuations are not given: Cardington was worth twenty-four marks; Goldington ten marks; Great Barford twenty-four marks; Renhold twelve marks; and Willington twenty marks.[40] Willington's value was therefore about average. The valuation for Willington in the cartulary states that at that time:

> The benefice of the vicar of Willington is able to exist totally with the altar dues and with all the small tithes and the tithes of the mill and will owe nothing. Therefore it has a sufficient holding and is able to pay two marks and so is valued for a tax of seven marks. The valuation of the whole church is twenty marks.[41]

There is no mention of a school in Willington in the fifteenth century although canon law required every rural parish to have a clerk to attend the priest, look after the church and keep a school for the children.[42] The surname 'Clerk' is first mentioned in 1397 but then disappears from the records until 1440, to reappear very regularly 1448–74. This surname may suggest links between the Clerk family and Newnham Priory, but there is no evidence that members of this family were professional clerks in Willington.

Clerks of the view are mentioned in 1426 when they, and many of the lord's tenants, said that in their estimate there remained almost one hundred rabbits in the lord's warren.[43] Also: 'through the clerks of the view and twelve sworn tenants of the lord, the enclosure of the lord's woodland called Le Shirehacthe [sic] was completely broken on all sides and similarly that of the Grove because of neglect by John Kempston.'[44] He was declared to be at the mercy of the lord and was ordered to repair the said enclosures, 'well and sufficiently' before the next Easter under penalty of one hundred shillings. The clerks of the view in 1426 are not named, but three clerks are named in subsequent records: Robert Tayllour, in 1448; Richard Whythove, who was the vicar 1452–57, in 1453; and John Yarwey, in 1473–82.

In forty-three of the forty-nine records of the views of frankpledge or views with court still extant the prior of Newnham Priory is listed as being in default, that is, of not coming to the court. It is unlikely that he ever came. At first, in 1395 and 1397, he paid 4d. for absences in two years, but in the early fifteenth century it seems to have been accepted that he would not pay. It was usually said that he was, 'given a day to pay' and in 1420 the word 'constantly' (presumably referring to his default of court) was written above his name.[45] There are no further records of fines paid

---

40 Godber, *Cartulary of Newnham Priory*, entry numbers 111–21. These appear to be a complete series of records including taxation details for the vicarages of seven churches. Three of these, Renhold, Stagsden and Great Barford have two entries for which the first records date from 1260, 1253 and 1252 respectively and are followed by undated records in which the amounts of taxation are very different. The single taxation figures for Salford, Cardington, Willington and Goldington were each undated. The records in the cartulary are not easily accessible because they are transcriptions in Latin, and although Miss Godber has written summaries at the beginnings of many of them, these summaries are very brief. Miss Godber observes that the cartulary is incomplete; that it seems to have been copied by a team of scribes; and that, 'it cannot be said that the standard of exactitude is high.'
41 Godber, *Cartulary of Newnham Priory*, entry number 116.
42 W. W. Capes, *The English Church in the Fourteenth and Fifteenth Centuries* (London, 1920), p. 334.
43 BARS, Box R212, Roll 36, September 1426.
44 *Ibid.*
45 BARS, Box R212, Roll 29, October 1420.

by him before the long gap in the records, from 1426. After 1448 he still did not attend court, but he regularly paid a fine of 2d. a year for not doing so. There are very few other mentions of any prior. One was fined 4d. and instructed to repair a wall between Willington vicarage and the lord's land in 1448, which must have been in need of repair for some time as the lord's assessors of fines threatened to charge him a penalty of 40s. if it was not put right before Michaelmas the following year.[46]

In 1409, Queen Joan instituted a series of occasional fines for offences to be paid both to her and to the church. In that year the tenants were ordered to repair a road under the threat of a penalty of 40d. to her and 40d. to the church.[47] There is no evidence that the penalty, which was much larger than those usually charged, was paid. After that date there were seven other occasions when penalties of different amounts, payable to both the lord and the church, were threatened. These double amounts meant that the lord increased the penalties for tenants who did not obey the custom of the manor and possibly avoided some of the resentment which such payments must have generated by providing a source of income for the church. In 1411, Queen Joan threatened smaller penalties of 6d. payable to both herself and the church on people who allowed their animals to roam so that they damaged their neighbours' crops.[48] In 1415, five orders were included in the manor court rolls which threatened penalties of either 6d., or 12d. to both John Mowbray and the church, but there is no evidence that the penalties were incurred.[49] Double penalties were incurred later in 1415 and in 1422 when tenants allowed some of their animals to roam free.[50]

There are no more double charges recorded relating to the custom of the manor, but in 1450 and 1451 the brewers each incurred fines of 40d. paid to both the lord and the church for brewing ale at the time of the church service.[51] Thereafter it seems that the threat of punishment using heavy payments jointly to the lord and the church was reserved for only the most serious matters. The final mention of these penalties was in 1457 when it was ordered: 'That the labourers by the day who are resident and belong to the Lete are not to accept labouring outside the vill. They are able to have sufficient services and payment within.'[52] The penalty for this was punitive: 'Forty pence payable to the lord and the Church in equal portions, as and when they are found guilty to the contrary.'[53] There is no mention of labourers working outside the manor in the later records.

It seems that, like other tenants, the vicars were required to attend the manor court and were subject to the custom of the manor. There is no evidence that they asked to be excused or were fined for non-attendance at court. The Willington vicars appear in the manor court rolls on a number of occasions, but there is no indication of the role they played in the spiritual and pastoral care of the community.

Some vicars were affluent enough to lend money to other tenants, and at least one of them let out some land. William Hieygue and Bartholomew Fermour, the

[46] BARS, Box R212, Roll 38a, October 1448.
[47] BARS, Box R212, Roll 11, April 1409.
[48] BARS, Box R212, Roll 13, April 1411.
[49] BARS, Box R212, Roll 18a, Michaelmas 1415.
[50] BARS, Box R212, Roll 19, October 1415; Roll 31, October 1422.
[51] BARS, Box R212, Roll 39a, October 1450; Roll 40a, October 1451.
[52] BARS, Box R212, Roll 46a, October 1457.
[53] *Ibid.*

vicars of Cardington and Willington respectively, made loans to other tenants which were not repaid.[54] Five years later, the rolls note that 'the Reverend Robert' held an illegal dovecote on his manor.[55] Dovecotes were a sign of status, usually only held by lords of the manor or their superior lords. It is unusual to find a reference to tenants holding them. Richard Whythove, named in the rolls 1453–54, and listed as vicar 1452–57,[56] took a tenant to court alleging that he had not paid in full for lands which he, the vicar, had granted him.[57] In October 1454 Richard Whythove was ordered to enclose a piece of land between the vicarage and the, 'holding in which John Clerk lives'.[58] Richard Dalby, the vicar of Cardington, in rather unclerical behaviour, assaulted a man with a harvest knife, drawing blood in 1462 and was fined 12d.[59] He was also fined 12d. for a brewing of ale. In 1470 the vicar is not named, but he stood surety for the repairs to William Rydy's barn, hall and bakehouse, which the latter was ordered to repair before the Feast of All Saints later that year or pay a penalty of twenty shillings.[60]

The Newnham Priory Terrier
Although the references to Newnham Priory and the vicars of Willington in the manor court rolls and bailiffs' accounts for Willington are very sketchy, in the early sixteenth century a scribe or scribes at Newnham Priory wrote a series of detailed land books, or terriers, with clear details of the priory's lands in some parts of Bedfordshire.

The Willington terrier is very similar to the Bedford rental dated 1506–7 and to the rental and terrier for Biddenham dated 1505–6.[61] The early history of these three documents is largely unknown.[62] Although both the Biddenham and Willington documents may be neat copies of the originals, there is no reason to suppose that they were not both prepared in the early years of the sixteenth century. The script of both is in a very similar hand.

The terrier for Willington is written on ten folios of paper, four of which are blank. Two folios have bunch of grapes water marks similar to those seen on French paper dating from the fifteenth century. No folio numbers were originally written on the pages, but numbers have been added in pencil on the top, right-hand corners. The folios measure approximately 11 x 16.5 inches and are sewn into a cover made from parchment measuring just over 16.5 x 22 inches.[63]

---

54   BARS, Box R212, Roll 18a, Michaelmas 1415; Roll 28, May 1420.
55   BARS, Box R212, Roll 35, October 1425. The Reverend Robert is not found in the *Fasti Ecclesiae Bedfordiensis* cited by Vowles, *The Parish of St Lawrence, Willington*, p. 65. He was named in the rolls in 1425, and so was either Robert Calyser or Robert Chapman.
56   Vowles, *The Parish of St Lawrence, Willington*, p.65.
57   BARS, Box R212, Roll 42a, October 1453; Roll 43a, October 1454.
58   BARS, Box R212, Roll 43a, October 1454.
59   BARS, Box R212, Roll 50a, October 1462.
60   British Library, Add.Ch.26813/8, May 1470.
61   Barbara Cook, 'Newnham Priory: Rental of Manor at Biddenham, 1505–6', in *Publications of Bedfordshire Historical Record Society*, vol. 25 (Streatley, 1947), pp. 15–17 and W. N. Henman, 'Newnham Priory: a Bedford Rental, 1506–7', in *Publications of Bedfordshire Historical Record Society*, vol. 25 (Streatley, 1947), pp. 82–3.
62   No rental for Willington has been found.
63   Parchment is made from the skin of a sheep and vellum from that of a calf or cow. Although this skin is large, the marks of hair follicles suggest that it is parchment.

Fifteen tenants or land-holders are mentioned in the text. The major land-holders in the manor appear to have been Newnham Priory, John Gostwyke, William Gost-wyke and John Myton. The list does not include representatives of other religious institutions or members of the county families which were prominent in the Bedford rental, although they may have rented land in the village which did not abut on to the Newnham lands. The family names of most of the villagers mentioned in the terrier appear in the court rolls from the end of the fourteenth century. The exceptions are Thomas Passewater, whose ancestors appear in the Willington court rolls from the mid-fifteenth century, and Richard Dyke and Thomas Rees, whose families have not so far been traced. On several occasions the scribe is unsure who holds pieces of land. The name of the holder of the land is left blank on ten occasions, and two names have been given on four occasions, indicating uncertainty about the identity of the tenant.

Exact calculation of holdings is difficult because of approximate measurements of fields and of variations in sizes. Although virgates may vary in size from fifteen to sixty acres in different parts of the country, in Bedfordshire Dr Fowler accepted that they are usually thirty acres, which may also be called a yardland.[64] A quarter yardland is a quarter virgate and may be approximately eight acres. Four roods make an acre.

The medieval open-field system was still in use in Willington in 1507. There seem to have been three arable fields, plus Brookefeild which seems to have been arable and pasture, and meadows, enclosures and common grazing land elsewhere. Newnham Priory held 134 parcels of land and two crofts as follows: in Millfield, twenty-eight parcels, said to amount to fifteen acres, three and a half roods;[65] in Fulwellfeld, thirty-five parcels, said to amount to twenty-seven acres and three roods; in Midlemarshfeild, forty-six parcels, said to amount to about thirty-three acres; in Brookefeild, seventeen parcels of land amounting to about ten acres, one rood of arable and some pasture; in Willington meadows, eight parcels of land, about ten acres, one rood; in Balles Croft and Chanons Croft, four acres each, probably pasture. The total land area was calculated by the scribe as about 105 acres, but this figure may need further consideration. The lands held by the priory were mostly arable but included about ten acres of meadow and about nineteen acres of pasture, some in Brookefeild and the rest in the two crofts.

The earliest detailed map of Willington is the 1779 estate map.[66] In this map the parish is shown to be divided south-east to north-west by a road from the crest of the greensand ridge through the Willington cross-roads and on to the Ouse. Today this is Wood Lane and Station Road.

In 1507, Millfield formed the north-east part of the manor, extending from the Ouse and Willington mill to the south, possibly crossing the road leading towards Great Barford and extending towards the waterway called The Denes. No early sixteenth-century names of fields or landscape features in this field, mentioned in the terrier, appear on the 1779 map.

---

[64]   G. Herbert Fowler, *Bedfordshire in 1086: An Analysis and Synthesis of Domesday Book, BHRS,* Quarto Memoirs, vol. 1 (Aspley Guise, 1922).
[65]   These spellings of 'field' are as in the original.
[66]   Gostelow, *A Plan of the Estate of her Grace the Duchess of Bedford and Robert Palmer Esquire ... 1779.*

Fulwellfeld lay to the south of Millfield and had been renamed Conduit Field by 1779. The name of part of this field called Lynhill, or Lynehyll, in the sixteenth century had become Lime Hill by this date. In the early sixteenth-century this field was divided up into many narrow strips. A baulk, or raised boundary feature, is shown aligned with these strips on the 1779 map.

Midlemarshfield had been renamed Michaelmas Field by 1779. Its northern boundary is not clear; it may have extended northwards from the boundary with the Cottnum fields as far as the The Denes and across what is now the main road from Willington to Bedford, which is not mentioned in the terrier. The northern part of this field may have been divided into doles and allocated annually by drawing lots. Other sixteenth-century names have disappeared. There is another baulk in the middle of this field, running approximately north/south, shown on the 1779 map.

Brookefeild is not shown as an open-field in 1779, but in 1507 it may have extended from the Tudor manor house site, adjacent to the church, northwards to the Ouse. The meadowlands of Willington can still be seen as a series of strips in 1779, but the locations of Balles Croft and Chanons Croft are not shown. They may have been situated either in the piece of land in the north-west of the manor, containing the church, the moated site and probable manor site, or in the land described as pastures or enclosures on the map. It seems that in 1507 the Willington commons were situated either side of the two streams running roughly east-west from Cople parish and along the verges of the lanes in the manor. The river Great Ouse and the island, The Holme, appear in both the 1507 terrier and on the 1779 map. In 1507 the island was described in the terrier as 'lord Latymer's holme'.

Tenants or land-holders named in the Willington terrier

Names	Millfield	Fulwellfeld	Midlemarshfeild	Brookefeild	Meadowland	Crofts	Total
Dyke, Richard		1					1
Fesaunt, John			1				1
Gostwyke, John	6	13	12	5	4	1	41
Gostwyke, William	4	6	7	4			21
Lord of Latymer					1		1
Myton, John	9	5	10	1			25
Passewater, Thomas			1		2		3
Prior of Newnham			1		1	1	3
Rees, Thomas				2	1		3
Vicar of Willington		1	2	1		1	5
Warner, John	2		2	1	1		6
Warner, Robert	1	4	4	2			11
Yerway, John	1		1				2
Yerway, William				1			1

Medieval manor houses were often built near the church, and the terrier mentions Bury Mead Knoll in Brookefeild, Bury Mead in the meadows and Bury Balke in Midlemarshfield, suggesting that the medieval manor house in Willington was built in the north-west of the manor.

There is no evidence in the court rolls to show that the Priory paid common fines; nor is there evidence in the accounts to show whether or not the priory paid any rents for its holdings. The terrier makes no mention of a park, the warrens and fisheries, the woodlands, the cottnums or of the lands held by the miller showing that they had no financial interest in any of those lands.

It is not possible to state with any certainty the influence Newnham Priory and the vicar of Willington had on life in the manor. The prior chose not to attend the manor court, and while the vicar enjoyed a certain status, and seems to have attended the court regularly; his influence on the tenants is unknown. There is no evidence that religion dominated the lives of the population in the fourteenth and fifteenth centuries.

The Newnham Priory terrier for Willington shows that the prior held substantial lands there in 1507. However, it seems that life in the village had been less influenced by the church in the years after the Peasant's Revolt than by members of local families, such as the Gostwyks and the Mitons.

In 1538, shortly before the dissolution of Newnham Priory in January 1541, Robert Reve, who had been vicar of Willington since 1508, died in office and the patronage of Willington church passed to the new lord of the manor, John Gostwyk.[67] He has been described as a servant of Henry VIII who valued a: 'well-chosen complex of properties and a good name more than financial gain.'[68] In advice to his son he recommended moderation in all things; in particular he advised against leasing out lands for more than twenty years, and charging an entry fine of more than one year's rent to his tenants.[69]

---

[67]   Vowles, *The Parish of St Lawrence, Willington*, p.27.

[68]   Joyce Youings, 'The Church', in E. Miller, ed. *The Agrarian History of England and Wales*, vol. 4 (Cambridge, 1991), p. 347.

[69]   Dickens, 'Estate and Household Management in Bedfordshire c 1540', pp.42–5.

Chapter Eight

After the Peasants' Revolt

This volume tells the story of a rural Bedfordshire manor following the changes in English society brought about by the drastic reduction in population in the mid fourteenth-century and the uprisings and disturbances of 1381, the Peasants' Revolt. Although the structure and language of the manorial records suggests continuity and a hierarchical system of control, the history of Willington 1382–1522 reveals how tenants took opportunities to better themselves and their families. The lords of the manor sought to retain the value of their property and income – not necessarily successfully – while the tenants lived a relatively peaceful life within the structure of the Mowbray administration.

Willington emerges as a stable community where the custom of the manor prevailed, and the local bailiff, almost always a resident, was a pivotal figure. It was a single manor parish with an absentee landlord, so the bailiff and the tenants jointly controlled the use of the open fields from before 1066 until the purchase of Willington by a local man in 1529. There is no evidence in the medieval documents that the absentee landlords exploited their tenants or that religion dominated the lives of the population – quite the reverse. In contrast, the story of Willington's near neighbour Blunham was more vibrant, and sometimes more violent. It had a commercial legacy from a market held there during the fourteenth-century, and life may have been influenced by the presence of the small Fraternity of Blunham.[1]

The land

Willington manor was on the western edge of what has been described as some of the best agricultural land in England, and although it had no mineral resources except clay, gravel and sand, it had a: 'mixed and variable nature of soil types over a short distance which supported successful, mixed farming of the former demesne, the three-field system of open fields, the commons, and the woodlands.'[2] The tenants' prosperity was primarily dependent on agriculture and was determined by the type and fertility of the soil and sub-soil, on the weather, and on the opportunities for the sale of produce and materials. Their arrangements for working the open fields and commons, the pasture and meadows followed unwritten customary practices. Once established, these practices were slow to change. Each type of soil was exploited: the heaviest clay on the greensand ridge was used for woodland; the arable fields were on the sloping clay soils; there was grazing on the gravel terraces; and hay and grazing on the riverside meadows. Land was enriched by animals being

---

[1] Two wardens nominated a priest to pray for the souls of the founders and all Christian people. The Fraternity had a cottage with a yard and was dissolved in the sixteenth-century, VCH, vol. 3, p. 233.
[2] Brian Kerr, *An Unassuming County* (Bedford, 2014), p. 90.

turned into the fields after harvest, and animals also grazed on common lands along the river, along the waterway called The Deans, and on the herbage along the tracks and headlands.

The records show that some individual tenants tried to extend their holdings 1397–1416 and tried to increase productivity by what might be described as pre-enclosure behaviours. They were fined for making illegal enclosures, sometimes surrounding them with hedges, and for obstructing access by others to their lands by ploughing up the track to the mill and blocking up tracks along the boundaries between fields.[3] This sort of behaviour was again recorded after May 1448.[4] The manor court rolls 1463–70 contain further examples of encroachment by the ploughing of extra strips of land.[5] John Warnere, the constable, 'enclosed the common way to the township', and John Myton was accused of digging a new ditch as wide as the common.[6] Five important tenants also neglected to clear their ditches so that they denied water to other arable fields, or tried to close footpaths across their lands and made enclosures without the permission of the court.[7] Hedges round some of these enclosures denied other tenants access with their ploughs to their own fields. There were also disagreements about arrangements for the pasturing of animals in the fields and on the commons.

The people

There were significant differences in wealth on the manor and some indications of difference in status by the erection of dovecotes. A few prosperous families had large holdings, and many families had substantial farmhouses described as inset-houses in the early fifteenth century and hall-houses later on, but some tenants were described as cottagers and may have lived on the holdings of others and been unable to work regularly. Records of thefts suggest that some families fell on hard times.

The documents reveal a reciprocal relationship between the lord's officials and the leaders of the manor community and an acceptance that they depended on each other. Two juries, usually of twelve men each, served at most views of frankpledge with court, held in the autumn, ensuring that twenty-four households were involved in the court process during much of the fifteenth century. In the first quarter of the fifteenth century some tenants provided pledges, or guarantees, to others less fortunate than themselves to enable them to be granted holdings or repair buildings. In 1425 six fathers repaired buildings for their sons.[8] There is much less evidence of such forms of support after that date.

There are occasional mentions of trade, but the most lucrative form of activity appears to have been brewing. The development of this skill from a cottage activity for many, perhaps using a communal brew-house in the manor, to a specialised

3   BARS, Box R212, Roll 2, October 1394; Roll 3, October 1395; Roll 9, October 1407; Roll 14b, May 1412; Roll 15 October 1413; Roll 21, October 1416.
4   BARS, Box R212, Roll 38a, May 1448.
5   British Library, Add.Ch.26813/1-8.
6   British Library, Add Ch. 26812/3, October 1467; Add Ch. 26812/6, April 1469.
7   British Library, Add Ch. 26813/3, October 1467; Add Ch. 26813/4, May 1468; Add Ch. 26813/5, April 1468 or later; Add Ch. 26813/6, April 1469; Add Ch. 26813/7, October 1469; Add Ch. 26813/8, May 1470.
8   BARS, Box R212, Roll 35, October 1425.

activity for two or three is clearly documented. Brewing is one of the main areas which throws some light on the lives of women on the manor, who are otherwise only occasionally mentioned.

The buildings

The documents do not provide a complete list of the buildings on the manor; the buildings on free holdings held by free men were never included. The buildings on customary holdings, whether held by free men or villeins, were only listed when they needed repair. The medieval manor house was described in 1376, and there are details of several insethouses on the manor in the first quarter of the fifteenth century. The rolls contain details about the construction of the mill on several occasions and reveal that the machinery, the dam and the mill-pond were damaged periodically by floods and bad weather.

Although there is a detailed description of the manor house shortly before the Peasants' Revolt,[9] there is only one vague reference to it in the court rolls; the 'hall yard' was mentioned in May 1449.[10] It may have been the administration centre for the Mowbray's Bedfordshire properties, and the bailiff and his family may have lived there, William Launcelyn's family may even have lived there at one time. The manor courts may have been held in the hall, and the brew-house may have been used by all the tenants, but there is no evidence for any of these activities in the manorial accounts or court rolls. The manor house was demolished by John Gostwyk in the late 1530s.

Inset houses appear occasionally elsewhere in medieval wills and other documents and are frequently listed in the Willington manor court rolls 1408–23.[11] During those years the records show that twenty-one tenants had at least one of them on their holding. The names of the men holding them suggest that, in Willington, many of them were held by families who, in addition to farming their lands, also practiced rural trades.[12] The layout and construction of this type of building is unknown, but in Willington the living accommodation may have been inset between the domestic service rooms on one side and a workshop or occupational store on the other. Fewer such buildings are mentioned in the second half of the fifteenth century, when there are more mentions of hall-houses.

The responsibility for repairs to the most important manorial asset, the mill, was made explicit when the lease was granted for periods of years. The lease arrangements show evidence of attempts to ensure that the tenant undertook his responsibilities, but at the same time the lord provided some support for its maintenance. When John Ussher took over the lease of the mill in 1413, he and his assigns agreed to provide the millstones and all of the machinery and to repair the mill dams and the holding and put them right at his own expense. The lord's officials agreed to provide:

9   Bailey, *The English Manor*, pp. 58–9.
10   BARS, Box R212, Roll 38b, May 1449.
11   BARS, Box R212, Roll 10, October 1408 – Roll 33, October 1423, inclusive.
12   John Goffe was a brewer, Richard Lygtfot was described as a carpenter, and the names Rider, Smith, Tayllour, Thresshere and Wright suggest other rural trades.

one limb for the same John to repair and put right the said Dam during the aforesaid term. And the said John and his assigns will hand over the said mill, the stones for milling and all the Machinery pertaining to the said mill and the mill Dams at the end of the term of the tenancy well and sufficiently repaired.[13]

John gave a deposit of twenty pounds and was not asked to provide pledges or guarantors. By 1452, when the mill was leased to Thomas Myller, the terms of the lease were much more generous, suggesting that the mill had become less profitable and that the lord's officials had difficulty finding a miller. The rent had been reduced to £3 13s. 4d. a year, and Thomas was allowed to quarry gravel near the mill. He could also keep fish in the mill pond and benefit from the willows and the underwood growing round it. The lord would provide 'all the stuffs' for repairs, but Thomas would provide all the carpentry works and iron and hand the mill back 'well prepared.'[14]

In addition to detailed information about repairs to important buildings on the manor, lists of timber, granted by the steward and delivered by the bailiff to the tenants to repair their buildings, are included from April 1409.[15] The records show a substantial number of buildings of various sizes and uses which, during most of the fifteenth century, the lords of the manor were determined to keep in good repair. Large numbers of buildings appear in the rolls at intervals of approximately ten years, with follow-ups two years later, suggesting that the Mowbrays' councils arranged for regular surveys to take place.

The issue of ruined buildings was exploited by the entrepreneurial William Launcelyn, 1448–52, who negotiated a variety of arrangements with tenants whose buildings needed repair, although he did not then deliver on the agreements. In 1450 seven holdings were vacant, and five were still vacant in May 1452 when the lord's stewards and surveyors stayed overnight with the Launcelyn household. The numbers of vacant holdings gradually reduced to one in May 1453 and two in May 1454 after which the lists of vacant holdings on the manor ceased to be recorded in the court rolls.

The largest number of buildings needing repair is found in the court roll of September 1515 when more than twenty tenants were named as needing to repair at least sixteen halls, eighteen barns, one kitchen, twelve bake-houses, seven stables and a hay-house.

Manorial control and the decline of serfdom
The lords of the manor made efforts to manage the manor and maintain the value of their assets by a variety of techniques. They appointed an experienced local man as bailiff, and the steward, surveyors and other members of the Mowbray council visited twice a year with occasional extra visits when there were suspicions of dishonesty or other problems. The lord and his council were willing to modernise and abandon the punitive effects of medieval serfdom, supporting the custom of the manor and the maintenance of a participative pattern of life where at least twenty-four tenants were regularly involved in the court process; two juries at the views of frankpledge date from 1404. This was supported by the tithing system into which all men over

---

13   BARS, Box R212, Roll 15, October 1413.
14   BARS, Box R212, Roll 40b, May 1452.
15   BARS, Box R212, Roll 11, April 1409.

twelve were enrolled and were responsible for the good behaviour of their fellows. The practice of appointing two constables from among the tenants at regular intervals from the 1440s also ensured local involvement in manorial affairs.

Modifications to the terms of tenancy for holdings were also made in response to social and financial changes and the periodic difficulties in finding tenants. In the late fourteenth century many holdings were let 'at will' and were insecure. In 1415, for the first time, a holding was let for two lives, to a man and his wife, a practice which was used increasingly throughout the fifteenth century. In 1452 a holding was granted for three lives, that is to a man, his wife and one other, with an additional year after the death of the last tenant. A system of charging penalties to ensure that tenants repaired buildings and cleared ditches was still employed, but there appears to have been a long-term patience with tenants ensuring that they complied by increasing the threatened penalty annually until the repairs or clearances took place. This seems to have led to a relatively peaceful solution to the arrears but, combined with the falling income from rents, led to dwindling incomes for the lords of the manor as a result.

The last reference to lands held 'in bondage' in the court rolls was in October 1395, and the last use of the word 'villein' was in April 1426, although most of the rolls between this date and October 1448 have not survived.[16] The use of the word 'serf' is almost unknown. A William Toky was described as a serf in October 1394.[17] In September 1417, after the list of sworn men at the start of the court roll, the ambiguous phrase 'born in the demesne' was used. It implied that the man concerned was tied to the manor of his birth but did not make it clear whether he was a serf or was of villein status.[18] Although the word was seldom used in the documents, serfdom lingered on, as implied in October 1457 when the court ordered that: 'the labourers by the day who are resident within the precinct of the Lete are not to accept labouring outside the vill while they are able to have sufficient services and payment within.'[19] Heavy penalties of 40d. payable to the lord and the church in equal portions were threatened for breaking this order.

The records suggest that the Mowbrays abandoned direct farming of their demesne in Willington at about the time of the Peasants' Revolt. Their former demesne lands were granted to, 'various bondsmen tenants and certain tenants of will'. The bailiff's account of that year states that messuages and other lands were formerly held in bondage, some by molemen and cottars. After that date most villein tenants paid cash for their rents and performed few customary services, but they were still tied to the manor of their birth. Villeins who were members of the Rider and Tele families left the manor in 1417, 1419 and 1420 and were ordered to return; although there is no evidence that they did so.[20]

Even so, the men who held the former demesne lands became more independent over time, partly as a result of the difficulties in finding sufficient and good tenants. In April 1421, about the time that Lord Mowbray returned after five years in France,

16   BARS, Box R212, Roll 3, October 1395; Roll 36a, April 1426; Roll 38a, October 1448.
17   BARS, Box R212, Roll 2, October 1394.
18   BARS, Box R212, Roll 22, September 1417.
19   BARS, Box R212, Roll 46a, October 1457.
20   BARS, Box R212, Roll 22, May 1417; Roll 26, May 1419; Roll 28, May 1420.

two quarters of the demesne lands and four messuages each with half a virgate of land were untenanted, with a resultant loss of income of more than 27s. The steward must have been concerned and he stayed overnight to agree new rents with the tenants. The new rents for the quarters of demesne land may have been reduced to £20 a year, although they were not noted in the court roll.[21] Difficulties in attracting tenants may have been linked with the poor state of buildings, but there were undoubtedly other factors; one particular messuage was often challenging to let, suggesting that it was on land that was infertile or which regularly flooded. Three quarters of the demesne lands remained untenanted until 1423.

In October 1425 eighteen tenants were listed as having buildings needing repair, at least seven of which had defective thatch. Only William Taillour was said to have done the repairs well.[22] Although ruined buildings were often seen as the root of the problems in finding tenants the lords of the manor seem to have become more reluctant to provide timber for repairs as the fifteenth century progressed.

In 1449 the four parts of the former demesne lands were subdivided into twelve lots. They were granted to thirteen tenants, and the total annual rent was reduced to £18.[23] All was still not well, for in May 1454 these tenants gave notice of their intention to hand the lands back to the lord in March 1455. There are no further references to the demesne lands in the court rolls after this date, but in the bailiff's account 1457–58 it notes that £18 was paid for: 'various lands of Wilyngton so handed over to tenants of the same vill by the steward this year.' These rents of £18 continued to be paid until at least 1480–81.

Change on the manor was not driven by national events or by a domineering lord of the manor in the fifteenth century. It took place in a series of small steps within a stable environment in which members of the manor elite negotiated terms with manorial officials, a process which had begun in 1382. The gradual changes in the terms of tenancy for tenants gave most of the customary tenants almost as much security as free tenants. By the early 1450s the payment of entry fines to the lord when being granted a holding had reduced from several pence at the end of the fourteenth century to a capon, probably worth about 3d. From 1454 heriots were no longer paid by a tenant's heirs after his death or on the surrender of a property.

The four surviving court records from the sixteenth century, 1515–22, suggest change in the management of the manor. There were no longer two juries of twelve men, although the number of sworn jury men in the views of frankpledge was larger, thirteen in March 1520, fifteen in March 1522, and fourteen in December 1522. There is only one record of a change in constables; in December 1522. These changes may hint that the Howards were less committed to the management of Willington than Katherine Neville and her husbands had been in the past. However, there was some continuity, the constables who retired and those who were appointed came from established Willington families; William Yarwey and John Myton replaced John Warner and Edmund Totnam.

---

[21]   BARS, Box R212, Roll 30, April 1421. A note is appended to the end of the roll to say that the overnight stay was on 17 June but the year is not given.
[22]   BARS, Box R212, Roll 35, October 1425. The end of the roll is missing, but the amount of detail about repairs may be attributed to the appointment of a new steward, named in the following two rolls as Roger Hunte of nearby Roxton.
[23]   BARS, Box R212, Roll 39b, May 1449.

Leading families

Well-established influential free families included the Maryons and the Mitons. Because of their free status there is less information about them in the court rolls, but they lived on the manor for several generations, and the Mitons regularly served on the jury of the manor court and held manorial offices. Two families of villein status, the Riders and the Yarweys, also dominated the manor for many years. The Rider family appears in the records of the manor in 1309 and continues to be recorded until 1451. The Yarweys are recorded in the manor court rolls from 1394 until the 1600s. This core of free and villein families, with the use of two juries on the manor court, the tithing system and the appointment of men to manorial office, supported stability on the manor.

Although the year 1500 has been thought to mark: 'a significant stage in the move from a society of communities to one based on the individual', at Willington it could be argued that some individuals had effectively influenced life on the manor from before the end of the fourteenth century.[24] The Gostwyks, a free family, were the thread which held the story of Willington together 1382–1731, until the manor passed into the hands of Sarah, Duchess of Marlborough. They ensured continuity at a local level, often as bailiffs, from the early fourteenth century, if not before, eventually becoming lords of the manor in 1529. The manor court rolls contain few details of their agrarian activities, but in 1507 the Newnham Priory terrier shows that the brothers John and William Gostwyke held much of the land on the manor.

By the early 1500s the family was preparing to play a national role. John Gostwyk had married a daughter of the Leventhorpe family[25] whose ancestor had been receiver general of the duchy of Lancaster and whose family had close links with the Mowbrays.[26] Their son, also named John, is thought to have been born 1480–90 when Willington was held by the Howards. He was laying the foundations of his successful career as a merchant in the service of Cardinal Wolsey and King Henry VIII when the four surviving court rolls from the Howard period were written.[27] He and his wife Joan bought the manor in 1529 from the Duke of Norfolk, and the directions which he wrote for their son suggest that their good name, and that of their son, was at least as important to them as the acquisition of land and the accumulation of wealth.[28]

Although the Gostwyks might have moved into the modern world by 1500 the medieval pattern of the lives of some tenants continued until at least 1599. This was witnessed by the twelve orders and penalties agreed for the use of the commons which were written in English for the first time that year. A further twelve were agreed in 1605.[29] In 1609, nineteen orders and penalties were listed which made it clear what was expected from the tenants when keeping animals, cultivating fields, clearing ditches and gleaning in the fields. This document contains the names of twenty-six tenants and five widows with the dues they paid and the numbers of animals that they were allowed to keep on the commons. This

24 Dyer, *Country Merchant*, p. 2.
25 Finberg, 'Gostwicks of Willington', p. 57.
26 Moye, *The Estates and Finances of the Mowbray Family*, p. 403.
27 Finberg, 'Gostwicks of Willington', pp. 58–9.
28 Dickens, 'Estate and Household Management in Bedfordshire c 1540', pp. 38–45.
29 BARS, Box R212, Roll 77, October 1609.

increase in documentation about the common fines and the use of the commons at the beginning of the seventeenth century suggests that there may have been an increase in disputes about the rights of tenants.

It is not known how long the vestiges of the customs of the manor and use of the commons endured as insufficient documents survive. However, the enclosure of Willington's open fields by the then Duke of Bedford, without Act of Parliament, in about 1800, while increasing agricultural efficiency and production, may have led to the customary rights of the tenants being finally extinguished.

Appendix One

Terrier of the prior and Convent of Newnham of its Land and Tenements in Wellyngton, made there on the 12th day of July in the twenty second year of the reign of King Henry the seventh [1507]

The transcription of the Willington terrier that follows mirrors the original in its lack of punctuation, erratic use of capital letters and erratic spellings of family names, field-names and landscape features. Willington was spelt 'Welyngton' in the bold headings of the folios but three other different spellings of the name were used in the text. The first names of tenants or land-holders have been given modern forms in the translation. The line breaks in the original have been adhered to in the transcript, except in one case, but are not used in the translation.

The use of occasional English phrases may suggest that the scribe was not a fluent Latin scholar, but the use of five different prepositions following forms of the verb *abutto* in both the Biddenham and Willington documents does not support this. In the Bedford terrier the use of prepositions following forms of *abutto* is more limited suggesting that it was written by a different scribe.

Transcription

(folio 3 dorso)   **Welyngton**

Territorium prioris et Conventus de Newenham de terris et tenementis suis in Wellyngton factum ibidem duodecimo die Julij anno regni regis Henrici Septimi Vicesimo Secundo

> In les Millfeild Una acra et dimidia super ympeorum furlong inter
> terram domini de Wellington et utraque parte
> dimidia acra abuttans in Dadmore inter terram Johannis
> Myton ex parte boreali et terram domini ex parte australi
> una roda in Dadmore inter terram Willelmi Gostwyke ex parte
> boreali et terram domini ex parte australi
> dimidia acra super eandem inter terram domini ex parte
> australi et terram Johannis Myton ex parte boreali
> dimidia acra super eandem inter terram Willelmi
> Gostwyke ex parte boreali et terram domini ex parte
> australi
> una Roda_super eandem inter terram domini ex utraque parte
> dimidia roda inter Dadmore ex parte boreali et forera
> Johannis Gostwyke ex parte australi
> una roda iacens subtus tenementum Johannis Myton
> inter dictum tenementum ex parte occidentali et terram
> ipsius Johannis Myton ex parte orientali
> una roda et dimidia in uno selione iuxta dictam
> Rodam nisi uno selione Johannis Myton intermedio
> una roda et dimidia super Standweyfurlonge[1] inter
> terram Roberti Warner ex parte occidentali et terram
> domini ex parte orientali
> dimidia acra super eandem inter terram domini et
> Johannis Myton
> dimidia acra super eandem inter terram domini et
> Johannis Myton[2]
> ~~dimidia~~[3]
> una acra super eandem inter terram Johannis Myton
> ex utraque parte
> dimidia acra super eandem inter terram domini ex
> parte orientali et terram Johannis Yerway
> ex parte occidentali

(folio 4 recto)   **Welyngton**

> dimidia acra super eandem inter terram Johannis Gostwyke
> ex parte occidentali et terram domini ex parte orientali
> dimidia acra super eandem inter terram domini ex utraque parte
> dimidia acra super eandem inter terram Johannis Warner
> ex parte occidentali et terram domini ex parte orientali
> una roda super eandem inter terram domini ex utraque parte
> dimidia acra super eandem inter terram Willelmi Gostwyke

---

1   This may mean a road to a quarry or gravel pit.
2   This line is as written, a repeat of the previous line.
3   Not only is 'dimidia' crossed out, it is almost erased.

Translation

(folio 3 reverse) **Welyngton**

The Terrier of the prior and Convent of Newnham of its lands and tenements in Wellyngton, made there on the twelfth day of July in the twenty-second year of the reign of king Henry the seventh.

> In the Millfeild, One and a half acres on the furlong of saplings
> between the land of the lord of Wellington on either side
> half an acre abutting on Dadmore between the land of John
> Myton on the north side and the land of the lord on the south side
> one rood in Dadmore between the land of William Gostwyke on the
> north side and the land of the lord on the south side
> half an acre on the same between the land of the lord on the south side
> and land of John Myton on the north side
> half an acre on the same between the land of William Gostwyke on the
> north side and the land of the lord on the
> south side
> one Rood on the same between the land of the lord on either side
> half a rood between Dadmore on the north side and the headland of
> John Gostwyke on the south side
> one rood lying below the tenement of John Myton between the said
> tenement on the west side and the land of John Myton himself on
> the east side
> one rood and a half in one strip[4] next to the said Rood, but one strip
> belonging to John Myton comes in between
> one rood and a half on Standweyfurlonge between
> the land of Robert Warner on the west side and the land of the lord on
> the east side
> half an acre on the same between the land of the lord and of
> John Myton
> half an acre on the same between the land of the lord and of
> John Myton
> ~~half~~
> one acre on the same between the land of John Myton
> on either side
> half an acre on the same between the land of the lord on the east side
> and the land of John Yerway
> on the west side

(folio 4 front)   **Welyngton**

> half an acre on the same between the land of John Gostwyke on the
> west side and the land of the lord on the east side
> half an acre on the same between the land of the lord on either side
> half an acre on the same between the land of John Warner on the west
> side and the land of the lord on the east side
> one rood on the same between the land of the lord on either side
> half an acre on the same between the land of William Gostwyke on the

---

4   Of arable land in the common fields.

ex parte occidentali et terram domini ex parte orientali
dimidia acra super eandem inter terram domini ex parte
orientali et terram Yerway vel domini ex parte occidentali
una Roda super eandem inter terram Johannis Gostwyke
 ex parte orientali et terram Willelmi Gostwyke vel
domini ex parte occidentali
una acra super eandem inter terram Johannis Gostwyke
ex parte orientali et terram domini ex parte occidentali
dimidia acra super eandem iuxta terram domini ex parte occidentali
tres rode super eandem inter terram Johannis Gostwyke
et terram [blank]
dimidia acra super quarentenam versus le Verne[5] inter terram
domini ex parte occidentali et terram Johannis Warner
ex altera parte
dimidia acra super eandem inter terram domini ex parte
occidentali et terram Johannis Gostwyke ex parte orientali
una acra et una Roda terre super eandem inter terram Willelmi
Gostwyke ex parte occidentali et terram Johannis Miton[6] ex altera parte
una acra et una roda terre frisce simul iacens super Reefurlonge inter
terram [blank]
Summa Circa xv [15] acre tres Roda et dimidia

(folio 4 dorso)   **Welyngton**

In le Fulwellfeld dimidia acra iacens in Twelacres
iuxta terram domini ex parte orientali
dimidia acra super eandem inter terram Johannis Gostwyke
ex parte [blank]
vicarious de Wellington habet illam acram
dimidia acra super eandem abuttans in Stanway inter
terram domini ex parte orientali et terram Johannis
Gostwyke ex altera parte
una acra super eandem inter terram Johannis Gostwyke
 ex parte occidentali et terram Johannis Myton ex
parte orientali
dimidia acra super eandem inter terram Roberti Warner
ex parte occidentali et terram domini ex parte orientali
una acra super eandem inter terram Willelmi Gostwyke ex
parte occidentali et terram domini ex parte orientali
una acra super eandem inter terram Johannis Myton
ex parte occidentali et terram domini ex parte orientali
dimidia acra super eandem inter terram domini ex parte
occidentali et terram [blank]
due acre simul iacentes inter terram domini ex parte
orientali et terram Johannis Gostwyke ex parte occidentali
una acra simul iacens super eandem nisi dimidia acra
Johannis Warner intermedia inter terram Johannis Gostwyke
ex parte orientali et terram domini ex
altera parte
una acra super eandem inter terram Johannis Myton
ex parte occidentali et terram Johannis Gostwyke
ex parte orientali

<hr>

5   The *Oxford English Dictionary* says that Verne is an obsolete variation of Fern, meaning a windlass.
6   This is the only example of the spelling of this surname in the document. It is most probably the same John Myton, mentioned often elsewhere.

west side and the land of the lord on the east side

half an acre on the same between the land of the lord on the east side
and the Yerway land or the lord's on the west side

one Rood on the same between the land of John Gostwyke on the east
side and the land of William Gostwyke or
the lord on the west side

one acre on the same between the land of John Gostwyke on the east
side and the land of the lord on the west side

half an acre on the same next to the land of the lord on the west side

three roods on the same between the land of John Gostwyke and the
land [blank]

half an acre on the furlong against the Verne between the land of the
lord on the west side and the land of John Warner
on the other side

half an acre on the same between the land of the lord on the west side
and the land of John Gostwyke on the east side

one acre and one Rood of land on the same between the land of William
Gostwyke on the west side and the land of John Miton on the other side

one acre and one rood of uncultivated[7] land lying together on Reefurlonge between the land [blank]

In total About 15 acres, three and a half roods.

(folio 4 reverse) **Welyngton**

In Fulwellfield half an acre lying in Twelacres next to the land of the
lord on the east side

half an acre on the same between the land of John Gostwyke on the
[blank] side

the vicar of Wellington has this acre

half an acre on the same abutting on Stanway between the land of the
lord on the east side and the land of John
Gostwyke on the other side

one acre on the same between the land of John Gostwyke
on the west side and John Myton's land on
the east side

half an acre on the same between the land of Robert Warner on the
west side and the land of the lord on the east side

one acre on the same between the land of William Gostwyke on the
west side and the land of the lord on the east side

one acre on the same between the land of John Myton on the
west side and the land of the lord on the east side

half an acre on the same between the land of the lord on the west side
and the land [blank]

two acres lying together between the land of the lord on the east side
and the land of John Gostwyke on the west side

one acre lying together on the same, but that John Warner's half an acre
is in the middle, between the land of John Gostwyke on the east side
and the lord's land on
the other side

one acre on the same between land of John Myton on the west side and
the land of John Gostwyke
on the east side

---

dimidia acra super eandem ad finem Ville inter terram
domini et terram Johannis Myton
dimidia acra super eandem inter terram Johannis Myton
et terram Johannis Warner
dimidia acra iacens super lynhill inter terram domini
ex parte australi et terram Willelmi Gostwyke ex
parte boreali
una Roda super eandem inter terram domini ex parte
boreali et terram Johannis Gostwyke ex parte australi
due Rode iacentes apud Chambers inter terram Johannis
Gostwyke ex parte australi et terram Willelmi Gostwyke
ex altera parte

(folio 5 recto)   **Welyngton**
dimidia acra super Middlefurlonge extendens ultra Regiam
viam inter terram Johannis Gostwyke ex parte occidentali
et terram domini ex altera parte
dimidia acra super eandem inter terram domini ex utraque
parte extendens ultra Regian viam
dimidia acra super eandem inter terram Johannis
Gostwyke ex parte occidentali et terram domini ex
altera parte
dimidia acra super eandem inter terram domini ex utraque parte
dimidia acra super eandem inter terram Johannis
Gostwyke ex parte orientali et terram domini vel
Richardi Dyke ex altera parte
una Roda super eandem inter terram domini ex parte
orientali et terram Willelmi Gostwyke ex parte occidentali
una Roda et dimidia super Denefurlonge inter terram
Johannis Gostwyke ex parte orientali et terram domini
ex parte occidentali
dimidia Roda super eandem inter terram domini ex parte
orientali et terram Roberti Warner ex altera parte
una acra super eandem iuxta terram domini ex parte
occidentali
due Rode super eandem inter terram Willelmi Gostwyke
ex parte occidentali
dimidia acra super le Hay inter terram domini ex parte
orientali et terram Roberti Warner ex parte occidentali
dimidia acra super eandem inter terram domini ex utraque parte
una Roda super eandem inter Communem Divisam ex parte
occidentali et terram domini ex parte orientali
dimidia acra super eandem inter terram Johannis
Gostwyke ex utraque parte in escambium pro alia
dimidia acra super eandem inter terram domini ex parte
orientali
dimidia acra super eandem inter terram domini ex parte orientali[8]
una acra super eandem inter terram Roberti Warner
ex parte occidentali et terram [blank]
una acra super eandem inter terram domini ex parte
orientali et terram Willelmi Gostwyke ex parte occidentali
due seliones pro tribus Rodis simul iacentes super eandem
inter terram domini ex utraque parte

---

8   This line has been repeated, as in the original.

half an acre on the same at the end of the Township, between the land
of the lord and John Myton's land
half an acre on the same between the land of John Myton and the land
of John Warner
half an acre lying on lynhill between the land of the lord on the south
side and the land of William Gostwyke on
the north side
one Rood on the same between the land of the lord on the north side
and the land of John Gostwyke on the south side
two roods lying at Chambers between the land of John Gostwyke on
the south side and the land of William Gostwyke
on the other side

(folio 5 front)   **Welyngton**
half an acre on Middlefurlonge extending beyond the King's highway
between the land of John Gostwyke on the west side and the land of the
lord on the other side
half an acre on the same between the land of the lord on either side
extending beyond the King's highway
half an acre on the same between the land of John Gostwyke on the
west side and the land of the lord on the
other side
half an acre on the same between the land of the lord on either side
half an acre on the same between the land of John Gostwyke on the
east side and the land of the lord or of
Richard Dyke on the other side
one Rood on the same between the land of the lord on the east side and
the land of William Gostwyke on the west side
one Rood and a half on Denefurlonge between the land of John Gostwyke on the east side and the land of the lord
on the west side
half a Rood on the same between the land of the lord on the east side
and the land of Robert Warner on the other side
one acre on the same next to the land of the lord on the
west side
two Roods on the same between the land of William Gostwyke on the
west side
half an acre on the Hay between the land of the lord on the east side
and the land of Robert Warner on the west side
half an acre on the same between the land of the lord on either side
one Rood on the same between the Common Boundary on the west side
and the land of the lord on the east side
half an acre on the same between the land of John Gostwyke on both
sides in exchange for another
half an acre on the same between the land of the lord on the
east side
half an acre on the same between the land of the lord on the east side[9]
one acre on the same between the land of Robert Warner on the west
side and the land [blank]
one acre on the same between the land of the lord on the east side and
the land of William Gostwyke on the west side
two strips for three Roods lying together on the same between the land
of the lord on either side

---

[9]   This line is repeated as in the original.

due seliones pro tribus Rodis simul iacentes super
eandem inter terram domini ex utraque parte[10]
Summa Circa xxvij [27] acre tres roda[11]

(folio 5 dorso)   **Welyngton**
In le Midlemarshfeild dimidia acra terre super Stokebalk
furlonge inter terram Johannis Yerway ex parte occidentali
et terram domini ex altera parte
dimidia acra super Langeland inter terram domini Prioris
de Newenham ex parte boreali et terram Johannis Myton
ex altera parte
vicarious de Wellyngton tenet illam acram
una acra iacens super Dolefurlonge nisi dimidia acra domini
intermedia inter terram domini ex parte australi
et terram Willelmi Gostwyke ex altera parte
dimidia acra super eandem inter terram Johannis
Gostwyke ex parte boreali and terram Willelmi Gostwyke
ex altera parte
tres seliones simul iacentes abuttantes in le Dene
iuxta terram domini ex parte occidentali at terram [blank]
unus selio super eandem inter terram Johannis Gostwyke
ex parte orientali et terram Willelmi Gostwyke
ex parte occidentali
unus selio super eandem inter terram domini ex parte occidentali
et terram Johannis Myton ex altera parte, et isti quinque
sunt other half rode
una roda in Goseland inter terram domini ex utraque parte
dimidia rode beyond the Dene super Crowe Well inter
terram Johannis Gostwyke ex parte orientali et terram
domini ex parte occidentali
una acra super eandem inter terram Johannis Gostwyke
ex parte occidentali et terram domini ex parte orientali
dimidia acra super eandem Inter terram Johannis
Gostwyke ex utraque parte
dimidia acra super eandem inter terram Willelmi
Gostwyke ex parte occidentali et terram domini ex
parte orientali
dimidia acra super Middlemarsh iuxta terram Roberti
Warner ex parte australi
una Roda super Middlemarshed iuxta terram Johannis
Gostwyke ex parte occidentali

(folio 6 recto)   **Welyngton**
dimidia acra super eandem iuxta terram Johannis
Myton ex parte occidentali
una Roda super eandem iuxta terram Johannis Myton
ex parte occidentali et terram domini ex parte orientali
una roda super Woodway furlonge inter terram domini
ex parte boreali et terram Johannis Myton ex parte
australi
una Roda super eandem inter terram domini ex utraque parte
una roda super Stokebalkefurlonge inter terram domini

---

10   This line has been repeated, as in the original.
11   These figures may be inaccurate.

two strips for three Roods lying together on the same between the land
of the lord on either side
Total About 27 acres and three roods[12]

(folio 5 reverse) **Welyngton**

In the Midlemarshfeild half an acre of land on Stokebalk furlonge
between the land of John Yerway on the west side and the land of the
lord on the other side
half an acre on Langeland between the land of the lord Prior of
Newenham on the north side and the land of John Myton
on the other side
the vicar of Wellyngton holds this acre
one acre lying on Dolefurlonge, but that the lord's half an acre comes
in the middle, between the land of the lord on the south side and the
land of William Gostwyke on the other side
half an acre on the same between the land of John Gostwyke on the
north side and the land of William Gostwyke
on the other side
three strips of land lying together abutting on the Dene next to the land
of the lord on the west side and the land [blank]
one strip on the same between the land of John Gostwyke on the east
side and the land of William Gostwyke
on the west side
one strip on the same between the land of the lord on the west side and
the land of John Myton on the other side, and these five
were the other half rood
one rood on Goseland between the land of the lord on either side
half a rood beyond the Dene on Crowe Well between
the land of John Gostwyke on the east side and
the lord's land on the west side
one acre on the same between the land of John Gostwyke on the west
side and the land of the lord on the east side
half an acre on the same Between the land of John
Gostwyke on either side
half an acre on the same between the land of William Gostwyke on the
west side and the land of the lord on the
east side
half an acre on Middlemarsh next to the land of Robert
Warner on the south side
One rood on Middlemarshed next to the land of John
Gostwyke on the west side

(folio 6 front) **Welyngton**

half an acre on the same next to the land of John
Myton on the west side
one Rood on the same next to the land of John Myton on the west side
and the land of the lord on the east side
one rood on Woodway furlonge between the land of the lord on the
north side and the land of John Myton on the
south side
one Rood on the same between the lord's land on either side
one rood on Stokebalkefurlonge between the land of the lord

---

[12]   Calculated by the author as 23 acres 3 roods.

terram Johannis Myton ex parte occidentali
ex utraque parte et abuttat super forera Johannis
Gostwyke
una Roda super eandem inter terram domini ex utraque
parte
una acra super eandem inter terram domini ex parte
occidentali et terram Johannis Fesaunt ex parte
orientali
una acra super eandem inter terram domini ex parte
occidentali et terram Johannis Gostwyke ex parte
orientali
uno selio pro dimidia acra in Litlemarsh inter terram
domini ex parte occidentali et terram Roberti Warner ex parte orientali
una Roda in Litlemarsh inter terram Roberti Warner
ex utraque parte
una acra in Longlitlemarsh inter terram domini ex
parte australi et terram Johannis Myton ex parte boreali
una Roda super eandem inter terram domini ex parte boreali
et terram Willelmi Gostwyke ex parte australi
duo seliones pro tribus rodis apud Smalhedges
inter Burybalke ex parte occidentali et terram Willelmi
Gostwyke ex parte [blank]
dimidia acra super eandem inter terram Roberti Warner
ex parte occidentali et terram domini ex parte orientali
una acra et dimidia super Stokebalkefurlonge inter
terram domini ex utraque parte
dimidia acra super eandem inter terram domini ex parte
orientali et terram Roberti Warner ex parte occidentali

(Folio 6 dorso) **Welyngton**
una Roda super LongCroWell inter terram domini ex parte orientali et
terram Roberti Warner ex altera parte
dimidia acra super eandem inter terram domini ex utraque parte
una super Mansherd inter terram Johannis Gostwyke ex parte
occidentali et terram Johannis Myton ex altera parte
dimidia acra super Merefurlonge inter Burybalke ex parte orientali et
terram domini ex parte occidentali
dimidia acra super eandem inter terram domini ex parte orientali et
terram Thome Passewater ex parte occidentali
dimida acra in Goorebroode inter le balke ex parte occidentali et
terram domini ex parte orientali
dimidia acra super eandem inter terram domini ex utraque parte
tres Rode simul iacentes toward the Mere inter terram Johannis
Gostwyke et terram [blank]
due rode simul iacentes in Lonlangland nisi una roda et dimidia intermedia
inter terram vicarii ex parte australi et terram Willelmi
Gostwyke ex altera parte
tres Rode simul in superiore Lampitte inter terram domini ex parte
orientali et terram Johannis Gostwyke ex parte occidentali
una roda super eandem
tres Rode super Shortelongland inter terram domini ex parte australi
et terram Johannis Myton ex altera parte
dimidia acra super Stratefurlonge inter le Mare ex parte occidentali et
terram Johannis Gostwyke ex parte orientali
dimidia acra super eandem inter terram domini ex parte orientali et
terram Johannis Myton ex parte occidentali

the land of John Myton on the west side
on either side and it abutts on the headland of John
Gostwyke
one Rood on the same between the land of the lord on either
side
one acre on the same between the land of the lord on the west side and
the land of John Fesaunt on the
east side
one acre on the same between the land of the lord on the west side and
the land of John Gostwyke on the
east side
one strip for half an acre in Litlemarsh between the land of the lord on
the west side and the land of Robert Warner on the east side
one Rood in Litlemarsh between the land of Robert Warner on
either side
one acre in Longlitlemarsh between the land of the lord on the south
side and the land of John Myton on the north side
one Rood on the same between the land of the lord on the north side
and the land of William Gostwyke on the south side
two strips for three roods at Smalhedges
between Burybalke on the west side and the land of William
Gostwyke on the [blank] side
half an acre on the same between the land of Robert Warner on the
west side and the land of the lord on the east side
one and a half acres on Stokebalkefurlonge between
the lord's land on either side
half an acre on the same between the land of the lord on the east side
and the land of Robert Warner on the west side

(folio 6 reverse) **Welyngton**

one Rood on LongCroWell between the land of the lord on the east side
and the land of Robert Warner on the other side
half an acre on the same between the land of the lord on either side
one on Mansherd between the land of John Gostwyke on the west side
and the land of John Myton on the other side
half an acre on Merefurlonge between Burybalke on the east side and
the land of the lord on the west side
half an acre on the same between the land of the lord on the east side
and the land of Thomas Passewater on the west side
half an acre in Goorebroode between the baulk on the west side and the
land of the lord on the east side
half an acre on the same between the land of the lord on either side
three Roods lying together toward the Mere between the land of John
Gostwyke on the west side and the land [blank]
two roods lying together in Lonlangland, but that one rood and a half
is in the middle, between the land of the vicar on the south side and the
land of William Gostwyke on the other side
three Roods together in upper Lampitte between the land of the lord on
the east side and the land of John Gostwyke on the west side
one rood on the same
three roods on Shortelongland between the land of the lord on the south
side and the land of John Myton on the other side
half an acre on Stratefurlonge between the Mere on the west side and
the land of John Gostwyke on the east side
half an acre on the same between the land of the lord on the east side
and the land of John Myton on the west side

due rode super eandem inter terram domini ex parte orientali et
terram Johannis Myton ex parte occidentali
una Roda super eandem inter terram domini ex parte orientali et
terram Roberti Warner ex parte occidentali
Summa Circa xxxiij acre[13]

(folio 7 recto)   **Welyngton**
In le Brookefeild una acra terre simul iacet in
Brookefeild super le Middlefurlonge inter terram
Willelmi Yerway ex parte australi et terram domini
ex parte boreali. vicarius de Wellington habet illam
acram
una acra simul iacet abuttans super Smalway ad
Caput[14] occidentale inter terram Thome Rees ex parte
australi et terram Willelmi Gostwyke ex parte boreali
dimidia Roda super eandem inter terram domini ex parte
boreali et terram Johannis Gostwyke ex parte australi
et abuttat ad Caput occidentale super Smalway et
ad Caput orientale super terram domini que dicta
dimidia Roda extendit nisi usque ad medium dicte
quarentene
due Rode simul iacentes super Walyshedfurlonge inter
terram domini ex utraque parte et abuttant ad Caput
boreale super Walished et ad alud [sic] Caput super terram
Johannis Gostwyke
una acra simul iacens under Sandhill quarum una
est forera de Smalwayfurlonge iuxta terram Willelmi
Gostwyke vel domini de Wellington ex parte orientali
et abuttat ad Caput boreale super Yramleys
una Roda super eandem inter terram Willelmi Gostwyke
ex parte occidentali et terram domini ex parte orientali et
abuttat super Yramleys
dimidia acra iacens inter Pasturan vocatam Yramleys
ex parte orientali et terram Roberti Warner ex
parte occidentali et abuttat versus westmead de
Couphull ad Caput boreale
due Rode super eandem inter terram domini ex
parte orientale et terram Johannis Gostwyke ex
parte occidentali et abuttat ut supra
due Rode super Sandhill inter terram domini ex
parte boreali et terram Johannis Myton ex parte
australi et abuttant ad Caput orientale super Meadfurlonge

(folio 7 dorso)   **Welyngton**
due dimidie Rode ^iacentes^ super eandem[15] Meadfurlonge inter
pasturam vocatam Yram ex parte boreali et terram [blank]
una roda super eandem inter terram Thome Rees ex parte
occidentali et terram domini ex parte orientali et abuttat
super Coupelmead

---

[13]   Calculated by the author as about 23 acres.
[14]   It might be expected that 'Caput' would be written in the accusative, but it is not written so here, or
elsewhere in the text which follows
[15]   This word has been expunged, that is, not erased but removed from the document by writing a row
of dots beneath it

two roods on the same between the land of the lord on the east side
the land of John Myton on the west side
one Rood on the same between the land of the lord on the east side and
the land of Robert Warner on the west side
Total About 33 acres

(folio 7 front)   **Welyngton**

In the Brookefeild one acre of land lying together in
Brookefeild on the Middlefurlonge between the land of
William Yerway on the south side and the and of the lord
on the north side. the vicar of Wellington has this
acre
one acre lying together abutting on Smalway at the western Headland
between the land of Thomas Rees on the south side and the land of
William Gostwyke on the north side
half a Rood on the same between the land of the lord on the north side
and the land of John Gostwyke on the south side
and it abuts at the western Headland on Smalway and on
the eastern Headland on the land of the lord which said
half Rood extends only as far as the middle of the said
furlong
two Roods lying together on Walyshedfurlonge between the land of the
lord on either side and they abut at the northern headland
on Walished and at another Headland on the land of
John Gostwyke
one acre lying together under Sandhill of which one is the Headland of
Smalwayfurlonge next to the land of William
Gostwyke or the lord of Wellington on the east side
and it abuts at the northern Headland on Yramleys
one Rood on the same between the land of William Gostwyke on the
west side and the land of the lord on the east side and it
abuts on Yramleys
half an acre lying between the Pasture called Yramleys on the east side
and the land of Robert Warner on the
west side and it abuts against Couphull's westmead
at the northern Headland
two Roods on the same between the land of the lord on the east side
and the land of John Gostwyke
on the west side and it abuts as above
two Roods on Sandhill between the land of the lord
on the north side and the land of John Myton on the south
side and they abut at the eastern Headland on Meadfurlonge

(folio 7 reverse)   **Welyngton**

two half Roods ᵍˡʸⁱⁿᵍ in the same Meadfurlonge between
the pasture called Yram on the north and the land [blank]
one rood on the same between the land of Thomas Rees on the west
side and the land of the lord on the east and it abuts
on Coupulmead

una Roda super eandem inter terram domini ex utraque parte
una acra super eandem inter terram domini ex utraque parte
et abuttat super [blank]
una longa acra abuttans super Reemead inter terram
domini ex utraque parte
tres Rode terre simul iacentes super Gytemerefurlong
inter terram domini ex utraque parte et abuttant ad
unum Caput super Burymead Knoll et ad aliud Caput
super foreram Johannis Gostwyke
quinque seliones super eandem pro una acra et
dimidia inter terram domini ex parte orientali et
terram Willelmi Gostwyke ex parte occidentali et
abuttant ad Caput boreale super foreram[16] Johannis
Gostwyke et ad Caput[17] australe super
Communem pasturam de Wellington

Summa Circa x [10] acre una roda

(folio 8 recto)   **Welyngton**
In pratis de Welington tres rode prati simul
iacentes in le Reemead inter pratum Johannis
Gostwyke ex parte australi et pratum Roberti
Warner ex parte boreali et abuttant ad Caput
orientale super Dachedole et ad aliud Caput super
Communem de Wellyngton
Item una Roda iacens in Dachedole inter pratum
domini ex una parte et pratum Johannis Gostwyke
ex altera parte et abuttat super aquam de Ouse
Item sex acre prati in duabus pecijs vocatis
Stadholme una pecia iacet inter holmum domini
de Latymer ex parte australi et pratum Johannis
Gostwyke ex altera parte Et altera pecia iacet
inter pratum domini ex parte boreali et pratum
Thome Passewater ex parte australi
Item una acra prati iacet inter le Burymead
ex parte australi et pratum domini ex altera parte
Item una acra prati iacet in le Brookmead inter
pratum domini ex parte orientali et pratum Roberti
Warner ex altera parte
Item tres rode prati iacentes in eodem inter
pratum Johannis Gostwyke ex utraque parte
Item una pecia prati in eodem inter pratum
domini de Wellyngton ex utraque parte et abuttat
ad Caput australi super Clausum domini Prioris vocatum
Chanons Crofte et aliud Caput super Mytons brooke
Item dimidia acra prati iacet in Poorepitt inter
pratum Thome Rees ex parte orientali et pratum
Thome Passewater ex parte occidentali

Summa prati Circa x [10] acre una roda

---

[16] *Forera* is a headland formed in an open field, where the plough turned and deposited soil over time
[17] *Caput*, in this context it also means a headland, but as it has been written with a capital letter it may
have been constructed to form a boundary round a piece of land

one Rood on the same between the land of the lord on either side
one acre on the same between the land of the lord on either side
and it abuts on [blank]
one long acre abutting on Reemead between the land of
the lord on either side
three Roods of land lying together on Gytemerfurlong
between the land of the lord on either side, and they abut
at one Headland on Burymead Knoll and another Headland
on John Gostwyke's headland
five strips on the same for one acre and
a half, between the land of the lord on the east side and
the land of William Gostwyke on the west side and
they abut at the northern Headland on John
Gostwyke's headland and on the southern Headland on the Common
pasture of Wellington

Total about 10 acres 1 rood

(Folio 8 front) **Welyngton**
In the meadows of Welington three roods of meadow lying together on
the Reemead between the meadow of John
Gostwyke on the south side and the meadow of Robert
Warner on the north side and they abut at the eastern Headland
on Dachedole and at another Headland on
Wellyngton Common
Also one Rood lying in Dachedole between the meadow
of the lord on one side and the meadow of John Gostwyke
on the other side and it abuts on the river Ouse
Also six acres of meadow in two pieces called
Stadholme. one piece lies between the holme[18] of the lord
of Latymer on the south side and the meadow of John
Gostwyke on the other side And the other piece lies
between the meadow of the lord on the north side and the meadow of
Thomas Passewater on the south side
Also one acre of meadow lies between the Burymead
on the south side and the lord's meadow on the other side
Also one acre of meadow lies in the Brookmead between
the meadow of the lord on the east side and the meadow of Robert
Warner on the other side
Also three roods of meadow lying in the same between
John Gostwyke's meadow on either side
Also one piece of meadow in the same between the meadow
of the lord of Wellyngton on either side and it abuts
at the southern Headland on the Enclosure of the lord Prior called
Chanons Crofte and another Headland on Myton's brooke
also half an acre of meadow lies in Poorepitt between
the meadow of Thomas Rees on the east side and the meadow
of Thomas Passewater on the west side

The total of the meadow, About 10 acres one rood

---

18   holme may indicate an island, or piece of land surrounded by brooks and ditches.

(folio 8 dorso)   **Welyngton**

Item unum Croftum vocatum Chanons Crofte continens
quattuor acra iacet subtus manerium domini Prioris
inter terram domini de Wellyngton ex una parte et
terram pertientem ad vicarium ex altera parte et
abuttat Contra Brookemead
Item unum Croftum vocatum Balles Crofte continens
quattuor acras terre iacet inter terram Johannis
Gostwyke ex utraque parte et abuttat super Brookemead

Summa xlix [49] acre terre
    X acre una roda prati
octo acre pasture[19]

---

[19]   There appears to have been a scribal error here. The total given for acres of land does not match the
totals given for the different fields in the document.

(folio 8 reverse) **Welyngton**

Also one croft called Chanons Crofte, containing
four acres, lies below the manor of the lord Prior
between the land of the lord of Wellyngton on one side
and the land pertaining to the vicar on the other side and
it abuts Against Brookemead
Also one Croft called Balles Crofte, containing
four acres of land, lies between the land of John
Gostwyke on either side and abuts on Brookemead

Total 49 acres of land
   10 acres one rood of meadow
eight acres of pasture

Appendix Two

By-laws of the Manor, 1397–1540

The by-laws of the manor were understood by the tenants but not written in the manor court rolls. Below is a list of the customs for Willington, extracted from the manorial records. The customs were adapted over time according to changing circumstances.

Richard II
It is ordered by the steward that no-one shall play Quoits under a penalty of 12d.[1]

Henry IV
It was ordered by all the community that all the community should make up the road called Wadenye which road is exceedingly harmful in its use for all for their passage, and has been viewed by John Gostwyke, William Rydere, John Bande and John Rydere. And the [illegible] of the said community is not necessary for making the said way for the servants and assigns of the aforesaid John Gostwyke and William Rydere and all given the [illegible] 40d to the lady and the church 40d from [illegible] with the agreement of the community.[2]

It was ordered to all the tenants that no tenant [should] at any time [have] hounds within the demesne of the lady under a penalty of half a mark, [6s. 8d.] neither any dogs to go down the lady's Warren under a penalty of half a mark, [6s. 8d.].[3]

It was ordered by all the tenants that no-one is to permit any colts[4] to pass at large, that is to say, that they are to be penned with their mothers. So that [if] they are found to have been delinquent, they will be under a penalty of 6d.[5]

Also it was ordered by the same that no-one is permitted to let their sheep, pigs or calves roam in the fields [torn edge] without custody, allowing them to trespass on to the herbage and corn of the neighbourhood, under penalties, if they should have been found delinquent, of 6d to the lady and 6d to the church.[6]

---

[1]   BARS, Box R212, Roll 5, October 1397.
[2]   BARS, Box R212, Roll 11, April 1409.
[3]   BARS, Box R212, Roll 13, April 1411.
[4]   The document says 'pull' which could be an abbreviation for *pullanus*, a colt, or *pullus*, a chicken. Fom the context 'colts' is more likely.
[5]   BARS, Box R212, Roll 13, April 1411.
[6]   *Ibid.*

Henry V

It was ordered by all the lord's tenants that everyone whatsoever who has any land in the common fields [illegible] is to make one drain on their land before the feast of St. Mark [the Evangelist, 25 April] next in the future, so that the waters do not overflow the said fields but have been put in their watercourses outside the said fields, and that the [said] fields are not blackened by the aforesaid defective watercourses, under a penalty of 12d. paid [to the lord] and 12d. paid to the church.[7]

Also it was ordered by the same that everyone whatsoever should keep their sheep and calves within their enclosures so that neither their sheep nor calves cause any damage in either the grain or the grass of their neighbours. Under penalties of 12d. paid to the lord and 12d. to the church.[8]

Also it was ordered by the same that everyone whatsoever who holds any pigs in the township, who puts the said pigs in the keeping of the community keeper of pigs, just as most of the community's pigs are put, if this does not happen, [they] must pay the lord 6d. and 6d. to the church. And anyone who always keeps his pigs in his own custody has paid the salary and stipend of the community keeper of pigs for his neighbours in the township.[9]

Also it was ordered by the same that no-one is to tie any bullocks within the corn of their neighbours also that their foals make no damage. And if it should happen against this order he will pay 12d to the lord and 12d. to the church.[10]

Also it was ordered by the same that no bullocks are to be depastured or pastured for all the year in those fields in which horses are pastured. And if it should happen [he] will pay to the lord 12d. and 12d. to the church.[11]

It was agreed within the tenantry that those tenants who hold bullocks should have them in the field called Eastfeld which was cut this year, to sustain and pasture their bullocks. And that the said bullocks shall not be kept in any other [illegible] fields, under a penalty for each of 2s.[12]

And it was ordered [by] the steward and commanded in full court that no tenants henceforth dare to do nor make a plea either in the court of the king, neither in a Special court, under a penalty of 20s. [paid to the lord] as often as any against this ordered and commanded suit, without a special command granted by the lord or steward.[13]

7   BARS, Box R212, Roll 18a, April and September 1415.
8   *Ibid.*
9   *Ibid.*
10   *Ibid.*
11   *Ibid.*
12   BARS, Box R212, Roll 20, May 1416.
13   BARS, Box R212, Roll 29, October 1420.

Henry VI

It was ordained by all the tenants that none shall graze beasts in a certain field called Fulwellefeld and the field sown with barley, nor in the meadows with others for one month after the feast of the Nativity of the Blessed Mary the Virgin [8 September] under a penalty of 6d. paid to the lord and 6d. to the church.[14]

It was ordered by the lord's council and all the tenants that no-one shall put their animals in the several fields of the lord without the permission of the the tenants who hold the aforesaid fields, nor put pigs in the manor unless they are ringed. Also that none shall overthrow the pastures there.[15]

Also it was ordered to all the tenants that they should view a certain fence between the land of the lord and Thomas Maryon. And that the said Thomas alleges that the said fence should be made on the soil of the lord and which verdict should be decided on a day before the next [court] under a penalty for each of them of 4d.[16]

Also they present that Emma Skynner held a brothel. Therefore the bailiff was ordered to put her outside the demesne.[17]

Also it was ordered by the lord and all the homage that the labourers by the day who are resident within the boundary of the Lete are not to accept labouring outside the vill while they are able to have services and sufficient payment within under a penalty of 40d. payable to the lord and the church in equal portions as and when they are found guilty to the contrary.[18]

Edward IV

It was ordained in the court, by the agreement of all the tenants, that no tenant should prosecute another tenant outside the demesne for debts or trespass unless they should exceed 40s., under penalty of 20s. forfeited to the lady.[19]

And it is ordered that none shall carry away branches growing in the warren, without a license to remove them without permission, under a penalty of 12d.[20]

Also it is ordered that henceforth none shall play at tennis at anytime of the year if they are more than 12 years old and not as such unless at Christmas and not for money unless they have sufficient, within the vill, under a penalty for each of 40d. and a punishment of imprisonment for one day and a night.[21]

14   BARS, Box R212, Roll 31, October 1422.
15   BARS, Box R212, Roll 38b, May 1449.
16   BARS, Box R212, Roll 39b, May 1451.
17   BARS, Box R212, Roll 40a, October 1451.
18   BARS, Box R212, Roll 46a, October 1457.
19   British Library, Add Ch. 26813/1, October 1463.
20   British Library, Add Ch. 26813/2, May 1464.
21   British Library, Add Ch. 26813/3, October 1467.

It was ordered to all the tenants who possess hedges and make crofts to the north and south that they must remove them before 40 days under a penalty for each of 40d. so that each tenant should have access for their plough, except for Myllefelde which is only a footpath.[22]

And it was ordered to all the tenants that henceforth none of them is to pasture any animals or cattle in any one nor other individual pasture without agreement under a penalty for each of 12d.[23]

It was ordered in Court, following the agreement of all the tenants, that henceforth no commoners should pasture animals or their cattle in the pastures of the lady called Fulwell, Myttelmershe, Vyrtnell Furlong, Moutonswell Furlong, nor with their horses, before the feast of Saint Peter in Chains [1 August] under a penalty for each of them of 12d. for as many failings as are found.[24]

It was ordered that henceforth no commoners should make any footpath on Fulwell Headland which remains in the hand of Thomas Tayllour, under a penalty of 6d. for each of them.[25]

[No rolls survive from the reigns of Edward V, Richard III, or Henry VII]

Henry VIII
And it was presented to the villagers that they should well and faithfully scour their ditches next to the Rabbit Warren and the lane leading as far as the Mill under a penalty of 12d. for each offence according to the agreement of the tenants.[26]

And it is ordered [that] no-one is permitted [to put] his pigs in the common pastures of the vill without sufficient rings. With sufficient rings they will not stray from the pastures. Under a penalty for each of 3s. 4d.[27]

[torn edge] by the tenants to well and suffciently repair their holdings which they have from the lord either in part or by Copy [torn edge] before the next Court, under a penalty for each offence of 10s.[28]

[torn edge] by the tenants to show in this court before the Steward at the next court what acres of land and meadowland, [torn edge] he holds from the lord, both by copy and at the Lord's will, and how much of the demesne land, [torn edge] under a penalty for each offence of 6s. 8d.[29]

22   British Library, Add Ch. 26813/4, May 1468.
23   British Library, Add Ch. 26813/5, August 1468.
24   British Library, Add Ch. 26813/8, May 1470.
25   *Ibid.*
26   BARS, Box R212, Roll 61, September 1515.
27   *Ibid.*
28   BARS, Box R212, Roll 62, March 1520.
29   *Ibid.*

It was ordered, by the agreement of all the tenants within this demesne, that each tenant should scour his ditch next to the King's Road before the next Court under a penalty for each offence of 12d.[30]

It was ordered that each tenant within this Demesne will ring their pigs before the feast of Our Lord's Nativity [25 December] next in the future, under a penalty for each offence of 12d.[31]

It is ordained through the homage with the lord's consent that no-one may keep any ducks or drakes after the quarter fair at the start of Lent, that is Ash Wednesday under penalty of 3s. 4d.[32]

It is ordained that forthwith no tenant shall cut or lop any trees called elms or ashes unless the twigs and branches of these trees called lop should be of the age of sixteen years growth under penalty of forfeiture of 3s.4d. to the lord.[33]

It is ordained that whosoever may hold free tenements and lands shall bring and show his evidences for this to the next court that he may divide his free lands from the lord's lands under penalty of forfeiture of 10s. to the lord.[34]

Each tenant shall ring his pigs from time to time when it shall be necessary. No unringed pigs shall root upon pastures neither those held in severality nor upon common pastures within this demesne under penalty of forfeiture to the lord 3s. 4d.[35]

Each Tenant shall ring his pigs from time to time when it shall be necessary, so that they shall not root either upon pasture held in severalty or upon common pasture within this demesne under the penalty of forfeiture to the lord whenever and however many times etc. [this ruling shall be infringed] 4d.[36]

No-one shall trespass in the lord's wood by cutting down either wood or underwood or the boughs called hazel rods without licence from the lord or of his officials under penalty of 6d.[37]

No-one may kill any rabbits in the warren called the Conyngre nor in the close, neither shall he take any rabbits in the nests called rabbits' nests under penalty of forfeiture to the lord how often and whenever it shall be found that this has been done 12d.[38]

30   BARS, Box R212, Roll 64, 1522.
31   *Ibid.*
32   BARS, Box R212, Roll 65, October 1537.
33   *Ibid.*
34   *Ibid.*
35   BARS, Box R212, Roll 66, October 1538.
36   BARS, Box R212, Roll 67, October 1539.
37   *Ibid.*
38   *Ibid.*

No keeper of sheep within this demesne shall keep his sheep in the Deans nor in any other pasture called Severall pasture grounde before the Feast of St Michael the archangel [Michaelmas, 29 September] next in the future under the penalty of forfeiture of 20d. to the lord.[39]

Each tenant shall ring his pigs from time to time when it shall be necessary. Also that they shall not root upon pasture held in severalty nor upon common pasture within this demesne under penalty of forfeiture of 4d. to the lord whenever and however many times [this infringement shall occur].[40]

[39]   BARS, Box R212, Roll 68, October 1540.
[40]   *Ibid.*

Appendix Three

View of Frankpledge with Court Baron of William Gostwicke Esquire, held there on the twenty third day of October in the Forty first Year of the reign of the our lady Elizabeth, by the grace of god, Queen of England, France and Ireland, defender of the faith etc [1599]

The following court roll is divided into two sections, the view of frankpledge and the court baron. It was written by the Gostwicke's steward, William Butler, in Latin and English. As the seventeenth century progressed, English was used throughout the court rolls with only the heading and the concluding sentences being written in Latin.

At the end of the sixteenth century the few surviving court rolls show increasing concern about the use of the commons in Willington. By 1599 the roll contained a list of twelve orders; evidence that the lord and his steward wished the medieval rules for the use of the open fields and common lands to continue to be observed. It also contains a list of about thirty tenants with the amounts of common fine that they each paid.[1]

This view of frankpledge was written in Latin, although some English words were used, and there is very little punctuation. It has been translated into modern English with punctuation marks added to make it easier to read, using upper and lower case letters as in the original.

The orders, which form the bulk of the record of the court baron, were written in English and have been transcribed using the original spellings and upper and lower case letters. Latin numerals have been replaced throughout by Arabic numerals.
Where details of saints' days have been given in the footnotes, they are taken from C. R. Cheney's *A Handbook of Dates*.[2]

---

[1]   BARS, Box R212, Roll 73 April 1594 listed eighteen tenants and the animals which they kept on the manor, but did not show how much they each paid; Roll 77, October 1609, listed nineteen orders and twenty-six or more tenants, with the animals which they kept on the common and the common fines which they paid.

[2]   C. R. Cheney, ed., *A Handbook of Dates: For Students of British History*, 2nd ed. (Cambridge, 2000).

View of Frankpledge with Court Baron of William Gostwicke Esquire, held there on the twenty-third day of October in the forty-first Year of the reign of the our lady Elizabeth, by the grace of God, Queen of England, France and Ireland, defender of the faith.

The first Court of William Butler, gentleman, Steward there

Essoins
None on this day

Sworn now for the lady Queen, from the Homage, by the Sworn Men

William Yarwaye	William Sylbey	Thomas Shadbolt
William Ball	Thomas Gayton	Robert Dey
John Hilles	William Osmond	Richard Rozell
Thomas Cleyton	George Fadlett	Peter Inyce
William Mason	Thomas Rozell	John Rogam

They present common fines for head silver and land silver 8s. 11d.[3]

Firstly the aforesaid Men presented on their oath that the Inhabitants gave 8s. 11d. to the Lord as Common fine for hed sylver and Land silver on this day, as from ancient Custom. This paid in Court, into the hand of the aforesaid lord, as follows: from the holding of William Yarwaye 15d., from the holding of George fadlett [*sic*] 8d., from the holding of William Ball 7d., from the holding of Michael Meyse 4d., from the holding of Thomas Rozell 3d., from the holding of Thomas Shadbolt 8d., from the holding of William Sylbey 7d., from the holding of Peter Inyce 5d., from the holding of William Osmond 4d., from the holding of Thomas Gayton 4d., from the holding of Edward Cleyton 10d.,[4] from the holding of William Mason 5d., from the holding of Thomas Hilles 10d., from the holding of Richard Rozell 3d., from the holding of Robert Dey 2d., from the holding of Richard Reynoldes 1d., from the holding of Peter Cowper 1d., from the holding of John Goodwyn 1d., from the holding of Robert Craft 1d., from the holding of Thomas Man 1d., from the Tytford holding 1d., from the holding of Thomas Bacon 1d., from the holding of Stephan Momford 1d., from the holding of two widows 1d., from the holding of John Wren 1d., from the holding of widow Gye 1d.

Making default of Suit of court and is amerced

Also they say that the Earl of [4d.] Kent, Nicholas [4d.] Luke esquire, Giles [4d.] Allen gentleman, Agnes [4d.] Richardson, Richard [4d.] Reynoldes, and the parson of [4d.] Bromham owed suit at this Court and made default on this day. Therefore each of them is at mercy to the lord as appears above their Heads

---

[3]   The total of the fines below is 8s. 10d., a corrected list, which is easier to read, is written in different ink at the end of the roll.
[4]   This number is unclear. It may have been intended as 'ix' that is 9d., but it appears as 10d. in the list at the end of the document.

We present certain inhabitants within the Jurisdiction of this Lete have not provided Arrows with longbows, according to the terms of the Statute thereof. Therefore being at mercy to the lord   2d.

Furthermore the aforesaid Sworn Men say that the aforesaid inhabitants have not got their own[5] according to the form of the statute thereof, therefore they are at mercy to the lord for   12d.

Also they present that Thomas Shadbolt has not cleared his watercourse sufficiently. Therefore he is at mercy to the lord   4d.

Election of Constable
At this lete Thomas Shadbolt and Robert Dey were elected into the office of Constable and Sworn in.

Now the Court Baron

Penalties put[6]
1. **Firstly**, it was ordered by the aforesaid Sworn Men *That the whole Inhabitants shall before the feast of Saint Murtine[7] the Bishoppe next cominge Dreane the feylds where nede shall require with the Common plough, upon payne of everie farmer makinge default to forfayt 2s and every cottager*   *12d*
2. **Item** *that none shall suffer their Sheepe to go into the Stubble fielde untill one wicke before Saint Matthew's daye[8] and that no man shall[9] let their beastes be abrode in the night, untill the same tyme without consent of the whole Inhabit- ants or the most parte of them, upon payne of everie one offendinge to forfayt for everie defaulte*   *12d*
3. **Item** *that everie man shall Ringe his hogges before the feast of Saint Luke[10] uppon payne to forfayt for very hogge unringed*   *4d*
4. **Item** *that there shalbe no bie heardes kept after the hearde goeth forth with the beastes, upon payne of everie one offendinge to forfayte for everie time so offending*   *3s 4d*
5. **Item** *it is agreed that if thinhabitants, or the most parte of them, do consent to preserve and kepe anie one fielde severall at such tyme as there harvest is ended, for their plough Cattell, that whosoever shall breake up the same contrarie to the order and agreement by them sett downe, shall forfayte*

10s

---

5   This phrase has been difficult to translate. It has been assumed that an abbreviation h'nt is 'habent'
6   Orders 1–12 are mostly written in English. The English passages are shown in italics. There are a variety of spellings for every-day words.
7   The feast of Saint Martin (Murtine) was either 11 November or 4 July, but it is most likely that fields would need to be drained before the winter.
8   St Mathew's day was either 24 February or 21 September.
9   'shall' has been written in this transcription in the lower case, but the scribe has written 'sh' in an unusual way, so that on some occasions words which begin with these two letters could be transcribed as either upper or lower case.
10   The feast of Saint Luke is 18 October.

6. **Item** *that none shall suffer their Cattell to go uppon the Common of Myll field before the tyme appointed upon payne of everie one makinge default to forfayte for everie tyme that they are there taken*   *12d*

7. **Item** *that everie man shall dytch his landes in the tilth and breach fieldes before Saint Andrewe thapostle next[11] and in anie other place or places upon lawful warninge given to them they maye for not dytchinge be annoyance to thinhabit-ants. Uppon payne of everie one makinge default to forfayte*   *12d*

8. **Item** *that none shall kepe any geese to go into their neighbours grayne upon payne to forfayte for everie tyme that they are taken in any grayne 12d, that is to say 6d to the Lorde and 6d to the owner of the graine*

9. **Item** *that none shall kepe any oxen or other Cattell in Mychaelmas field, but such as shalbe tyed uppon their owne grounde, uppon payne of everie one offending to forfeit for everie default*   *12d*

10. **Item** *that none shall gleane any beanes nor pease upon payne of everie one offending to forfeit 12d, that is to say 4d to the Lorde and 8d to the owner of the Land.*

11. **Item** *that none shall gleane any other grayne without lycens of the owner untill the grayne be carried, upon payne to forfeite for everie default 12d, that is to say 4d to the Lord and 8d to the owner of the grayne.*

12. **Item** *if any man encroche upon his neighbours land in plowinge, by the Judge-ment of two indifferent men, then the offender shall laye it out againe and shall likewise forfeit to the Lord for everie such defaulte*   *12d*

If any of these orders be broken by the Lord of the Manner (the depasturinge of 40 Lambes in the stubble field at the Lords pleasure onely excepted) that then the sayd orders shall stand voyd.

Overseers of the Fields
At this Court William Yarwaie, Edward Cleyton, John Hilles and William Silbey were elected to the office of overseers of the Fields and Sworn in.

Assessors of fines: John Hilles, Thomas Shadbolt, Sworn Men
A particular of the fine Certaine[12] belonging to this manner what everie tenante payeth for his Tenemente to the Lord, at the feast of Saint Michael Tharchangel onely

William Yarwaie a year	15d	**Richard** Reynolde	1d
George Fadlett	8d	Peter Coper	1d
William Ball	7d	John Goodwyn	1d
Michael Mease	4d	Robert Craft	1d
Thomas Rosell	3d	Thomas Man	1d
Thomas Shatbolt	8d	Richard Tytford	1d
William Sylbey	7d	Thomas Bacon	1d
Peter Inyce	5d	Stephen Momford	1d

[11] The feast of Saint Andrew is 30 November.
[12] A fixed fine.

William Osmund	4d	John Manton	1d
Thomas Geyton	4d	John Wren	1d
Edward Cleaton	10d	Wyddowe Gye	1d
William Mason	5d	for the tenement in which two widows	
Thomas Hille	10d	live	1d
Richard Rosell	3d	Robert Dey	2d
		sum total 8s 11d	

Appendix Four

A New Barn for Thomas Wyltshyre and Other Buildings
Roll 37, 22 April 1440

This court roll is the only one to survive after 26 September 1426 and before 14 October 1448. By this date Katherine Neville had been widowed for a second time and was holding Willington manor in her own right as part of her dower.

The court roll is short and written on parchment approximately 25 cms square, but there are two other documents: the memorandum of costs for Thomas Wyltschyre's barn, on a scrappy piece of repaired parchment measuring about 18 x 21 cms; and Richard Pecke's, the bailiff's, allowances and expenses for Cardington and Willington, on parchment measuring 16 x 25 cms.

The court of Lady Katherine Duchess of Norfolk, held there on Friday in the Vigil of Saint George the Martyr in the eighteenth year of the Reign of King Henry the sixth after the conquest

Sworn men

John Taylor	John Tryket	Robert Partryche
John Yarwey the elder	William Dryngwell	Thomas Sterlyng constable
John Rotlond	Richard Bawdewyn	John Palmer constable
John Fesaunt	John Palmer the younger	William Sterlyng

Amercements 15d.
They present that William defect now well Dryngwell, Thomas put right Wyltschyre, David $^{2d.}$ Whytchyrche, John $^{2d.}$ Yarwey the elder, Robert $^{2d.}$ Partryche, John $^{2d.}$ Clerk, John $^{2d.}$ Bodynho William $^{2d.}$ Sterlyng, John $^{2d.}$ Fesaunt, Robert $^{1d.}$ Fesaunt have ruined tenements, therefore they are amerced. And they are ordered to put them right against the next [court] under a penalty for each of them of 2s.

Amercement 2d. penalty
Also they present that John $^{2d.}$ Maryon has an overflowing ditch next to the holding of Thomas Sterlyng, causing a nuisance to the neighbours. Therefore they are at mercy. And both are ordered to put it right against the next [court] under a penalty of 6s. 8d.

Amercement 2d. penalty
Also they present that the same John $^{2d.}$ Maryon has another overflowing ditch below Dudlescroft, causing a nuisance. Therefore he is at mercy. And he was ordered to put right the aforesaid ditch against the next [court] under a penalty of 6s. 8d.

Amercement 2d. penalty

Also they present that David [2d] Whytchyrche has a ditch below his tenement, not flowing sufficiently, causing a nuisance. Therefore he is amerced. And furthermore he was ordered to put it right against the next, under a penalty of 2s.

Amercement 2d. penalty

Also they present that John [2d.] Myton has another damaged ditch at the end of the township causing a nuisance in the neighbourhood. Therefore he is at mercy. And furthermore he was ordered to put it right against the next [court] under a penalty of 4s.

Attachments none

Names of the assessors of fines: John Rotlond, John Yarweye the younger,
Sum of this court 23d.
Expenses of the steward and of other surveyors 7s. 6d.

Welyngton

Memorandum of various costs and expenses made as regards the barn of Thomas Wyltschyre there for new reparations paid for by lady Katherine, Duchess of Norfolk in the 18th year of Henry VI [1 September 1439–31 August 1440]

Firstly for felling 27 sole posts[1] and wall-plates and secondly for 300 spars 4s.
Also for paying John Cook of Cople, carpenter, for making the said barn £3 13s. 4d.
Also to John Wright for buying reeds for the same 5s. 2d.
For to John Wright working the same reeds 11 days taken for 4d a day 3s. 8d.
Also to John Wody for one roof, for thatching the same jointly, with the Ridging of the same, 8s. 6d.
Also to William Drynkwell for hiring 1 man for carrying straw for roofing to the same 7s. in full
Also in straw to John Myton, Thomas Wyltshire bought for the same barn 33s. 4d.
Also in Laths for Winding to John Bodenhowe and Daubing, in full 11s.
Also to to William Drinkwell in digging and carrying land for the same 2s. 6d.
In hinges and hooks to Thomas Ranaldes bought for the doors and shutters 22d.
In raising the same xijs 7s.
In a month for the said roofer and his servant for 20 day 6s. 8d.[2]
Total £8 4s. [almost invisible, at the bottom of the sheet]

Welyngton Richard Pecke, bailiff there
The same Richard makes allowance of 32s. 4d. paid to the lord king both from the Views in Cardington and in Welyngton this year the 18

Decay of rent rendered 10s. 1d.

Also for an allowance of 3s. 4d. charged on the tenement lately in the holding of John Gabriell for which he paid per annum 13s. 4d. and now demised for 10s. by Richard Phille.

---

[1]   These may have been posts (*Solys postys*) which were set in the ground or rested on it.
[2]   That is 4d. a day for two men.

And for 3s.charged on the tenement lately in the holding of Henry Lord for which he rendered 8s. a year and now let for 5s.by the same Richard Phille,
And for 20d.charged on the tenement lately in the holding of Stephen Colet for which he was answerable for payment of 6s. 8d. a year and now let for 5s. by the same Richard Phille.
And for 2s. 1d. free rent in decay of one tenement lately belonging to Adam Warde, because it is devastated, and in the hand of the lord because of no tenant this year.

And for 12s. of income from the rabbits this year to the above from David Whytchy-rche as from part of his fee to the lord this year 18 Et cetera

[torn edge] John Waryner 15s. 2d.
Also the cancelled[3] account of W Drynkwell for 28 spars for the repairs of the tenement lately belonging to Dynyell 4d.
And for carrying the same 8d.
And for carrying T W [torn edge] of Blunham them to the lord 3s. 4d.
And in reeds Robert [Wollyface] bought for the same 2s.
And for making the same Robert Feasaunt in Willington 10d.
Also in straw bought from Thomas Maryan for the same 4s.
Also for cutting Katherine Ireland the same straw 12d.
And in 1 thatcher John Benet for thatching the same straw 16d.
And for the servant John Abell of the same for carrying the aforesaid straw to him 16d.
And for 400 nails bought at Bedford for the same tenement 4d.

And for £8 4s. for constructing one barn for Thomas Wyltschire as appears above in various parcels of a certain schedule annexed and specified.

Costs of the houses in the holding of Robert Tayllour alias clerk   £4 6s. 6d.
Also on the cancelled account to William Drynkwell
For 25 ground studs, wall-plates and beams and also for 50 spars for the tenement with carriage of John Yarwey   7s.
And for one carpenter Thomas Wryght to construct, in full, and underpin the Inset-house ¹³s. ⁴d. and putting together the sides assembled for the same building and for putting together ¹⁶s. ⁸d. one door by his new master carpenter, in full   30s.
Also in reeds [illegible] bought for the same   2s. 6d.
Also in straw W Drynkwell bought for the same for the said 2 buildings   17s.
And for 1John Benett roofer, constructing for 9 days on the same tenement   3s.
And for 1 servant W Drynkwell for the aforesaid for the aforesaid time   3s.
In 1 servant for the roofer [illegible] Robert Taillour   2s. 6d.
Also payment for the reeds William Peck chiefly from Webb's   12d.
In the costs concerning the raising of the said door-frame   15d.
And in digging land W Drynkwell and carrying [it] for the same   12d.
 Also in cutting down and carrying withies for putting on the said buildings 18d.
 Also for Winding and Binding Robert Fesond and Dawbing the same, in full 9s.

---

3   The words written in the document as *inprestacione* or *in prostarcione* have been translated as 'imprest' meaning 'cancelled.'

Also in hinges and hooks Thomas Regynald bought for the doors and windows 2s.

Also [illegible] for 350 nails bought for the same doors and windows   15d.[4]

Also in separating 1 rood of boards for the aforesaid buildings and the mill ~~vs~~ 4s. 6d.

Costs of the mill

W Drinkwell, William Shakeston and W Pecke for scouring one watercourse on the western side of the mill

Also the account of various expenses made round the millpond there this year the
                                                                        18 7s.

Fee account [5]

The same account [hole torn] for accounting for the fee itself   30s. 4d.

and for the Court of Bedford [hole torn]

And for wood [hole torn] for the same   6s. 8d.

---

4   These nails cost slightly more than those bought at Bedford, which were 4d. for 100.
5   Fee used in its medieval sense, these are the lord's accountancy costs.

Appendix Five

Manor Officials

Stewards 1384–1482

Year(s)	Lord or lady of the manor	Stewards
1384–86	Thomas Mowbray	Lord Robert Plesyngton named as head steward. Named as former head steward 1386–91.
1388–89	Thomas Mowbray	Sir William Bagot named as steward and as former head steward 1389–90.
1389–1410	Thomas Mowbray to 1398, the Crown to 1410	William Rees named as steward 1389-October 1403. Described as head steward in bailiff's account 1392–93 for Haynes. May have continued in post until 1410.
1397	Thomas Mowbray	John Lancaster, of Bressingham, Norfolk, may have been chief steward, but is not named in the Willington records.
1410–15	The Crown to c.1413, John Mowbray (and Katherine Neville) to 1415	John Boteler named as steward. Said to be under-steward in 1418 and 1421 after Thomas Bekyngham was appointed.
Before 1417	John Mowbray (and Katherine Neville)	John Preston named as former steward in 1417, other dates unknown.
1416–24	John Mowbray (and Katherine Neville)	Thomas Bekyngham named as steward and as head steward in 1417. He was said to be 'formerly steward' in 1426. John Boteler named as under-steward in 1418 and 1421.
1425–32	John Mowbray (and Katherine Neville)	Roger Hunte named as steward in 1425 but is thought to have worked for the Mowbrays before and after this date.
1457–74	John Beaumont (and Katherine Neville) to 1460, Katherine Neville to 1465, John Woodville (and Katherine Neville) to 1469, Katherine Neville to 1474	Thomas Rokes named as steward 1461–74. He stayed overnight with his family in Shefford in 1457 and it is probable that he was steward from this date.
1480–81	Katherine Neville	The steward is mentioned in the bailiff's account 1480–81, but is not named.

Receiver Generals and Receivers 1382–97

Year(s)	Lord or lady of the manor	Receiver Generals
1382–83	John Mowbray	Thomas Tuttebury.
1384–85	Thomas Mowbray	Thomas Tuttebury.
1385–86	Thomas Mowbray	Roger Mareschal, clerk.
1386–93	Thomas Mowbray	Thomas Yokflete, clerk.

Year(s)	Lord or lady of the manor	Receivers for Bedfordshire
1382–83	John Mowbray	John Olney, named as previous receiver.
1384–93	Thomas Mowbray	Roger Parker of Shefford.
1393–97	Thomas Mowbray	Roger Tunstall.

Bailiffs 1382–1487

Year(s)	Lord or lady of the manor	Bailiffs
1382–93	John Mowbray to 1383, Thomas Mowbray to 1393	Robert Gostwyk named as bailiff.
1393–94	Thomas Mowbray	William Pecke named as bailiff.
1394–1418	Thomas Mowbray to 1399, the Crown to 1412/13, John Mowbray (and Katherine Neville)	William Ridere named as bailiff (may have been a father and son with the same name).
1416	John Mowbray (and Katherine Neville)	Richard Marable named as bailiff.
1420	John Mowbray (and Katherine Neville)	John Pratt named as bailiff.
1440	Katherine Neville	Richard Pecke named as bailiff.
1448–57	John Beaumont (and Katherine Neville)	A bailiff managed the manor but is not named.
1457–62	John Beaumont (and Katherine Neville) to 1460, Katherine Neville	John Gostwyk named as bailiff. He was also named as bailiff for Bromham in the same year. In 1459 he collected dues and rents for four parishes including Willington.
1462–69	Katherine Neville to 1465, John Woodville (and Katherine Neville) to 1469	John Yarwey the younger named bailiff in 1462 and 1469. John Yarwey the elder named as bailiff in 1463 and 1464.
1480–81	Katherine Neville	William Paryssh named as bailiff. In addition to being described as bailiff and reeve of Willington, he was collector of payments at a court at Bedford Castle and bailiff and rent collector at Bromham. John Gostwyk named as 'lately Bailiff' in 1481.
1486–87	Lord John Howard	William Otley named as bailiff, William Gostwyk named as deputy. William Otley came from outside the manor.

Constables 1394–1522

Year(s)	Lord or lady of the manor	Constables
1394	Thomas Mowbray	Constable not named. He pledged for nine people who called the hue and was himself fined six times.[1]
1397	Thomas Mowbray	Constable not named. Paid three fines of 2d. each.
1404–12	The Crown, during the minority of John Mowbray	Adam Warde named as constable in 1404, an unsuitable choice. There is recorded evidence of his petty crimes over the years. He was a constant brewer on the manor. He was not named again as constable so it is not known how long he held the post. William Rydere named as constable in 1407.
1413–1425	John Mowbray (and Katherine Neville)	John Bande the elder and younger named as constables October 1413-September 1423. John Warner served alongside 1413-October 1415. Robert Partryche served alongside October 1416-October 1425. In October 1425 John Bande is not mentioned. Constables served as jurors, assessors of fines or ale-tasters during these years.
1440	Katherine Neville	Thomas Sterlyng and John Palmer named as constables.
1448	John Beaumont (and Katherine Neville)	John Cook and John Myton named as constables.
1450	John Beaumont (and Katherine Neville)	John Yarwey the younger and John Rodland named as constables.
1450–52	John Beaumont (and Katherine Neville)	John Yarwey the younger and John Rodland replaced by John Clerk and John Flaunders.[2]
1452–53	John Beaumont (and Katherine Neville)	John Clerk and John Flaunders replaced by John Taylour and Randolph Bawdywyn.
1454	John Beaumont (and Katherine Neville)	John Taylour and Randolph Bawdywyn replaced by Robert Cook and John Flaundrers as constables.
1455	John Beaumont (and Katherine Neville)	Robert Cook and John Flaundrers replaced by John Redy and John Tylere as constables.
1456	John Beaumont (and Katherine Neville)	John Redy and John Tylere replaced by John Yarwey the younger and John Taylour as constables.
1457–58	John Beaumont (and Katherine Neville)	John Yarwey the younger and John Taylour replaced by John Yarwey and John Warner.
1461–62	Katherine Neville	John Flaunders and John Starlyng named as constables and tasters of ale.[3]
1463	Katherine Neville	John Flawndrys and Robert Cooke retired, John Yerwey and John Warner named as constables.
1464	Katherine Neville	John Yerwey retired and Henry Parker took his place.
1465	John Woodville (and Katherine Neville)	John Warner and Henry Par[ker] named as constables. Henry Parker retired and Robert Cooke named as constable.

[1] The meaning of this phrase is unclear in this roll, but in later rolls he is fined for not asking for the fine from tenants who either called the hue unjustly or were rightly accused by the hue.
[2] Their names were spelt as John Clerke and John Flaundre in Roll 41a, October 1452.
[3] Their names were spelt as John Flaundrys and John Sterlyng in Roll 50c, October 1462.

1467–68	John Woodeville (and Katherine Neville)	Robert Cooke and John Warnere named as constables.
1469	Katherine Neville	Robert Cooke and John Warner named as constables, replaced by John Flawndres and John Yerwey the younger.
1471	Katherine Neville	John Flaundres and John Yerwey retired, John Bardolfe and Thomas Tayllour sworn in as constables.
1473–78	Katherine Neville	No constables named.
1481	Katherine Neville	Henry Parker and John Yarewey the younger named as constables and ale-tasters.
1482–1522	Katherine Neville to 1482/83, Thomas Howard until 1529	The few surviving records do not include names of constables until December 1522, when William Yarwey and John Myton seem to have replaced John Warner and Edmund Totnam.

Warreners and Keepers of Sheerhatch Wood 1394–1482

Year(s)	Lord or lady of the manor	Warrener/Keeper
1394	Thomas Mowbray	John Disworth (or Dysworth) named as warden of the lord's warren and warden of Sheerhatch.
1394–97	Thomas Mowbray	John Tunstall appointed by letters patent at Epworth on 1 September 1395 as warden of the lord's warren and warden of Sheerhatch.
1404	The Crown	Unnamed warrener reported an offence of trespass.
1408	The Crown	John Gostwyk named as the keeper of the Wood of the Shire.
1409 and 1411	The Crown	John Tunstall named as the keeper of the Wood of the Shire.
1413	John Mowbray (and Katherine Neville)	William Cook named as keeper of Willington Wood. He was said to to be lately warrener in 1417.
1414–18	John Mowbray (and Katherine Neville)	Keeper referenced but not named. John Warner was said to be former warrener in 1417.
1419–21	John Mowbray (and Katherine Neville)	Robert de Wyllyton named as warrener and keeper of Sheerhatch for life. William Walter is said to have been the former warrener, but no other details of him have been found in the records.
1421–26	John Mowbray (and Katherine Neville)	William Rydere named as keeper of Sheerhatch. John Kempston named as keeper of Sheerhatch (Shirewode) 1423.
1423	John Mowbray (and Katherine Neville)	There seem to have been two short term appointments of keeper and warrener. John Kempston was employed as woodward 1418–26.
1450–51	John Beaumont (and Katherine Neville)	Keeper referenced but not named.
1461	Katherine Neville	John Morborne named as 'sworn warrener'.
1472	Katherine Neville	William Dyet (or Dyat, Dyot, Dyette) named as 'sworn keeper of the common', a post not mentioned elsewhere. He is mentioned six times in the rolls 1467–82.
1475	Katherine Neville	Thomas Passewater leased the fisheries and the warren for forty years.
1482	Katherine Neville	Richard Godfrey Esquire and William Fitzhave Gentleman granted the warren for life.

Ale-tasters and Assessors of Fines

Year(s)	Lord or lady of the manor	Assessors of fines	Ale-tasters
April 1394	Thomas Mowbray	John Cartere and John Southmuln.	Not named.
October 1394	Thomas Mowbray	Adam Warde and William Ridere.	Not named, fines for brewing 7s. 4d.
October 1395	Thomas Mowbray	Thomas Miton and Thomas Ridere.	Not named, fines for brewing 12s. 6d.
May 1396	Thomas Mowbray	John Maryon and Adam Warde.	Not named.
October 1397	Thomas Mowbray	John Bande and Thomas Ridere.	Not named, fines for brewing 6s 4d.
October 1403	The Crown	Robert Miton and Thomas Ridere.	Not named, fines for brewing 4s.
October 1404	The Crown	Robert Myton and Thomas Rydere.	Not named, fines for brewing 5s.
October 1406	The Crown	Thomas Rydere and Robert Myton.	They 'have not diligently performed their office.' Fines for brewing 4s. 1d.
April 1407	The Crown	John Bande and Robert Myton.	Not named.
October 1407	The Crown	Robert Myton and John Rydere.	William Ryder and Robert Myton. Brewing fines 4s. 5d.
May 1408	The Crown	Thomas Rydere and John Myton.	Not named.
October 1408	The Crown	Thomas Rydere and Robert Myton.	Robert Myton and Thomas Rydere. Brewing fines 4s. 2d. plus 4d. for keeping an ale house.
April 1409	The Crown	Thomas Rydere and Robert Myton.	Not named.
October 1410	The Crown	Robert Myton and Thomas Rydere.	Probably Thomas Rydere and Robert Myton. Brewing fines may be 1s. 5d. but document torn.
April 1411	The Crown	Robert Myton and Thomas Rydere.	Not named.
October 1411	The Crown	John Bande, Robert Myton.	William Ryder and Robert Myton. Brewing fines 3s 4d.
May 1412	The Crown	Not named.	Not named.

October 1413	John Mowbray (and Katherine Neville)	Robert Myton and Thomas Rydere.	William Rydere and Robert Myton. Brewing fines 2s. 4d.
April 1414	John Mowbray (and Katherine Neville)	Not named.	Not named.
October 1414	John Mowbray (and Katherine Neville)	John Gaubryel and Thomas Rydere.	William Ryder and Robert Myton. Brewing fines 10d.
April and September 1415	John Mowbray (and Katherine Neville)	John Bande and Thomas Rydere.	Not named.
October 1415	John Mowbray (and Katherine Neville)	John Myton and Thomas Rydere.	William Rydere and Robert Myton. Brewing fines 18d.
May 1416	John Mowbray (and Katherine Neville)	Not named.	Not named.
October 1416	John Mowbray (and Katherine Neville)	Robert Myton and John Rydere.	William Rydere Robert Myton. Brewing fines 14d.
May 1417	John Mowbray (and Katherine Neville)	Copy of roll incomplete.	Not named.
October 1417	John Mowbray (and Katherine Neville)	John Gostwyk and John Myton.	William Rydere and Robert Myton. Brewing fines 12d.
April 1418	John Mowbray (and Katherine Neville)	John Myton and John Gaubryl.	Not named.
October 1418	John Mowbray (and Katherine Neville)	John Bande and Robert Myton.	William Rydere and Robert Myton. Brewing fines 4s.
May 1419	John Mowbray (and Katherine Neville)	Not named.	Not named.
October 1419	John Mowbray (and Katherine Neville)	Robert Myton and Robert Partrych.	William Ryder and Robert Myton were replaced by John Bande the younger and John Myton. Brewing fines 2s. 4d.
May 1420	John Mowbray (and Katherine Neville)	Not named.	Not named.

Date	Lord (and Lady)	Affeerers / Officers	Remarks
October 1420	John Mowbray (and Katherine Neville)	Robert Myton and John Bande the younger.	John Bande the younger and John Myton. Brewing fines 3s. 4d.
April 1421	John Mowbray (and Katherine Neville)	Not named.	Not named.
October 1422	John Mowbray (and Katherine Neville)	Robert Myton and John Gostwyk.	John Bande the younger and John Myton. Brewing fines 15d.
June 1423	John Mowbray (and Katherine Neville)	John Bande and John Myton.	Not named.
October 1423	John Mowbray (and Katherine Neville)	John Bande the elder, William Tayllour.	Not named.
September. 1423	John Mowbray (and Katherine Neville)	John Bande the elder and Robert Myton.	John Bande the younger and John Myton. brewing fines 2s. 2d.
October 1425	John Mowbray (and Katherine Neville)	End of roll missing.	John Miton and John Bande have not performed their offices. They each paid 2d. Brewing fines 1s 10d.
September 1426	John Mowbray (and Katherine Neville)	Robert Miton and William Taillour.	Not named.
April 1426	John Mowbray (and Katherine Neville)	John Miton and John Bande the elder.	Not named.
April 1440	Katherine Neville	John Rotlond and John Yarweye the younger.	Not named.
October 1448	John Beaumont (and Katherine Neville)	John Flaundres and John Taylour.	John Cook and John Myton. Brewing fines 12d.
May 1449	John Beaumont (and Katherine Neville)	John Myton and John Taylour.	Not named.
October 1450	John Beaumont (and Katherine Neville)	John Myton and John Yarwey.	John Cook and John Myton. Brewing fines 1s. 10d. and two penalties each of 40d. for men brewing at times of the church service.
May 1451	John Beaumont (and Katherine Neville)	John Yarwey and John Rodland.	One man paid a penalty of 40d. for brewing at the time of the church service.
October 1451	John Beaumont (and Katherine Neville)	John Cook and John Myton.	John Yarwey the elder, John Gostwyk, John Redy or John Yarwey the younger. Brewing fines 1s. 4d.

May 1452	John Beaumont (and Katherine Neville)	John Yarwey the younger and Randolph Bawdewyn.	Not named.
October 1452	John Beaumont (and Katherine Neville)	John Flaunders and Randolph Bawdewyn.	John Gostewyk and John Yarwey the elder. Brewing fines 2s. 1d.
May 1453	John Beaumont (and Katherine Neville)	John Flaunders and Randolph Bawdewyn.	Not named.
October 1453	John Beaumont (and Katherine Neville)	John Taylour and John Redy.	John Yarwey.
May 1454	John Beaumont (and Katherine Neville)	Not named.	Not named.
October 1454	John Beaumont (and Katherine Neville)	John Flaunder and John Taylour.	John Yarwey and John Gostewyk. Brewing fines 2s. 9d. 'John Cook and John Myton were then elected as tasters of ale and took the oath.'
May 1455	John Beaumont (and Katherine Neville)	Not named.	Not named.
October 1455	John Beaumont (and Katherine Neville)	Not named.	John Cook and John Myton. Brewing fines 1s. 7d.
April 1456	John Beaumont (and Katherine Neville)	Not named.	Not named.
October 1456	John Beaumont (and Katherine Neville)	Randolph Bawdweyn and John Flaunders.	Mentioned but not named. Brewing fines 2s. 2d.
April 1457	John Beaumont (and Katherine Neville)	John Yarwey and John Flaunders.	Not named.
October 1457	John Beaumont (and Katherine Neville)	John Clerk and John Taylor.	John Cook and John Myton. Brewing fines 2s. 4d.
July 1458	John Beaumont (and Katherine Neville)	John Yarwey the younger and John Taylour.	Not named.
October 1458	John Beaumont (and Katherine Neville)	John Cook and John Myton.	Mentioned but not named. Brewing fines 12d.
July 1459	John Beaumont (and Katherine Neville)	John Cooke and John Myton.	Not named.

Date	Lord	Officers	Notes
October 1461	Katherine Neville	John Cooke and John Myton.	John Flaunders and John Starlyng. Brewing fines 1s. 2d. They are also the constables.
October 1462	Katherine Neville	John Cooke and John Myton.	John Flaundrys and John Sterlyng. Brewing fines 1s. 2d. They are also the constables.
May 1463	Katherine Neville	John Yerwey and Randolf Bawdewyn.	Not named.
October 1463	Katherine Neville	John Tayllour and John Myton.	John Myton and John Sterlyng. Brewing fines 3s. 2d.
May 1464	Katherine Neville	John Flawndrys and John Tayllour.	Not named.
October 1464	Katherine Neville	John Myton and John Flandrys.	John Myton and John Cooke. Brewing fines 3s. 2d.
April 1465	Katherine Neville	John Fla(u)drys and John Morbourne.	Not named.
October 1465	John Woodville (and Katherine Neville)	John Flandrys and John Tayllour.	John Warner and Henry Parker. Brewing fines 18d. 'In their place were elected John Flaundrys and Randolph Bawdewyn'.
April 1466	John Woodville (and Katherine Neville)	John Yerwey the elder and Randolph Baudewyn.	John Flaundrys and Randolph Baudewyn. Brewing fines 2d.
October 1466	John Woodville (and Katherine Neville)	John Myton and John Warner.	John Flaundres and Randolph Bawdewyn. Brewing fines 22d.
April 1467	John Woodville (and Katherine Neville)	Randolph Bawdewyn and Thomas Tayllour.	Not named.
October 1467	John Woodville (and Katherine Neville)	John Flaundris and John Yerwey.	Robert Cooke and Robert Warner. Brewing fines 22d.
May 1468	John Woodville (and Katherine Neville)	John Roper and John Bawdewyn.	Not named.
April or later 1468	John Woodville (and Katherine Neville)	John Flaundres and Nicholas Waren.	John Warner and Robert Cooke. Brewing fines 20d.
April 1469	John Woodville (and Katherine Neville)	John Yerwey and John Waren.	Not named.

Date	Lord/Lady	Ale-tasters	Notes
October 1469	Katherine Neville	John Yerwey the elder and John Waren.	John Warner and Robert Cooke. Brewing fines 18d.
May 1470	Katherine Neville	John Flawndrys and John Yerwey the younger.	Not named.
October 1471	Katherine Neville	John Myton and Thomas Tayllour.	John Flaundres and John Yerwey the younger. Brewing fines 18d.
May 1472	Katherine Neville	John Flaundres and Henry Parkere.	Not named.
October 1473	Katherine Neville	John Flaunders and John Warner.	John Warner and William Fesaunt. Brewing fines 12d.
April 1474	Katherine Neville	Not named, roll incomplete.	Not named.
October 1474	Katherine Neville	John Warner and Henry Parcer.	Not named. Fines for brewing 10d. Two brewers pledged by the steward.
March 1475	Katherine Neville	Not named.	Not named.
October 1475	Katherine Neville	Not named.	Not named. Three brewers. Brewing fines 18d.
April 1476	Katherine Neville	Not named.	Not named.
October 1477	Katherine Neville	Henry Parcar and John Yarewey.	Not named. Three women brewers. Brewing fines 18d.
March 1478	Katherine Neville	Not named.	Not named.
November 1478	Katherine Neville	John Flaundres and John Yarewey.	Not named. Three brewers (two women, one man). Brewing fines 12d.
April 1479	Katherine Neville	Not named.	Not named. Brewing fines 12d.
October 1481	Katherine Neville	John Warnere and John Yarewey the younger.	Henry Parker and John Yarewey the younger are both ale-tasters and constables. Three women brewers. Brewing fines 10d.
May 1482	Katherine Neville	Not named.	Not named.
September 1515	Thomas, Duke of Norfolk	William Gostwyk and Richard Smaleway.	Not named.
March 1520	Lord Thomas, Earl of Surrey	William Yarwey and Thomas Resse.	Two women brewers. Brewing fines 4d.
March 1522	Lord Thomas, Duke of Norfolk	Thomas Parker and William Yarwey.	Two women brewers. Brewing fines 4d.
December 1522	Lord Thomas, Duke of Norfolk	Thomas Parker and Thomas Reysley.	Two women brewers. Brewing fines 3d.

Appendix 6

People and Families

The leading roles in the story of Willington manor after the Peasants' Revolt were played by members of the Gostwyk family and by the dowager Duchess of Norfolk, Katherine Neville, who held Willington, and a substantial part of the Mowbray estates, as her dower for about fifty years. They were supported by hundreds of individuals: stewards, surveyors, receivers, auditors, accountants, bailiffs, craftsmen, tenants and others. Summaries of the lives of some of them are given below.

Goffe, John

There seem to have been two generations of men with the same name.[1] A John Goffe the elder, who was a brewer, is referred to in October 1410.[2] John Goffe 'the younger' is not mentioned but is implied. It is not known which of these men was the husband of Mariota Goffe mentioned in October 1416.[3]

John Goffe is named in thirty rolls 1397–1426. In 1397 he was granted a messuage and ten acres of land in Willington and was one of twenty one brewers.[4] He paid 4d. for two brewings. From 1406–13 he is listed as a juror and described as a sworn man or tithing man, showing that he was a respected member of the community. He paid 2d. for John Wright, who may have been a young servant or member of his extended family, to join a tithing in 1410.

He, perhaps with the help of his wife, brewed on the manor for about thirty years, usually paying between 4d. and 8d. a year.[5] He paid more, 12d., in both 1410 and 1413;[6] and was described as a constant brewer 1411–18. In 1418 he paid 18d. for brewing and was also fined as follows:

> … and that the same John [2d] sold old ale as he was ordered by the tasters of ale. And that [2d] the same John sold old ale and put a sign and afterwards it was withdrawn, therefore he was amerced. And that the same [2d] John sold ale by the barrel and cup. And the same John [2d] sold ale by measure without a seal. Therefore he is amerced.[7]

[1]   The text is based on John Hutchings' work prepared for Colmworth and Neighbours Historical Society, as part of his research into medieval brewing practices.
[2]   BARS, Box R212, Roll 12, October 1410.
[3]   BARS, Box R212, Roll 21, October 1416.
[4]   BARS, Box R212, Roll 5, October 1397.
[5]   BARS, Box R212, Rolls 5, October 1397; Roll 6, October 1403; Roll 7, October 1404; Roll 8, October 1406; Roll 10, October 1408; Roll 14a, October 1411; Roll 15, October 1413; Roll 17, October 1414; Roll 19, October 1415; Roll 21, October 1416; Roll 23, October 1417; Roll 25, October 1418; Roll 27, October 1419; Roll 29, October 1420; Roll 31, October 1422; Roll 33, October 1423; Roll 35, October 1425.
[6]   BARS, Box R212, Roll 12, October 1410; Roll 15, October 1413.
[7]   BARS, Box R212, Roll 25, October 1418.

Life did not run smoothly for him. He and his wife were accused of stealing from the bailiff in October 1416.[8] He was often accused and fined for not repairing his farm buildings, which included a house, grange, barn, shippon, sheep pen, malt kiln, bake house and insethouse, although the lord or lady gave him timber for his repairs. In May 1419 he also took on a cottage.[9] In October 1422 his ditch needed to be cleared.[10] The Goffe family was not recorded in any later rolls, and there is no information about where they came from or where they went to.

Gostwyk (or Gorstwyk, Gostewik, Gostwick, Gostwyke) family
In 1309 members of the Gostwyk family were second only in wealth to the lord of the manor but were less prosperous by 1332. As free tenants they were rarely mentioned in the court rolls, although they worked for the Mowbrays in various administrative roles over the centuries.

After the Peasants' Revolt they served as bailiffs for at least three periods: Robert Gostwyk was bailiff from 1382–93, and a John Gostwyk was bailiff 1457–62. At this time he was also bailiff for Bedford Castle and Bromham and collected rents for the lord from Cople, Cardington and Barford.[11] In 1481 a man with the same name was described as 'lately Bailiff and Reeve' with substantial arrears of 38s. 7d.

John Gostwyk was named as keeper of the wood of the shire in October 1408, when he also paid 4d. for brewing and was found guilty of sharing a debt of 10d. with John Bande. John Gostwyk, father and son, were jurors from 1416–26. A later John Gostwyk was ale taster 1451–52. Men of this family appear in fifty-seven court rolls 1394–1522.

John Gostwick (born before 1490, died 1545) joined the household of Cardinal Wolsey and was rewarded with the purchase of Willington manor from the Duke of Norfolk in 1529. Following Wolsey's fall he entered the service of Thomas Cromwell where he acted as treasurer and administrator. Despite some political and religious controversy he was knighted in 1540 and honoured in October 1541 when the King lodged at Willington. A more detailed history of the Gostwick family has been published elsewhere.[12]

Hunte, Roger
Roger Hunte was a local man from Roxton who became a Member of Parliament in 1407. He worked 'of counseill' for John Mowbray, second Duke of Norfolk, Earl of Nottingham and Earl Marshall from 1415 and was steward of Willington 1425–32, during which time he was paid £10 a year from the Willington accounts.[13] In 1425, when John Mowbray was engaged in a dispute over precedence with the Earl of Warwick, Roger Hunte was entrusted with pleading his case in parliament.[14] Roger Hunte's work led to the title of Duke of Norfolk being restored to Lord Mowbray.

---

8   BARS, Box R212, Roll 21, October 1416.
9   BARS, Box R212, Roll 26, October 1419.
10 BARS, Box R212, Roll 31, October 1422.
11 British Library, Add Ch. 657.
12 Finberg, 'Gostwicks of Willington', pp. 48–138.
13 Moye, *The Estates and Finances of the Mowbray Family*, p. 389.
14 *Ibid*, p. 58.

Roger Hunte is named once in the Willington court rolls, on 10 October 1425, but it is likely that he was steward in April and September 1426. Distinguishing features of these two rolls are the generous meals which were provided on the day the courts were held. On 22 April 1426 the meal provided for the steward and other surveyors consisted of: 'bread 5d., ale 10d., in beef meat 5½d., in calf and piglet 12d., for 4 pullets 4d., 1 capon 3d., in pepper and saffron 1d., in supplies for the same 3d., and in parchment for the rolls and ink for writing 6d. Sum [torn corner] 4s 1½d.'[15] On 29 September 1426, the meal was for the expenses of the steward and many other visitors, and consisted of: 'bread 6d., beer 15d., various fish and salt 4d., in fresh fish 11d., eels 3d., in flesh of castrated beef 14d., also 2 capons 8d., 1 goose 4d., 1 chicken 1d., in pepper and saffron 1d., 2 bushels of oats 6d. Sum 6s. 4d.'[16]

Roger Hunte became a distinguished speaker of the House of Commons and second baron of the exchequer.[17] His grave, and very worn memorial, can be seen in Roxton church; he died 1455–56.[18]

Launcelyn, William

William Launcelyn appears in the rolls 1426–82 and is mentioned seventeen times. The Launcelyn family held Wood End manor in Cople from the Mowbays and were an influential gentry family.[19] There is no evidence that William became bailiff at Willington, but he was an important figure on the manor during the 1450s. In May 1452 the steward and his party stayed overnight with the Launcelyn household.[20]

From 1448–57 William Launcelyn benefited from buildings which needed to be repaired. Thomas Wyltshyre's former holding, Trykats, was granted to him in 1448 free of charge on condition that he made the necessary repairs.[21] He later stood bail for repairs on one holding, and continued to promise to repair buildings in Trykats and other tenements. In later court rolls the list of buildings which he promised to repair grew. He continued to have the use of several holdings rent-free while delaying refurbishments.

The Launcelyn family had a long-term interest in the fisheries, the rabbit warren, and the game of the warren of Willington. They were leased to a Walter Launcelyn for ten years in 1457[22] and then for the term of his life in April 1467.[23] They were leased to a John Launcelyn for forty years in April 1476.[24]

Ann Launcelyn, a daughter of the family, is said to have been nurse to Henry VIII when young, and later lady of the bedchamber to Catherine of Aragon.

---

15   BARS, Box R212, Roll 36a, April 1426.
16   BARS, Box R212, Roll 36, September 1426.
17   Moye, *The Estates and Finances of the Mowbray Family,* p. 397.
18   Julian Lock, 'Hunt, Roger (d. 1455/6), Lawyer and Speaker of the House of Commons', *Oxford Dictionary of National Biography* (date of access 8 September 2018), http://www.oxforddnb.com/view/10.1093/ref:odnb/9780198614128.001.0001/odnb-9780198614128-e-14204.
19   VCH, vol. 3, p. 238.
20   BARS, Box R212, Roll 40b, May 1452.
21   BARS, Box R212, Roll 38a, October 1448.
22   British Library, Add Ch. 657.
23   BARS, Box R212, Roll 53a, April 1467.
24   BARS, Box R212, Roll 57b, April 1476.

Lygtfot (or Lyeghtfoot, Lyghtfoot, Lygtfoot) family
Members of the Lygtfot family appear twenty times in the Willington court rolls
1390–1423.

William Lyghtfoot, a carpenter, appears in the bailiff's account 1389–90 when
Roger Parker, the lord's receiver for Bedfordshire, paid 40s., 'over making a Grange
at Hynton.'[25] The grange is presumed to have belonged to Thomas Mowbray; 23s.
for wood and cuttings of various oaks were allowed for the repairs.

Cristiana Lyeghtfoot paid 2d. for one brewing in 1394;[26] in April 1409 Cristiana
Verne, who may have been the same person after marrying a second husband:

> surrendered one Messuage and half a virgate of land into the hands of the lady
> for the use of John Lygtfot. To be held by the same John by Court roll according
> to the custom of the Manor for the term of his life, rendering therefrom to the
> lady 13s. 4d. a year, and all the customs and services owed therefrom. And the
> aforesaid John will well and sufficiently provide the said Cristiana with mixed
> grain and money in proportion to a tenth of his estate during all her life. [27]

This appears to be the only recorded occasion on which a tenant provided a pension
for a woman in Willington in the fifteenth century. Neither Cristiana nor John appear
again in the Willington records.

In October 1415 a Richard Lygtfot surrendered his messuage and one virgate
of land and meadow and took a messuage with half a virgate of land and appurtenances.[28] He appears sixteen times in the court rolls 1410–23. His widow is
mentioned in 1418, so the Richard of 1419–23 was probably the earlier Richard's
son. During these years he is described as having a ruined insethouse and later
having a holding which is described as being devastated. He served on the second
jury, was sometimes excused from attending court and was obliged to mend his
overflowing ditch. Finally, in October 1422 he surrendering his holding, which was
described as being ruinous in June 1423.[29]

Maryon (or Maryan, Marion) family
Members of this family appear more than forty times in the rolls 1395–1475. A
John Marion is mentioned in eighteen rolls 1395–1455 and may be a father and
son, and perhaps even grandson. Thomas Maryon is named in eight rolls 1440–55
after which it appears that the male line of the family died out in Willington. Felecia
Maryon is mentioned once in 1455,[30] the dowager Lady Elizabeth Maryon fourteen
times 1456–71,[31] and Isabella Maryon is mentioned in 1474 and 1475.[32]

In October 1425 John Marion was one of the three men who were found to have

---

[25]   BARS, Box R213, R8/62/2/7. The reference to timber for this grange has been incorrectly transcribed as being at Lynton, but in both cases the lowercase 'h' is used at the start of the village name.
[26]   BARS, Box R212, Roll 2, October 1394.
[27]   BARS, Box R212, Roll 11, April 1409. The document seems to read *mesculent* and *pecilent*. Her
surrender of her holding to his use, and his agreement to pay her a pension, suggests that she may have
been his mother-in-law, or his mother who had remarried and been widowed a second time
[28]   BARS, Box R212, Roll 19, October 1415.
[29]   BARS, Box R212, Roll 32, June 1423.
[30]   BARS, Box R212, Roll 43b, May 1455.
[31]   Elizabeth is described in the rolls as *domina*. The title has several different meanings, but 'dowager'
seems the most appropriate in this context.
[32]   BARS, Box R212, Roll 55a, October 1474; Roll 57a, October 1475.

a dovecote on their land which he was said to have made, 'about the fourth year of the reign of the late king Henry IV' (30 September 1402 – 29 September 1403). The rolls do not tell us whether he was allowed to keep it.[33] John Maryon also appears on the lists of jurors on the second jury before 1426.

In 1465 tenants encroached on the lands of the dowager Lady Elizabeth Maryon and she successfully appealed to the court to regain them.[34] Although she was expected to attend the manor court she was often excused attendance by the bailiff or another member of the manor elite. It is not clear whether this was because of her social position or because she was infirm.

Although the rolls do not make it clear, it seems that the Maryons were free, and possibly substantial, tenants. They were often fined at the courts for having ditches which overflowed, and in 1413 the roll records that their ditch at Coppyd Hall Croft was not wide enough.[35] They mended it immediately to avoid paying a fine of 20s. 'Coppyd' is a dialect word linked to an elevated position, and in 1779 the Gostelow map still showed a small estate with three fields and a piece of woodland on the greensand ridge at the extreme south of the manor to the east of Sheerhatch Wood which may have belonged to this family in the fifteenth century.

Miton (or Myton) family

Members of this family frequently appear in the court rolls 1394–1425. Three men with this name appear in the roll of October 1394: Robert served on the jury of sworn men, Thomas paid a fine for brewing and provided a pledge for another tenant and John was unjustly accused of an offence. The family provided an assessor of fines in 1395 and consistently throughout 1403–26. They were also assessors of fines at other times, especially 1458–66.

John Myton, possibly a father, son and grandson, appears twenty times in the rolls from April 1440 (when he was described as constable and ale-taster) to November 1478, as well as in the Newnham Terrier of 1507. From 1448 he was sometimes a juror and was named as one of the assessors of fines on eleven occasions. A later John is named as assessor of fines in 1537 and 1539.

Other members of the family are named as Margeria Myton 1479–81, who may have been a widow, Richard and his wife Christiane 1474–76, and Thomas and William who were each involved in assaults in 1456, 1473, 1475 and 1478. Robert and John Miton were both included in the list of free men on the manor included in the bailiff's account 1457–58.

A recently discovered piece of parchment, relating to the transfer of two messuages on the manor in 1543, indicates that a Thomas Miton was still illiterate on that date.

Neville, Katherine

Katherine Neville was lady of the manor of Willington, a royal lady, and a member of the extended royal house of Lancaster, being the eldest daughter of Ralph Neville, First Earl of Westmorland, and a legitimised grand-daughter of John O'Gaunt. She was born c. 1400 and married four times.

---

[33]   BARS, Box R212, Roll 35, October 1425.
[34]   BARS, Box R212, Roll 51b, April 1465.
[35]   BARS, Box R212, Roll 15, October 1413.

She lived much of her life at the Vinegarth, in Epworth on the Isle of Axholme in north Lincolnshire, and her association with Willington dated from her marriage to John Mowbray in 1412 until her death in 1483. During her first marriage she was often left alone while her husband served abroad.

> There are only occasional glimpses of her active in administering Mowbray property during these years, but as the three surviving Mowbray receiver-general's accounts all cover years when the earl was absent for all or most of the year, and as his receiver-general travelled regularly to Epworth, it must be presumed that she was largely responsible for overseeing the estates between 1415 and 1423.[36]

After John Mowbray's death in 1432 about a third of the Mowbray estates were given to her as her dower, and during the next fifty years she shared it with three further husbands, or held it in her own right. Her second marriage to Sir Thomas Strangeways is first mentioned in January 1442 but was not of long duration as Katherine was married to John Beaumont, first Viscount Beaumont, by August 1443. John Beaumont was killed at the battle of Northampton on 10 July 1460.

Katherine's marriage sometime after 1465 to her fourth husband was described at the time as 'a diabolic marriage' and would still raise eyebrows today. She was over sixty and Sir John Woodville was a youngster in his early twenties. This too was a short marriage as he was executed on 12 August 1469 following the battle of Edgcote.

Katherine outlived all her husbands, her son, her grandson and her great grand-daughter, Anne Mowbray, who had been married in January 1478 to Richard, Duke of York, when they were aged five and four respectively. Anne died in 1481 and Richard became one of the 'Princes in the Tower' and disappeared in 1483.

Katherine Neville's influence on Willington manor can be seen in the building of a new barn and some repairs in 1440. Her third and fourth husbands seem to have been efficient administrators, but the manor was also efficiently managed by her and her stewards when she held it in her own right; although by the end of her life the amount of detail in the court rolls, especially in the halmoots, reduced. In October 1481 and May 1482 an increase in detail suggests new management making preparations for her death and a change in ownership.

Rider (or Ridere, Ryder, Rydere) family
The family was recorded in the 1309 subsidy roll for Willington when three men with this name concealed their taxable goods – their tax assessments were subsequently increased nearly three-fold.[37]

Men with the forenames John, Thomas, Walter and William appear about one hundred times in the manor court rolls from 1394 , although Walter appeared only once in 1394.

Thomas Rider of Barford held a messuage and nine acres of land in Barford 1386–97, or later, under a more formal arrangement than usual. It was: 'thus

---

36   Rowena E. Archer, 'Neville [married names Mowbray, Strangways, Beaumont, Woodville], Katherine, duchess of Norfolk (c. 1400–1483), noblewoman', Oxford Dictionary of National *Biography* (date of access 8 September 2018), http://www.oxforddnb.com/view/10.1093/ref:odnb/9780198614128.001.0001/odnb-9780198614128-e-54432.
37   Hervey, *Two Bedfordshire Subsidy Lists 1309 and 1332.*

allowed by the lord, as appears in the court roll of Bedford for this year, to be held by the same Thomas and his descendants at the lord's will.'[38] William Ridere had been appointed bailiff 1394–95 but may have been appointed part way through the previous year, for which the bailiff's account is missing. By this time, Thomas and William both appear to have been powerful individuals even though the family had been referred to as serfs in the 1309 subsidy list. However, in 1414 John Rydere was the only person in the records obliged to pay a fine of 2s. for his daughter's marriage, 'and no more as he is exceedingly poor and in need.'[39] If this was a plea to be granted a reduced payment, it was not heeded.

William Ridere appears at least thirty-one times in the records 1394–1426 and may have been a father and son. 'He' served three different lords of the manor and one lady of the manor, Queen Joan. He was bailiff of Willington in the bailiff's account 1394–95 until about 1418 and also served as a juror throughout this period; he was mentioned once as constable in October 1407.[40] A man of the same name was an ale-taster October 1411-October 1416. The receiver's accounts for Willington 1421–22 also refer to William Rydere as bailiff, though the text is ambiguous, it says: 'And for £30, received as part of the arrears of William Rydere, from the hand of William Gillow, bailiff of the manor of Fennystanton, from 2 tallies, sealed with the seal of William Gillow himself, of which the first contained £14 and the other £16.' Later in the account entries refer to the 'said bailiff,' but this is probably William Gillow. William Ridere paid at least £54 13s. 4d. as arrears. He is referred to as keeper of Sheerhatch wood, 1421–26.

Two John Rideres, possibly father and son, were mentioned forty-five times in the records April 1394-April 1426 and were usually members of the jury. One of them was an assessor of fines in October 1416.[41] They were involved in fights in 1395 and 1418, and a man with the same name left the village in 1419, dying soon afterwards.[42]

A Thomas Ridere was mentioned in the Willington bailiffs' accounts 1384–97 and at least twenty-five times in the court rolls 1394–1419. His death was recorded in October 1417, and some of his lands were at first taken over by his widow, but new tenants had been found by October 1419. A man of the same name still lived on the manor at that time but is not mentioned in any later documents.

In 1409, when Queen Joan was lady of the manor, John Rider was allowed forty trees to repair his buildings.[43] Thomas Rider was allowed forty beams in 1411[44] and a further thirty-two trees to make a new house in 1414.[45] These significant numbers imply that the buildings on the family holdings were large and that they were prosperous. The family may have begun to abuse their position, and life for them may have become more difficult after the manor was returned to John Mowbray in 1413.

Members of the Rider family are recorded in the manorial records until 1451, and a small piece of woodland called Riders' Croft appears on the 1779 estate map

[38] BARS, R8/62/2/4–11.
[39] BARS, Box R212, Roll 16, April 1414.
[40] BARS, Box R212, Roll 17, October 1414.
[41] BARS, Box R212, Roll 21, October 1416.
[42] BARS, Box R212, Roll 3, October 1395; Roll 26, May 1419.
[43] BARS, Box R212, Roll 11, April 1409.
[44] BARS, Box R212, Roll 13, April 1411.
[45] BARS, Box R212, Roll 14, October 1411.

of Willington – the only visible evidence in the eighteenth century that they had ever been there.

de Wyllyton (Welyngton, Wilton) , Robert

This man was appointed keeper of the warren of Willington and the wood of Sheer-hatch by John Mowbray (the fifth) at Rouen, 24 January 1419, and was paid by him, at the least, throughout 1419–32. He was described as surgeon and warrener of Willington (*surgeyn et warrenario de Williton*).[46] His wife Margaret received his payments while he was away in France and he appears in the manorial documents 1421–22 and 1426:

> Also that Robert Welyngton made an allowance of 12 oaks to William Launce-leyn, and John Kempston is to allow 12 oaks to the same William about the next feast that is said [to be] St Peter in chains, but which are cleared for fuel

> Also Robert Welyngton sold 1 oak to John Kempston for 3s from the lord's wood called Le Shirehatch.[47]

At some point before the death of John Mowbray, Robert's wages were raised from 60s. 8d to £6 16d. each year for his good service. His name, written Robert Wilton, is believed to have been signed fifth on the list of original members of the fellowship of surgeons whose ordinances were drawn up in May 1435.[48]

No further details of his career as a surgeon have been found, except that a Robert Warreyn, master and royal surgeon, is recorded in about 1454 as having been chosen by the Duke of York that year to serve on a medical commission of five practitioners to administer to King Henry VI. [49] If this was Robert de Wyllyton he would have been very elderly when he was pardoned eleven years later in 1465 by Edward IV for an unspecified offence.[50]

Yarwey (or Yarewy, Yareway, Yarway, Yerwey) family

This was a large family whose name appears in the court rolls about eighty times 1394–1426 and approximately 150 times 1448–83. The mentions of the Yarweys were most numerous at the end of the 1470s.

Before 1400 five men with this name are mentioned in the court rolls: Henry and Richard from 1394; John from 1395; Thomas once in 1396 and William once in 1397. Henry died in 1417 and John was referred to as 'the elder' in 1422 but died in 1425. Three generations of men named Walter Yarwey appear in the rolls 1407–11. Father and son are mentioned in a land transfer in 1407 when: 'John Watte came to this Court and took from the lady one Messuage and half a virgate of land which lately was held by Walter Yarwey, to be held the same John by Court roll, according to the custom of the Manor for the term of his life.'[51] One of John Watte's pledgers was a Walter Yarwey

[46] Arundel Castle Archives, A1642, full transcript by Moye, *The Estates and Finances of the Mowbray Family*, pp. 259, 418.
[47] BARS, Box R212, Roll 36, September 1426.
[48] Moye, *The Estates and Finances of the Mowbray Family*, p. 389.
[49] It is possible that 'warrener' was an alias.
[50] Charles Hugh Talbot and Eugene Ashby Hammond, *The Medical Practitioners in Medieval England. A Biographical Register* (London, 1965), p. 305.
[51] BARS, Box R212, Roll 8b, April 1407.

and a young man of the same name joined a tithing in 1411. It is not possible to say which Walter, with Robert Myton and John Gaubryell, illegally, 'grazed their beasts' in 1422 resulting in a fine of 6d. to the lord and 6d. to the church each.[52]

Four other tenants died in the same year that Walter, 'closed the days of his existence' in October 1408. This unusually large number suggests plague or famine on the manor at that time. The lord claimed heriots from the estates of all five men, but Walter's was the largest; his bullock was worth 12s. The heriots claimed from the other four tenants were valued between 5s. and 7s.

Four widows from the Yarwey family held their late husband's holdings until their own death. Matilda Yarwey, widow of Richard, held land 1404–10 during which time the messuage fell into repair. Other un-named Yarwey widows held their late husbands' lands for short lengths of time, but Henry Yarwey's widow, Joan, held lands from 1417 to at least 1420. She was reported as having defective buildings in 1419 and 1420.

John Yarwey was mentioned more than a hundred times 1448–83, described variously as John the elder; John the younger; John the middle, October 1474–April 1479; or John Yarwey, alias Clerk, October 1473–October 1482. John the elder and younger were bailiffs 1463–69; John the elder was ale-taster1450–54, and John the younger was named as ale taster in 1471 and 1481; John Yarweys were constables in 1450, 1456–58, 1463, 1469–71 and 1481; they were also occasionally assessors of fines. In October 1477 three men named John Yarwey sat at the same court on the main jury and one was assessor of fines.[53] In November 1478 three John Yarweys sat on the main jury, one sat on the second jury, one was a brewer and one was an assssor of fines.[54]

Men of the family named John or William continue to appear less frequently in the court rolls which survive 1515–1605. During this period they were jury men or assessor of fines. William was named as overseer of the fields in October 1599. His was the first name in the list of jurors in October 1603, but by October 1605 he was no longer a juror and was fined 3s. 4d. for cutting down willows from the lord's land. Nevertheless he still appears to be an important man on the manor because it was agreed: 'that yt shalbe Lawfull for William Yarway to keepe any Cattle uppon his Walleheade.' He seems to have been the only tenant to ever be given this privilege, but his name is not found in any later rolls.

[52]   BARS, Box R212, Roll 31, October 1422.
[53]   BARS, Box R212, Roll 58a, October 1477.
[54]   BARS, Box R212, Roll 59a, November 1478.

Glossary of Terms

Acreman: type of low status, unfree tenant; a small-holder. The use of the term is uncertain and probably has differing meaning according to the local use of the term in a particular manor.

Advowson: the perpetual right of patronage to present to a vacant church or benefice, being either a rectory or vicarage.

Affeeror: local officer and suitor appointed by the manorial court to advise on and moderate the levels of amercements and fines set by the court. They were also known as assessors of fines.

Ale-taster: local officer and suitor appointed by the manorial court to monitor and regulate the price and quality of ale brewed within the jurisdiction of the manor.

Amercement: monetary penalty levied by the manorial court for an offence or infringement within the jurisdiction of the court. Tenants found guilty and fined were said to be 'at the mercy of the lord, or lady' *(in misericordia)*.

Appurtenance: something that belongs or 'appertains' to land, that is buildings, outhouses, yards, gardens, orchards, and/or the rights, liberties and responsibilities that might also 'appertain' to it.

Assart: land cleared from woodland or waste for cultivation.

Assessor of fines: see Affeeror.

Assize of bread and ale: session, or assembly of local officials, supported by national statute and held to regulate the price and quality of bread and beer.

Attachment: taking and/or apprehending a person to appear in court to answer a summons. An individual who did not appear as summoned might then be distrained.

Bailiff: paid official responsible to the lord or his steward for day-to-day management of the manor; such as rent collection, levying fines and amercements, and the local administration of justice. Often the bailiff was appointed from outside the manor.

Bondsman: general word for an unfree tenant within a manor, bound or effectively enslaved to a lord and to the manor of his birth; also a person bound by a bond.

Boonwork: unpaid seasonal labour service on the lord's demesne. Boonwork ceased when the demesne was no longer farmed by the lord directly.

Bordar: cottager or smallholder, generally of a less servile condition within the manor than a bondsman, who may have built a cottage on the edge of the common land or waste.

Canon: member of an ecclesiastical community or a rule of law.

Capital messuage: high status property or dwelling house; the lord's main house or estate property in a manorial context.

Capon: cockerel that has been castrated to improve the quality of its flesh for food.

Cart(e)bote: common right of tenants to take timber from the woodland to make or repair carts and other instruments of husbandry.

Common fine: annual payment by tenants at the view of frankpledge or court leet to the lord of the manor, sometimes called head silver, land silver or rents of assize.

Common land: land common to a manor or lordship over which some tenants had shared beneficial rights such as the right to graze animals.

Constable: local official appointed at the view of frankpledge, with responsibility for keeping the peace and good order.

Copyhold: form of land tenure or holding that involved a form of registration of title whereby the tenant would have a copy of the entry on the court roll describing the transaction giving them their certified 'proof of title' to the land concerned. Although copyholders held land originally 'at the will of the lord according to the custom of the manor' over time copyhold became a recognised and legally secure form of tenure administered by a manor court and although perhaps dependent still to some degree on local custom was the subject of national case law and legal definition making it as capable of conveyancing for sale and inheritance as land of freehold tenure. Copyhold could be 'enfranchised' to become freehold, a process accelerated by statute law that eventually abolished it as a form of tenure in the twentieth century.

Cotland: small-holding of land attached to a cottage.

Cottar: small-holder or cottager.

Court baron: see manor court.

Court leet: see manor court.

Curtilage: yard or court and outbuildings attached to a dwelling house.

Custom of the manor: form of law and associated framework of rules established by long usage, governing and regulating the local administration of a manor and the conduct and activities of those resident there.

Customary court: see manor court.

Customary tenant: see customary tenure.

Customary tenure: form of land tenure or holding based on the custom of the manor often synonymous with 'unfree' or villein tenure (meaning land held by restrictive obligations and terms 'at the will of the lord' very unlike those of freehold tenure) that later became copyhold tenure.

Custumal: written list of the customs of a manor.

Demesne: land within the manor for the lord's own occupation and use; the lord's home farm. Many lords ceased to farm their demesnes directly in the years after the Black Death.

Distrain(t): seizing goods or property to compel the performance of an obligation, recover a debt, procure satisfaction for a wrong committed or enforce a court decision.

Dower: widow's right to hold a 'portion,' often proportionally a third, of her late husband's land for the rest of her life for her sustenance and the nurture and education of her children.

Engrossment: amalgamation of land holdings of two or more farms for occupation by one tenant leaving one farm house empty or reducing its status to a cottage.

Entry fine: payment by a tenant on taking possession of a land holding, also described as a relief. The size of entry fines, in comparison with the annual rents, varied between estates according to custom and procedure.

Escheat: reversion of a property to the lord or the Crown when the tenant died without heirs, or when the heir had not attained his or her majority, or had committed an offence which incurred the forfeiture of their land and estate. Escheators were officials appointed to collect revenues from escheated estates.

Essoins: excuses given by tenants for not being able to attend court in an action or to perform a suit to the court. If excused, tenants were not fined for non-attendance. If no excuses were given or agreed then the tenants who did not attend were fined for default of court.

Estreat: duplicate copy or extract of an original writing or record such as fines and amercements imposed by the manor court, written out and given to local officials for them to levy and collect the same.

Extent: formal recitation estimating and valuing the land, rents, services etc. of the manor.

Fealty: swearing or taking an oath of fidelity to the lord, an obligatory commitment associated with land holding and service within the manor.

Fee: hereditary land held from a superior lord in return for homage and service.

Fine: payment made to the court by tenants entering holdings, by tenants in default of court, by brewers for the right to brew ale and for minor offences.

Forfeiture: deprivation of land or property as a penalty for transgressing some act or law or for some other obligatory omission.

Frankpledge: pledged or promised responsibility, binding a group of men together to act as mutual sureties for the behaviour of the group members, for example, ensuring their attendance at court, keeping the peace, paying fines and rents.

Free warren: franchised right from the Crown granting the right to keep and hunt small game and game birds over a designated area of land, open or enclosed.

Glebe: land belonging to a parish church and benefice.

Hayward: local manorial officer charged with keeping and supervising the common herd of cattle and ensuring, in particular, that they do not break or crop the hedges of neighbouring enclosed lands or damage the common grass pasture; and with responsibility for overseeing harvesting.

Head silver: see common fines.

Heriot: form of death duty, being the customary entitlement of the lord of the manor to the best, or most valuable, beast or money payment in lieu, from the estate of a deceased tenant; also charged on the surrender or transfer of some pieces of land within the manor.

Hid(e) or hid(e)age: ancient land tax associated with area measurement of land; often a land measurement of approximately 120 acres, but dependent on local variations in the size of an acre. See also Shreeveshot.

Holme: river island or piece of fen ground surrounded by water.

Homage: submissive acknowledgement and obligation of service to a lord; 'homage jury' was a jury of tenants that do 'homage' to the lord and serve the court.

Honour: large lordship, or 'seignory' of several smaller lordships and manors, with some collective dependence for the performance of customs and services.

Hue and cry: ancient common law practice which allowed any tenant to accuse another of an offence and to seek the assistance of the constable in taking the offender to court.

Hundred: unit of local government smaller than a county and larger than a vill, often with an open-air meeting place. The area was originally so called as it consisted of a hundred 'hides' (the amount of land that would support a family) and freeholders organised into ten kinship 'tithings', with a 'public' court and jurisdiction concerned essentially with peace keeping. It was similar to the old county court in jurisdiction and procedure, either directly managed by the Crown or often later farmed out and franchised to lords by sheriffs acting for the Crown.

Insethouse: farm building, No clear descriptions of the use and layout of these buildings have been found.

Knight's fee or service: a form of feudal service by which tenants of the Crown held land (fee) in return for forms of military service – such as the provision of knights – and associated incidents.

Land silver: see common fines.

Lay subsidy rolls: records of taxation in England made between the twelfth and seventeenth centuries; said to have been administered by members of the local community and listing local tenants. They were known as the tenths and fifteenths,1290–1334, because the contribution of townsmen was based on one tenth of the valuation of their property and country dwellers on one fifteenth.

Leet court: see manor court.

Manor court: private court linked to ownership of a manor that was run to exercise certain rights of jurisdiction over the tenants holding land within the manor. The views of frankpledge or court leet devolved from royal jurisdiction to the lord of the manor. They dealt with disputes between tenants, land transactions, payment of dues such as heriot, upholding the custom of the manor and by-laws. The court baron or 'halmoot' administered the customs of a particular manor and regulated the tenure (including the transfer of land) and various aspects of the life of tenants. Its rights of jurisdiction were very important within the community and included managing the use of the common fields and settling disputes.

Manor court rolls: formal records of the court's judicial and administrative proceedings and the activities of the manor court; often sewn together in groups.

Merchet: fine or payment to the lord by a tenant for licence to allow his daughter to marry.

Messuage: legal term for a property including a dwelling house with adjoining land and appurtenances.

Mol(e)men: tenants paying rent for land (molland) on which services had anciently been commuted, that is, converted into a money payment.

Perquisites of court: profits arising to a lord of the manor from fines and amercements levied by the court.

Pledge: guarantor named by the court to ensure the upholding and execution of orders of the court e.g. payment of rents, fines, debts, repair of buildings etc.

Plough team: communal team usually comprising eight oxen and the plough itself.

Ploughbote: the common right to take timber to make or repair ploughs, carts and harrows, and to make rakes, forks etc.

Poll tax: tax upon every head or poll, i.e. on every person.

Quit rent: small monetary payment by tenants to the lord of the manor in lieu of labour services in order to be quit and free of some obligation.

Receiver: officer appointed to receive and collect money from a manor or manors.

Receivers' accounts: records of money collected by the receiver from a manor or a group of manors.

Reeve: officer term often synonymous with steward or bailiff. Elected from the manorial tenantry.

Relief: alternative term for an entry fine.

Rental: written record of the rents and services payable to the lord of the manor; used by officials given responsibility to collect them.

Rents of assize: see common fines.

Scutage: a tax levied on those holding land by knight service.

Seisin: possession of land.

Serf: an unfree or servile tenant.

Sheriff or Shire Reeve: the official responsible for the administration of a county on behalf of the Crown.

Sherreveshot: single tax which was the precursor of the modern rating system. The spelling of sherreve was irregular as was the medieval spelling of 'sheriff.'

Shilling: silver coin, to the value of twelve pennies. There were twenty shillings to the pound.

Shippon: cattle shed.

Socage: originally a type of free tenure without the obligation of military service. The holding could be sold or inherited, usually by the eldest son, who paid a fee to enter the holding and was obliged to attend the manor court. On some manors socage was of two kinds: free socage carried fixed and 'honourable obligations; villein socage carried obligations of a humbler nature. As the distinction between free and unfree tenure became less clear and copyhold tenure became more usual, the term 'socage' was less used. It was abolished in 1660.

Socman or Sokeman: tenants holding land in free socage.

Solar: upper chamber in a hall or relatively large house.

Steward: chief officer and administrator of a manor, or manors, directly responsible to the lord. The steward presided at sittings of the manor court.

Survey: document describing the land of a manor or estate in measured and evaluated form with details of land parcels, boundaries, tenure, rents and services.

Tenants at will: tenants with a limited security of tenure, synonymous with villeinage and 'unfree' tenure, and holding land literally 'at the will of the lord.'

Tenement: anything which might be held by a tenant; in this context a holding of land with a house.

Terrier: survey recording and detailing land and property.

Tithing: group of adult men over the age of twelve who were each responsible for the good behaviour of the others.

Toft: place or piece of ground on which a messuage or house stood or formerly stood.

Toll: payment in towns, markets and fairs for goods and cattle bought and sold, and for passing over a highway, bridge or ferry.

View of frankpledge: see manor courts.

Vill: local unit of administration, that is, the manor or the village.

Villein tenant: see tenants at will.

Virgate: measure of land varying in extent but frequently averaging thirty acres (a quarter of a hide).

Warrener: official appointed to keep and supervise a warren.

Woodward: manorial official responsible for maintenance of the lord's woodland and for preventing offences against the same, including poaching.

Bibliography

Primary Sources

The Anglo-Saxon Chronicles, translated by Anne Savage (London, 1982)

Blunham Manor Court Rolls, Bedfordshire Archives and Records Service (BARS), L26/51, L26/52, L26/53, L26/54

Blunham Rental 1457, BARS, L26/154

Blunham Survey 1498, BARS, L26/212

Cirket, Alan, *Sketch Map based on Gostelow Map 1779*, BARS, R1/75

Compoti of all the Ministers of Thomas, Earl of Surrey, for Manors of Framlingham at the Castle, Kettleburgh, Hacheston, Peasenhall, Kelsale, and Willington (Bd.), Suffolk Record Office, HD 1538/225/6

Cook, Barbara, 'Newnham Priory: Rental of Manor at Biddenham, 1505–6', in *Publications of Bedfordshire Historical Record Society*, vol. 25 (Streatley, 1947), pp. 82–103

Eggington Court Rolls, BARS, X301/1/1–16

Fenwick, Carolyn, ed., *The Poll Taxes of 1377, 1379, and 1381. Part 1 Bedfordshire – Lincolnshire*, Records of Social and Economic History, new ser., 27 (Oxford, 1998)

Godber, Joyce, ed., *The Cartulary of Newnham Priory*, Bedfordshire Historical Record Society (BHRS), vol. 43 (Bedford, 1963–64)

Gostelow, Thomas, *A Plan of the Estate of Her Grace the Duchess of Bedford and Robert Palmer Esquire, lately purchased of His Grace the Duke of Marlborough, in the Parish of Willington in the County of Bedford 1779*, and the map book, BARS R1/75

Hamilton-Thompson, A. ed., *Visitations of Religious Houses in the Diocese of Lincoln*, vol. 1.: *Injunctions and other Documents from the Registers of Richard Flemyng and William Grey, Bishops of Lincoln, A.D. 1420 to A.D. 1436*, Canterbury and York Society (Horncastle, 1914)

Hamilton-Thompson, A. ed., *Visitations of Religious Houses in the Diocese of Lincoln*, vol. 3.: *Visitations of Religious Houses (concluded) by Bishops Atwater and Longland and by their Commissaries, 1517–1531.*, Lincoln Record Society (Hereford, 1940–47)

Hamson, J., 'Grant of Free Warren to Newnham Priory', in *Publications of Bedfordshire Historical Record Society*, vol. 5 (Aspley Guise, 1920), pp. 97–100

Henman, W. N., 'Newnham Priory: a Bedford Rental, 1506–7', in *Publications of Bedfordshire Historical Record Society*, vol. 25 (Streatley, 1947), pp. 15–81

Hervey, S. H. A., ed., *Two Bedfordshire Subsidy Lists 1309 and 1332*, Suffolk Green Books 18 (Bury St Edmunds, 1925)

Jamieson, D., *The Terrier of the Prior and Convent of Newnham of its Land and Tenements in Willington 1507*, unpublished transcription and translation of BARS, AD 325

Jefferys, Thomas, *The County of Bedford* (London, 1765)

Morris, John, ed., Veronica Sankaran and David Sherlock, *Domesday Book 20: Bedfordshire* (Chichester, 1977)

Terrier of the Prior and Convent of Newnham of its Land and Tenements in Wellyngton, made there on the 12th day of July in the twenty second year of the reign of King Henry the seventh, BARS, AD328a

Thompson, J. S., ed., *Bailiffs' Accounts for Willington and Certain Other Manors, 1382 to 1397*, BARS, CRT 130 Willington 11

Thompson, J. S., ed., 'The Hundred Rolls of 1274 and 1279', in John Thompson, ed., *Hundreds, Manors, Parishes and the Church: a Selection of Early Documents for Bedfordshire*, BHRS, vol. 69 (Bedford, 1990)

Thompson, J. S. and K. T. Ward, 'Eggington Court Rolls (1297 -1572)', in John Thompson, ed., *Hundreds, Manors, Parishes and the Church: a Selection of Early Documents for Bedfordshire*, BHRS, vol. 69 (Bedford, 1990), pp. 184–228

The Trewe copye of Blunham Charter, made unto them by Edmonde, Late Earle of Kent, BARS, L26/229, CRT 130 Blunham 7.

Willington Bailiff's Account, 1457–58, British Library, Add Ch. 657

Willington Bailiffs' Accounts, 1382–97, BARS, R8/62/2/1-11

Willington Manor Court Rolls, 1394–1674, BARS, Box R212, Rolls 1-80a

Willington Manor Court Rolls, 1394–1674, translated by Dorothy Jamieson, BARS, http://bedsarchives.bedford.gov.uk/ CommunityArchives/Willington/WillingtonManorCourtRolls/ WillingtonManorCourtRollsIntroduction.aspx

Willington Manor Court Rolls, 1463–72, British Library, Add Ch. 26813/1-8

Willington Manor Court Rolls 1463–72, transcription by Joyce Godber, BARS, CRT 130 Willington 4

Willington Receiver's Accounts 1421–22, Arundel Castle Archives, A1642

Wyllyngton Account of William Paryssh, Bailiff and Reeve there at the Time Within, Arundel Castle Archives, A1328

Secondary Sources

Airs, Malcolm, *The Tudor and Jacobean Country House: A Building History* (Stroud, 1995)

Albion Archaeology, *Archaeological Desk-based Assessment, Bedford River Valley Park Bedfordshire* (unpublished, 2007)

Alcock, W., 'The Meaning of Insethouse', *Vernacular Architecture*, vol. 27, issue 1 (1996), pp. 8–9

Archer, R. E, *The Mowbrays, Earls of Nottingham and Dukes of Norfolk, to 1432* (unpublished PhD thesis, 1984), University of Oxford

Archer, Rowena, 'Rich Old Ladies: the Problem of Late Medieval Dowagers', in A. J. Pollard, ed., *Property and Politics: Essays in Later Medieval History* (Gloucester, 1984) pp.15–35

Archer, Rowena E., 'Neville [married names Mowbray, Strangways, Beaumont, Woodville], Katherine, duchess of Norfolk (c. 1400–1483), noblewoman', Oxford Dictionary of National Biography (date of access 8 September 2018), http://www.oxforddnb.com/view/10.1093/ref:odnb/9780198614128.001.0001/odnb-9780198614128-e-54432

Bailey, M., *The English Manor, c1200 – c1500* (Manchester, 2002)

Bailey, M. 'The Rabbit and the Medieval East Anglian Economy', *Agricultural History Review,* vol. 36 (1998), pp. 1–20

Bollongton, Robert, *Willington and the Russells* (Willington, 2012)

Britnell, R., 'Land and Lordship: Common Themes and Regional Variations', in B. Dodds and R. Britnell, eds, *Agriculture and Rural Society after the Black Death; Common Themes and Regional Variations* (Hatfield, 2008), pp. 149–67

Britnell, R., 'Markets and Incentives: Common Themes and Regional Variations', in B. Dodds and R. Britnell, eds, *Agriculture and Rural Society after the Black Death* (Hatfield, 2008), pp.3–20.

Capes, W. W., *The English Church in the Fourteenth and Fifteenth Centuries* (London, 1920)

Cheney, C. R., *Handbook of Dates: For Students of British History,* 2nd ed. (Cambridge, 2000)

Clanchy, M. T., *From Memory to Written Record: England 1066–1307*, 3rd ed. (Oxford, 2013)

Coleman, S. R., 'Monuments Protection Programme', *South Midlands Archaeology*, vol. 20 (1990), pp. 3–5

Dickens, A. G., 'Estate and Household Management in Bedfordshire, c. 1540', in BHRS, vol. 36, *The Gostwicks of Willington and Other Studies* (Streatley, 1956), pp. 38–45.

Dyer, Christopher, *A Country Merchant 1495–1420* (Oxford, 2012)

Dyer, Christopher, 'English Peasant Buildings in the later Middle Ages', *Medieval Archaeology*, vol. 30 (1986), pp. 19–45.

Dyer, Christopher, *Everyday Life in Medieval England* (London, 1994)

Dyer, Christopher, *Standards of Living in the Later Middle Ages: Social Change in England c1200 – 1500* (Cambridge, 1989)

Edgeworth, Matt, *Fluid Pasts: Archaeology of Flow* (London, 2011)

Edmondson, G. and A. Mudd, 'Medieval Occupation at 'Danish Camp', Willington', *Bedfordshire Archaeology*, vol. 25 (2004), pp. 208–21

Edwards, James F. and Brian Paul Hinde, 'The Transportation System of Medieval England and Wales', *Journal of Historical Geography*, vol. 17, no. 2 (April 1991), pp. 123–34

Finberg, H. P. R., 'The Gostwicks of Willington', in BHRS, vol.36, *The Gostwicks of Willington and Other Studies* (Streatley, 1956), pp. 48–138

Fleming, Robin, *Lords and Kings in Conquest England* (Cambridge, 1991)

Fowler, G. Herbert, *Bedfordshire 1086: An Analysis and Synthesis of Domesday Book*, BHRS Quarto Memoirs, vol. 1 (Apsley Guise, 1922)

Fryde, E. B. and N. Fryde, 'Peasant Rebellion and Peasant Discontents', in E. Miller, ed., *The Agrarian History of England and Wales*, vol. 3, 1348–1500 (Cambridge, 1991), 8 vols.

Gardiner, Mark, 'Vernacular Buildings and the Development of the Later Medieval Domestic Plan in England', *Medieval Archaeology*, vol. 44 (2000), pp.159–79

Godber, Joyce, *History of Bedfordshire, 1066–1888* (Bedford, 1969)

Great Britain, Public Record Office, *Calendar of Inquisitions Miscellaneous (Chancery) Preserved in the Public Record Office 1377–88*, vol. 4, no. 123 (H.M.S.O., 1957)

Gwynn, Peter, *The King's Cardinal: The Rise and Fall of Cardinal Wolsey* (London, 1990)

Harvey, P. D. A., *Manorial Records*, Archives and the User, no. 5 (London, 1999)

Harvey, P. D. A., 'Tenant Farming and Tenant Farmers - The Home Counties', in E. Miller, ed., *The Agrarian History of England and Wales*, vol. 3, 1348–1500 (Cambridge, 1991), 8 vols.

Hassall, Jane, 'Excavations at Willington, 1973', *Bedfordshire Archaeological Journal*, vol. 10 (1975), pp. 23–40

Hatcher, John, *Plague, Population and the English Economy 1348 – 1530*, Studies in Economic and Social History (London, 1977)

Herbert Fowler, G., *Bedfordshire in 1086: An Analysis and Synthesis of the Domesday* Book, BHRS, Quarto Memoirs, vol.1 (Aspley Guise, 1922)

Holmes, G. A, *The Estates of the Higher Nobility in Fourteenth Century England* (Cambridge, 1957)

Hoskins, W. G., *The Making of the English Landscape* (London, 1995)

Jamieson , D., *Willington: Manor and the Honour of Mowbray* (unpublished dissertation for the Advanced Research Diploma in Local History, 1999) University of Cambridge

Jones, A. C. *The Customary Land Market in Fifteenth Century Bedfordshire* (unpublished PhD thesis, 1975), University of Southampton

Kerr, Brian, *An Unassuming County* (Bedford, 2014)

Latham, R. E., *Revised Medieval Latin Word-list* (Oxford, 1965)

Lock, Julian, 'Hunt, Roger (d. 1455/6), Lawyer and Speaker of the House of Commons', *Oxford Dictionary of National Biography* (date of access 8 September 2018), http://www.oxforddnb.com/view/10.1093/ref:odnb/9780198614128.001.0001/odnb-9780198614128-e-14204.

Marsom, F. W., 'The Meeting Place of Wixamtree Hundred', *The Publications of Bedfordshire Historical Record Society*, vol. 25 (Streatley, 1947), pp.1–3

McKisack, May, *The Fourteenth Century*, Oxford History of England, vol. 5 (Oxford, 1959)

Moye, Lucy B., *The Estates and Finances of the Mowbray Family, Earls Marshall and Dukes of Norfolk, 1401 to 1476* (unpublished PhD thesis, 1985), Duke University, USA

Musson, Anthony, *Medieval Law in Context: the Growth of Legal Consciousness from Magna Carta to the Peasant's Revolt* (Manchester, 2001)

Page, William, ed., *Victoria County History of Bedfordshire*, vol. 3 (London, 1912)

Pollard, A. J., ed., *Property and Politics: Essays in Later Medieval History* (Gloucester, 1984)

Poos, L. R. and R. M. Smith, 'Legal Windows into Historical Populations', in Z. Razi and R. Smith, eds, *Medieval Society and the Manor Court* (Oxford, 1996)

Rackham, O., *Trees and Woodland in the British Landscape* (London, 1973)

Richardson, John, *The Local Historian's Encyclopedia* (New Barnet, 1986)

Roberts, Marilyn, *The Mowbray Legacy: The Story of one of England's Great Medieval Families; with Genealogical Tables of Famous Descendants including Anne Boleyn, Elizabeth I, Sir Winston Churchill, Diana, Princess of Wales, Audrey Hepburn, George Washington, Thomas Jefferson and George W. Bush* (Scunthorpe, 2004)

Simco, Angela, *Archaeological Field Visit, Sheerhatch Wood* (unpublished site report, February 2003)

Summers, Dorothy, *The Great Ouse – The History of a River Navigation* (Newton Abbot, 1973)

Talbot, Charles Hugh and Eugene Ashby Hammond, *The Medical Practitioners in Medieval England. A Biographical Register* (London, 1965)

Thirsk, Joan, *Tudor Enclosure*, Historical Association 41 (London, 1958)

Thirsk, Joan, C. G. A. Clay and Christopher Clay, eds, *Rural Society: Landowners, Peasants and Labourers 1500 -1750* (Cambridge, 1990)

Vowles, Gordon, *The Parish of St Lawrence, Willington, Its Church and its Vicars* (Willington, 2016)

Ward, Kevin, *Society of Archivists Diploma Training Manual, Module G 'Estate Archives' Units 2–9* (unpublished, 1995)

Watts, John L., ed., *The End of the Middle Ages: England in the Fifteenth and Sixteenth Centuries* (Sutton, 1998)

Welldon-Finn, R., *Domesday Book, a Guide* (London, 1973)

White, R., *Willington Parish Essay* (unpublished, 1978), BARS, PL/AC2/57

Youings, Joyce, 'The Church', in E. Miller, ed., *The Agrarian History of England and Wales*, vol. 4, 1348–1500 (Cambridge, 1991), 8 vols

Index

Wadlowe, Edmund 50
wage rates 80, 142
Walys, Richard 104
Warde, Adam 70, 71, 115
Warden Abbey 46
Warden (Wardon), Abbot of 97, 142, 146
wardship 59–60
Warenere, John 158
Wareyn, Robert 98
Warner family 70, 115, 116
Warner, John 70, 83, 85, 87, 91, 115, 143, 162
Warner, Robert 115
Warner, Thomas 143
Warner, William 83
warren
 extent of 39, 132
 lease of 17, 36, 46, 82, 112, 127, 130
 maintenance of 124
 poaching 40, 54
 protection of 51, 80, 96–97, 133
warreners 68, 96, 115, 142
Wars of the Roses 77, 108
water transport 79
watermill 43
Watt, William 82, 130
Wattes, John 136
Wattes, Nicholas 96
weather 118, 136, 157, 159
weavers 59, 80
Webbe, William 28, 66
wheat 65, 76, 96
Whythove, Richard 151, 153
widows 29–30, 32, 44, 46–47, 87, 142, 163
Wileton, Nicholas de 145
William the Conqueror, King of England 100
Willington Grove 107
Willington Mere 78, 80
Williton, Robert 142
windmill, Haynes 124–125
Wing 110, 114
Wingfield, Sir Robert 104–105
withies 28

Wixamtree Hundred 3, 4, 8, 38
Wodec, John 57
Wodehyll, John 55, 82
Wodeward, John 99, 137
Woketon, John 129
Wolsey, Thomas, Cardinal 67, 163
women 44, 62, 79, 87–88, 158. *see also* widows
Wood Lane 4, 154
woodlands
 extent of 39, 157–158
 management of 27–29, 120, 133–135
 protection of 51, 56–57, 79
 trespass in 67, 103
Woodville, Elizabeth, Queen of England 108
Woodville, Sir John 11, 24, 68, 92, 108, 138
woodwards 22, 39, 83–84, 99, 115, 135, 138
wool 82
Wootton, William 150
Wrest Park 38, 44
Wryght family 98
Wryght, Walter 98
Wryght, William 82
Wryght, William the younger 137
Wyllyton church 97
Wyllyton, Robert de 20, 22, 68, 73, 99, 115
Wyltshyre, Thomas 23, 24, 120, 138, 141
Wyneld, Agnes 34
Wyneld, Richard 34

yardland 154
Yarwey family 85, 95, 98, 116, 117, 163
Yarwey, Henry 82, 93, 113
Yarwey, Joan 93
Yarwey, John
 as ale-taster 86
 animals of 90
 as bailiff 111, 114, 146
 bake-house of 80
 building repairs 28, 137